WITHDRAWN
Sno-Isle Libraries

Presidential
Diversions

Also by Paul F. Boller, Jr.

Presidential Inaugurations

Presidential Wives

Presidential Anecdotes

Presidential Campaigns

PRESIDENTIAL DIVERSIONS

Presidents at Play from George Washington to George W. Bush

☆ ☆ ☆ ☆ ☆

Paul F. Boller, Jr.

Harcourt, Inc.

ORLANDO   AUSTIN   NEW YORK
SAN DIEGO   TORONTO   LONDON

Copyright © 2007 by Paul F. Boller, Jr.

All rights reserved. No part of this publication may be reproduced
or transmitted in any form or by any means, electronic or mechanical,
including photocopy, recording, or any information storage and retrieval
system, without permission in writing from the publisher.

Requests for permission to make copies of any part of the work
should be submitted online at www.harcourt.com/contact or mailed
to the following address: Permissions Department, Harcourt, Inc.,
6277 Sea Harbor Drive, Orlando, Florida 32887-6777.

www.HarcourtBooks.com

Library of Congress Cataloging-in-Publication Data
Boller, Paul F.
Presidential diversions: presidents at play from George Washington
to George W. Bush/Paul F. Boller, Jr.—1st ed.
p. cm.
Includes bibliographical references and index.
1. Presidents—United States—Biography—Anecdotes.
2. Amusements—United States—Anecdotes.   I. Title.
E176.1.B884   2007
973.09'9—dc22   2006019662
ISBN 978-0-15-100612-0

Text set in Century Old Style
Designed by Kaelin Chappell Broaddus

Printed in the United States of America

First edition
A C E G I K J H F D B

For Dorothy Eister
and
David and Jenny

Contents

Preface

The hard-working James K. Polk once wrote solemnly in his diary: "No President who performs his duties faithfully and conscientiously can have any leisure." Polk was just about the only U.S. President who felt that way, though the uptight John Adams tended to have guilt feelings if he strayed too long from his duties as America's devoted public servant. "I cannot well bear the Thought of putting the public to an Expense," he once said, "merely for the Sake of my Pleasure, Health or Convenience."[1]

Most Presidents found that taking time off from their official responsibilities in order to have a little fun now and then was essential to their physical well-being and mental equanimity. Some Americans grumbled if they thought their leaders were having too good a time of it, but others thought that presidential vacations were good for the country as well as for the Chief Executive. Years ago, Arizona congressman Morris K. Udall, in a thoughtful speech on the American presidency, insisted that "we need Presidents who have diversions. I'd rather see someone who played a little poker or climbed a mountain or backpacked or hit a golf ball or had some diversions once in a while than these kinds of intense 18-hour-a-day Presidents we've had in modern times." Actually, there have been few workaholics in the White House. Polk was certainly one of them, and Lyndon B. Johnson another. But even LBJ played golf and attended sports events on occasion, though he talked politics even when he was supposed to be relaxing.[2]

The hobbies and diversions of the Presidents were as varied as the Presidents themselves. They ranged from stamp collecting to letter writing, from swimming to piano playing, and from fishing to painting. George Washington liked horseback riding, dancing, attending plays, and collecting paintings. John Adams devoured books and enjoyed instructing his son John Quincy in the art of reading. Thomas Jefferson took walks and rode horses for exercise, but to satisfy his boundless curiosity about the nature of things he also delved into just about every field of knowledge, ranging from science and religion to literature and the arts. For Abraham Lincoln, humor—amusing stories and jokes—was a psychological necessity to offset his sensitivity to the "sadness of things." Shakespeare was also indispensable to Lincoln; he read the plays, quoted from them, saw them performed, and had a great time discussing passages from them with his friends and associates. Grover Cleveland sought refreshment in fishing; so did Herbert Hoover and dozens of his successors. William Howard Taft played golf; and Woodrow Wilson, Dwight D. Eisenhower, John F. Kennedy, and most of the Presidents after them followed in his footsteps. But Taft, Wilson, Eisenhower, and Kennedy liked to read, too, as did many of our other Presidents.

Some Presidents, like Gerald R. Ford, were truly sportsmen; others, like Harry Truman, preferred books and music. Theodore Roosevelt was both a sportsman and an intellectual. His energies were unbounded. He was a bird watcher, a hiker, a camper, a professional cowboy, a soldier, a boxer, and a wrestler. But he was also a voracious reader (history, biography, politics, novels, and poetry) and a fine writer (letters, speeches, articles, and books). The night before his inauguration, in 1905, he boxed with a professional prize fighter in the White House and the next day delivered a nicely written address of his own composition. He had a "corking time," he said, when he was in the White House. He loved his work and he loved his play. Not all our Presidents could say the same.[3]

In examining the games, sports, and cultural activities that each of the Presidents, beginning with George Washington, turned to for their relaxation and renewal, I discovered much about their health, as well as their attitude toward work and play. But my main interest has been in what the Presidents did when they took time off from their work. "Sports," journalist Heywood Hale Broun once said, "do not build character. They reveal it." The same is true, I think, of cultural interests. There is no doubt that the sports, games, and cultural activities that the Presidents choose to engage in when they take time off tell us a great deal about their personas—and about their presidencies.[4]

There is history in all of this, as in all things human. The story of presidential diversions, from George Washington to George W. Bush, reveals a steady movement away from the colonial Puritan belief that time off from work was a "mispense of time" and toward the view that amusements are an essential part of human existence. At the same time, certain leisure activities have been incorporated into the President's work schedule. During the twentieth century it became increasingly imperative for Presidents to attend sports events, throw out the first baseball of the season, and sponsor cultural events in the White House. But many Presidents' leisure activities went far beyond these mandatory public appearances. They played golf because they loved it, read books for pleasure, and watched movies for the same reasons everybody else did. And they seem to have been the Presidents who enjoyed their work the most.

The Dignified George Washington

George Washington took an austere view of human relations. "It is easy to make acquaintances," he once wrote, "but very difficult to shake them off, however irksome and unprofitable they are found to be after we have once committed ourselves to them...." His solution? "Be courteous to all but intimate with few, and let those few be well tried before you give them your confidence; true friendship is a plant of slow growth." Not surprisingly, America's first President became famous for his dignity and reserve; some people felt awkward and tongue-tied in his presence.[1]

But Pennsylvania's Gouverneur Morris thought people exaggerated Washington's aloofness. Once, for the fun of it, he made a bet with Alexander Hamilton that he "could be as familiar" with the stately Virginian as he was with his closest friends. To prove his point, he walked up to Washington at a reception a few days later, put a hand on his shoulder, and cried merrily: "My dear General, how happy I am to see you looking so well." The reaction was unnerving. Washington "stepped suddenly back," according to some of the people in attendance, "fixed his eye on Morris...with an angry frown, until the latter retreated, abashed, and sought refuge in the crowd. The company looked on in silence." Morris learned his lesson the hard way; he vowed never to approach Washington so informally again.[2]

Unfortunately for Washington, many people found him forbidding even when he was trying to be friendly. Members of his own family sometimes felt ill at ease in his presence. His "presence," confessed Nelly Custis, Washington's adopted granddaughter, "generally chilled my young companions" and even "his own near relatives feared to speak or laugh before him." This was because of "the awe and respect he inspired," she explained, "and not from his severity. When he entered a room where we were all mirth and in high conversation, all were instantly mute. He would sit a short time and then retire, quite provoked and disappointed, but they could not repress their feelings." It's not surprising that after Washington's death, when John Marshall came to write the first serious book about him, it turned out to be "a Mausoleum," as John Adams put it, "100 feet square at the base, and 200 feet high."[3]

Washington was certainly no glad-hander, but he was no stuffed shirt, either. As a youngster he took his farm work at Mount Vernon seriously, but he also had plenty of fun. Spending long hours in the saddle, he came to love horses, riding them for pleasure as well as for work, and came to be regarded as the best horseman in Virginia. He enjoyed fox hunting, as did most planters; attended and bet on horse races, and even bred and raised race horses himself. He did a lot of fishing, too, for fun as well as profit, went to cockfights, and took in circuses whenever he could. When it came to sports, Washington was a good wrestler, and he excelled at games like quoits and rounders, which called for hurling stones and iron bars. He never actually threw a dollar across the Rappahannock River, as legend has it (President Truman said Washington would have been too stingy to do that), but he did throw a stone to the top of Natural Bridge, a 215-foot high rock in the Shenandoah Valley.

In 1772, artist Charles Willson Peale visited Mount Vernon, where he got to "pitching the bar" with some young friends one afternoon. Suddenly, to his surprise, Washington—a forty-year-old colonel at the time—appeared and asked to join in. "No sooner did the heavy iron bar feel the grasp of his mighty hand," wrote Peale later on, "than it lost the power of gravitation, and whizzed through the air, striking the ground far, very far, beyond our utmost limits. We were indeed amazed, as we stood around stripped to the buff, with shirt sleeves rolled up, and having thought ourselves very clever fellows, while the colonel, on retiring, pleasantly observed, 'When you beat my pitch, young gentlemen, I'll try again.'"[4] During the American Revolution, a soldier at Valley Forge observed that for relaxation Washington "sometimes throws and catches a ball for hours with his aide-de-camp."[5]

But Washington's recreations weren't entirely outdoor activities. On rainy days he liked to play cards, making small bets; he took up billiards, too, and became quite proficient at the game. Even more to his liking, however, was dancing. He learned to dance as a youngster, and it became one of his favorite diversions, though his wife, Martha, seems never to have joined him on the dance floor. When he was at Mount Vernon, Washington liked to go to dances in Alexandria, ten miles away. Not all of them met with his approval. In his diary he wrote disparagingly about one party he dubbed "the Bread & Butter Ball" because of its threadbareness. "Went to the ball at Alexandria," he wrote, "where Musick and Dancing was the chief Entertainment. However, a convenient room detached for the purpose abounded in great plenty of Bread and Butter, some biscuits with Tea, and Coffee, which the Drinkers of could not distinguish from hot water sweet- 'ned—Be it remembered that pocket handkerchiefs served the pur- pose of Table Cloths & Napkins and that no apologies were made for either. I shall therefore distinguish this Ball by the stile and title of the Bread & Butter Ball."[6] Washington liked good food and drink (though he was a moderate drinker) at his parties, as well as attrac- tive partners. During the American Revolution, his camp set aside a day of celebration for the signing of a treaty of alliance with France, and at the party that evening, he danced more than three hours, "with- out once sitting down," with the young wife of General Nathanael Greene, whose stiff knee kept him off the dance floor.[7]

When Washington became President in 1789, he was forced to give up or curtail some of his favorite recreations. But from almost the beginning, he took time off from work to keep in shape by riding horseback for a couple of hours each morning and taking afternoon walks. He also "exercised in a Carriage," as he put it in his diary, taking his wife Martha, and sometimes his two grandchildren, for the fourteen-mile ride around Manhattan, which was then the nation's capital.[8] When Congress was not in session, he took vacations in Mount Vernon, where he could entertain his friends and for a time indulge in one of his greatest pleasures: making daily rounds of his plantation on horseback. Once, just before leaving for Mount Vernon, Washington told the members of his cabinet that he wanted to dispose of all public business before heading south because he wanted "to have my mind as free from public care as circumstances will allow." He also arranged to have thirty-six dozen bottles of port sent ahead in preparation for the entertaining he planned to do when he got home.[9]

In 1790, Washington was seriously ill for several weeks, and upon recovering he persuaded two of his associates—Thomas Jefferson and Alexander Hamilton—to join him on a five-day trip to Long Island and New Jersey for some sightseeing and fishing. His trip did not go unnoticed. One newspaper reported that "yesterday afternoon the President of the United States returned from Sandy Hook and the fishing banks, where he had been for the benefit of the sea air, and to amuse himself in the delightful recreation of fishing. We are told that he has had excellent sport, having himself caught a great number of sea-bass and black fish—the weather proved remarkably fine, which, together with the salubrity of the air and wholesome exercise, rendered this little voyage extremely agreeable, and cannot fail, we hope, of being serviceable to a speedy and complete restoration of his health."[10] It wasn't the only fishing trip he worked into his schedule while President. In tours he took of the country soon after taking office, to demonstrate his broadly national outlook at a time when provincial loyalties were still powerful, Washington managed to work in some dancing as well as fishing. In Charleston, South Carolina, he was warmly welcomed one night at a fancy dance party at which he took happily to the floor, and the following night he was vociferously hailed at a concert, where, he recorded in his diary, he was surrounded by "at least four hundred ladies, the number and appearance of which exceeded anything of the kind I had ever seen."[11]

If Washington enjoyed the company of women, his greatest social pleasure, he once said, was get-togethers with "my intimate friends and acquaintances."[12] In the circle of his friends, Thomas Jefferson observed, Washington abandoned his taciturnity; mingling with people he knew and liked, James Madison noticed, "he was talkative" and sometimes "fluent and even eloquent."[13] At Mount Vernon he and Martha did a lot of entertaining, and at times, he once complained, their home became a "well resorted tavern."[14] Once they moved into the President's House in New York, they felt obliged to do some entertaining for the general public, but it was necessarily far more formal and restrained than what they were used to in Virginia, and much less fun. They decided on three major weekly events for the public: the President's levee, a reception for men on Tuesday afternoons; Mrs. Washington's reception, Friday evenings, for both men and women; and state dinners every Thursday at four, to which government officials and members of Congress were invited. It took some time before Washington derived any pleasure from these events.

For Washington, the first levee was undoubtedly the worst. After a sizeable number of gentlemen filled the reception room, David Humphreys, one of his secretaries, ostentatiously threw open the door, announced loudly, "The President of the United States!" and beckoned for Washington to enter the room. Washington was surprised and irked by what he regarded as unnecessary ceremoniousness, and he told Humphreys afterward, "Well, you have taken me in once, but, by God, you shall never take me in a second time."[15] After that, he always arrived first for the levee and stood waiting in front of the fireplace, facing the entrance, ready to receive the visitors with a dignified bow, and "with hands so disposed of as to indicate that the salutation was not to be accompanied with shaking hands."[16] Some people criticized his bows as a bit too kingly for a republic, but Washington insisted he did the best he could with them. Wouldn't it be better "to throw the veil of charity over them," he asked, "ascribing their stiffness to the effects of age, or to the unskillfulness of my teacher, rather than to pride and dignity of office, which God knows has no charms for me?"[17]

Washington found his wife's receptions more pleasurable, partly because he enjoyed chatting with women and partly because he felt more at ease with Martha on deck with him. At Martha's receptions, she remained seated, as did the women who called on her, while the men remained standing. She was of course the center of attraction at these occasions, but Washington doffed his sword and cocked hat to circulate amiably among the women, and he did so, according to Abigail Adams, "with a grace, dignity and ease that leaves Royal George far behind him."[18] When the clock in the hall struck nine, Mrs. Washington usually stood and announced: "The General always retires at nine, and I usually precede them." The two of them then took their leave.[19]

As for the state dinners, Washington's level of enjoyment varied depending on the guests. Some people found the dinners stiff and uncomfortable. At the dinners that Pennsylvania Senator William Maclay attended, he thought the food was excellent and appreciated the attention the President gave him, but he found him cold and formal. "It was the most solemn dinner I was ever at," he said of one experience at the President's House. Washington filled a glass of wine, he reported, and "with great formality drank to the health of every individual by name round the table." Then, in an effort to amuse the guests, he told a story about a clergyman who lost his hat and wig while passing a river called Brunks, and succeeded in eliciting a bit of polite laughter over the tale. After that, he "now and then said a sentence or two on some common subject," and during awkward silences "played with the fork, striking on the edge of the table with it."[20] Maclay was probably overly nit-picky about Washington's dinners; a fervent democrat, he was extremely sensitive to any sign of aristocratic hauteur in the President's behavior. Washington tried hard to be dignified but not overbearing at these gatherings. Still, he couldn't help being irked when some members of Congress straggled in late for dinner one night. "Gentlemen...," he said, "we are too punctual for you. I have a cook who never asks whether the company has come, but whether the hour has come."[21]

Washington's dinners gradually improved. They always went well when a couple of his best friends—Philander Knox and Robert Morris—were there. A little wine helped, too. "He is generally sedate and serious," recalled one of his guests, "and only after having two or three glasses of wine and when roused by the conversation around him, does his face assume an expression of liveliness." With champagne, apparently, Washington became even more sociable. Including young people at the dinners—the grown-up sons, daughters, and in-laws of the guests—also lifted Washington's spirits, because the events were then more like the parties he threw at Mount Vernon. For a long time, however, he found it hard to balance amiable hospitality with the "republican dignity" he was anxious to display in public. He once confessed he would rather be at Mount Vernon with a good friend or two than surrounded by the officers of state and all of Europe's grandees in the President's House.[22]

Sometimes Washington treated guests to a play, rather than dinner, at the John Street Theater in New York, and later, when the capital moved to Philadelphia, to a play at the new theater there; it was one of his chief delights. He saw his first play as a youngster and at once became a theater lover. As an adult he came to like Shakespeare, especially *Hamlet,* and, like so many other Americans at the time of the Revolution, he became a devoted fan of Joseph Addison's *Cato,* a play set in ancient Rome that celebrated republican values. Washington saw the play many times, liked to quote from it, and even arranged for a performance for his soldiers at Valley Forge during the American Revolution. Another favorite was Richard B. Sheridan's *School for Scandal,* a racy play that upset prudish people in America. Washington made the mistake of asking Senator Maclay to join him and Martha for a performance of the play in New York, and ended up offending rather than entertaining the prim Pennsylvanian. "I never liked it," Maclay confided to his diary; "I think it an indecent representation before ladies of character and virtue."[23] But Maclay was an exception. Most of Washington's guests were flattered to share the stage box with him and Martha, and they enjoyed taking in the friendly references to the President that turned up in some of the newer productions. Washington's immense pleasure seeing plays was marred only by the fuss people made over him when he appeared at the playhouse.

The Washingtons attended concerts as well as plays, but music seems to have played only a minor part in their lives. There was a legend that Washington played the flute, but Washington himself told Jefferson emphatically that he couldn't "raise a single note on any instrument."[24] He did, though, buy his wife's granddaughter, Nelly Custis, a "forte Piano" as well as a harpsichord, and he thoroughly enjoyed listening to her sing and play on these instruments, especially when she performed for guests. He was enormously pleased when composer Francis Hopkinson sent him a copy of his *Seven Songs for Harpsichord and Forte Piano,* which he had dedicated to Washington.[25]

Washington seems to have found more pleasure in art than in music. He was deeply interested in architecture, sculpture, and painting, and became an art collector when he was twenty-eight. He acquired busts of military leaders like Alexander and Julius Caesar, designed Mount Vernon himself, and collected paintings by such American artists as Benjamin West, John Trumbull, and Charles Willson Peale, as well as by foreign artists. Washington added many paintings to his collection while President, and when he was living in Philadelphia he transformed the President's House into a kind of art museum, exhibiting important works of art to the public. "To encourage literature and the arts," he insisted, "is a duty which every good citizen owes to his country."[26]

Neoclassicism—historical art centered on ancient Greece and Rome—was the fashion in Washington's day, and Washington appreciated some of its achievements, but his preference was for landscape painting depicting natural settings in America instead of the ancient world. In this he was ahead of his time, observed historian James Thomas Flexner, who went on to pronounce Washington the "grandfather (or perhaps great-grandfather) of that most indigenous of American artistic movements, the Hudson River School," which emerged in the 1820s.[27] In 1785, the French neoclassical sculptor Jean Antoine Houdon visited Mount Vernon to make a study of Washington before returning to France to create a full-length statue of him. Worried that Houdon would drape his figure in a Roman toga, Washington wrote Jefferson, then in Paris, about his misgivings. He acknowledged that he lacked "sufficient knowledge of the art of sculpture to oppose my judgment to the taste of connoisseurs," but wondered whether "some little deviation in favor of the modern costume" might be possible. He added that departures from neoclassicism "had been introduced in painting by Mr. West," and "received with applause and prevails extensively."[28] Houdon omitted the toga, but years later Horatio Greenough did a posthumous huge marble statue of Washington, presenting him as an old Roman, stripped to his waist, with a toga draped over his knees, which, when unveiled in the Capitol Rotunda, produced such a storm that it was soon moved to the basement of the Smithsonian Institution where it wouldn't embarrass the nation anymore. Washington would have approved of the move.

Washington acquired books as well as paintings, but although his library at Mount Vernon (almost nine hundred volumes) contained novels, biographies, historical works, and the Greek and Roman classics, his tastes ran to practical treatises on farming, raising horses, agriculture, and, above all, military matters. When his stepson, George Washington Parke Custis, enrolled at Princeton University, Washington urged him to read books of lasting importance. "Light reading...

may amuse for the moment," he told him, "but leaves nothing behind."[29] Washington himself apparently did little reading for pleasure.
When he was President, he conscientiously subscribed to several
newspapers—among them the *Gazette of the United States,* the *American Advertiser,* the *Pennsylvania Gazette,* the *New York Magazine,*
and the *Aurora*—to keep up on current events. But he lamented the
fact that the editors stuffed their papers with "scurrile and nonsensi-
cal declamation" instead of "publishing the debates in Congress on
all great national questions." He came especially to dislike Benjamin
Franklin Bache's *Aurora* and Philip Freneau's *National Gazette* because of their harsh criticisms of his presidential policies, and at one
cabinet meeting he exploded in wrath at the slanders that "rascal Freneau" had been hurling at him, swearing that "*by god* he had rather
be on his farm than to be made *emperor of the world* and yet that they
were charging him with wanting to be a king."[30] Washington cut
down on his subscriptions when he retired, but kept up with the news
until his death. In his last illness, he sat in a room with his wife and
secretary, Tobias Lear, reading the papers. "He was very cheerful,"
Lear recalled, "and when he met with anything he thought diverting
or interesting, he would read it aloud as well as his hoarseness would
permit."[31]

In retirement, Washington resumed the activities he'd loved at
Mount Vernon before he became President: riding around his plantation every morning to check on the farm work; entertaining friends,
and strangers, too, in the relaxed and informal way he preferred; and
taking little trips to nearby places from time to time. There's a story
that one day, while returning from a visit to the region where the Federal City was to be located, he saw an old-fashioned chaise containing a young couple and much baggage suddenly overturn and dump
the woman onto the road, and he quickly galloped up, dismounted,
and rushed to her aid. About the same time, the British actor John
Bernard, who had been performing in Philadelphia, arrived on the
scene, saw the accident, and, according to his memoirs, at once
joined Washington in helping the couple. They revived the woman

with water from a nearby spring and after ascertaining that neither she nor her husband was seriously hurt, "grasped the wheel" of the chaise, Bernard wrote later, and "to the peril of our spinal columns, righted the conveyance," put the luggage back on the vehicle, and sent the couple off on their way. "All this helping, hauling, and lifting occupied at least half an hour," Bernard recalled, "under a meridian sun in the middle of July, which fairly boiled the perspiration out of our foreheads." After the couple left, Washington offered to dust Bernard's coat and Bernard did the same for Washington. Bernard took a good look at Washington, who was still a stranger to him, and observed "a tall, erect, well-made man, evidently advanced in years, but who appeared to have retained all the vigor and elasticity resulting from a life of temperance and exercise."[32]

But Washington was looking the actor over, too, Bernard remembered, and suddenly he smiled and exclaimed, "Mr. Bernard, I believe?" Bernard nodded and Washington went on: "I had the pleasure of seeing you perform last winter in Philadelphia." He then invited the actor to ride home with him for some rest and refreshment, and when he indicated where he lived nearby, it was Bernard's turn to be pleasantly surprised. "Mount Vernon!" he cried, having passed the place the day before, "have I the honor of addressing General Washington?" Offering his hand, Washington returned, "An odd sort of introduction, Mr. Bernard, but I am pleased to find you can play so active a part in private, and without a prompter." Bernard of course accepted the invitation, and he spent the next hour and a half at Mount Vernon plying the former President with questions about the young American nation.[33]

Washington never mentioned the encounter with Bernard in his diary or in any of his letters, and some historians question the authenticity of the tale Bernard told some years after Washington's death. Still, the actor's admiration for Washington was genuine enough, and it was the main point of his story. Washington, he said, "spoke like a man who had felt as much as he reflected, and reflected more than he had spoken." He also portrayed the first President as a country gentleman who, unlike most planters, would rush to help the young couple instead of summoning his servants to do the job. Like most people, moreover, he placed great emphasis on Washington's noble bearing. "Whether you surveyed his face, open yet well defined," he wrote, "dignified but not arrogant, thoughtful but benign; his frame, towering and muscular, but alert from its good proportion—every feature suggested a resemblance to the spirit it encased, and showed simplicity in all alliance with the sublime." It never occurred to Bernard to slap Washington on the back when they parted. A "feeling of awe and veneration," he said, stole over him.[34]

☆ ☆ ☆ 2 ☆ ☆ ☆

The Conscientious
John Adams

In July 1783, when John Adams was in Holland negotiating a trade treaty for the United States, he was impressed by the "hobby horse" (*Lief-hebbery*), meaning "hobby," to which the Dutch men seemed to be addicted, and he decided he would "rather ride a Dutch Hobby Horse than an English or a French." He also thought that having a hobby was "the most wholesomest Exercise in the World." The Dutch, he said, "live to great Ages by the strength of it....They pitch in early Life upon some domestick Amusement, which they follow all their days at Leisure." One day he visited an elderly Dutchman named Lionet who seemed to be brimming with health, strength, and energy because, Adams thought, of his lifelong hobby centered on "natural knowledge."[1]

Adams spent over two hours with Lionet, examining his collection of marine shells and looking through his folio on caterpillars. He was convinced that Lionet would have died fifty years earlier had it not been for his hobbyhorse. Still, despite his admiration for the Dutchman's accomplishments, Adams wasn't inclined to take up a hobby of his own, for, as he told his wife Abigail, "I have too much to do to study Men, and their mischievous Designs on Apple Trees and other things...."[2] Adams's work centered on people and politics, not on nature and her wonders. His labors for his country, during the American

Revolution and after, took precedence over hobbyhorses, and frequently over relaxation and refreshment even when he badly needed them. Adams was beset by Puritan guilt if he neglected work for long. His Manichean viewpoint—centered on the conflict between good and evil—translated into one between work and play.

As a youngster, growing up on his father's farm in Braintree, Massachusetts, Adams spent a lot of time outdoors fishing, hunting, swimming, and ice skating, as well as doing farm work for his father. He also wrestled with friends, shot marbles, and flew the kites that he and his brother made themselves. He didn't find Braintree's Latin School very exciting, so he played hooky whenever he could, going off to hunt and fish. Adams wasn't particularly anxious to go to college, but his father insisted, and once he arrived at Harvard, he fell in love with the place. It was "gay, gorgeous," he exulted; it "invigorated my Body, and exhilarated my soul."[3]

At Harvard, Adams soon acquired a "Love of Books and…fondness for Study," and lost interest in boyhood sports.[4] He also became exceedingly concerned about his future. He was anxious to avoid the fate of "the common Herd of Mankind, who are born and eat and sleep and die, and [are] forgotten," and he determined to become "a great man" some day, renowned for his "Honour or Reputation." He was "not ashamed," he confessed, "to own that a Prospect of an Immortality in the Memories of all the Worthy to [the] end of Time would be a high Gratification to my Wishes."[5] It was a dazzling goal that young Adams chose, and it was clear he was going to have to labor diligently if he were to achieve it. But the Puritanism he had imbibed from his parents required that the goal be social, not self-centered, and in the end he found himself striving hard to serve his country as best he could. Unfortunately, he didn't always seem to get much fun out of his endeavors.

Time and again Adams chastised himself in his diary for getting mired in trivialities. "Sloth and negligence," he feared, "will be the ruin of my schemes."[6] He studied law after leaving Harvard, passed the bar exam, and soon became active in the patriot cause on the eve of the American Revolution. At the same time, he continued to whap away at himself and the "idle diversions" that tempted him. "A habit of Indolence, and listlessness is growing very fast upon me," he wailed one day. Another time: "Wasted the Day, with a magazine in my hand." And again: "This Day has been lost in much the same, Spiritless manner." In one entry in his diary, he listed the distractions—"Guns, girls, cards, flutes, violins"—and lamented: "I am too lazy to rise early and make a fire; and when my fire is made at ten o'clock, my passion for knowledge, fame, fortune, or any good is too languid to make me apply with spirit to my books, and...my mind is liable to be called off from law to a girl, a pipe, a poem, or love-letter, a Spectator, or play...." In November 1760, with another year almost gone, he felt he hadn't accomplished much. "Most of the time," he sighed, "has been spent in Rambling and Dissipation. Riding and Walking, Smoking Pipes and Spending Evenings, consume a vast Proportion of my Time, and the cares and Anxieties of Business, damp my Ardor and scatter my attention. But I must stay more at home—and commit more to writing."[7]

Adams scoffed at the fun and games that tempted him. "Let others," he wrote, "waste their bloom of life at the card or billiard table among rakes and fools." As for dancing, "I never knew a dancer who was good for anything else." He worked hard to stifle his bent for pleasure. "Let no trifling diversion or amusement or company decoy you from your books," he implored himself, that is, "let no girl, no gun, no cards, no flutes, no violins, no dress, no tobacco, no laziness decoy you from your books."[8] Years later, when he met with Benjamin Franklin and Thomas Jefferson to discuss the design for the Great Seal of the United States, Adams suggested featuring Hercules, the Hero, choosing between virtue and vice: "The Hero resting on his Clubb. Virtue pointing to her rugged mountain, on one Hand, and persuading him to ascend. Sloth, glancing at her flowery Paths of Pleasure, wantonly reclining on the Ground, displaying the Charms both of her Eloquence and Person, to seduce him into Vice."[9] It's no wonder that the high-strung Adams had a nervous breakdown as a young lawyer and rode off to the mineral springs in Stafford, Connecticut, to recuperate. But he soon became restless. "I begin to grow weary of this idle, romantic Jaunt," he wrote his wife, Abigail. "I want to see my Wife, my Children, my Farm....I want to hear the News, and Politicks of the Day."[10] He was happy to be back at home in Braintree and at work again in Boston.

In 1778, when Adams went to France for the first time to seek a treaty of alliance for his country, he was overwhelmed by its magnificence. "The delights of France are innumerable," he wrote his wife. "The Politeness, the Elegance, the Softness, the Delicacy, is extreme." As stern and haughty as he was, he added, "I cannot help loving these People, for their earnest Desire, and Assiduity to please."[11] He was impressed by their handiwork as well, especially in Paris and Versailles: the public buildings, gardens, sculptures, paintings, and music. "The Richness, the Magnificence, and the Splendor, is beyond all Description," he told his wife, and they extended to "private homes" as well, and to "Furniture, Equipage, Dress, and especially Entertainments." But Adams suddenly caught himself up short; he didn't want to get carried away. "But what is all this to me?" he interjected. "I receive but little Pleasure in beholding all these Things, because I cannot but consider them as Bagatelles, introduced, by Time and Luxury, in Exchange for the great Qualities and hardy manly Virtues of the human heart. I cannot help suspecting that the more Elegance, the less Virtue in all Times and Countries." He went on to express the fear that his own country would some day achieve "the Power and Opportunity" to be "elegant, soft, and luxurious" too. His own luxuries, he insisted, were simpler: the company of his wife, children, and friends who were good conversationalists.[12]

Fortunately, Adams didn't always resist his inclination to enjoy himself in France. He acknowledged there was "an infinity of Curiosities" there, and he regretted he didn't have more time to take them in. There were so many "elegant Entertainments" in the theaters, he noted, and such an abundance of "good company and excellent Books" available, that if his wife were with him and his country were at peace, he would be "one of the happyest of men in France."[13] A few days later Adams wrote Abigail a lively letter about a long ramble he took in Paris with son John Quincy, visiting gardens and castles, and inquiring into their historical associations. When the two of them reached home, he said, they were "much pleased with our Walk and better for the Air and Exercise."[14] Being Adams, however, he felt impelled afterward to wonder whether he should have been studying French instead of hiking around Paris with his son and writing about it at such length for his wife. "Suppose," he said, "I should describe the Persons and Manners of all the Company I see, and the fashions, the Plays, the Games, the sports, the spectacles, the Churches and religious Ceremonies—and all that—should not you think me turned fool in my old Age—have I not other Things to do of more importance?"[15]

Adams expressed his delight more than once in walking and riding around Paris, though he almost invariably ended by wondering whether his friendly forays were of any use to his country and himself. "To take a walk in the Gardens of the Palace of the Tuilleries, and describe the Statues there, all in marble, in which the ancient Divinities and Heroes are represented with exquisite Art, would be a very pleasant Amusement, and instructive Entertainment, improving in History, Mythology, Poetry, as well as in Statuary. Another Walk in the Gardens of Versailles, would be usefull and agreeable." But—the inevitable little word intervening whenever Adams started feeling good about something—"to observe these objects with Taste and describe them so as to be understood, would require more time and thought than I can possibly spare." Furthermore, he went on, it is not the fine arts "which our country requires." It's the "Usefull, the mechanic Arts" that a young country like the United States needs most.[16] If he had the time, Adams continued, he could fill volumes with descriptions of temples, palaces, paintings, sculptures, tapestry, and porcelain, but he couldn't do it "without neglecting my duty." His duty, he reminded Abigail, was "the Science of Government," which is "the Art of Legislation and Administration, and Negotiation." Then he added one of the most quoted passages in all his correspondence: "I must study Politicks and War that my sons may have liberty to study Mathematicks and Philosophy. My sons ought to study Mathematicks and Philosophy, Geography, natural History, Naval Architecture, navigations, Commerce and Agriculture, in order to give their children a right to study Painting, Poetry, Musick, Architecture, Statuary, Tapestry and Porcelaine."[17] Adams was a voracious reader on such subjects as history, religion, philosophy, the classics, and politics, but painting, music, and architecture never played a large part in his life. He did, though, enjoy the operas, concerts, and theatrical performances he was seeing for the first time in Paris.

Adams was a compulsive worker, as lawyer, politician, diplomat, Vice President, and President, but he was not exactly a sedentarian. He knew that physical activity was good for him, and he was convinced that horseback riding in particular cured his ailments and preserved his health. From the Hague he wrote Abigail that by "frequent Exercise on Horseback and great Care, I seem to have recovered my Health, strength and Spirits beyond my Expectation," and that riding was "the only Way of guarding against Fevers...." So he rode every day, he told her, even in wretched weather; "shaking on horseback," as he put it, helped keep him in good shape.[18] Still, Adams couldn't help worrying about taking time off from work for his physical well-being. Once, when some of his associates urged him to take an excursion for his health, he admitted to his wife that "I cannot well bear the Thought of putting the public to an Expense merely for the Sake of my Pleasure, Health or Convenience."[19] But after a bout with the flu, when a doctor suggested going to Bath, the popular health resort in England, for a few weeks, he crossed the Channel with his son, and when they reached London, he was so fascinated by the big, bright, busy city that he spent two months there before proceeding to Bath. There were twinges of guilt, to be sure, but there was plenty of fun all the same.

When Washington became President in 1789 and Adams began presiding over the Senate as Vice President, he almost drove the senators crazy with his worries about whether official procedures were noble and dignified enough for the new republic and by his agonizing over how two Presidents—President Washington and President of the Senate Adams—should behave when they were in the same room. Adams acknowledged that the vice presidency was the most insignificant office ever dreamed up by the mind of man, but there was no way he was going to lie down on the job even if it didn't amount to much. At first, though, he spent more time in Braintree than in the nation's capital, walked and rode around his farm, and, above all, indulged himself in his greatest love: reading. More than anything else, he once wrote Abigail, "except for my wife and children, I want to see my books."[20]

Adams was not only an indefatigable reader; he had rules for reading, too. "Can any man," he once asked, "take a book in his hand, in the Morning and confine his Thoughts to that till Night?" Surely not; such "uniformity" would be tiresome. Wouldn't "Variety" be "more agreable, and profitable?" He proposed a reading routine. First, he said, read a book for an hour, then think about it for an hour, and then do some "exercise" for an hour—dine, smoke, walk, cut wood—and then repeat the process and, the second time, perhaps read aloud. "I never spent a whole Day upon one Book in my life," he once bragged. But Adams did other things with his books.[21] Sometimes he skimmed them; other times he filled the margins of the pages with comments that were variously commendatory, explosive, angry, scornful, or sarcastic. Years later, Zoltan Haraszti filled a sizeable (and stimulating) book with Adams's lively marginalia.[22]

Adams enjoyed reading Latin as well as English, and he once gave his son John Quincy, a young lawyer at the time, instructions on how best to read the classics: Livy, Cicero, Polybius, Plutarch, and Sallust. "Take your book, your dictionary, your grammar, your sheet of paper, and pen and ink," Adams wrote him. "Begin at the beginning and read the work through—put down in writing every word with its meaning.... You will find it the most delightful employment you ever engaged in. When you have finished the 35th book you will say that you have learned more wisdom from it than from five hundred volumes of the trash that is commonly read."[23]

Writing was as dear to Adams as reading. "The more I write, the better," he told Abigail. But as with reading, he stressed what he learned from writing rather than the joy he derived from it. "Writing," he added, "is a most useful improving Exercise."[24] On another occasion, he told Abigail he had "a great Deal of Leisure, which I chiefly employ in Scribbling that my Mind may not stand still or run back like my Fortune." Adams composed political treatises, pamphlets, public documents, and speeches, but he wasn't always at his best when he was trying to be dead serious. His inaugural address in 1797 was unremarkable except for a sentence that went on and on for more than seven hundred words. His invective was always more stimulating than his solemnities: He brushed Alexander Hamilton off as "the bastard brat of a Scotch peddler"; dismissed Thomas Paine's influential *Common Sense* as "a poor, ignorant, malicious, short-sighted, crapulous mass"; and emitted a long list of words to convey his scorn about the eighteenth century—"the Age of Folly, Vice, Frenzy, Brutality, Daemons, Buonaparte, Tom Paine, or the Age of the Burning Brand from the Bottomless Pit, or anything but the Age of Reason."[25]

Adams's forte was in fact letter writing. He poured out wondrous letters—vivid, lively, funny, emphatic, satirical, affectionate, sentimental—to Abigail, family members, relatives, and friends. "Letter-writing is, to me, the most agreable Amusement" he ever found, he once admitted. He instructed his son John Quincy in writing as well as reading. There is no accomplishment more useful, he told him, "or which conduces more to the happiness of life...than the art of writing letters." The basic rules, he declared, were "simplicity, ease, familiarity and perspicuity," but these were not achieved without long and hard work and study. "Suffer no careless scroll ever to go out of your hand," he advised his son. "Take time to think even upon the most trifling card. Turn your thoughts in your mind, and vary your phrases and the order of your words [so] that taste and judgment may appear even in the most ordinary composition."[26] Adams worked diligently on his own correspondence. For many of his letters he prepared a first draft and then edited it carefully before putting it in final form and sending it off. His letters to Abigail during their long separations while he was serving as a delegate in the Continental Congress and as America's representative abroad sparkled with love for the English language; so did her responses. His exchanges with Thomas Jefferson, another splendid letter writer, during their declining years are a delight to read today. Adams wanted to be remembered for his contributions to the public good, but his letters are surely one of his greatest legacies.

In retirement at Quincy, Adams did some work on his farm, walked daily, rode horseback, read a lot, as always, and carried on a lively correspondence with friends like Thomas Jefferson, Benjamin Rush, and Benjamin Waterhouse, exchanging opinions on religion, philosophy, politics, and the arts, as he always loved to do. The renowned British writer Samuel Johnson, he recalled, once said that when he "sat upon his throne in a tavern," he "dogmatized and was contradicted, and in this he found delight." Adams felt the same way. "My throne is not in a tavern but at my fireside," he said. "There I dogmatize, there I laugh and there the newspapers sometimes make me scold; and in dogmatizing, laughing and scolding I find delight, and why should not I enjoy it, since no one is the worse for it and I am the better."[27]

Adams doubted that he would achieve the goal of fame he had set for himself as a young man. He thought that Benjamin Franklin and George Washington would get more credit for American independence than he would despite his mighty efforts for the cause from the very beginning of the struggle. "The history of our Revolution," he once wrote, "will be one continued Lye from one end to the other. The essence of the whole will be that Dr. Franklin's electrical rod smote the Earth and out sprang General Washington. That Franklin electrified him with his rod—and thence forward these two conducted all the Policy, Negotiations, Legislatures and War." Then he added self-consciously: "If this letter should be preserved and read a hundred years hence, the reader will say, 'The envy of...JA could not bear to think of the truth.'"[28]

More than two hundred years have passed since Adams wrote his letter about the history of the American Revolution, and the judgments about his stature as one of the Founding Fathers are more generous than they were in his own day. In recent years some historians have come to rate him as "near great" among the Presidents and to praise him for the courage he showed in preserving peace with France while holding that office. Would the approval have pleased Adams? Probably. But there doubtless would have been some guilt along with the pleasure.[29]

☆ ☆ ☆ **3** ☆ ☆ ☆

The Gifted
Thomas Jefferson

Thomas Jefferson was known as the "Sage of Monticello"; he seemed to know something about everything. Once, when he was traveling in Virginia and got into a conversation with a stranger at an inn where he spent the night, he astonished the man with his versatility. The stranger mentioned some mechanical operations he had witnessed recently, and Jefferson's familiarity with them led him to think that Jefferson was an engineer. Then they got to talking about agricul ture, and the stranger decided that Jefferson was a farmer. More talk convinced the stranger that he was a lawyer, and then a physician, and when they reached the subject of religion, he concluded that Jefferson was a clergyman, though he wasn't quite sure of what denomination. The next morning he asked the landlord for the name of the remarkable man he met the night before. "What," exclaimed the landlord, "don't you know the Squire?—that was Mr. Jefferson." "Not President Jefferson?" cried the stranger. "Yes," nodded the landlord, "President Jefferson." Years later, when President John F. Kennedy entertained some Nobel prize winners at a White House dinner, he introduced them as "the most extraordinary collection of talents that has ever been gathered at the White House with the possible exception of when Thomas Jefferson dined alone."[1]

Jefferson didn't dine alone much; he was a sociable as well as an erudite fellow. He preferred dining in the President's House with members of his family, relatives, friends, and guests who shared his passion for the arts and sciences. Historians today insist that Jefferson's skills, particularly as an inventor, have been overrated, but there is no doubt that his endless quest to understand the world about him as best he could enabled him to acquire a tremendous amount of knowledge and skills in an impressive number of fields: chemistry, botany, music, architecture, sculpture, painting, gardening, mathematics, astronomy, and religion. In his own way, Jefferson liked to "twist the tail of the cosmos," as U.S. Supreme Court Justice Oliver Wendell Holmes, Jr., once put it, but he also thought that the increase of knowledge about natural phenomena would produce wiser, better, and happier human beings.

But Jefferson was no couch potato. He was active physically as well as intellectually. He was convinced, in fact, that body and mind were closely related. "If the body be feeble," he warned, "the mind will not be strong." Sometimes he even asserted that a healthy body was more important for a person than a learned mind. "Exercise and recreation," he declared, "are as necessary as reading; I will say rather more necessary, because health is worth more than learning. A strong body makes the mind strong."[2]

In 1993, *Runner's World,* the highly regarded magazine for America's multitudinous runners, singled out the learned Virginian as the "Founding Father of Fitness," and went on to show that the third President of the United States, who did some running in college, was a firm believer in regular exercise for every American. Jefferson recommended walking, the magazine noted, as one of the best ways for a busy person to keep in good shape. "No one knows, till he tries, how easily a habit of walking is acquired," Jefferson told Thomas Mann Randolph, the young man who was to marry his daughter Martha in 1786. "A person who never walked 3 miles will in the course of a month become able to walk 15 or 20 without fatigue. I have known some great walkers and never knew nor heard of one who was not healthy and long-lived." Jefferson also insisted, "Not less than 2 hours a day should be devoted to exercise, and the weather should be little regarded. I speak from experience, having made this arrangement of my time."[3]

Jefferson was choosy about his exercise. He didn't rate ball games high. "Games played with the ball, and others of that nature," he declared, "are too violent for the body, and stamp no character on the mind."[4] He was friendlier toward hunting, having taken it up early in his life. When he was only ten, his father gave him a gun and ordered him to go into the woods and not return until he'd killed some game. Eager to please his father, he went out and searched far and wide without finding anything to shoot. Finally he came across a wild turkey trapped in a pen, and in no time released it, tied it to a tree, shot it, and carried it home on his shoulder to give to his father. Doubtless he improved as a hunter as he grew older, but as an adult he thought hunting gave only "moderate exercise" for the body, though it "gives boldness, enterprise, and independence to the mind."[5]

Walking, in short, seemed to be Jefferson's favorite exercise, and he insisted that one's heart should be in it. "Never think of taking a book with you," he advised. "The object of walking is to relax the mind. You should therefore not permit yourself even to think while you walk; but divert yourself by the objects surrounding you." And since walking was "the best exercise," people should "habituate themselves to taking long walks." He also advised people to take their outings in the afternoon, "not because it is the best time for exercise, but because it is the best time to spare from your studies."[6]

Jefferson enjoyed horseback riding, but he thought it did far less for the body than walking. "The Europeans value themselves on having subdued the horse to the uses of man," he noted. "But I doubt whether we have not lost more than we have gained by the use of this animal. No one has occasioned so much degeneracy of the human body." But though Jefferson deprecated riding for exercise, he actually loved horses, kept his stable filled with fine steeds, and rode them frequently for recreation, as well as for doing the chores on his plantation at Monticello. He had his accidents, to be sure, once taking a fall while on a fast gallop, breaking his arm and collarbone, and another time almost drowning when his horse slipped while crossing a river. But most of the time, he was, people said, "a complete master of a horse." When he was President, he rode every day from one to three in the afternoon, and he continued the practice at Monticello after leaving the President's House. "I am too feeble to walk much," he wrote a friend when he was seventy-six, "but ride without fatigue six or eight miles a day and sometimes thirty or forty."[7]

Occasionally Jefferson went fishing. In June 1790, he accompanied President Washington on a three-day fishing trip off Sandy Hook, New Jersey, which attracted the attention of the newspapers, and in the spring of 1791 he and James Madison took a nine-hundred-mile journey in the Northeast, during the course of which they fished in Lake George, in eastern New York. But the lengthy Jefferson-Madison excursion was more than a fishing trip. Jefferson was feeling out of sorts at the time, and he decided to take a vacation from his labors as President Washington's secretary of state in order to "get rid of a headache which is very troublesome, by giving more exercise to the body and less to the mind." Still, he planned to exercise his mind as well, by observing trees and plants along the way at the request of the American Philosophical Society (a scientific organization to which he belonged) and by visiting farmers on Long Island and in other parts of New York to find out how they coped with the depredations of the Hessian fly on their crops. As for Jefferson's friend Madison, then a Virginia congressman, "Health, recreation, and curiosity" were "his objects" in joining Jefferson on the trip.[8]

The trip to the Northeast, which took a little over a month, was great fun for the two Virginians. They traveled by ship, horseback, and carriage, stopping at inns along the way, with Jefferson making detailed records of plants and trees he had never seen before for the APS. But he accomplished much more: He visited factories around Albany that produced salted herring, rum, and nails; discovered a new species, the red squirrel, near Lake Champlain; studied maple sugar production in Vermont; and learned that farmers in the Hudson Valley had developed a new variety of wheat that resisted the Hessian fly attacks. Jefferson was elated by his findings, and his headache was long gone by the time he returned to New York City to resume his work at the State Department. Madison thought his friend was in great shape by the end of the trip.[9]

Before getting back to New York City, then the nation's capital, Jefferson placed a large order for trees and shrubs, including maples, from a nurseryman in Flushing, Long Island, and when they arrived in Monticello he planted sixty maples on his farm, hoping to develop a maple orchard. The orchard failed, to his disappointment, but he had success with many of his other plantings. "No occupation is so delightful to me as the culture of the earth," Jefferson wrote a friend, the artist Charles Willson Peale, "and no culture comparable to that of the garden." The "greatest service which can be rendered any country," he declared, "is to add a useful plant to its culture." When he was in Europe, he made similar journeys for recreation, scientific inquiry, and just plain fun.[10]

At Monticello, Jefferson cultivated some of his gardens for food and others for beauty. "I have often thought," he wrote Peale, "that if heaven had given me choice of my position and calling, it should have been on a rich spot of earth, well watered, and near a good market for the production of the garden." Sometimes considered the first serious gardener in the United States, Jefferson continually exchanged seeds, plants, and botanical information with other gardeners around the country, and took the opportunity when he was abroad to collect plants he thought might be of use to American farmers. He was a "tree-hugger," too, sometimes called the "Father of American Forestry." He hated to see trees wasted, and when he was President, he is said to have exclaimed: "I wish I was a despot that I might save the noble, beautiful trees that are daily falling sacrifice to the cupidity of their owners and the necessity of the poor.... [The] unnecessary falling of a tree, perhaps the growth of centuries, seems to me a crime little short of murder." Jefferson was planting trees and designing treescapes almost to the end of his life. "Too old to plant trees for my own gratification," he said, when he was in his eighties, "I shall do it for posterity. Though an old man, I am a young gardener."[11]

Jefferson was an architect as well as a gardener. Learning from books and from buildings he observed while in Europe, he was continually renovating his home, Monticello, located on a small, densely wooded mountain in the Virginian Piedmont. "Architecture is my delight," he said, "and putting up and pulling down one of my favorite amusements." Through it all, he designed his mansion in such a way as to make the slave quarters almost invisible. He was strongly influenced by the Renaissance architect Andrea Palladio, who looked to Roman antiquity for his models. Monticello, as Jefferson designed it, was a modified Palladian villa, and his later architectural masterpieces were in the Palladian style: the Virginia Capitol in Williamsburg; "Poplar Forest," a small retreat house in Bedford County; and the University of Virginia. Professional architects place the buildings for the University of Virginia—his "academical village"—among the greatest of all American architectural achievements.[12]

At Monticello, Jefferson was an inventor as well as a gardener and architect, but his achievements were mainly modest. His most important invention was a "moldboard of least resistance" that increased the effectiveness of the plow and received acclaim in Europe as well as in the United States. One French authority proclaimed Jefferson's plow to be "mathematically exact, and incapable of further improvement," and saw to it that Jefferson received a gold medal for his achievement. Justly proud, Jefferson wrote Robert Fulton that it was "the finest plough which has ever been constructed in America," adding that the plow "is to the farmer what the wand is to the sorcerer." And since the farmer "produces the most essential things of life," the plow was "the most useful of the instruments known to man."[13]

Jefferson's other contrivances—including a dumbwaiter for bringing wine up from the cellar, music and writing stands adjustable in various ways, and a revolving or swivel chair—were minor labor-savers, almost as fun to look at as to utilize. Jefferson was always on the lookout for new labor-saving devices, and he corresponded with, and even sought out, people who he'd learned were tinkering with various gadgets that might be of some use. He kept a set of carpenter's tools and garden instruments in the President's House, "from which he derived much amusement." When he was in France, he insisted on having with him a "box containing small tools for wooden and iron work, for my own amusement." In 1807, Jefferson showed a British diplomat an "odd but useful contrivance" that looked like a turnstile, placed at the foot of his bed, "with 48 projecting hands on which hung his coats and waistcoats and which he could turn round with a long stick, a knickknack that Jefferson was fond of showing with many other mechanical inventions." But Jefferson was interested in large projects, too, like balloon travel, dry docks, submarines, steam power, and odometers, though he never got seriously involved in designing any of them.[14]

In 1797, when Jefferson was elected president of the American Philosophical Society, located in Philadelphia, he called it the "most flattering incident of his life," and in accepting the honor expressed an "ardent desire to see knowledge so disseminated through the mass of mankind, that it may at length reach the extremes of society, beggars and kings." In his proposals for public education and in the curriculum he drew up for the University of Virginia, which he played a major part in founding, he placed special emphasis on the natural sciences. Jefferson didn't believe in "pure" science; he thought that science had intrinsic social significance. Not only did it lead to practical improvements in daily life; he also thought it encouraged diligence, honesty, and zeal for the truth.[15]

While Jefferson liked to tinker with his mechanical instruments and tools, he also spent hours studying and exchanging views with other researchers in a wide variety of disciplines: astronomy, geology, archeology, climatology, mineralogy, botany, optometry, paleontology, chemistry, meteorology, and medicine. In his *Notes on Virginia,* he went to great lengths to disprove the contention of Buffon, a

leading French naturalist, that plants, animals, and even human beings indigenous to the New World were smaller than those in Europe.
He took science into his own home, too, arranging the entrance hall
in his mansion at Monticello as a kind of museum. On the walls
and on tables he displayed peace pipes, wampum belts, moccasins,
rattlesnake-skin insignia, and other Indian artifacts; the antlers of an
elk; the stuffed head of a bighorn sheep; the upper jaw of a mammoth
found in Kentucky; and other fossils. One guest thought there was
"no private gentleman in the world in possession of so perfect and
complete a scientific, useful, and ornamental collection." After delv-
ing into Jefferson's work in science, twentieth-century astronomer
Harlow Shapley concluded that the Virginian "had caution and dar-
ing inquisitiveness and a willingness to change his mind in the light
of new facts or as a result of further thought. What we would now call
proper scientific methods appeared to be instinctive with him."[16]

Jefferson's interests were not all scientific; he was attracted to the
arts, too, and regarded them, like science, as playing an important
part in promoting virtue and happiness among people. He was an
amateur when it came to painting and sculpture, in which his tastes
were eclectic, but with music he was something of a professional.
Music, he said, was "the favorite passion of my soul," and he spent
hours practicing the violin as a young man. Apparently a competent
performer, he joined two or three other young men in playing for
Francis Franquier, the colonial governor, in weekly concerts at the
Palace in Williamsburg. He also played for "sympathetic listeners"
at Monticello, which included Benjamin Franklin and Francis Hopkinson, one of America's earliest composers. When he was in Paris,
Maria Cosway, the Englishwoman with whom Jefferson fell deeply in
love, sent him a piece of music that she had composed, and he wrote
to John Trumbull: "Kneel to Mrs. Cosway and lay my soul on her
lap."[17]

While it has been taken for granted that Jefferson was an able violinist, it is only fair to point out that one of his contemporaries
sneered that Patrick Henry was the "worst fiddler" in Virginia, "with

the exception of Thomas Jefferson." But this may have been a political, not a musical, putdown, for Jefferson seems to have played some of the best violin music from Europe—Vivaldi, Corelli, Boccherini, and Handel—with zest and skill. In any case, Jefferson's wife, Martha, adored his violin playing. When he was courting her, he liked to play the violin at her home, as she accompanied him on the harpsichord and they both sang. One day, two of Martha's suitors happened to call on her when Jefferson was there, but when they heard the violin music, they looked resignedly at each other, and one of them exclaimed: "We are wasting our time. We may as well go home." Jefferson married Martha Skelton, a well-to-do widow, in 1772, and soon after he decided to organize a musical group that could play for him and his wife whenever they wanted some music. Not finding the talents he sought in Virginia, he sent to France for a gardener who could play the French horn, a weaver who played the clarinet, a cabinetmaker who had mastered the hautboy (oboe), and a stonecutter who could handle the bassoon. He didn't get quite what he wanted, but he did have a small ensemble for a time among his household workers, and he occasionally joined them in playing.[18]

When Jefferson became President in 1801, he took his preference for "Republican simplicity" with him and abolished the weekly levees and formal drawing rooms, replaced formal bows with handshakes, opened the President's House to visitors of all classes every morning, and, when asking guests to dinner at four at the executive mansion, substituted "Thomas Jefferson invites" for "The President of the United States" on the invitation cards. He dressed simply and plainly, particularly in the morning, even when welcoming foreign diplomats who came to pay formal calls on him and were splendidly attired. Some diplomats were offended, but Andrew Merry, the Envoy Extraordinary and Minister Plenipotentiary of His Britannic Majesty, was infuriated. He complained that Jefferson met him in his slippers and that the informal etiquette (which he called "pell-mell"), recognizing no status distinctions, at the first presidential dinner for Merry was a deliberate insult to him and his wife.[19]

But most people found Jefferson's dinners enormously satisfying. Though Jefferson was mostly a vegetarian and a moderate wine drinker, his dinners, often featuring French cuisine, were elegant. One guest reported that "never before had such dinners been given in the President's house, nor such a variety of the finest and costly wines." The "absence of splendour, ornament and profusion," he added, "was more than compensated [for] by the neatness, order and elegant sufficiency that pervaded the whole establishment." Jefferson not only entertained every day (usually having fourteen guests), but he also took care that all the guests felt comfortable and at home in the President's House. "I dined a large company once or twice a week," former President John Adams observed, "and Jefferson dined a dozen every day." In fact, Adams added, "I held levees once a week, and Jefferson's whole eight years was a levee." Jefferson claimed he enjoyed the family get-togethers the most and held the dutiful dinners for members of Congress and foreign diplomats without much enjoyment. His fun came in picking other kinds of guests: distinguished travelers, scientists, writers, explorers, and just plain citizens. Once he invited his butcher to dinner. When the man learned that one of Jefferson's guests was ill and that meant an extra place at the President's House, he decided to bring his own son with him. Jefferson was unfazed; he introduced both of them to his other guests and kept an eye on them during the dinner to be sure that they were having a good time.[20]

In addition to wining and dining his guests, Jefferson liked to show them his library, both at the President's House and at Monticello. He regretted not having time as President to do much reading, but he continued to add books to his collection. "I cannot live without books," he confessed. By 1815, when he sold his books to Congress (to pay some debts) as the nucleus of a congressional library, he had accumulated more than seven thousand volumes. Jefferson's enemies were critical of the transaction, insisting there were subversive books in the collection. "It might be inferred," growled Cyrus King, a die-hard Federalist, "from the character of the man who collected it, and France, where the collection was made, that the library contained irreligious and immoral books, works of the French philosophers, who caused and influenced the volcano of the French Revolution....The bill would put $23,900 into Jefferson's pocket for about 6,000 books, good, bad, and indifferent, old, new, and worthless, in languages many can not read, and most ought not [to]." As for Jefferson, after turning his collection over to the Library of Congress, he resumed collecting books.[21]

Jefferson's books included the ancient classics, of course, as well as books on scientific, legal, historical, political, religious, and philosophical subjects and on the fine arts. Jefferson took a practical approach to his library. Books, he thought, were tools to help people master serious disciplines. "Nothing of amusement," he said solemnly, "should lumber a public library." He did, though, read fiction, as well as poetry, for pleasure, and he regarded Shakespeare as indispensable for anyone "who wishes to learn the full power of the English language." For Jefferson, reading and writing were closely allied. In giving advice to a young friend on how to read, he urged him to criticize "the style of any book whatsoever, committing the criticism to writing. Translate into the different styles, to wit, the elevated, the middling, and the familiar,... Undertake at first short compositions... paying great attention to the elegance and correctness of your language."[22]

Jefferson stressed "elegance and correctness" in his own writing. It was his "peculiar felicity of expression," John Adams said, that led him to be chosen to write the first draft of the Declaration of Independence. Adams, who entered into an extensive correspondence with Jefferson later in life, also praised Jefferson's letters. He thought they ought to be published, for, he said, "they will exhibit a Mass of Taste, Sense, Literature and Science, presented in a sweet simplicity and a neat elegance of Stile, which will be read with delight in a future age." Jefferson once said that "an hour of conversation would be worth a volume of letters," but in this instance he was egregiously mistaken, for the Adams-Jefferson letters, available since the 1950s in a handsome edition, are one of the great pieces of writing that appeared in the early years of the American republic.[23]

On June 24, 1826, Jefferson wrote his last letter. It was a reply to a request by Roger C. Weightman to attend an Independence Day celebration in Washington planned for the fiftieth anniversary of the Declaration of Independence. Regretting his inability to be present because of illness, Jefferson went on to make his final pronouncement on the issues and values that had concerned him for most of his life. "All eyes are opened or opening to the rights of man," he told Weightman. "The general spread of the light of science has already laid open to every view the palpable truth that the mass of mankind has not been born with saddles on their backs, nor a favored few booted and spurred ready to ride them legitimately, by the grace of God." Less than two weeks later, on July 4, he was dead. John Adams had died a little earlier that day.[24]

$$\star \ \star \ \star \ 4 \ \star \ \star \ \star$$

The Learned
James Madison

It would never have occurred to anyone to ask James Madison, the "Father of the Constitution," what his hobbies were or what sports he liked best. Small and delicate as a young man, Madison looked "sedentary and studious," according to Edward Coles, a friend who was to become his private secretary. When "little Jemmy" (five foot six), as he was called, was a student at the College of New Jersey in Princeton, he studied so hard in order to finish his last two years in a year that he got only four or five hours' sleep a night. He succeeded, graduating in 1771, but was thoroughly worn out.[1]

Madison was never robust. Throughout his life he suffered from "epileptoid hysteria," an illness that produced sudden attacks, somewhat like epilepsy, that temporarily clouded his mind. He was also plagued by "bilious fever," or malaria, from time to time, and from attacks of rheumatism as he grew older. Madison's poor health kept him from entering the service during the American Revolution, prevented him from crossing the Atlantic to visit his friend Thomas Jefferson in Paris in 1785, and made it impossible for him to become much of an athlete, though he took walks and horseback rides upon the advice of his doctor. He also took trips in the summer to Berkeley Warm Springs, north of Winchester, Virginia, to avail himself of the medicinal waters there. Madison's enormous achievements as a statesman despite his physical handicaps were a tribute to his fine mind, great diligence, and deep dedication to the development of a new nation based on republican principles.

Madison was raised on his father's farm in Montpelier, Virginia, where he became fond of horses, learned a great deal about agriculture, enjoyed gardening, and in his travels around the countryside acquired a scientific interest, like Jefferson's, in trees, plants, rocks, and animals. "In my walks for exercise or amusement," he once explained, "objects frequently presented themselves which it might be a matter of curiosity to inspect."[2] Sports like fishing and swimming and games like whist and chess played a minor part in his life, and he carefully avoided gambling and excessive drinking. Aside from his life with his wife, Dolley, he seemed to get his greatest pleasure from his work as a major architect of the U.S. Constitution; author (with Alexander Hamilton and John Jay) of the *Federalist Papers;* chief formulator of the Bill of Rights in Congress; organizer, with Jefferson, of the Democratic-Republican Party; secretary of state for President Jefferson; and finally, President of the United States. Historian Gordon Wood pronounced Madison "the most profound and original political theorist not only in the Revolutionary and Constitution-making period, but also in all of American history."[3] He was an assiduous reader and a thoughtful writer whose social insights have withstood the test of time.

When Madison went to Philadelphia in 1770 as a delegate from Virginia to the Continental Congress, he received a mixed reception from the people he encountered. Pale, a bit awkward, and with a weak voice, he struck some as "a gloomy stiff creature," but others as "wise, temperate, gentle" and, of course, "studious."[4] Madison was shy and reserved when he was with strangers or in large crowds but relaxed, friendly, and good-natured in small groups and among friends. "I admire the mildness of Mr. Madison's manners," wrote Washington writer Margaret Bayard Smith in her memoirs, "and his smile has so much benevolence in it, that it cannot fail of inspiring good will and esteem."[5] Edward Coles admitted that Madison's "form, features, and manner were not commanding," but insisted that "his conversation was exceedingly so," and that "few men possessed so rich a flow of language, or so great a fund of amusing anecdotes, which were made the most interesting from their being well-timed and well-told."[6] Madison, said writer James K. Paulding, who knew him well, was "a man of wit, relished wit in others and his small bright blue eyes twinkled most wickedly when lighted up by some whimsical conception or association."[7]

Madison's sense of humor went back at least to his college days. At Princeton, he was a member of the American Whig Society, a student organization founded for "the cultivation of eloquence and literature," and he took a prominent part in a "paper war" with another student group, the Cliosophian Society, founded, like the Whig Society, for students who wanted to meet, talk, and compete for attention while in college. There were rules for the war between the Whigs and the Clios: One society attacked the other in writing, usually doggerel, to which the other replied, and then the verses of both sides were read aloud to an assembly of all the Princeton students and some of their professors. In September 1771, shortly before Madison's graduation, a fierce doggerel war, authorized by the faculty, took place in which Hugh Henry Brackinridge, Philip Freneau, and James Madison took the lead for the Whigs in attacking the Clios. Of the nineteen satirical putdowns sent to the Clios, Madison wrote three, and, by general agreement, they displayed the worst poetry and contained the most vulgar lines. In his pieces, Madison called the Clios "screech owls, monkeys and baboons," predicted that "each one's stench will kill his brother," and had this to say about one of the Clios who was planning to become a clergyman:

> "The lecherous rascal there will find
> A place just suited to his mind,
> May whore and pimp and drink and swear
> No more the garb of Christian wear."

He also attacked the Clios' poet laureate, who, he said, was emasculated by one of the Muses, and then had this to say:

> "Urania threw a chamber pot
> Which from beneath her bed she brought
> And struck my eyes and ears and nose
> Repeating it with lusty blows.
> In such a pickle then I stood
> Trickling on every side with blood
> When Clio, ever grateful muse
> Sprinkled my head with healing dews
> Then took me to her private room
> And straight out Eunuch out I come
> My voice to render more melodious
> A recompense for sufferings odious..."[8]

Before the Whig–Clio war ended, one of the students read these and other verses from both sides aloud in the Princeton Prayer Hall to the entire student body. The result was that Madison never attempted poetry again; he admitted to John Quincy Adams years later that he had "never...been favored with the Inspiration of the Muses."[9] But he did enjoy slipping ribald remarks into letters he wrote to his best friends after leaving college. John Witherspoon, the Scottish Presbyterian clergyman who headed the College of New Jersey, apparently never knew anything about this side of Madison. He was mainly impressed by the young man's intelligence and earnestness, and he once told Jefferson that during Madison's three years at Princeton, he "never knew him to do, or to say, an improper thing." Jefferson liked to tease Madison by quoting Witherspoon's remark about him on appropriate occasions.[10]

After Madison married Dolley Payne Todd, a pleasant young Quaker widow from Pennsylvania, in 1794, he began to come out of his shell and to feel more at ease in public, with his "beloved" by his side. Before the marriage, people said Madison, who always wore black, looked like a man on his way to a funeral; afterward, they commented on his amiability when appearing in public. When he took his oath as President in March 1809, he arranged for Dolley to attend the ceremony (the first President's wife to do so), and after that to take charge of the receptions, dinners, and entertainments that he was expected to sponsor in the President's House. At the inaugural ball, the writer Washington Irving was more impressed by Dolley than by her husband. She was "a fine, portly, buxom dame, who has a smile and a pleasant word for everybody," he wrote afterward, but "as for James Madison—ah! poor Jemmy! He is but a withered little apple john!"[11]

Margaret Bayard Smith was charmed by Dolley, too, but she also had a nice exchange with the new President. When Madison came over to greet her at the inaugural party, she recalled, he teased her some, as was his wont, and then asked how she was coming with the well she and her husband were having dug on their property. "'Truth is at the bottom of a well' is the old saying," he reminded her, "and I expect when you get to the bottom of yours, you will discover most important truths. I hope you will at least find water." As time passed and the ballroom became more crowded, Madison seemed to have faded. Later in the evening Mrs. Smith thought he seemed "spiritless and exhausted." When asked to stay for supper he agreed to do so, but, turning to Mrs. Smith, sighed that he "would much rather be in bed."[12]

Dolley's *courtesie de coeur* charmed just about everyone during Madison's eight years as President, and when the couple retired to Montpelier in 1817, they continued to please their guests by their ability to present high-class entertainments without abandoning the "Republican simplicity" that their friend Jefferson prized so highly. After attending one of the Madison dinners, Pennsylvania congressman Jonathan Roberts remarked that his "impression respecting the deportment of Mrs. Madison and the whole arrangement of the feast is that it was conducted with much ease and plainness. Nor do I think that the sternest democrat amongst us would be dispos'd to condemn the practice with much severity were he to witness it."[13]

At Montpelier, Madison liked to take his horse, Liberty, for a ride every morning around the plantation, and on rainy days he took walks on the porch for exercise. Sometimes he and Dolley ran races for the fun of it, and both seem to have done well for their age. In the afternoons they visited relatives and then returned home to serve dinner to guests that usually lasted two hours. At the table, according to Margaret Smith, Madison "was the chief speaker....He spoke of scenes in which he himself had acted a conspicuous part and of great men who had been actors in the same theater....Franklin, Washington, Hamilton, John Adams, Jefferson, Jay, Patrick Henry and a host of other great men were spoken of and characteristic anecdotes of all related. It was living History!" Only in the presence of strangers, Mrs. Smith wrote, did "this entertaining, interesting and communicative personage" become "mute, cold, and repulsive."[14]

Madison, according to Mary Cutts, Dolley's niece, was "a dear lover of fun and children." Though he had no children of his own, he liked quoting the whimsical things they said, telling amusing stories about them, and on occasion playing games with them. Mary's little brother Richard was one of the former President's favorites. He liked to pretend that the boy was a businessman and that he was the boy's agent, and in a playful letter he addressed him as "Richard Cutts, Tobacco Planter, Washington." Richard's entire tobacco crop, Madison reported dutifully, was net weight three ounces and ready for marketing, and he needed some instructions. Did Richard want the tobacco sold in England or in the United States? If manufactured, should it be pigtail, twist for chewing, or made into snuff? As partial payment, Madison enclosed a penny in the envelope, regretting that he "could not send you small change." He went on to say that he was eagerly awaiting Richard's visit to Montpelier and urged him to bring his sisters with him. "All your friends," he concluded, "white, yellow and black, send compliments."[15]

For as long as Madison's health held out, he continued his favorite activities: He read, wrote, oversaw his plantation, served as president of the local agricultural society, joined the board of visitors of Jefferson's beloved University of Virginia in Charlottesville, and became a member of a convention that drafted a new constitution for Virginia.

By 1831, however, his health had declined so seriously that he stayed in bed most of the time with rheumatism. "I am still confined to my bed," he wrote a friend, "with my malady, my debility and my age, in triple alliance against me."[16] The time came when his wife began reading to him and taking dictation from him, for he still had things to say about the development of the country.

Despite a life of poor health, Madison lived to the age of eighty-five. His last message to the nation, "Advice to My Country," written shortly before his death in 1836, was in Dolley's handwriting.[17]

☆ ☆ ☆ 5 ☆ ☆ ☆

The Unpretentious
James Monroe

James Monroe's vocation was the public service; so was his avocation. Beginning as a young man at the time of the American Revolution, he held one government position after another—local, state, and national—during the next forty years, with little time off, until he reached the presidency in 1817. Monroe has been called America's first important "professional politician," whose career was politics and whose private life was submerged in public affairs. He wrote hundreds of letters through the years, but they dealt almost entirely with political activities rather than personal and family matters. His son-in-law once told him that if he wrote an account of his life and times it would be "interesting and valuable." Monroe seemed surprised; "such was his modesty and self-depreciation that he had never thought of it before." Toward the end of his life, when he finally took time off to write his autobiography, his main purpose was to set the political record straight, not to reveal anything of interest about himself as a person.[1]

Monroe's boyhood is almost a blank. The records are so sparse that biographers are reduced to describing the social context of his early years in some detail, and then resorting to speculative phrases about what he was doing at the time. It is on the record, though without any details, that he sailed as a youngster, fished, rode horseback, and followed the hounds and bird dogs. At sixteen, Monroe left his home in Westmoreland County, Virginia, for Williamsburg, to enter the College of William and Mary. He dropped out to join the army at the outbreak of the War for Independence, was wounded in the left shoulder, and was promoted to captain for "bravery under fire." As an adult he was described as "six feet tall, broad, square-shouldered, and impressive in personal appearance. He was a man of rugged physique, raw-boned and by no means handsome." People spoke of his "great physical strength and endurance," and though he was usually quiet, modest, and reserved, he refused to be intimidated at any time in his life. Once, during Monroe's presidency, his secretary of the treasury, William H. Crawford, went to his office to request prompt action on appointments for some of his friends. When he found that the President wanted time to think it over, Crawford lost his temper, raised his cane, and shouted, "I will not leave this room till my request is granted." "You will not?" cried Monroe, seizing the tongs. "You will *now* leave the room or you will be thrust out." Crawford backed down at once, apologized profusely, and insisted on a friendly handshake before leaving.[2]

When Monroe became President, he was forced to take time off from politics to do some socializing. He didn't mind mingling with people on occasion; it was one of the President's obligations. But he was too tied up in political work to care much about whether or not Washington's social season was a success. At times, he liked to ride out into the countryside and pause to engage people along the way in conversation in order to learn something about them, as a pleasant change from engaging White House visitors in small talk. "Nature," wrote Maryland politician William Wirt, in a much-quoted appraisal of Monroe, "has given him a mind neither rapid nor rich, and therefore he cannot shine on a subject which is entirely new to him. But to compensate him for this, he is endued [*sic*] with a spirit of restless emulation, a judgment strong and clear, and a habit of application which no difficulties can shake, no labours can tire."[3]

Monroe strove to do his best at presidential dinners and receptions. He was courteous and thoughtful, and he never tried to dominate the gatherings. Justice Joseph Story dined at the White House one evening and found that the President "retains his plain and gentle manners; and is in every respect a very estimable man." When Harrison Gray Otis, Federalist leader in Massachusetts, attended a dinner for political bigwigs at the White House and sat out of the way at the foot of the table, he was impressed by the way Monroe sought him out and insisted on having a friendly glass of wine with him.[4]

Baron Axel Klinkoström, visiting Washington from Sweden, was also favorably impressed with Monroe. He delivered a letter from Stockholm to the President, and then asked to visit the naval docks in the United States to see if he could learn something that might be useful for his own country. Monroe smiled, gave his permission, and then said he would be happy if someone from Europe found anything "new and instructive in so young a country as the United States." The baron responded by saying that the day would come when Europeans could visit the United States, not to bring over inventions of their own, "but to fetch information and instruction about new things regarding which in the old world one had incomplete ideas or none." Klinkoström enjoyed his encounter with Monroe, but he was a little upset by the motley crowd that turned up at the President's reception. It was, he wrote, a "large gathering of all classes and ranks of the community; amid the smartly dressed were others, badly and slouchily dressed, who seemed to want to display themselves in a costume less tidy and less suitable to the occasion. I noticed some farmers or other men in stained clothes, uncombed hair, unbrushed and muddy boots, just as they had come from the street."[5]

But it wasn't only humble Americans who ignored the White House proprieties. At a dinner Monroe gave for foreign diplomats, the sociality went downhill rapidly soon after the guests were seated. Sir Charles Vaughan, the British minister, sat opposite Count de Sérurier, the French minister, and after the dining commenced, the Brit noticed that whenever he made a remark, the Frenchman bit his thumb. Finally he asked angrily, "Do you bite your thumb at me?" "I do," said the count coldly. At that point, the two men jumped up, rushed into an adjoining room, and had their swords crossed when

Monroe, who had hurried after them, entered the room and threw up their swords with his own. He then called for his servants, ordered the two men into separate rooms, and sent for their carriages. After that he returned to the dinner table, and the evening ended quietly. The following morning the two diplomats sent their apologies.[6]

With this dramatic exception, Monroe's dinner parties rarely sparkled. They seem to have been primarily tedious duties for the President, not occasions for pleasant relaxation. George Ticknor, a writer and educator from Boston, attended a small dinner party in honor of America's friend, the Marquis de Lafayette, then visiting the United States, and found it "extremely agreeable," but admitted this was "quite out of the common course." Judge E. R. Watson thought Monroe lacked the sophistication to be an outstanding host. "He always used the plainest, simplest language," according to Watson, "but was not fluent....He lacked the versatility and I should say also the general culture requisite for shining in the social circle...." Still, the judge thought that Monroe was "always interesting and instructive," and that whenever he was with "good listeners," he "led in conversation and talked of the scenes and events through which he had passed, *et quorum magna pars fuit* [of which he was a major part]."[7]

Monroe might have enjoyed the social side of the presidency more if his wife, Elizabeth, had been at his side for most receptions and dinners. Unfortunately, Mrs. Monroe was a chronic invalid (she may have had epilepsy) and was forced to turn over much of her responsibility for entertaining to her older daughter, Eliza Hay. The custom at the time Monroe became President in 1817 was for the President's wife to pay calls on the wives of senators and representatives, as well as on the wives of foreign dignitaries, and then receive their calls in return. But because of her poor health, Mrs. Monroe decided to abandon first calls, to the consternation of Washington society, and she also gave up the practice of holding continuous open house for visitors, scheduling precise and limited hours to meet them instead. In retaliation, the ladies of Washington boycotted her for a time, and saw to it that one of her "drawing rooms," the first event of the 1819 autumn season, opened to a "beggarly row of empty chairs; only five women attended, three of whom were foreigners." Later that year, Monroe held a cabinet meeting to discuss the etiquette of presidential visits, and the decision was made that neither the President nor his wife was obliged to make either first calls or return calls.[8]

Only gradually did people accept the new rules, and when they began meeting Mrs. Monroe at her stated hours, they found they liked her. She was "serene and aristocratic," said one observer, "…too well-bred to be moved by anything—at least in public." The Monroes' last big reception—New Year's, 1825—went swimmingly, and they both received compliments. "My impressions of Mr. Monroe are very pleasing," wrote one woman afterward. "He is tall and well-formed. His dress was plain and in the old style….His manner was quiet and dignified. From the frank, honest expression of his eyes…I think he well deserves the encomium passed upon him by the great Jefferson, who said, 'Monroe was so honest that if you turned his soul inside out there would not be a spot on him.'" As for Mrs. Monroe, her "manner is very gracious and she is a regal-looking lady."[9]

By the end of Monroe's second term as President, both he and his wife were eager to retire to Oak Hill, the home he had built in Virginia for retirement. "I shall be heartily rejoiced," he wrote Jefferson, "when the term of my service expires, and I may return home in peace with my family, on whom, and especially on Mrs. Monroe, the burdens and cares of my long public service have borne too heavily." When he left Washington, he was at long last ready to relax. Settled comfortably at Oak Hill, Monroe entertained family and friends, supervised work on his plantation, enjoyed his friendships with Jefferson and Madison, busied himself with his books, and did some writing. Every day he took time off in the morning and evening to ride around the countryside, either alone or with a friend. He refused to discuss politics with visitors and turned down suggestions that he run for Vice President with John Quincy Adams in 1824.[10]

In 1830, Elizabeth died suddenly, and Monroe was shattered. An injury from falling off his horse added pain to his sorrow. Unable to live alone at Oak Hill, he moved to New York City and spent his last days with his daughter Maria and her husband. For a time he was able to take leisurely walks in the neighborhood without anyone being aware that a former President of the United States was in their midst. As his vitality declined, he took to bed and soon developed a racking cough. "I am free from pain," he said, "but my cough annoys me much, both night and day." He died on July 4, 1831, the third President to die on the Fourth, and there was a great ceremony in City Hall in his honor, attended by thousands of people.[11]

Monroe's close friendship with Madison, after Jefferson died, added a great deal of pleasure to his life in his later years. "Mr. Monroe was warmly attached to his friends," recalled Judge E. R. Watson of Charlottesville. "He never forgot a service rendered him, whether in public or private life. But in his friendship and affection for Mr. Madison there was something touching and beautiful. Washington and Jefferson he greatly admired, but Mr. Madison he loved with his whole heart....I have several times seen them together at Montpelier, and, as it seemed to me, it was only in Mr. Madison's society that Mr. Monroe could lay aside his usual seriousness and indulge in the humorous jest and merry laugh, as if he were young again."[12]

☆ ☆ ☆ **6** ☆ ☆ ☆

The Aquatic John Quincy Adams

John Quincy Adams, the son of John Adams, was the first President to wear trousers instead of knee breeches. He was also the first—and only—President to take them off and swim nude in the Potomac River.

Adams was a powerful swimmer, and he took a dip in the Potomac just about every day. One warm June morning, when Thurlow Weed, a New York politico, was in Washington, he saw "a gentleman in nankeen pantaloons and a blue pea-jacket walking rapidly from the White House toward the river," and he realized at once it was President Adams. "I moved off to a respectful distance," he recalled. "The President began to disrobe before he reached a tree on the brink of the river, where he deposited his clothes, and then plunged in, head first, and struck out fifteen or twenty rods, swimming rapidly and turning occasionally on his back, seeming as much at his ease in that element as upon *terra firma*. Coming out he rubbed himself thoroughly with napkins, which he had brought for that purpose in his hand. The sun had not yet risen when he had dressed himself and was returning to the presidential mansion."[1]

Adams didn't always have as uneventful a swim as the one Weed witnessed. One morning a tramp stole his clothes while he was swimming, and he had to ask a boy who happened by to run to the White

House to get some clothes for him from his wife, Louisa. On another occasion he planned to paddle across the river in a canoe and swim back, but the canoe filled with water halfway across and sank. Adams was partly dressed this time, and his clothes filled with water and "hung like fifty-two pound weights upon my arms," he wrote later, making it difficult for him to swim. By the time he reached shore, he had lost most of his clothes in the water and had to return to the White House only half dressed. His losses: one shoe, one waistcoat, two napkins, and two handkerchiefs. Afterward, he wrote in his diary that while "struggling for life and gasping for breath" in the water, he had "ample leisure to reflect upon my own indiscretion" in using a leaky old canoe. Still, he continued to take chances. Sometimes, when he swam in bad weather, against the protests of his wife, he almost drowned.[2]

The most famous JQA swimming story, possibly spurious, involved a perky newspaperwoman named Anne Royall, who published two small papers called *Paul Pry* and *The Huntress*. Determined to get an interview with President Adams about his bank policy, she followed him to the Potomac one morning and plunked herself down on his clothes after he hopped into the river. "Come here!" she yelled. Taken by surprise, Adams returned to the shore and asked: "What do you want?" "I'm Anne Royall!" she announced. "I've been trying to see you to get an interview out of you for months on the State Bank question and I have hammered at the White House and they won't let me in, so I watched your movements, and this morning I stalked you from the Mansion down here. I'm sitting on your clothes and you don't get them till I get the interview. Will you give it to me or do you want to stay in there the rest of your life?" "Let me get out and dress," begged Adams, "and I'll promise to give you the interview. Please go behind those bushes while I make my toilet." "No you don't," replied Royall. "You are President of the United States and there are a good many millions of people who want to know and ought to know your opinions on this Bank question. I'm going to get it. If you try to get out and get your clothes I'll scream, and I just saw three fishermen around the bend. You don't get out ahead of that interview!" So, the story goes, she got her interview while Adams stood chin-deep in the Potomac River.[3]

Sometimes Adams took a horseback ride at dawn instead of a swim in the Potomac, and then, back in the President's mansion, read the Bible and went over the newspapers before having breakfast. On occasion, later in the day he attended horse races, partly to get away from people. "The races," he said, "relieved me of many visitors." Fishing was another sport he enjoyed, and he never felt more relaxed and contented than when working in the White House garden. He'd taken up billiards in Europe, and when he was President he purchased a billiard table, some cue sticks, and billiard balls for the White House and billed the federal government for them. This produced such an uproar among his enemies in Congress—they charged Adams with wasting the public's money on "gaming tables and gambling furniture" that corrupted the nation's youth—that he finally assumed the expense himself.[4]

One of Adams's greatest pleasures was dining with close friends and enjoying good food, wine, and conversation. He was something of an oenophile; he cherished fine wines and was knowledgeable about them. In 1832 his doctor urged him to cut down on his drinking, but he continued to take two or three glasses of Madeira after dinner. At one fancy dinner to which he was invited, he and the other guests drank a glass of hock with oysters on the half shell, a glass of sherry after the soup, and champagne with the meats. Then the host brought out fourteen bottles of Madeira for them to taste, and Adams was able to identify eleven of them correctly, to the surprise and delight of his companions.[5]

Despite JQA's fondness for good food and drink, he was by no means an epicurean. He was as earnest and diligent as his father was, and as self-critical, too, when he thought he was not doing his best. He was even harder on himself and more miserable at times than his father ever was, in great part because he clashed with his parents over his choice of a career. When he was a student at Harvard,

Adams decided he wanted to become a man of letters, known for his poetry and literary reviews rather than for his public service, as his parents preferred. He wrote poetry at Harvard that was creditable but not outstanding, and he worked hard to improve it. But his parents made it clear that they expected him to be a great statesman someday, not a litterateur. His father pressed him hard. "You come into life with advantages which will disgrace you if your success is mediocre," he wrote JQA in April 1794, when the latter was working as a lawyer in Boston and dreaming of a literary life. If "you do not rise to the head not only of your profession, but of your country, it will be owing to your own *Laziness, Slovenliness,* and *Obstinacy.*"[6]

A few years earlier, when JQA was at Harvard, he was genuinely happy. He enjoyed his studies, his friends, and his amusements: dancing, drinking, singing, playing the flute, and going to the theater. He looked forward to the life of a literary gentleman, producing writings that would be read with respect and pleasure. But after graduation in 1787, when he began studying law in Theophilus Parson's Academy in Newburyport, his spirits fell precipitously. Adams found law far less stimulating than literature, and the idea of making it a career or using it as a stepping stone to public office had no appeal for him at the time. The pressures—to make law his profession, to seek public office, to become famous—became too much for him, and he finally succumbed to a serious attack of anxiety and depression and had to drop out of law school for a time. "God in Heaven…," he wrote in his diary, "take me from this world before I curse the day of my birth." He spent sleepless nights, worried about trifles, and despaired over his worthlessness. To pull himself out of his misery, he tried valerian root tea and quinine, copied out passages from his favorite poets and playwrights, including Shakespeare, and did a lot of walking, riding, and swimming. Adams found succor in sociability, too. With friends and family he could be an amiable chap, relaxing and feeling at ease eating, drinking, and chatting. With outsiders, however, he was stiff, cold, and even seemingly hostile, leaving them puzzled by his demeanor. He once admitted that he was "reserved, cold, austere," and with a "forbidding manner" that bewildered people. Years later, even his son, Charles Francis Adams, said that JQA wore an "Iron Mask."[7]

In time, JQA recovered from his illness, resumed his law work, and then, after all his agonizing, finally made his choice: public service. He made the decision in 1794, when he was practicing law in Boston, after President Washington, knowing his talents, appointed him as minister to Holland (an assignment later changed to Portugal). After thinking it over, Adams decided to accept the post. Returning to Europe had a strong appeal for him. Having spent some time with his father there when he was a boy, Adams had been captivated by its cultural riches. The prospect of associating again with cultivated people and taking in more of Europe's art, literature, music, and theater more than made up for postponing, or perhaps even relinquishing, his plan to become one of America's illustrious literati. Adams's decision to accept a diplomatic post led to a distinguished career for the ambitious young man: He was minister to Holland, Portugal, England, and Russia; then, back in the United States, U.S. senator from Massachusetts, followed by a stint as professor of rhetoric and oratory at Harvard, secretary of state for President Monroe, and finally, the highest prize, President of the United States. After retiring, his service as a congressman from Massachusetts won him respect and acclaim. With him during both the happy days and the hard times was his wife, Louisa, an attractive, intelligent, and musically talented woman whom he had met in London and married in 1797.[8]

Adams, who entered the White House in 1825 at the age of sixty-one, was one of the few Presidents who might rightly be called an intellectual. In addition to swimming, riding, and hiking, he took as much free time as he could to read the classics, write poetry, attend the theater, take in operatic performances (which he'd learned to love in Paris), and delve into astronomy. One of his favorite diversions was to translate the ancient classics from Latin into English. Adams also shared his wife's love for music. "I am extremely fond of music," he said, "and by dint of great pains have learnt to blow very badly the flute—but I could never learn to perform upon the violin, because I never could acquire the art of putting the instrument in tune." Drawn to Louisa at the outset because of her musical talent, he sang and played with her when he was courting her, and when he became President he liked to have her perform on the harp and piano for his guests. The Adamses' dinners received much praise for their refinement.[9]

When Adams presented his agenda to Congress after his inauguration as President in 1825, he included cultural as well as economic proposals for developing the United States: scientific expeditions, an astronomical observatory, and a national university, as well as the building of roads, canals, and bridges binding the country together. The majority of congressmen were hostile to the kind of government activity that Adams proposed; they were also hostile to Adams himself, bent on replacing him with Andrew Jackson in the next election and determined to denigrate him as much as they could while he was in the White House. Badly defeated by Jackson in his quest for a second term in 1828, he thought his "character and reputation" were "a wreck." The "sun of my political life," he lamented, "sets in the deepest gloom." Opera music accompanied his gloom. "In the French opera of Richard Coeur-de-Lion," Adams wrote years later, "the minstrel Blondel, sings under the walls of his prison a song beginning:

> O, Richard! O, mon roi!
> L'univers t'abandonne.

When I first heard this song forty-five years ago, at one of the first representations of that delightful play, it made an indelible impression upon my memory, without imagining that I should ever feel its force so much closer home. In the year 1829 scarce a day passed that did not bring it to my thoughts."[10]

But Adams wasn't miserable for long. In September 1830 he was elected to the House of Representatives from the Plymouth District in Massachusetts, and his seventeen years in Congress were exciting and productive. Recognition of Adams's tremendous ability, which eluded him as President, finally came to him for his work in Congress, particularly for his energetic fight against the "gag rule" that prevented members of the House from discussing the slavery issue. It took eight years, with numerous speeches and ingenious procedural maneuvers in the House, before Adams mustered enough votes to repeal the rule in 1844. By this time even many of his opponents couldn't help admiring him for his courage and determination when it came to following his principles. From being called the "Madman of Massachusetts" (and being threatened with censure, expulsion from the House, and even death), he came to be called "Old Man Eloquent."

Adams hated to miss a day in Congress, and once, when he walked into the House, a bit unsteady after recovering from a stroke, everyone stood and applauded, and two congressmen helped him to his seat. He was at his seat in the House when he collapsed and he died a little later, in February 1848, and Missouri senator William Hart Benton, a Jacksonian who liked some of Adams's poetry, exclaimed, "Where else could it have found him, at any state of his career, for the fifty years of his illustrious public life?"[11]

Always on the job, yes, except when he wanted to swim. In his eightieth year, Adams had an "irresistible impulse" to swim in the Potomac again. As he entered the water, he overheard some boys murmur, "There is John Quincy Adams." The boys had left their clothes on one of Adams's "old standard rocks," but he found another rock to put his on and had a good swim. It was one of his last.[12]

The Two-Fisted
Andrew Jackson

Andrew Jackson's friend John McNairy, a judge who studied law with him in Salisbury, North Carolina, in the early 1790s, didn't think Jackson was much of a sportsman. "The truth is, as everybody here well knows," he said, "General Jackson never was fond of any kind of sport, nor did he indulge in any except occasionally for amusement, but horse-racing." McNairy was only partly right. Jackson loved horses and he even bred race horses at the Hermitage, his plantation near Nashville, Tennessee, to enter in the races. But he also indulged in other sports as a young man.[1]

As a boy, Jackson was a tough little fellow, and people soon learned that they mistreated or even teased him at their peril. He rarely picked fights, but he was quick to defend his honor if he thought he had been insulted. And he fought hard when challenged in a game. In wrestling matches, a former schoolmate recalled, "I could throw him three times out of four, but he would never stay *throwed*. He was dead game even then, and never would give up." Once, some of the boys he played with secretly loaded a gun up to its muzzle and gave it to him to fire off so they could see the explosion "kick" him over. When Andy fired and, to his surprise, landed on his back, he jumped up and thundered, "By God, if any of you laughs, I'll kill him." There was no laughter. On another occasion, when a building in Jonesboro caught fire, Jackson quickly took charge and organized a water-bucket line of people to fight the fire, and when a drunk began annoying the bucket carriers, Jackson whacked him senseless with a bucket and ordered the line to resume its work. "He saved the town!" exclaimed one observer. On another occasion, when someone interrupted a speech he was giving by crying "pshaw!," Jackson stopped talking and cried: "Who dares to say pshaw to me? By—, I'll knock any man's head off who says pshaw to me!" There were no more pshaws.[2]

Jackson's admirers called him a hero for having whipped the British in New Orleans at the end of the War of 1812, and they lauded him for his boldness, determination, courage, and manliness. Some of them wanted to believe that he never ventured beyond the bounds of propriety, and, as his friend John Eaton put it, that his "moral character" was "without reproach." But when Andy was a law student in Salisbury, one of his acquaintances insisted he was "the most roaring, rollicking, game-cocking, horse-racing, card-playing, mischievous fellow that ever lived in Salisbury." Jackson did not "trouble the law books much," it was said, and he spent "more time in the stable than in the law office." He was, in short, "the head of all the rowdies hereabouts." One December, he had the job of organizing a Christmas ball, his town's fancy annual social event. For the fun of it, he sent tickets to two prostitutes, a mother-and-daughter team, but when they showed up at the party, not many of the guests were amused. Jackson had to apologize.[3]

Jackson loved gambling. There wasn't much that he wouldn't bet on. While living in Charleston, South Carolina, he took a stroll one night, happened on some people shooting craps, and stopped to watch. After a while, one of the players challenged him to a game, betting two hundred dollars against the fine horse that had brought Jackson to town. Jackson accepted the challenge, won the game, and headed for home two hundred dollars richer. "My calculation," he told friends, "was that, if a loser in the game, I would give the landlord my saddle and bridle, as far as they would go towards the payment of his bill, ask a credit for the balance, and walk away from the city; but being successful, I had new spirits infused into me, left the table, and from that moment to the present time I have never thrown dice for a wager."[4]

Years later, when Jackson was living at the Hermitage, nearby Nashville was becoming something of a "sin city," with billiards played for money on such a large scale that the Tennessee legislature banned the game. There were horse races to bet on, too, and plenty of card games. For a time cockfights became immensely popular and Jackson got into the swing of things, raising gamecocks, training them, and entering them in fights in Nashville. "In all these sports— the innocent, the less innocent, and the very bad," wrote James Parton, one of Jackson's earliest chroniclers, "Andrew Jackson was an occasional participant. He played billiards and cards, and both for money. He ran horses and bet upon horses of others. He was occasionally hilarious over his whiskey or his wine when he came to Nashville on Saturdays. At the cock-pit no man more eager than he."[5]

Parton talked to people who remembered seeing Jackson frequently at the cock pit in Nashville's public square, cheering on some of his favorite birds in a loud voice: "Hurrah! My Dominica! Ten dollars on my Dominica! Hurrah! My Bernadotte! Who'll take me up? Well, done, my Bernadotte! My Bernadotte forever!" Once, Colonel Weightstill Avery saw one of Jackson's chickens revive after being cut down in a fight and, by a lucky stroke, kill his antagonist. "There," cried Jackson, "is the greatest emblem of bravery on earth. Bonaparte is not braver!" Everyone, Avery noticed, was consuming large quantities of mint julep while playing the birds.

Jackson gave up many of his youthful amusements after he became a soldier, and then President. While he was running for President, however, his early-life shenanigans came to plague him. "What!" cried one woman, when she heard there were plans to nominate Jackson for President. "Jackson for President! *Jackson! Andrew Jackson!* The Jackson that used to live in Salisbury? Why, when he was here he was such a rake that my husband would not bring him into the house. It is true, he *might* have taken him out to the stable to weigh horses for a race, and might drink a glass of whiskey with him *there*. Well, if Andrew Jackson can be President, anybody can!"[6]

When Jackson became President in 1829, he continued his love affair with horses. He brought more than a dozen race horses to Washington from his Hermitage plantation and enlarged the White House stables to house them. Though he kept in touch with the training of his horses at the Hermitage as well as at the White House, he turned the management of his racing affairs over to Andrew Jackson Donelson, his wife Rachel's nephew, whom he had adopted when he became President. He continued to be a good judge of horses, purchasing his best-known horse, Truxton, when he saw him lose a race but realized he was poorly reared and needed retraining. After putting the horse through the best training he could devise, he decided it was ready for a race and challenged the owner of Greyhound, the horse that had defeated Truxton in the first place. The stakes were high, both for Jackson and all the Tennessee farmers who had made bets, mostly on Greyhound. Truxton won handily, and Jackson and his friends held a big party to celebrate their winnings. A little later, Jackson ran Truxton against an unbeaten horse, Ploughboy, and though his own horse became lame two days before the race, he refused to postpone the event. Truxton won the first heat, and Jackson worked hard on the horse's legs in the half hour between heats. To his enormous delight, Truxton ran well enough to achieve victory by sixty yards in the second heat.[7]

Jackson didn't always win. A mare, Maria, seemed unbeatable. Truxton's son, Decatur, failed to beat her, as did several other horses owned or backed by Jackson. When someone asked the President if he'd ever failed at anything, he replied, "Nothing that I can remember except Maria. I could not beat her." Jackson sometimes experienced trouble at the racetracks. Once, he suspected that someone was trying to fix a race in which he was competing, so he took a position, well armed, at the starting point, and announced he would shoot anybody he observed trying to interfere with the race. On another occasion, he took his Vice President, Martin Van Buren, to the track with him. When one of the jockeys mounted a large stallion named Busirus, he lost control and Jackson quickly jumped in front of Van Buren, crying, "Get behind him, Mr. Van Buren! They will run over you, sir!" After Busirus calmed down, Jackson berated his trainer for not doing a better job with the horse.[8]

When Jackson entered the White House, a friend gave him a plain-looking "sulky"—a light two-wheeled vehicle with a seat for the driver—for use in riding around Washington. Some people thought the vehicle fit "Old Hickory" to a T. Poet N. P. Willis put it this way: "Some eccentric mechanic has presented President Jackson with a sulky made of rough cut hickory, with the bark on. It has very much of the everlasting look of 'Old Hickory' himself, and if he could be seen driving a high-stepping, bony old iron-gray stud in it, any passenger would see that there was as much fitness in the whole thing as in the chariot of Bacchus.... Some curiously-twisted and gnarled branches have been ingeniously turned into handles and whip-box, and the vehicle is compact and strong." Some people noted that Jackson's rough-hewn sulky was simple and unpretentious compared to the elegant carriages that most of the other Presidents had used.[9]

Jackson did little entertaining when he first became President. He was still grieving over the loss of Rachel, who had died of a heart attack just three months earlier. At the Hermitage, he and Rachel had enjoyed entertaining visitors as well as friends, whom they treated almost as members of the family. "There was lots of merriment and fun of the homely sort," according to one chronicler. Rachel was fond of "the hearty diversions of the homely sort," he reported, "particularly in the vigorous, old-fashioned dances." Since she was short and plump and Jackson was tall and slender, "the spectacle is said to have been extremely curious when they danced a reel together, which they often did." But Rachel became more pious and puritanical as she grew older, and she eventually gave up dancing. She never gave up her pipe, though. Neither did Jackson, though one doctor suggested he do so for his health. "Now, Doctor," Jackson told him, "I can do anything you think proper to order, and bear as much as most men. There are only two things I can't give up; one is coffee and the other is tobacco."[10]

Jackson was a pipe collector. He accumulated a large collection of pipes from around the world, but he always confessed that he liked best the sweet taste of his plain corncob pipe. When he became President, a congressman, eager for an appointment to a post abroad, decided to capitalize on the President's fondness for pipes. One day, he called on Jackson (who was of course smoking his pipe) and said, "General Jackson, I am about to ask you a favor—a favor, sir, that will cost you nothing, and the government nothing, but will gratify me exceedingly." "It's granted, sir," said Jackson. "What is it?" "Well, General," said the congressman, "I have an old father at home who has as great an esteem for your character as one man can have for another. Before I left home, he charged me to get for him, if possible, one of General Jackson's pipes, and that is the favor I now ask of you." "Oh, certainly," said Jackson, laughing and ringing the bell. When a servant appeared, Jackson told him to bring him two or three clean pipes. "Excuse me," interrupted the congressman, "but may I ask you for that very pipe you have just been smoking?" "This one?" said Jackson. "By all means, if you prefer it." He began to empty out the ashes, but the congressman stopped him. "No, General," he said, "don't empty out the tobacco. I want that pipe, just as it is, just as it left your lips." When Jackson readily handed it to him, the congressman carefully put it in a piece of paper, thanked Jackson for his generous gift, and left the room beaming with pleasure. Three weeks later he received his appointment and left for South America.[11]

When Jackson got around to entertaining regularly in the White House, he persuaded his adopted son's wife, Emily Donelson, to become his hostess, and he began holding levees every other Thursday when Congress was in session and fairly sizeable supper parties. Jackson seems to have enjoyed himself on these occasions, but more than once he confessed he was happiest when Mrs. Donelson's children were with him or when he got to meet the children of some of his guests. He and Henry Clay's little girl got along fine even though he detested her father. One visitor saw Jackson seated in his rocking chair one afternoon, trying to read the newspaper, with a chubby boy wedged on each side of him and a third on his lap. Senator Thomas Hart Benton was deeply moved one cold and rainy night when he saw the President go outdoors and return with a lamb because a child who was with him cried piteously when he heard the creature was out in the cold. "They are the only friends I have," Jackson once said of the children, "who never pester me with their ambitions or tire me with their advice." Jackson sometimes kept government officials and foreign diplomats sitting in the executive waiting room while he was exchanging pleasantries with a group of schoolgirls.[12]

Jackson had a limited education, and he never became much of a reader of books for pleasure. Most of the books he owned dealt with military matters or agricultural subjects. The only fiction he ever touched, reportedly, was Oliver Goldsmith's *The Vicar of Wakefield,* a popular eighteenth-century British novel. Biographer John Spencer Bassett wrote that Jackson's "attainments in scholarship were very meagre. He knew no more Latin than he could pick up in the practice of his profession of lawyer; his spelling and grammar were devoid of regularity...his acquaintance with literature is a negligible quantity. Occasionally one finds in his papers some oft-quoted phrase as *Carthago delenda est,* but it is always one he must have heard on a hundred stumps in Tennessee."[13]

When Harvard awarded Jackson an honorary degree in 1833, John Quincy Adams (whom he beat in the presidential election of 1828) was furious. Jackson, he inveighed, was "a barbarian who could not write a sentence of grammar, and hardly could spell his own name." Adams naturally exaggerated; the Jacksonians in Congress had done much to wreck his presidency. Jackson could, in fact, express himself clearly and forcefully when he needed to do so, and as for spelling a word four different ways in one paragraph, as Jackson is alleged to have done, it surely takes a certain amount of ingenuity to come up with such verbal variety. The doctorate of law that Harvard bestowed on Jackson was written in Latin, and when the students addressed him as "Doctor Jackson" after the ceremony, he told them, "I shall have to speak in English, not being able to return your compliment in what appears to be the language of Harvard. The only Latin I know is *E Pluribus Unum*."[14]

Jackson had plenty of enemies, but he was one of our most popular Presidents, and he received countless gifts, mainly food, during his eight years in the White House. The largest and most famous present, sent by Colonel Thomas S. Meacham of Sandy Creek, New York, in 1835, was an enormous piece of cheese, four feet in diameter, two feet thick, weighing fourteen hundred pounds, decked in roses and bearing the label "Our Union, it must be preserved." Jackson put it aside for aging and ripening, and just before leaving office in March 1837, he invited the public to come to the White House to share it with him on February 22, Washington's birthday, from one to three in the afternoon. At the appointed hour, people swarmed into the Executive Mansion from Washington and surrounding towns— men, women, and children, blacks as well as whites—with knives, forks, and spoons in their hands, and in the course of slashing off hunks of the cheddar to devour or take home they spilled cheese all over, ground it into the carpets, smeared it on the walls, furniture, and even draperies, and left the corridors dangerously slippery. "Although there has been considerable excitement of late," cried the *Washington Sun,* "the abolition excitement, the Texas excitement— the cheese excitement is the greatest of all."[15]

Martin Van Buren, recently elected to replace Jackson in the White House, was thoroughly disgusted when he saw the unsightly mess the cheese-devourers had left behind. He took a solemn vow that he would never serve such a massive refreshment in the White House when he became President.[16]

☆ ☆ ☆ **8** ☆ ☆ ☆

The High-Toned
Martin Van Buren

One day, when Congress was debating a tariff bill sponsored by Henry Clay, Martin Van Buren, then a senator from New York, was asked what his views on the tariff were. Van Buren replied that he opposed an "oppressive inequality" and favored a "conciliatory measure." It was a typical Van Buren statement: evasive, ambiguous, and noncommittal. He became so famous for his lack of commitment—"vanburenish," for a time, came to mean "noncommittal"—that people tried to smoke him out on trivialities just for the fun of it. "Matt," said a senator who had made a bet he could get a straightforward answer out of him, "it's been rumored that the sun rises in the East. Do you believe it?" "Well, Senator," returned Van Buren, "I understand that's the common acceptance, but as I never get up till after dawn I can't really say." He was having his fun, too, but that didn't mean he wasn't seriously "vanburenish" whenever he thought it helpful to his career. He ended up with nicknames not especially complimentary: "The Little Magician," "the American Talleyrand," and "the Red Fox of Kinderhook."[1]

Van Buren came up the hard way. His father was a small farmer in Kinderhook, New York, near Albany, who used his house as a tavern, where Matt was born and raised. As a youngster he worked in the tavern as a pot boy. He spent a few years in the village academy learning the fundamentals, and then became a clerk in the law office of

Francis Sylvester. From there Van Buren began his gradual ascent from local attorney and county officeholder to state senator, U.S. senator, secretary of state, Vice President, and finally President of the United States. He was extremely ambitious and possessed qualities that were helpful for rising in the political world: tact, caution, shrewdness, graciousness, courtesy, and the ability to work quietly behind the scenes to achieve his objectives. Virginia senator John Randolph of Roanoke said Van Buren "rowed to his object with muffled oars." Like Monroe, he was a professional party politician, and he played an important part in the development of the Democratic Party.[2]

Van Buren wasn't known for his sports or recreations. As a boy, it is said, he went fishing in the ponds and streams around Kinderhook, but as a young adult he seems to have been too busy pursuing his career in politics to take time off for relaxation. New York City changed all that. When he moved to Manhattan in 1801 to work in the law office of William P. Van Ness, he was introduced to entertainments never dreamed of in his hometown. He did a lot of sightseeing in his free time; made friends who liked to go out on the town; frequented gaming houses, dance halls, and theaters; and also had "an instructive education in matters closer to his heart." In the years that followed, Van Buren continued to take in the theater and came to like opera. He also developed a taste for wine with his meals, usually a fine Madeira or an Italian Montepulciano. He didn't smoke a pipe the way Andrew Jackson and his wife did, but he did take snuff. Once, when he was presiding over the Senate as Vice President, Henry Clay tried to annoy him by delivering a passionate polemic against Jackson's bank policy. Van Buren looked impassive through it all, but when Clay finished, he put down his gavel, asked one of the senators to take his chair, descended from the rostrum, and, instead of defending the President, went over to Clay's seat and said, "Mr. Clay, may I borrow a pinch of your excellent snuff?" Taken by surprise, Clay nodded dazedly and handed over his snuff box. Van Buren took a pinch of it, applied it to his nostrils, bowed, and left the Senate chamber. He had muffled his oars again.[3]

In 1831, President Jackson appointed Van Buren ambassador to Great Britain, and the latter made plans for his first trip abroad. His months in Britain had a major impact. When he arrived in London, he asked writer Washington Irving, America's chargé d'affaires in the embassy, to join him and his son (whom he had brought with him) on a tour of the literary and historic places of interest. After that they ventured into the country, visiting historic sites like Oxford, Blenheim, Stratford-on-Avon, and Warwick Castle, and ended up for Christmas at Barlborough Hall in Derbyshire with Irving's friend Reverend Cornelius Bode, who treated them to an old-fashioned Christmas with mummers, morris dancers, glee singers from neighboring villages, the wassail bowl, yule logs, and snapdragon dancing. As Irving observed, Van Buren indulged in "all kinds of merriment"; the writer's impression was that he was "a success-wearied man, rushing to pleasure and play with a childlike delight." Back in London for New Year's, Van Buren paid a call on the British foreign secretary and then accepted a series of social invitations. "His gaiety and charm," noted biographer Holmes Alexander, "soon captivated the Town. No other American minister...had ever shown such aptitude for the superficial graces of courtiership. Mr. Van Buren was a social success from the start and diplomatic London clutched him to her bosom."[4]

Van Buren was proud of his social success, impressed by the "glamour of court life," and elated to be the guest of knights, earls, dukes, and princes. When he learned that the Senate had refused to confirm his appointment as ambassador, he lingered two more months in London before returning home. It turned out to be a "prolonged fiesta" for him. He filled his letters and, later on, his autobiography with the names of the respectable people he met and with reports on the fashionable dinners and receptions to which he was invited. Van Buren had not ceased to be a Jacksonian Democrat, but he had come to believe that even in a democratic country there ought to be less informality and more style and dignity in the President's relations with the public than President Jackson displayed.[5]

When Van Buren succeeded Jackson as President in 1837, the change from Jackson's informality to Van Buren's formality began at once. "Coming into the presidency with no thought of doing any more than enjoying it," declared Holmes Alexander, with some exaggeration, "Mr. Van Buren proceeded to do so." This much is clear: Van Buren felt that he could not take pleasure in living in the White House without decent surroundings and a comfortable and enjoyable schedule for his time away from work. Persuading Congress to appropriate $27,000 for renovation, he had the place thoroughly cleaned, repainted, redecorated, and refurnished. Then he fashioned a code of etiquette that some people thought resembled that of a German principality. There were to be no more episodes like the near-riot that took place at Jackson's inaugural reception in 1829, or the one that reduced the White House to a pigpen when Jackson shared a big cheese with his rowdy followers. The new code of etiquette ended the custom of serving food at public receptions, open to everyone, except on New Year's Day and the Fourth of July. Van Buren also hoped to improve relations between high society in Washington ("the cliff-dwellers") and the President, which had declined during Jackson's presidency, by throwing small, elegant dinner parties for socially esteemed people. From the "People's Shrine" under Jackson, the White House, complained some Jacksonians, was becoming the "Palace" under Van Buren. "A few years ago," observed Frederick Marryat, "a fellow could drive his hackney coach up to the door, walk into the saloon in all his dirt and force his way to the President...," but Van Buren "has prevented the mobocracy from intruding itself upon his levees. The police are now stationed at the door to prevent the intrusion of any improper person."[6]

For those fortunate enough to share in Van Buren's bounty, the experience was a stimulating one. Washington journalist Nathan Sargent thought Van Buren had mastered "the high art of blending dignity with ease and gravity." Since Van Buren's wife, Hannah, had died many years before, he asked their daughter, Angelica Singleton, to serve as hostess on social occasions, and she was, one diplomat exclaimed, "fit to grace any court in Europe." Some people, though, wondered whether she wasn't becoming too courtly when she started receiving guests at receptions by sitting in an armchair on a raised platform. Van Buren himself dressed handsomely for his social appearances, but he was always relaxed, friendly, and good-humored, and he tried to make every one of his guests feel quite at home. Unlike Jackson, he also invited members of the opposition party and treated them cordially. One evening, when Henry Clay was a guest at one of Van Buren's sumptuous dinner parties at the White House, a servant suddenly rushed in to report that the kitchen was on fire. After a few buckets of water quenched the flames, Clay got up, put his hand over his heart, and announced: "Mr. President, I'm doing all I can to get you out of this house, but I assure you I do not want to burn you out." Van Buren responded with a friendly bow. Clay later praised the President for his "generous liberal hospitality."[7]

Van Buren's enjoyment of the good things in life eventually worked against him. On April 18, 1840, Pennsylvania congressman Charles Bogle rose in the House of Representatives and launched into a speech lasting three days in which he blasted Van Buren for installing a "Royal Establishment" in Washington, "as splendid as that of Caesar's, and as richly adorned as the proudest Asiatic mansion." He went on to examine the President's life from the "cabbage patch" at Kinderhook to his "present grandeur" as a "lily-fingered aristocrat," then did an inventory of all the expensive furniture Van Buren had acquired for the White House, and finally described in great detail his epicurean meals and costly clothing. "Is not all this enough to sicken an old-fashioned Democrat?" he wanted to know. "And this is *Van Buren democracy*?"[8]

Bogle's speech, entitled "The Regal Splendor of the President's Palace," circulated widely in pamphlet form during the campaign of 1840, in which Van Buren sought a second term and the Whigs ran William Henry Harrison as challenger. The campaign didn't deal much with serious issues; the Whigs turned it into a contest between their candidate, the plain, simple, and down-to-earth Harrison, and the Democrats' candidate, the high-toned, snobbish, and sybaritic Van Buren. With the country suffering from a deep depression following the financial Panic of 1837, it was not hard for the Whigs to portray the President as a self-centered, unfeeling man who flaunted his luxury while the masses suffered. Harrison won the election handily, and the Whigs happily celebrated the unseating of a President who, they said, was "a monarchist in principle, a tyrant and a despot in practice."[9]

Van Buren took his defeat gracefully, and even broke precedent by returning the President-elect's call at the White House and chatting pleasantly with him at Gadsby's Hotel. On his way back to Kinderhook after Harrison's inauguration, he stopped in New York City for some fun. At the Bowery Theater he saw a lengthy equestrian performance, during which the audience cheered for the former President as well as for the performers. At the Park Theater later on, he saw the popular Mrs. Seaton take the leading role in a play, *The Ladder of Love;* perform the lead in the opera *Norma;* sing the popular "Woodman, Spare That Tree"; and finally appear in a farce called *Shocking Events.* When he got back to Kinderhook he received a big reception, and after he had been living there a while, visitors noticed he ate apples instead of sweets, mounted horses with the agility of a young person, took a ride every morning before breakfast, and fished in the Kinderhook ponds and streams with rods that Samuel J. Tilden sent him from New York.[10]

Van Buren spent the next few years trying, without success, to become President again. But he also continued to enjoy fine living. He built a magnificent mansion near Kinderhook called Lindenwald, which he hoped would become as well known as Jefferson's Monticello and Jackson's Hermitage. He also spent two years in Europe, mingling with "the great, the fashionable, the royal and the holy," wearing the best suits, and staying in the finest hotels. Because his family was Dutch, he requested and received a family coat of arms from the ruler of Holland, which he adored. He lived in Sorrento, Italy, for a time, working on his memoirs, and then returned to

Kinderhook hoping to develop his estate at Lindenwald into a major social center, with ornate carriages, groomed horses, and high-class social events at which guests were expected to use finger bowls. Missouri senator Thomas Hart Benton dropped by once and was a bit perplexed. "I am chary of new customs," he said later, "but when I saw Mr. Van Buren dip the tips of my fingers in the bowl and wipe them daintily on a napkin, I just raked back my sleeves and took a good plain Republican wash."[11]

Van Buren's interest in politics declined as he grew older, but he remained companionable to the end. "Of a social and cheerful temper," wrote one Van Buren admirer, "he not only liked the decorous gaiety of receptions and public entertainments, but was delighted and delightful in closer and easier conversation and in the chat of familiar friends."[12]

☆ ☆ ☆ **9** ☆ ☆ ☆

The Amiable
William Henry Harrison

William Henry Harrison, at sixty-eight the oldest man to become President before Ronald Reagan, looked forward to assuming the highest office in the United States; he expected to do great things after entering the White House. "He is as tickled with the Presidency," observed the outgoing Martin Van Buren, "as a young woman with a new bonnet." But John C. Calhoun thought that Harrison "was as unconscious as a child of his difficulties and those of his country."[1]

One difficulty Harrison had much on his mind was his age. During the 1840 campaign he had to work hard, he complained, "to counteract the opinion, which has been industriously circulated, that I was an old broken down feeble man." Harrison was no sportsman, to be sure, but he took daily morning walks and did a lot of horseback riding to keep himself in good shape and demonstrate to the voters, as he put it, "that I was never in better health in my life." When he arrived in Washington a few weeks before the inauguration, he was anxious to live up to his campaign image as a physically active, lively, good-natured, and democratic person. He was especially eager to show the public that he was strong and healthy and had the stamina to cope with the responsibilities he had to face as chief executive. Though it was snowing when he arrived by train in Washington, he insisted on walking to City Hall, hat in hand, to meet William W.

Seaton, the mayor of the city, greeting people on the street amiably along the way.[2]

While awaiting Inauguration Day, Harrison kept busy—too busy, some people thought, for a man of his age—conferring with party leaders, selecting his cabinet, and placating pushy office-seekers. He also made a short trip to Virginia to visit relatives and get some rest. When he returned to Washington, he enjoyed taking brisk walks every morning, lightly dressed despite the cold, while charming the citizens he encountered with his big smile and small talk. Philip Hone, a Whig merchant from New York in town for the inauguration, was out for a stroll two days before Inauguration Day and suddenly noticed "an elderly gentleman dressed in black, and not remarkably well dressed, with a mild, benignant countenance, a military air, but stooping a little, bowing to one, shaking hands with another, and cracking a joke with a third; and this man," he learned to his surprise, "was William Henry Harrison, the President-elect of this great empire...there he was, unattended, and unconscious of the dignity of his position,—the *man* of men, the sun of the political firmament. People may say what they will about the naked simplicity of Republican institutions; it was a sublime moral spectacle."[3]

The weather on Inauguration Day was, unfortunately, "excessively disagreeable," according to one participant in the day's events, with "a sharp cold northeast wind prevailing the whole day." The Tippecanoe Clubs of Baltimore presented Harrison with a fine carriage and four handsome horses for the ride down Pennsylvania Avenue to Capitol Hill, but Harrison decided against using such a fancy conveyance. Instead, he mounted his spirited white charger, "Old Whitey," and rode to the Capitol at the appointed time, gloveless and with hat in hand, nodding, bowing, and waving to the people cheering him along the way.[4]

When Harrison appeared on the platform erected on the Capitol's east portico, hundreds of his admirers stood shivering in the cold before him, eagerly awaiting what he had to say. He said plenty. "He stood bareheaded, in a frock-coat, without overcoat, with bare hands, facing the keen nor'easter, a full hour and a half," observed journalist Nathan Sargent, "everyone but himself suffering from exposure to the piercing blast. Of this I can speak feelingly, as I sat within a few feet of him." While Harrison was droning on, revealing his deep knowledge of ancient history, some of the important people sharing the platform with him got up from time to time to stamp their feet and slap their sides in an effort to keep warm.[5]

Harrison seemed unfazed by the weather. There were three inaugural balls that evening, and the doughty new President danced at all three with the wives of prominent Whig leaders. His own wife, Anna, was absent; she was ill at the time and remained in Ohio, hoping to join her husband in Washington when she felt better. At the balls, according to one guest, "the indefatigable President...for hours made the rounds of a hundred little circles, all so many eddies of delight in which he sported unrestrained." Philip Hone attended one of the balls and was pleased again by seeing the President in action. "The President," he wrote afterward, "came in about half-past ten o'clock, with a numerous escort, and was marched through the files of ladies up and down the room. This ceremony, with his previous visits to two other public balls, added to the severe labours of the day, had tried the old soldier's stamina; but he appears to stand it very well." Added Hone: "If the opponents of the administration expect to make capital of his imbecility of either body or mind, they make a woeful mistake. He'll do his duty well and faithfully." But when Harrison returned to the White House late that night, thoroughly exhausted, he walked over to the fireplace and stood there rubbing his hands. "Are you all right?" asked one of the servants. "Yes," said Harrison. "Just a chill."[6]

Despite the chill, Harrison continued to expose himself to the elements as he launched the new administration. He rose early, took his customary daily walks, and sometimes brought people he met back to the White House for breakfast with him. He liked to do his own marketing and frequently went out to get chops and steaks for breakfast. He was famous for his hospitality—he and Anna had continually entertained guests at their mansion in North Bend—and he wanted to make himself just as available to people in Washington as he had been in Ohio. One stormy day, a farmer called to see President Harrison when he was at dinner, and one of the servants made him wait in a room where there was no heat. Afterward, Harrison rebuked the servant. "Why did you not show the man into the dining room, where it is warm and comfortable?" The servant mumbled something about soiling the carpet, and Harrison said sternly, "Never mind the carpet another time. The man is one of the people and the carpet and the house, too, belong to the people!"[7]

One day, when he was out on one of his walks, Harrison got caught in a rain shower, delayed changing into dry clothes, and developed a headache, then chills, and finally a fever. The physician who examined him at the White House thought he had a bad cold, but Harrison didn't respond to his treatment. The fever increased and the President began to show signs of pneumonia, and the final diagnosis was "bilious pleurisy." On April 3, four more doctors came to look him over and soon realized there was little chance for recovery. By ten that night Harrison had lapsed into a coma, and his last words were: "Sir, I wish you to understand the true principles of government. I wish them carried out. I ask nothing more." He died the following morning, April 4, 1841, and John Tyler was the first Vice President to become an "accidental President."[8]

Journalist Nathaniel P. Willis turned poetic upon Harrison's passing. "What!" he cried. "Soared the old eagle to die at the sun? Lies he stiff with spread wings at the goal he has won?" Then:

> "Death, Death in the White House?
> Oh never before
> Trod his skeleton foot on the President's floor."

Had Harrison lived to complete his term of office, he probably would have walked every day, taken rides on "Old Whitey," read the classics, and held even more receptions than Van Buren. But he probably would have served sweet, not hard, cider at his dinners. Alcohol had ruined the life of one of his sons, and he eventually closed down the corn distillery on his farm in Ohio and turned prohibitionist. "Dark, unsightly manufactories of a certain poison," he explained, ill suited the "heart-cheering prospect of...fields of grain inviting the spiritual proof that the seed has been cast on good ground." And he added penitently: "I have been a sinner myself; *but in that way I shall sin no more.*"[9]

☆ ☆ ☆ **10** ☆ ☆ ☆

The Hospitable
John Tyler

John Tyler's hero was Thomas Jefferson. When he was a little boy, he was thrilled when Jefferson visited his father, then governor of Virginia, at the governor's residence in Richmond and stayed for dinner. When the time came for dessert, the door flew open and a black servant came in holding up a dish of plum pudding, which he placed with a grand sweep in front of the governor. No sooner had he left than another servant burst into the dining room with another plum pudding and, at the signal from young John, placed it ceremoniously down in front of Jefferson. "Two plum puddings, John," exclaimed Governor Tyler, "two plum puddings! Why, this is rather extraordinary!" "Yes, sir," said the boy; "it is extraordinary, but," as he got up and bowed to Jefferson, "it is an extraordinary occasion."[1]

As an adult, Tyler admired Jefferson for his learning, his dislike of big government, his preference for agrarian over industrial society, and his devotion to states' rights. But he overlooked one other important preference in Jefferson's view of American government: "Republican simplicity." In April 1841, when Tyler first entered the White House after the death of William Henry Harrison, he was shocked by how run-down it had become and made it a priority to persuade Congress to approve funds to renovate the place, contributing money of his own to help cover expenses. His first wife, Letitia, was an invalid and unable to act as his hostess, but when he remarried a year or so after her death, his second wife, Julia, a beautiful young woman from New York thirty years his junior, enthusiastically took over as hostess. Strongly impressed by the elegant customs of the royal courts of Europe, she quickly introduced—with the full approval of her husband—some of the most high-toned practices that the White House had ever seen.

Jefferson would have been amazed. Julia received guests in "almost regal splendor," it was said. She sat in a large armchair on a slightly raised platform and nodded with great dignity to the guests as they were formally announced and passed in front of her. "The lovely lady Presidentress," as F. W. Thomas, a reporter for the *New York Herald,* called her, "is attended on reception day by twelve maids of honor, six on either side, dressed all alike." He added that the headdress she wore was "formed of bugles and resembling a crown." Tyler himself was friendly and informal, though dignified, but he enjoyed the praise Julia received as hostess and was angered by the criticism. Only one of the practices she introduced into the White House entertainments bothered him at first, though he gradually came to accept it: dancing. Somewhat puritanical, he was upset the first time he saw a waltz. In a letter to his thirteen-year-old daughter, he told her it was "a dance you have never seen, and which I do not desire to see you dance. It is rather vulgar I think." But Julia could do no wrong as far as Tyler was concerned, so when she began dancing with ambassadors and cabinet members at presidential parties he gave it his imprimatur, though he didn't do any dancing himself. He even accepted the lively polka, which she had learned in Europe and which was becoming popular in the United States. A New York musician, hoping for an appointment as foreign consul, composed some dance tunes for the President's wife, which he called "The Julia Waltzes"; he received a polite thank-you note instead.[2]

Like Julia, Tyler himself was a good host, and he looked upon the social side of the presidency as a respite from the hard work he put in meeting his responsibilities as Chief Executive. Colonel John S.

Cunningham, the U.S. Navy pay director, who came to know him fairly well, described Tyler as "the most charming man in conversation and the most bewitching in his hospitality, and winning in his eloquence that I have ever had the good fortune to witness." The refreshments were excellent at Tyler's dinners, and there was usually a lot of good talk. Tyler took great pleasure in lively but nonconfrontational exchanges with his guests. And he took time out for informal hospitality, too. He always took visitors into the dining room and invited them to help themselves to drinks "from a side-board well garnished with decanters of ardent spirits and wines, with a bowl of juleps in the summer and of egg-nog in the winter." Even his enemies acknowledged his skill at entertaining the public.[3]

At times, though, Tyler wearied of the routine. Once he made a bleak summary of what a day in the life of a President could be. "My course of life," he wrote a friend, "is to rise with the sun, and work from that time until three o'clock. The order of dispatching business pretty much is, first, all diplomatic matters; second, all matters connected with the action of Congress; third, matters of general concern falling under the executive control; then the reception of visitors, and dispatch of private petitions. I dine at three-and-a-half o'clock, and in the evening my employments are miscellaneous—directions to secretaries and endorsements of numerous papers; I take some short time for exercise, and after candlelight again receive visitors, apart from all business, until ten at night, when I retire to bed. Such is the life led by an American President. What say you?—would you exchange the peace and quiet of your homstead for such an office?"[4]

But blue moods seem to have been rare with Tyler. He was deeply dedicated to his work, though he did take time off, when he felt he could do so, for a little fun and relaxation. He went on daily drives, according to his daughter Letitia, "to escape from all the environments of political and social cares and duties," and he "took delight" in shooting, fishing, and riding, though he didn't get to do much of them while he was President. He loved animals, as did Julia, and the two of them collected a menagerie of pets ranging from a canary named Johnny Bly to an Italian greyhound called Lebeau, which gave them a great deal of amusement. Above all, they had music to rouse their spirits; Tyler, a violinist, and Julia, a guitar player, were both musically gifted. Sometimes Julia played the guitar and sang popular songs at presidential parties, and every so often the Tyler family assembled in the Green Room to play and sing together. Tyler enjoyed writing poetry, too, and when he was courting Julia he wrote a serenade he entitled "Sweet Lady, Awake," to which she later added music. Tyler also liked hearing his daughter Letitia sing, and he sometimes took her for a ride in the country and asked her to perform his favorite songs, the old Scotch ballads, for him.[5]

Soon after Tyler became President, the Bohemian-born composer Anton Philip Heinrich, known as "America's Beethoven," got to play portions of his grandiose *Jubilee,* celebrating American history from the founding of the Plymouth Bay colony onward, at the White House for the Tylers and their guests. The composition, according to one of Heinrich's friends who accompanied him on the visit, contained "wild and unearthly passages" that baffled most of the people in the audience, though they listened patiently for some time. "The composer labored hard to give full effect to his weird production," according to Heinrich's friend; "his bald pate bobbled from side to side, and shone like a bubble on the surface of a calm lake. At times his shoulders would be raised to the line of his ears, and his knees went up to the keyboard, while the perspiration rolled in large drops down his wrinkled cheeks." Finally Tyler got up, walked over to the piano, and put his hand on Heinrich's shoulder. "That may all be very fine, sir," he murmured, "but can't you play us a good old Virginia reel?" Heinrich was astonished. He arose from the piano, rolled up his manuscript, took his hat and cane, and headed for the door, exclaiming: "No, sir; I never plays dance music!" As his friend joined him outside, he cried: "Mein Gott in himmel! De peebles vot made Tyler Bresident ought to be hung! He knows no more about music than an oyshter!"[6]

Tyler enjoyed reading more than he did music, and he was extremely well read for a man who devoted his life to politics. "Have *hours* for reading," he advised one of his sons, "and *minutes* for playing." As a young man at the College of William and Mary, Tyler became familiar with the Greek and Roman classics and developed a deep appreciation for English literature and history. He was convinced that good reading produced good writing, and told one of his daughters who was struggling to improve her writing style that to "write anything well, it is necessary to overcome all restraint, to feel perfectly at ease, and to give the mind full play. By reading Pope, Addison, Johnson, and especially the *Spectator,* you will acquire an easy and happy diction. Nothing can surpass their epistolary style." Tyler's favorite writer was Shakespeare. He referred to him in letters and in speeches, and insisted that "there was not a thought in the human mind, or a feeling in the human heart, that did not find the best expression in some portion of the master poet's writings." From Shakespeare he found a rule for his own behavior: "Still in thy right hand carry gentle peace, to silence envious tongues."[7]

Tyler's presidency was mostly a failure. Elected, with Harrison, as a Whig, he asserted his states'-rights preferences as a Southern Democrat once he became President, and was read out of the party by Whigs who favored federal action to improve the nation's economy, after which he came to be called "the Presidency without a party." In February 1845, shortly before leaving the White House, the Tylers decided to throw the biggest bash they could organize, no matter what it cost them, as a kind of farewell to Washington. They sent out two thousand invitations, but three thousand people came. "We were," recalled Julia's sister Margaret, "as thick as sheep in a pen." The Tylers received guests in the Blue Room—high government officials, foreign diplomats, fashionable people from Washington and other cities—and saw to it that a Marine band in scarlet uniforms furnished music for the waltzes, polkas, and cotillions that were then the vogue. Announcement of supper at ten produced "such a rush, crush and smash to obtain entrance as was never seen before at a Presidential entertainment," but only two glasses were broken. Meanwhile, superb wine and champagne "flowed like water," Julia reported, "eight dozen bottles of champagne were drunk with wine by the *barrels*." Afterward, when Tyler was congratulated on the opulence of his final entertainment, he smiled and exclaimed, "Yes, they cannot say now that I am *a President without a party*."[8]

☆ ☆ ☆ **11** ☆ ☆ ☆

The Assiduous
James K. Polk

James K. Polk, the first President from Tennessee, preferred work to play. One day, a magician was scheduled to entertain some guests in the White House, and Secretary of the Navy George Bancroft persuaded Polk to attend the show. Everyone got a big kick out of the magician's performance but Polk; he felt he was wasting his time. "I was thinking," he wrote in his diary, "more about the Oregon and other public questions which bear on my mind than the tricks of the juggler." Some people called Polk "a man who never smiled."[1]

At some things, though, Polk did smile, at least to himself. His main target was the pretentious customs observed by the royal courts in Europe. He thought the practice of making an official announcement about the birth of foreign princes to the President of the United States was "supremely ridiculous." Solemnly notifying the American President about a death in the Russian royal family also struck him as being so silly that he could "scarcely preserve his gravity." Ceremonies like these, he confided to his diary, "seem to be regarded as of Great Importance by the Ministries of the Foreign Monarchies, though to me they are amusing and ridiculous." That Europeans might regard some of the customs of the American presidency a bit strange, too, never occurred to him.[2]

For the most part, though, humor played a minor part in Polk's life. He was extremely ambitious, dead serious, conscientious, hard-working, introverted, and austere. His poor health probably had something to do with his lack of warmth, as did the fact that he took his responsibilities as congressman, speaker of the House, governor of Tennessee, and President so seriously that he had little or no time for either leisure or amusements. He engaged in no sports or games, never read for pleasure, and had little or no interest in painting, music, or the theater. Politics was his great love; it came close to being an obsession.[3]

As a boy, Polk was frail and sickly. He couldn't keep up with the other farm boys in Mecklenburg, his hometown, in running, jumping, swimming, and wrestling, and he was looked down upon as a weakling. He had a gallstone operation when still a child (without anesthetics), suffered from stomach and bowel trouble most of his life, and never became robust. Gradually he learned to put forth all the efforts he could muster in his quest for success in the political world, taking time off only when he reached the breaking point; he would resume his heavy schedule as soon as he began feeling better. "No President who performs his duty faithfully and conscientiously can have any leisure," Polk insisted. "If he entrusts the details and small matters to subordinates, constant errors will occur. I prefer to supervise the whole operations of the Government myself rather than entrust the public business to subordinates and this makes my duties very great." He hadn't been President very long before he confided to his diary that "I am the hardest working man in the country."[4]

But there was a price to pay. Polk's diary is filled with entries revealing how sick, weak, tired, exhausted, and fatigued he felt after periods of unusual exertion, and how relieved he was to be back on his feet and at work again after a spell of serious illness. "My confinement to my office," he wrote after a year as President, "has been constant and unceasing, and my labours very great." But he didn't complain about it; he came close to bragging about it. He even expressed satisfaction with the setting aside of two evenings each week to hold informal receptions for the public, mainly because it gave him "an opportunity to devote the other evenings to business."[5]

On June 1, 1846, however, Polk took a little time off for a change. "Being much wearied by my long confinement for several months, I took a ride on horseback with my private secretary in the evening," he recorded. In August, he boarded the steamer *Osceola* for an excursion to Fortress Monroe and explained to his diary just why: "My intention is to take an excursion of only three or four days. It is my first absence from Washington since I have been President, except a single day in the spring of 1845 when I visited Mount Vernon going and returning on the same day. My long confinement to my office has considerably enfeebled me and rendered some recreation necessary." On Christmas Day, 1846, he worked in his office, while his wife, Sarah, went to church; and on New Year's Day, 1847, when the White House was open for the reception of visitors, he stood gamely for four hours shaking hands with the horde of people that showed up. Afterward he moaned to his diary: "I was very much exhausted by the fatigue of the day."[6]

Polk may have been worn out by the New Year's reception, but his hands were still in good shape when it was over. By this time he had mastered the "great art" of hand-shaking, and boasted that he could shake hands all day without suffering any ill effects. He explained to people that if a man surrendered his arm to be shaken, by some horizontally, by others perpendicularly, and by others with a strong grip, he could not fail to suffer severely from it, but that if he would shake and not be shaken, grip and not be gripped, taking care always to squeeze the hand of his adversary as hard as he squeezed him, then he suffered no inconvenience from it. "I told them also that I could generally anticipate when I was to have a strong grip, and that when I observed a strong man approaching, I generally took advantage of him by being a little quicker than he was and seizing him by the tip of his fingers, giving him a healthy shake, and thus preventing him from getting a full grip upon me." Outwitting aggressive hand-shakers at tiresome receptions seems to have been one of Polk's major pleasures while he was President.[7]

Most of the time, President Polk rose at dawn, took a short walk, and then plunged into his work. He took dinner at five and then resumed his work, sometimes staying up until late at night. If there was a reception in the morning he felt obliged to get up even earlier the next day, "to make up the amount of time" which he felt "belonged to the nation." Polk hated to waste time making small talk at receptions, but he realized that it was one of the President's duties to mingle with the people on stated occasions, and that if he refused to do so his administration would suffer harsh criticism. "I feel that I am compelled to yield to it," he admitted, "and to deprive myself of the ordinary rest, in order to attend to the indispensable duties which devolve on me." Sometimes his friends persuaded him to take a horseback or carriage ride for relaxation, and on rare occasions he even decided to take a little time off on his own. "This afternoon I took a ride on horseback," he once wrote, almost in triumph. "It is the first time I have mounted a horse for over six months. I have an excellent saddlehorse, and have been much in the habit of taking exercise on horseback all my life, but have been so incessantly engaged in the onerous and responsible duties of my office for many months past that I have had no time to take such exercises." Once, his wife remonstrated, "You work too hard." His response was to hand her a newspaper and say, "Sarah, here is something I wish you to read." Very early in his presidency she began to help him out, going over papers for him and advising on speeches.[8]

Sarah Polk, a Presbyterian Calvinist, permitted wine at presidential dinners, but she absolutely forbid dancing in the White House and prohibited the discussion of politics there on Sunday. If one of Polk's associates was so careless as to call on him Sunday morning, she usually hauled the fellow off to church with her. Once, one of Polk's friends inadvertently dropped by on the Sabbath to talk to the President, and when Sarah invited him to join her at church because an unusually fine preacher was going to be in the pulpit, he exclaimed irritably, "Then I would like to go with you, Madam, for I have played cards all night with him many a time." Some people found Mrs. Polk cold and formal, but others praised her intelligence and high-spiritedness.[9]

Polk never regretted the four years of "incessant labour and anxiety and of great responsibility" he had put in for his country. He had achieved his objectives—a lower tariff, the creation of an independent treasury, the settlement of the Oregon dispute with Britain, and the acquisition of California as a result of the Mexican War—and he looked forward to rest and relaxation in retirement. In February 1849, a couple of weeks before his successor, Zachary Taylor, was to be inaugurated, he expressed happiness that his term of office would soon be over and he would "cease to be a servant and become a sovereign" again. "I am sure I will be happier in this condition than in the exalted station I now hold." Unfortunately, Polk suffered "great fatigue" during his journey home, overwhelmed by the parties, receptions, ceremonies, and entertainments that his well-wishers held for him everywhere, developed a severe cold and then serious stomach and bowel trouble, and died at fifty-four in June, barely three months after leaving Washington.[10]

✩ ✩ ✩ 12 ✩ ✩ ✩

The Unpretentious
Zachary Taylor

In February 1849, General Zachary Taylor resigned his commission, after forty years of service in the U.S. Army, and began preparing his trip to Washington to take the oath of office as President. He told his well-wishers in Baton Rouge that he "should have preferred to retain the office I am now about to vacate, and remained among you." His wife, Margaret, certainly felt that way; electing her husband President, she thought, was "a plot to deprive me of his society; and to shorten his life by unnecessary care and responsibility."[1]

Known for his casual, even at times slovenly attire, Taylor, at the advice of his son-in-law, Colonel William Bliss, ordered two new suits, and when he arrived in Washington he found himself already presidential: the pockets of both suits were stuffed with letters from office-seekers who had paid the tailor handsomely for access to the President-to-be. Taylor's inaugural address, quite Whiggish, angered the Democrats but pleased the Whigs (a New Hampshire paper said it was "neither mule nor jackass, but a sort of hybrid"), and after putting in an appearance at the three balls that night in his honor he joined his wife in the White House, where they sat in rocking chairs in front of the fire to chew a little tobacco before retiring. Taylor, the "Hero of Buena Vista," was known for his "marksmanship" when expectorating.[2]

Taylor was born in Virginia and grew up in the frontier wilderness of Kentucky, and he was a farm boy before becoming a soldier. He developed agility, strength, and endurance as a youngster by driving the plow, yoking oxen, and harnessing and riding horses. In his spare time "Little Zach" went hunting and fishing, and once, during the winter, he swam the ice-cold Ohio River to the Indiana shore and back just to show people he could do it. "It was an active and happy life," biographers Silas Bent McKinley and Silas Bent believed, "mingling the execution of taking home venison or a basket of fish with the chores of sowing, reaping, harvesting and feeding and watering the stock." At the same time, young Taylor received instruction in mathematics and the classics from an itinerant Connecticut schoolmaster and developed a love of books, particularly those dealing with great military leaders and their campaigns. His tutor pronounced him "quick in learning" and "patient in study."[3]

After Taylor launched his career as a professional soldier, there was far less time for reading and for engaging in the sports he loved as a boy. But he managed to spend time in the libraries at the forts where he was stationed; sometimes fished with the soldiers, joined them in hunting prairie chickens; and also attended the amateur plays they put on for entertainment. Taylor's formal education was limited, but he took a serious interest in the education of his children and grandchildren, and tried to encourage "a taste for reading" in them. "There is nothing more important to insure a young man a high standard either in the army or navy than literary attainments," he told one of his son-in-laws, "& a taste for study if he had books... will be a source of amusement as well as occupation" that will prevent him from getting bored and keep him from "resorting to certain means to kill time which so frequently results in the destruction of so many young men in both arms of the public service."[4]

There was nothing pompous about Taylor. He lived and dressed simply wherever he was stationed and treated the men under his command with kindness and concern. He rarely wore a uniform or anything else that showed he was an officer, and on occasion this led to confusion when saluting was appropriate. "Taylor is short and very heavy," wrote a young officer from Illinois, "with pronounced face lines and gray hair, wears an old oil-coth cap, a dusty greencoat, a frightful pair of trousers, and on horseback looks like a toad." A wounded soldier who had been with him at the Battle of Monterey during the Mexican War found that Taylor was accessible to his men any time of day or night. "He will sit and talk with the commonest soldier in the most affable manner...," he reported, "enter minutely into the private affairs of the soldiers under his command, give them his advice when asked, as it frequently is, and when that is over, read to them from the newspapers the anecdotes of the army, which have made their way into print in the northern cities, at which he would laugh as heartily as any of them." The soldiers who fought under him during the war with Mexico called him "Old Rough and Ready."[5]

Shortly after Taylor's victory over Democratic candidate Lewis Cass in the 1848 election, he boarded a steamboat headed for his plantation, and a passenger, not knowing who he was, started talking politics with him. He'd voted for Cass, the passenger said, and though he thought well of Taylor as a man, he always voted Democratic and, besides, "did not think that Gen. T. was qualified" for the presidency. According to a reporter, when the man asked whether the general was a Taylor man, the President-elect replied, "not much of a one— that is, he did not vote for him—partly for family reasons, and partly because his wife...was opposed to sending 'Old Zack'...to Washington," where, he added straight-facedly, "she would be obliged to go with him!" At that moment another passenger recognized Taylor and greeted him by name, upon which the Cass supporter looked "a little wild" and disappeared into the crowd. Taylor "was in fine health and spirits," according to the newspaper that reported the tale; he "talked...little about politics and less about the elections, but was otherwise...quite sociable." The reporter also noted that he was neatly dressed.[6]

When Taylor became President, he felt as uncomfortable with the formalities of the White House as he did with those of the army. He liked best the simple, down-to-earth conversations he had with the average American at his receptions and state dinners, but he was friendly and courteous to everyone he encountered. A visitor from New York who called the wrong night at the White House was welcomed by Taylor anyway, and treated as hospitably as he would have been on a regular reception day. A Democratic congressman from Kentucky dropped by one morning and found Taylor "polite, cordial and talkative." The President "talked about cotton and hemp crops," he recalled, "but not a word on the subject of politics. Any other topic suits him better than matters of state. I confess that he is rather more polished and entertains gentlemen with more ease, than I expected." Gideon Welles, a Connecticut Democrat, was similarly impressed. Invited to a White House dinner for cabinet members, senators, and other government officials, he arrived early, introduced himself, and was cordially received. He found Taylor "affable and unassuming" as well as "guileless and very rightly disposed," and added that he "put on no airs, and could wear none were he to attempt it...." After Taylor greeted Welles by name, he took him over to a seat by the fire where they chatted pleasantly until the other guests began arriving.[7]

Taylor escaped the White House whenever he could, but it wasn't often enough for him. He liked to take morning walks in the city and, better still, ride a white charger he called "Old Whitey" (the same name as that of William Henry Harrison's favorite horse) on the wooded roads of the District of Columbia. Taylor let "Old Whitey" roam the White House grounds to his heart's content and didn't mind it a bit if visitors helped themselves to pieces of hair from the horse's tail to take home as souvenirs. Whig senator William Seward of New York took a lot of teasing for playing up to the President by giving him a silver-toothed currycomb as a gift to use on the old war horse.[8]

Taylor took a liking to the nation's military bands when he was living in the White House. In the summer, when the bands held forth on the White House grounds every Saturday afternoon, he usually went out to join the crowd, listen to the music, and talk informally to people. Frederica Bremer, a Swedish novelist visiting the United

States, found him "kind and agreeable, both in appearance and manner, and...simply, almost negligently dressed." He was "delighted," she noticed, "with children who leaped about so joyously...."[9]

Taylor didn't get to make many trips, for business or pleasure, when he was President. On one rare trip to the Northeast, to visit some of the states there for the first time, he traveled in a regular coach car instead of the special luxurious train offered him, because he wanted to mingle with the passengers. Another trip took him to Baltimore because of his interest in agriculture; he visited the Fair and Cattle Show there as well as the Maryland Institute Fair, and felt renewed as he returned to Washington.

Long before his presidency ended, Taylor was tiring of the political strife in Washington and the bitter attacks on his integrity by his opponents in Congress, and, with his wife, was beginning to look forward to settling down to peace and quiet in Cypress Grove, their plantation in Mississippi. Late in June 1850, New York's Thurlow Weed visited the President and got the impression that the aspersions cast on Taylor's integrity had "greatly disturbed his nervous system." Afterward he told Colonel Bliss, Taylor's son-in-law, that the President "was excited and feverish and ought, if possible to get a few days' repose." Taylor never did get the repose, but he seemed to be feeling good when, a few days later, he attended the Fourth of July ceremony at which the laying of the cornerstone of the Washington Monument took place. It was an unusually hot day and the orations were lengthy, and soon after Taylor got back to the White House he took sick; a few days later died, presumably of gastroenteritis. His last words were: "I am about to die. I expect the summons very soon. I have endeavored to discharge all my official duties faithfully. I regret nothing, but I am about to leave my friends." In the funeral procession three days later, "Old Whitey" marched behind the President's funeral car, with his master's boots in the stirrups. "Poor fellow!" wrote one reporter. "He stepped proudly."[10]

☆ ☆ ☆ **13** ☆ ☆ ☆

The Earnest
Millard Fillmore

Millard Fillmore was a modest fellow. He began his autobiography by saying he didn't think his birth "was marked by any striking signs in the Heavens above or the earth beneath…" In 1823, when he was a young lawyer in East Aurora, New York, the townspeople asked him to deliver the Independence Day address on July 4, and in his speech he practically apologized for agreeing to speak because he "trod the humble walks of life," lacked "genius and learning," and was unable to "charm the ear" by "sweet eloquence" or "please the eyes" by "graceful gestures." He did, though, speak well of the Declaration of Independence. Decades later, when he was visiting England as a retiree, Oxford University offered to confer an honorary degree on Fillmore as a former President, and he politely declined to accept it on the ground that it was written in Latin and he had never studied the language. "I have not the advantage of a classical education," he declared, "and no one should, in my judgment, accept a degree he cannot read."[1]

Fillmore deeply regretted the lack of a classical education. His father owned only three books—an almanac, a hymnal, and the Bible—and whatever schooling there was in the recently settled town of Locke, New York, where he grew up, was scanty and irregular. "My father's residence was not only in a new country," he recalled, "but remote from all the great thoroughfares of travel, and my life had been spent in obscurity. I knew nothing about the world, never having been from home for two successive days, nor formed the acquaintance of any beyond the few scattered neighbors of the vicinity." Learning to read in a nearby log-cabin schoolhouse opened up a new world for Fillmore. Bursting with eagerness to learn, he paid the two dollars required to use the little library in a nearby town and acquired a dictionary so he could look up every word in his reading that he didn't understand. Reading became one of his greatest loves, and as an adult he became a book collector.[2]

Fillmore had little time for sports when he was a boy, for there was work to be done on his father's farm. But when he found the time, he fished, went swimming, and did some hunting (when he was able to borrow a gun), even though his father warned him that such activity "was not profitable." For a time he worked for a cloth-maker, taking his precious dictionary with him every day to sneak in some learning while tending the carding machine. When a new academy opened up near his hometown, Fillmore began dividing his time between farming and schooling, then got a position as a law clerk, passed the bar, and finally set up his own law office in East Aurora, near Buffalo. He was married by then to Abigail Powers, a schoolteacher who shared his love of books. Together they began building up a little library of their own, with Fillmore, now a member of the New York State Assembly, browsing in the bookstores of Albany as often as he could.[3]

Fillmore tried to pass his love of books on to his law clerks as well as to his children. One of his former clerks remembered the way Fillmore arrived early at the law office, "cheerful with a springy step bidding him good morning. He would have a book under his arm which he had read the night before. He would comment how much he liked it and how he brought it down to the office to read." Once Fillmore became an assemblyman, however, the pressure of work cut deeply into his romance with books. "I have little time for reading...," he complained to his wife during one long session of the Assembly. "I attend no places of amusement but spend all my time in business." Another time he wrote her: "I have been at the theater but once this winter and at the museum but two or three times and I have visited no other places of amusement." And when politics came to dominate his life—as a congressman from New York, then as Vice President, and finally as President upon Zachary Taylor's death—he found less and less time for his favorite recreation.[4]

One of the most popular presidential myths has it that Fillmore installed the first bathtub in the White House. It was the famous early-twentieth-century writer and satirist H. L. Mencken who put the bathtub story in circulation, in a parody of scholarly writing that he didn't expect anyone to take seriously. He was astonished when the tale caught on with the American public, and it seemed to prove his long-held belief that no one ever lost any money underestimating the intelligence of the American people, whose heart's desire would be achieved, he once said, if a downright moron (with or without bathtub) became President. It was Andrew Jackson, not Fillmore, who first installed running water in the White House, thus making it possible to construct a bathroom in the East Wing containing a hot bath, a cold bath, and a shower bath.[5]

If Fillmore wasn't responsible for the first bathtub in the White House, he and his wife did arrange for a new stove to be put in the kitchen, despite the protests of the old-time cook. More important, since previous Presidents all took their books home with them when they vacated the White House, Fillmore decided that, with the help of his wife, he would establish the first permanent library in the executive mansion. It was a labor of love. When Congress, at his request, voted two thousand dollars to purchase books, he arranged for the largest room on the White House's second floor to be set aside as the library and began acquiring the kind of books he thought the President's house should possess. The first three books he ordered were Webster's dictionary, the Bible, and an atlas. Following in rapid succession were Shakespeare's plays, *Aesop's Fables,* the *Arabian*

Nights, Gulliver's Travels, writings by Tocqueville, the *Federalist Papers,* and a vast array of other books devoted to history, science, the arts, the classics, and literature. There were current periodicals, too: the *Democratic Review* and *Nile's Register.*[6]

In time, the room set aside for books in the White House became more than a library. It was a music room, too, containing the Fillmores' talented daughter Mary's piano, harp, and guitar, where she played for her parents and some of their special guests. It was Mrs. Fillmore's favorite room, and the President himself insisted on spending an hour there at night with his family after he finished his work, browsing in the library, listening to his daughter play, and sometimes joining in a songfest with his wife and children. In his entertainments for the public, Fillmore placed more emphasis on music than any of his predecessors in the White House had. At morning receptions the U.S. Marine Band played waltzes and polkas, music from operas, and patriotic tunes like "America," "Hail Columbia," "The Star-Spangled Banner," and "Hail to the Chief." At some of the smaller presidential dinners Mary played and sang for the guests, and on important occasions celebrities such as Jenny Lind, the "Swedish Nightingale," performed. Washington society was sent into ecstasy when Lind appeared in a White House recital attended by some of the most prestigious people who could be rounded up in the nation's capital. "If rank be measured by intellect alone," exclaimed one commentator, "the audience at her concert was essentially one of the very noblest before which Jenny Lind ever sang in any part of the world." Lind had a good chat with Fillmore and his family, too, and according to her biographer, only when she left "did she recollect that she had been in the presence of the man who controlled the most powerful and vigorous government that had ever arisen in the short lapse of a single century."[7]

Fillmore has never been rated highly as a President, but he certainly has his admirers, especially in his hometown, East Aurora, now a suburb of Buffalo. "Around here," announced Virginia B. Vidler, the town historian, some years ago, "we don't take Millard Fillmore lightly." In citing reasons for praising the President from East Aurora, the Fillmore-boosters usually mention the White House library first and then say something about cultural events like Jenny Lind's recital. Together they represented Fillmore's favorite diversions: books and music.[8]

The Convivial
Franklin Pierce

Franklin Pierce was the first, and thus far only, President to affirm, rather than swear, that he would faithfully execute the office of President and uphold the Constitution of the United States. He broke precedent, too, by mentioning his personal sorrow in his inaugural address (which he delivered from memory) on March 4, 1853. He had reason enough to be sorrowful. A few weeks before the inauguration, when he, his wife Jane, and their little boy Benjamin were traveling by train from Andover, Massachusetts, to their hometown of Concord, New Hampshire, the car on which they were riding suddenly slipped off the tracks and plunged down an embankment. Frank and Jane were only slightly hurt, but their eleven-year-old son was crushed to death in the wreckage as they looked on in horror. The Pierces never fully recovered from the loss of their son. Pierce blamed his own shortcomings for the tragedy, and his wife wore black for the rest of her life and spent a great deal of her time in solitude, writing love letters to Bennie.[1]

When Pierce was growing up, he hunted, fished, swam, and skated in Hillsborough, New Hampshire, where he was born, but as he grew older and entered the fields of law and then politics, his favorite diversion soon became having a few drinks with his buddies after work, especially if he felt out of sorts. He couldn't hold his liquor, his friends said, but his sociability, especially when he was in Washington, first as a congressman and then a U.S. senator from New Hampshire, impelled him to keep up with the serious drinkers, leaving him in pretty bad shape long before they were ready to call it a night. He took up drinking when he was in college. His father had warned him against "merriment" when he sent him off to Bowdoin College in Brunswick, Maine, in 1820, but his youthful "spirits were exuberant," Pierce recalled, and before long he was cutting classes to explore the nearby forests, shoot birds, fish and swim in the river, and, above all, visit the tavern—though it was officially off limits to Bowdoin students—to do a little imbibing and to acquire cans of liquor to take surreptitiously back to the campus. He did poorly in his studies until his third year, when, after reading John Locke and learning something about rationalism, he pulled himself together, started working hard, and managed to rise from last place to finish fifth in his class by the time of graduation.[2]

When Pierce got to Washington as a member of Congress he continued with his "merriment," which included Sunday-afternoon "cutups," at which he and his friends argued, horsed around, played practical jokes on each other, and indulged in crackers, cheese, and wine. During the racing season, Pierce and his friends headed for the track, where there was gambling "in all its mood and tenses," along with plenty of julep and raw whiskey. They took rowdy excursions, too, including one to Harper's Ferry by railroad, eating and drinking so much along the way that it made some of them, John Quincy Adams noticed, "loquacious and some drowsy." On the return to Washington, a Kentucky congressman entertained them with "facetious humors and coarse jokes and a very frequent and copious consumption of whisky drams." One evening, later on, Pierce and two of his friends got into a drinking bout and then decided to go to the theater. They ended up in a box with an army officer who had recently quarreled with one of Pierce's friends. The two resumed their fight and disrupted the show. When Pierce finally got dazedly to bed late that night, he found he had developed pleurisy and had to call the doctor. In 1852, when he ran for President on the Democratic ticket, his Whig opponents made much of drinking incidents like these during the campaign. He was "a hero of many a well-fought bottle," they said, when he was a soldier during the Mexican War.[3]

Not all of Pierce's diversions in Washington involved roughhouse. He attended plays and recitals with the best of them and was deeply moved by some of the performances. When he saw the popular actress Fanny Kemble play the part of Julia in *The Hunchback,* he was almost in ecstasy over her performance. About this time he decided to go on the wagon. Prodded by his wife and his own Calvinistic conscience, Pierce forswore drinking and tobacco just before leaving the Senate, became chairman of the New Hampshire temperance society when he got home, and succeeded in persuading Concord to ban drinking within the town limits. Years later, when he ran for President, someone wrote asking him "not to allow another glass of intoxicating liquor of any description" to enter his lips as a "beverage," and he responded by saying that there was no occasion for him to make such a resolution, because the decision to give up drinking was "formed long since" and would "never be shaken."[4]

Mrs. Pierce was delighted with her husband's decision to stop drinking. She was pleased, too, to see him leave Washington at the end of his senatorial term for she disliked the place, not only for its climate but also for the social whirl there that bored her and might, she feared, lead her husband astray. But above all, she was happy to see her husband settle down to law work in Concord, for she hated politics and had long hoped he would leave the political world once and for all and concentrate on law. But Pierce loved politics; after leaving Washington, he kept in touch with his friends in the Democratic Party and gave them the impression that he would become politically active again if the opportunity arose. Even his service in the Mexican War, from 1846 to 1848, failed to kill his interest in politics. In 1852, when his wife learned that he had actively sought the Democratic nomination for President without telling her, she was outraged. She stayed away from his inauguration in March 1853 and couldn't bring herself to move into the White House until two months later. Once there, she begged off from her duties as hostess, persuading her husband's aunt, Mrs. Abby Kent Means, to take her place, and spent most of her time sick and depressed in her bedroom, rarely going down to participate in White House entertainments.[5]

By general agreement, President Pierce's receptions and state dinners were a big disappointment to the Washington politicos and socialites who took White House social events seriously. "Everything in that mansion seems cold and cheerless," Charles Mason wrote in his diary after calling at the Executive Mansion. "I have seen hundreds of log cabins which seemed to contain more happiness." Without his wife by his side, Pierce did the best he could for the public. He still wasn't drinking, so he sought diversion in other ways: horseback riding (he called his black horse "Union"), calling on friends, and attending such public events as dedications of schools, commencements, and funerals of very important people. He took in plays and concerts, too, as during his senatorial years, accompanied by friends since his wife seldom went out. Now and then, however, she joined him for brief excursions to Cape May, Sulphur Springs, and other nearby places.[6]

One of Pierce's most ambitious trips, which included presidential speeches en route, took him—without Jane—to New York City, where he attended the nation's first world's fair, featuring a Crystal Palace like the one in Britain, to which Queen Victoria sent special representatives. Bad weather spoiled the trip for Pierce; he caught a severe cold in New York, and when he addressed the crowds, every word he uttered was "like a knife in his lungs." When he finally reached the Crystal Palace, he slipped into a nearby saloon for some brandy before entering the place. "Pierce has had a fine reception," wrote his friend John W. Forney, who had been with him most of the time, "but I deeply, deeply, deplore his habits. He drinks deep. My heart bleeds for him for he is a gallant and generous spirit. The place overshadows him. He is crushed by its great duties and," Forney trailed off, "he seeks refuge in..."[7]

Once, when someone asked Pierce what a President should do after leaving the White House, he sighed: "There's nothing left... but to get drunk." In retirement, he did his drinking, continued to hew to his "anti-anti-slavery" line, and during the Civil War opposed Abraham Lincoln and the Emancipation Proclamation so harshly that it was years after his death before his hometown of Concord, New Hampshire, put up a statue in his memory. During the war, Nathaniel Hawthorne, Pierce's classmate at Bowdoin, dedicated one of his books to Pierce, against the advice of the publisher, and many of Hawthorne's readers did what Ralph Waldo Emerson did: acquired the book but cut out the dedication before reading it.[8]

☆ ☆ ☆ **15** ☆ ☆ ☆

The Fastidious
James Buchanan

James Buchanan was a stickler for details. When a friend sent him a check for over $15,000 to settle an account, he refused to accept it because it contained an error of ten cents. As President, moreover, when he accidentally paid three cents less than he should have for some food he ordered for the White House, he insisted on sending the grocer the three cents even though the bill was marked as paid in full. He didn't want to pay too much or too little, he explained, but exactly the correct amount. With his passion for precision, Buchanan struck some people as being a small-minded fuddy-duddy who took the rules and proprieties too literally. But he certainly had been nothing like that as a young man.[1]

In 1807, when Jimmy, as he was called, entered Dickinson College in Carlisle, Pennsylvania, as a freshman, he at first worked hard on his courses but soon learned that "to be a sober, plodding, industrious youth" brought ridicule from his classmates, not praise, and left him without any friends. Determined to be a success on the campus, he deliberately began to misbehave. "Without much natural tendency to become dissipated," he recalled, "and chiefly from the example of others, and in order to be considered a clever and spirited youth, I engaged in every sort of extravagance and mischief." He defied the rules by drinking and smoking cigars on campus, and he

offended his professors by taking a smart-aleck attitude toward them
in the classroom. He also became a show-off. At an off-campus student
Fourth of July bash, he proudly proposed and downed no less than sixteen toasts to the holiday. Despite his mischief-making, Buchanan
continued to do well in his classes. To his dismay, however, he was ex-
pelled for disorderly conduct and reinstated only after solemnly promising to mend his ways. He did improve his conduct, but there was
something about him—perhaps a bit of arrogance he developed over
his ability to be both a good student and a roustabout if he so chose—
that offended his instructors. At graduation they denied Buchanan
first place on the commencement program despite his superior work.
He left Dickinson "feeling but little attachment toward the Alma
Mater." But one of his professors, Robert Davidson, who was a bit
vain, solemn, and precise himself, though kind and generous, left his
mark on Buchanan. One of the President's biographers was convinced
that as an adult, Buchanan was very much like Davidson.[2]

After college, Buchanan moved up steadily in the world, first as a
lawyer and then as a politician, and he eventually acquired a beautiful estate called Wheatland, near Lancaster, Pennsylvania, where he
entertained people in the fine style he preferred when he wasn't in
Washington. While studying law diligently in Lancaster, he relaxed in
the evening by taking walks to the edge of town and then, with no one
around, discussing out loud the material he had been going over all
day. More relaxing of course were sessions with his fellow students
in the local taverns, where he smoked black cigars, drank Madeira,
and got into lengthy bull sessions. As he rose in the profession
Buchanan acquired social standing, and, to his delight, it brought invitations to parties by people with status, admission to membership
in the Masonic Lodge, and appointment as one of the managers of the
annual social ball. He had an active social life in Washington, too,
after entering Congress in 1821, and, as a member of the Lower
House and then as a senator, he got in the habit of taking two-week
vacations in Bedford Springs, where he not only "took the waters" for
his health but also spent evenings in the resort's big ballroom, danc-

ing the schottische, the polka, and a new step called the "hop-trot" (or "rabbit-hop") with energy and enthusiasm.[3]

On assignments abroad Buchanan took his responsibilities seriously, but he also derived a great deal of pleasure from the social life that went with his position. As minister to Russia for President Jackson, he succeeded in persuading Emperor Nicholas to sign a commercial treaty with the United States, and was subsequently welcomed at the lively parties and fancy balls of the leading families in St. Petersburg. Much to his delight, the empress pronounced him a fine dancer. Before returning home Buchanan toured Europe and then visited Ireland, where he sought out the home of his ancestors at Ramelton and inevitably "sinned much," as he put it, "in the article of hot whiskey toddy which they term punch." A few years later he accepted a mission to England for President Pierce and almost immediately ran into a problem of etiquette. Pierce's secretary of state, William L. Marcy, had instructed Americans in the foreign service to perform their duties "in the simple dress of an American citizen," unencumbered by ribbons, gold lace, jewels, and the other fancy trimmings that prevailed in court circles. But England's Court of St. James, Buchanan knew, would be insulted if he followed Marcy's instructions, and he might end up being excluded from the prestigious English social world. While he was racking his mind about what to do, a friendly Brit suggested he appear in Court with a plain black-handled sword, which was the mark of a gentleman everywhere. Buchanan's appearance at court with the sword elicited a "benevolent smile" from the queen, and soon Buchanan was turning up at fashionable dinners at eight in the evening and at high-class parties at eleven.[4]

By the time Buchanan reached the White House, in 1857, he was well experienced in the art of social entertaining and looked forward to being a commendable White House host as well as a wise President. Since he was a bachelor, he asked his niece, Harriet Lane, an attractive woman in her twenties, to help him out as hostess, and by general agreement the two worked nicely together at the receptions and state dinners that Buchanan so enjoyed. Liquor flowed freely at his entertainments. A few weeks after the inauguration, he sent a note to his liquor suppliers chiding them for sending him champagne in small bottles. "Pints are inconvenient in this house," he told them, "as the article is not used in such small quantities." Newsman John W. Forney was astonished at Buchanan's capacity. "The Madeira and sherry that he has consumed would fill more than one old cellar," he wrote, "and the rye whiskey that he has 'punished' would make Jacob Baer's heart glad." Buchanan's wine was "stout and heavy," he noted, and "would make an old British sea captain weep joyful tears." Buchanan was by no means a single-bottle man, Forney noticed; he disposed of two or three bottles at one sitting, beginning with a "stiff jorum of cognac" and finishing with a couple of glasses of old rye. "And then the effect of it! There was no headache, no faltering steps, no flushed cheek. Oh, no! All was as cool, as calm and as cautious and watchful as in the beginning. More than one ambitious tyro who sought to follow his example gathered an early fall." When Buchanan's supplies ran low, he used the Sunday drive to church as an opportunity to stop at Jacob Baer's distillery after the service to pick up a ten-gallon cask of "Old J.B. Whiskey." He was amused to learn that some people thought the initials "J.B." stood for James Buchanan.[5]

To keep in shape, Buchanan took hour-long walks in the afternoon in the residential area around the White House and down Pennsylvania Avenue, sometimes stopping to talk to people. But he began to feel his age as he wrestled with the crisis over slavery that threatened to destroy the nation in the late 1850s. The stand that he took—that it was unconstitutional for states to secede from the Union, but equally unconstitutional for the President to use force to keep them in—satisfied no one and made resolution seem impossible. As his administration struggled on in desperation, Buchanan became fussy, short-tempered, and self-righteous. He banned dancing and card-playing in the Executive Mansion and began longing for retirement.

He was no longer "Jimmy"; he was "Old Buck," and his cabinet heads began deriding him behind his back.[6]

Buchanan did, however, carry off one triumphant social event in the waning months of his presidency. Learning that the Prince of Wales was scheduled to visit Canada, he arranged with Queen Victoria for her son to visit the United States, too, and spend some time as a guest of the President. When news of the visit got out, the social world in Washington was all a-twitter; it would be the first visit of a member of the British royal family to the President's house. When the prince reached Washington in the fall of 1860, Buchanan held a grand state dinner for him. It went very nicely until Buchanan got the impression that the prince was falling asleep at the table and hastily ordered the waiters to speed things up in order to keep him awake. After dinner the guests played cards (despite Buchanan's ban) and then retired. To Buchanan's chagrin, the royal family used all the beds in the President's mansion, forcing him to sleep on a cot.[7]

At Abraham Lincoln's inauguration on March 4, 1861, Buchanan looked "pale and wearied" to reporters, yet "his face beamed with radiance, for he felt relieved from the crushing care and anxiety he had borne for four years." Buchanan frankly confessed his relief to the new President. "If you are as happy, my dear sir, on entering this house," he is alleged to have said, "as I am in leaving it and returning home, you are the happiest man in this country." In retirement at Wheatland, Buchanan supported Lincoln when the war came, but he started work on a book that would explain and defend the policies he had followed during his four years as President. He did some reading, too, for he had assembled a nice library at Wheatland containing works by such favorites as Lord Byron, Sir Walter Scott, and Charles Dickens. He hosted friends at his estate, and from time to time made trips to Bedford Springs to take the waters for his gout and enjoy the relaxation. Like Pierce, his predecessor, Buchanan was soon forgotten.[8]

The Mirthful and Melancholy
Abraham Lincoln

One day in September 1862, Abraham Lincoln was leafing through a book by a popular American humorist as members of his cabinet assembled for a special meeting in his office. "Gentlemen," said Lincoln, when everyone was there, "did you ever read anything of Artemus Ward? Let me read a chapter that is very funny." He then began reading a short piece in the book called "High-Handed Outrage at Utica." Lincoln's apparent dilatoriness so irked Edwin Stanton, the secretary of war, that he almost got up and walked out of the room. But Lincoln continued reading with obvious pleasure, and when he finished, he laughed heartily while everyone else sat in silence. "Gentlemen," cried Lincoln disappointedly, "why don't you laugh?" And then, a little sadly, he told them, "With the fearful strain that is upon me night and day, if I did not laugh I should die, and you need this medicine as much as I do."[1]

Lincoln then turned serious. He took a piece of paper out of his tall hat and announced, "I have called you here on very important business. I have prepared a paper of much significance. I have said nothing to anyone, but I have made a promise to myself—and to my Maker. I am now going to fulfil that promise." He then read aloud what he had jotted down on the paper: "On the first of January, in the year of our Lord, 1863, all persons then held as slaves in any state or designated part of a state the people thereof shall then be in rebellion against the United States shall be then and thenceforth and forever free." Stanton was overwhelmed by the declaration. Rising and taking the President's hand, he exclaimed: "Mr. President, if reading a chapter of Artemus Ward is a prelude to such a deed as this, the book should be filed among the archives of the nation and the author canonized."[2]

Lincoln was the first "Phunny Phellow" (as humorous writers were sometimes called in his day) in the White House. Humor was health to his bones; it was his fun, his relaxation, and his medicine for coping with what the Japanese call "the sadness of things." During his presidency he took walks, did some horseback riding, and even went bowling on occasion. But Lincoln's dearest—his indispensable—diversion was humor. He liked to tell funny stories (some of them off-color), trade jokes with friends, come up with puns, and transmute experiences of his own into tales that people found hilarious. "He could make a cat laugh!" exclaimed one of his friends. "It was as a humorist that he towered above all other men it was ever my lot to meet," said another friend from Lincoln's youth. H. C. Whitney, who rode the circuit with Lincoln when they were lawyers in Illinois, was struck by his keen sense of the absurd: "He saw the ludicrous in an assemblage of fowls, in a man spading his garden, in a clothesline full of clothes, in a group of boys, in a lot of pigs rooting at a mill door, in a mother duck teaching her brood to swim—in everything and anything."[3]

Lincoln's law partner, William Herndon, was impressed with his friend's skill in telling stories. "In the role of a story-teller," he wrote, "I regard Mr. Lincoln as without an equal. His power of mimicry and his manner of recital were unique. His countenance and all his features seemed to take part in the performance. As he neared the pith or point of the story every vestige of seriousness disappeared from his face. His gray eyes sparkled; a smile seemed to gather up, curtain-like, the corners of his mouth; his frame quivered with suppressed excitement; and when the nub of the story—as he called it—came, no one's laugh was heartier than his." Journalist John W. Forney couldn't help noticing the mingling of joy and sorrow in Lincoln's personality. He was the "saddest of humanity," he wrote, and yet the sense of the ridiculous that Whitney observed was so keen, Forney thought, that it carried him through difficulties that would have destroyed almost any other human being. Forney was aware of the fact that Lincoln gave way to "uncontrollable fits of grief in the dark hours of the war," but he also knew that the President could "lift himself out of his troubles and enjoy…the old quirks and quips of the clown in the circus.…" Lincoln himself put it succinctly: "I laugh that I may not cry."[4]

Lincoln once called laughter "the joyous, beautiful, universal evergreen of life," and he felt much beholden to any person who contributed to his collection of witty remarks and droll tales. But humor wasn't always an end in itself for him. Both as a lawyer and as a politician he also found amusing stories enormously helpful in putting across important points he wanted to make. And as President, he used his gifts as a storyteller to put people at ease, to win them over to his point of view, or simply to distract them and get them out of his office without having to turn down their requests in so many words. Humor, he once said, was "an emollient" that "saves me much friction and distress." A group of people who went to the White House one day seeking jobs in the government reported resignedly afterward that "the President treated us to four anecdotes."[5]

During the Civil War, humor was crucial for Lincoln as a means of relaxing, getting away from his troubles for a time, and refreshing his spirits. John Hay, one of his secretaries, recalled how Lincoln once came running into his office a little after midnight with a book by Thomas Hood in his hand containing an amusing passage he wanted to read for Hay, "utterly unconscious that he with his short shirt hanging above his long legs & setting out behind like the tail feathers of an enormous ostrich was infinitely funnier than anything in the book he was laughing at." Hay was enormously impressed. "What a man it is!" he wrote later. "Occupied all day with matters of vast moment, deeply anxious about the fate of the greatest army of the world, with his own fame and future hanging on the events of the passing hour, he yet has such a wealth of simple bonhomie & good fellowship that he gets out of bed & perambulates the house in his shirt to find us that we may share with him the fun" he encountered in one of his books. Lincoln once told a friend that "a funny story, if it has the element of genuine wit," had the same effect on him that "a good square drink of whisky has on an old toper; it puts new life into me."[6]

Lincoln laughed at himself as well as at other people. When Stephen A. Douglas called him a "two-faced man" during a debate in Illinois in 1858, Lincoln said calmly: "I leave it to my audience. If I had another face, do you think I would wear this one?" A stranger came up to him one day, according to one of his favorite stories, and said, "Excuse me, sir, but I have an article in my possession which belongs to you." "How is that?" asked Lincoln, a bit puzzled. The stranger took a knife out of his pocket and said it had been given to him some time ago with instructions that he was "to keep it until I found a man *uglier* than myself. I have carried it from that time to this. Allow me now to say, sir, that I think *you* are fairly entitled to the property."[7]

Not everyone appreciated Lincoln's storytelling. People who detested his presidential policies were repelled by his sense of fun. They called him a low-level clown, a man who jokes while the nation mourns, and a crude, illiterate, barroom witling. "President Lincoln is a joke incarnate," declared James Gordon Bennett's *New York Herald,* a virulent enemy of Lincoln. "His election was a very sorry joke. The idea that such a man as he should be President of such a country as this is a very ridiculous joke. His debut in Washington society was a joke.... His inaugural address was a joke.... His cabinet is and always has been a standing joke. All his state papers are jokes. His letters to our generals, beginning with those to General McClellan, are very cruel jokes.... His title of 'Honest' is a satirical joke.... His intrigues to secure a renomination and the hopes he appears to entertain of a reelection are, however, the most laughable jokes of all."[8]

Some of Lincoln's enemies made up a story that in September 1862, shortly after the bloody battle of Antietam, Lincoln drove over the field in an ambulance with General George McClellan and Marshal Ward Hill Lamon, observing workmen burying the dead, and suddenly burst out, "Come, Lamon, give us that song about 'Picayune Butler'; McClellan has never heard it." "Not, now, if you please," McClellan is supposed to have exclaimed, as he shuddered at Lincoln's behavior, "I would prefer to hear it some other place and time." But Lincoln insisted, and Lamon went ahead with the silly song, much to the President's delight. "It would have been indecorous to name Lincoln the buffoon that he is," exclaimed the *New York World,* "if he had been merely the Chief Magistrate. But the truth must be told when he is a *Chief Magistrate seeking re-election....* The American people are in no mood to re-elect a man to the highest office whose daily language is indecent, and who, riding over the field of Antietam, where thirty thousand of his fellow citizens were yet warm in their freshly-made graves, could slap Marshal Lamon on the knee and call for the Negro song of 'Picayune Butler.'" The "story is incredible," exclaimed another anti-Lincoln paper, New Jersey's *Essex Statesman.* "The story can't be true of any man fit for any office of trust, or even for a decent society; but the story is every whit true of Abraham Lincoln."[9]

The story was of course every whit untrue, and Lamon (Lincoln's law partner in Illinois) pleaded with the President to issue a public denial. But Lincoln preferred ignoring the slander. "If I have not established character enough to give the lie to this charge," he told Lamon, "I can only say that I am mistaken in my own estimate of myself." But Lamon persisted, and finally composed a refutation of the story himself and showed it to Lincoln. "Lamon," said Lincoln, after reading it, "your 'explanation' is entirely too belligerent in tone for so grave a matter. There is a heap of 'cussedness' mixed up with your usual amiability, and you are at times too fond of a fight. If I were you, I would simply state the facts as they are. I would give the statement, as you have here, without the pepper and salt. Let me try my hand at it." So he jotted down a statement of his own, making it clear that the incident took place sixteen days after Antietam, several miles from the battlefield, and that it was "a sad little song" Lincoln had asked Lamon to sing. But he never got around to making the statement public.[10]

Ward Lamon's singing was important to Lincoln. Though Lincoln never learned to read music or play an instrument, listening to music was one of the great joys of his life. Noah Brooks, Washington correspondent for California's *Sacramento Union,* wrote that the President's "love of music was something passionate," and that his "tastes were simple and uncultivated, his choice being old airs, songs, and ballads....All songs which had for their theme the rapid flight of time, decay, the recollection of early days, were sure to make a deep impression." Lincoln frequently asked his musical friend Lamon to sing for him; sometimes he wanted spirited banjo tunes like "Picayune Butler" that raised his spirits, but more often he preferred melancholy songs like "Twenty Years After," dealing with the transience of life, that brought tears to his eyes after he visited the Antietam battlefield. "Many a time," Lamon recalled, "in the old days on the Illinois circuit, and often at the White House I was rendering in my poor way that homely melody."[11]

But Lincoln also liked serious music. He attended the opera in Washington nineteen times while President, and seems to have enjoyed productions of Mozart's *The Magic Flute,* Bellini's *Norma,* Weber's *Der Freischütz,* and Gounod's *Faust,* whose "Soldier's Chorus" he especially liked. He attended concerts, too, especially those of the popular composer-pianist Louis M. Gottschalk, who, though from New Orleans, was an abolitionist. He liked listening to the U.S. Marine Band as well, and regretted only that his appearance at the weekly concerts sometimes took attention away from the musicians. "I wish they would let [me] enjoy the music," he lamented. One afternoon, when he was working in his office, he couldn't help overhearing Meda Blanchard, the first opera singer to perform in the White House, singing for his wife, Mary, and her guests and went down to listen. Blanchard was about to finish her recital but stayed to sing for him, and four days later Lincoln attended her concert at the Willard's.

"Our Republican President seemed to have been oblivious to the cares of office," remarked the *Washington Star* snippily, "and wholly absorbed by the siren voice of the fair cantatrice." Criticized for attending operas in wartime, Lincoln said simply, "The truth is I must have a change of some sort or die."[12]

But Lincoln received bouquets as well as brickbats when he was in the White House. He had plenty of supporters who liked his lack of pretension, his bent for the light touch, and his affection for storytelling. "One advantage the Americans have," London's *Saturday Review* exclaimed, "is the possession of a President who is not only the First Magistrate, but the Chief Joker of the Land." During the Civil War, several joke books—with titles like *Abe's Jokes—Fresh from Abraham's Bosom* and *Old Abe's Jokes, or, Wit at the White House*—circulated in great numbers in the North and spread Lincoln stories, not all of them authentic, far and wide. Lincoln didn't mind; he thought good stories deserved a large circulation, though he denied authorship of some of them.[13]

Lincoln was of course far more than the Chief Joker of the Land. As President, he showed himself to be shrewd, selfless, dedicated, strong-willed, resourceful, compassionate, and extraordinarily magnanimous. The burdens he bore during the Civil War were far heavier than those of most American Presidents, and he undertook his responsibilities with remarkable patience, energy, and determination. Though his critics couldn't always see it, he remained steadfastly true throughout the war to his basic objectives: restoration of the Union (which he regarded as a great experiment in government of, by, and for the people) and the abolition of slavery (which he regarded as utterly incompatible with a decent democratic society). He was anxious, moreover, to get the ablest men, civilian and military, he could find to help him in realizing those objectives, and he did not mind if they personally held him in low esteem. When someone told him that Secretary of War Stanton had called him a damned fool, he said lightly, "If Stanton said I was a damned fool, then I must be one, for he is nearly always right and generally says what he means." Stanton came to hold Lincoln in high esteem, but some of his associates never did. They found it hard to understand that in pursuing his objectives—preserving the Union and freeing the slaves—Lincoln had to proceed cautiously to avoid alienating the border slave states (and driving them into secession) and keep from offending Northern public opinion (which was by no means sympathetic to abolitionism at first) if he was to avoid making futile and perhaps even counterproductive gestures.[14]

No President of the United States has been vilified the way Lincoln was during the Civil War. He was attacked from all sides: by abolitionists, Negrophobes, states' righters, strict constitutionalists, radicals, conservatives, armchair strategists, and by people who just did not like his looks or who resented his storytelling. From the day of his inauguration to the day of his assassination, the litany of invective was unrelenting. Among other things, Lincoln was called an ape, a baboon, a usurper, a traitor, a tyrant, an old monster, a Great Hog, a gorilla, an idiot, a demagogue, an imbecile, a lunatic, a despot, a plunderer, a charlatan, and a half-witted usurper. One New York newspaper regularly referred to him as "that hideous baboon at the other end of the avenue" and proposed that "Barnum should buy and exhibit him as a zoological curiosity."[15]

Once, when Lincoln was asked how it felt to be President, he responded: "You have heard about the man tarred and feathered and ridden out of town on a rail? A man in the crowd asked how he liked it, and his reply was that if it wasn't for the honor of the thing, he would much rather walk." But Lincoln wasn't thinking of the abuse heaped upon him when he said this. He was thinking of the terrible loss of life on the battlefield during his presidency and the heartbreakingly slow progress being made toward the achievement of his objectives. He had enjoyed politics enormously before he became President, and he had been eager, too, to hold the highest office in the land. But when he became President, he said, instead of glory he found "ashes and blood."[16]

Humor lightened the cares of office for Lincoln. So did music. And the theater also gave him great respite from his troubles. He attended Grove's Theater in Washington more than one hundred times, according to the manager, when he was President. He had a special fondness for Shakespeare. Once, when one of his assistants saw him in a Washington theater entranced by the gifted James Hackett's performance as Falstaff in *Henry IV,* he couldn't help thinking: "He has forgotten the war. He has forgotten Congress. He is out of politics. He is living in Prince Hal's time." Pleased by Lincoln's approval, Hackett sent him an autographed copy of a book he had written on Shakespeare, and when Lincoln wrote to thank him, he made some comments of his own on several of Shakespeare's plays. Delighted by Lincoln's letter, Hackett had it printed as a broadside entitled "A Letter from President Lincoln," to distribute to his friends. But the newspapers got wind of it, reprinted it in their columns, and Lincoln's enemies in the press made savage comments on Lincoln's remarks about Shakespeare. Greatly embarrassed, Hackett wrote Lincoln to apologize. "Give yourself no uneasiness on the subject," Lincoln told him. "I certainly did not expect to see my note in print; yet I have not been much shocked by the comments on it. They are a fair specimen of what has occurred to me through life. I have endured a great deal of ridicule, without much malice; and have received a great deal of kindness, not quite free from ridicule. I am used to it." For Lincoln, the pleasure of seeing Hackett play Falstaff far outweighed the pain of abuse from the press. But even this pleasure was short-lived. A little later Hackett sought a government job, and when Lincoln was unable to arrange one for him, he turned against the President and joined the ranks of the Lincoln-haters.[17]

Shakespeare was important to Lincoln. He was deeply moved by the language of the plays and tremendously impressed by their insights. "Some of Shakespeare's plays I have never read," he admitted; "while others I have gone over perhaps as frequently as any unprofessional reader. Among the latter are Lear, Richard Third, Henry Eighth, Hamlet, and especially Macbeth. I think nothing equals Macbeth." Lincoln often carried a copy of Shakespeare's plays around with him so he could read passages from them if the occasion arose. A young Frenchman who was on board the *River Queen* with the

President and some of his guests on Sunday, April 9, 1865, recalled that "we were proceeding up the Potomac. That whole day the conversation turned on literary subjects. Mr. Lincoln read aloud to us for several hours. Most of the passages he selected were from Shakespeare, especially *Macbeth*. The lines after the murder of Duncan, when the new king falls prey to moral torment, were dramatically dwelt on. Now and then [Lincoln] paused to expatiate on how exact a picture Shakespeare here gives of a murderer's mind when, the dark deed achieved, its perpetrator already envies his victim's calm sleep. He read the scene over twice." Only the Bible meant as much to Lincoln as Shakespeare did. Throughout his life he read and reread the King James Bible, especially the Old Testament, for its majestic language as well as its moral insights. "There's a lot of good wisdom in there," he once remarked as he patted the Bible by his side.[18]

For a man whose only formal education came from little "blab schools" in the country (where the youngsters recited their lessons aloud), Lincoln became astonishingly well read. As a young man he seemed to be reading all the time, when standing and sitting, and even when walking. Once a friend saw him strolling down the street, his nose in a book, stopping to chat with some people, and finally, as the conversation waned, resuming his walk and his reading. Lincoln's wife, Mary, got to worrying every time her husband took one of their little boys out for a ride in a cart. She knew he would start reading as he pulled the cart down the street and that sometimes when the child fell out, it was a long time before he noticed it.[19]

Lincoln once said his favorite people were those who brought him a new book that turned out to be full of wisdom. As a lawyer he was in the habit of reading newspapers and magazines, but he also found time to delve into some of the best books available in those days. In addition to the Bible and Shakespeare, he became familiar with such classics as Aesop's *Fables,* John Bunyan's *Pilgrim's Progress,* and Daniel Defoe's *Robinson Crusoe,* and he dipped into Mason Locke Weems's *Life of Washington,* the first biography of the first President, as well. Though he wasn't heavily into science, he did read Robert Chambers's

Vestiges of the Natural History of Creation from cover to cover when it came out in 1844, and expressed sympathy for its evolutionary view of the universe. But his favorite reading was poetry, and his favorite poet was Scotland's Robert Burns. Burns, he once said, "never touched a sentiment without carrying it to its ultimate expression and leaving nothing further to be said." At the request of the Burns Club in Washington, Lincoln composed a toast to the Scottish poet: "I cannot frame a toast to Burns; I can say nothing worthy of his generous heart and transcending genius; thinking of what he has said I cannot say anything which seems worth saying." He also liked reading Alexander Pope, Wordsworth, and Byron, as well as the American poets: William Cullen Bryant, John Greenleaf Whittier, Oliver Wendell Holmes, James Russell Lowell, and Edgar Allan Poe. He adored Poe's famous poem "The Raven" and took pleasure in reciting it for his friends and associates. He frequently read from Walt Whitman's *Leaves of Grass,* too. He liked Whitman's poetry for its "vitality and freshness and unique form of expression" and thought Whitman "gave promise of a new school of poetry." Lincoln was not widely read the way some of the other Presidents—such as John Adams, Thomas Jefferson, and Theodore Roosevelt—were, but the reading he did was mostly of a high quality and what he learned from it became an inseparable part of his being. "The truth about this whole matter," Billy Herndon averred, "is that Mr. Lincoln read less and thought more than any man in his sphere in America....I repeat, that he read less and thought more than any man of his standing in America, if not the world."[20]

Lincoln's taste in poetry ran to the melancholy. His favorite poem began with the line "Oh, why should the spirit of mortal be proud," and dwelt on the shortness of life and the folly of pride. Called "Mortality," it was written by William Knox, a Scotsman, in the early part of the nineteenth century, and was recited so often by Lincoln that people thought he wrote it himself. "Beyond all question, I am not the author," he wrote a friend. "I would give all I am worth, and go into debt, to be able to write so fine a piece as I think that is." He also liked Thomas Gray's "Elegy in a Country Churchyard" and Oliver Wendell

Holmes's "The Last Leaf," about an aging Revolutionary War soldier, which he committed to memory. In October 1844, when he visited his old neighborhood in southern Indiana, the "poetizing mood," as he called it, came over him and he wrote a pensive poem of his own. "That part of the country is, within itself, as unpoetical as any spot on earth," he acknowledged. "But still, seeing it and its objects and inhabitants aroused feelings in me which were certainly poetry; though whether my expression of those feelings is poetry is quite another question...." The first stanza set the mood:

> My childhood's home I see again;
>   And gladden with the view;
> And still, as memory crowds my brain,
>   There's a sadness in it too.[21]

Not all of Lincoln's verses were somber. Sometimes he amused himself by turning out comic lines. Two weeks after the Battle of Gettysburg (July 19, 1863), he took time off to dash off a bit of doggerel about General Robert E. Lee's invasion of the North from Lee's point of view:

> In eighteen sixty three, with pomp,
>   and mighty swell,
> Me and Jeff's Confederacy, went
>   forth to sack Phil-del,
> The Yankees they got arter us, and
>   giv us particular hell,
> And we skedaddled back again,
>   and didn't sack Phil-del.

It's not great writing, of course, but Lincoln didn't mean it to be. He was, after all, the kind of person, it was said, who liked the way Indianans described a crowded place: "There wasn't a room to cuss the cat without gittin' its hairs in your teeth."[22]

Lincoln adored good writing, and he worked hard to bring his own pieces down to earth, simplifying them and getting rid of what he called the "fizzlegigs and fireworks." By the time he became President, he had developed a distinguished prose style of his own: simple, clear, direct, forceful, rhythmical, poetic, and at times majestic. On the eve of his inauguration in March 1861, he asked William H. Seward, whom he had appointed secretary of state, to read the inaugural address he had written and make some suggestions for improvement. Seward liked the address but wrote a paragraph for him to add (if he approved it) at the end that he thought might help reduce the sectional tensions gripping the nation at that time: "I close. We are not, we must not be aliens or enemies but fellow countrymen and brethren. Although passion has strained our bonds of affection too hardly they must not, I am sure they will not be broken. The mystic chords which proceeding from so many battle fields and so many patriot graves pass through all the hearts and all the hearths in this broad continent of ours will yet again harmonize in their ancient music when breathed upon by the guardian angel of the nation." Lincoln liked the idea of ending the address with some conciliatory remarks for the South, but he transmuted Seward's rather prosaic paragraph into a shorter, but more moving statement, containing, as so often with his writing, a touch of poetry: "I am loth to close. We are not enemies, but friends. We must not be enemies. Though passion may have strained, it must not break our bonds of affection. The mystic chords of memory, stretching from every battlefield and patriot grave to every living heart and hearthstone, all over this broad land, will yet swell the chorus of the Union, when again touched, as surely they will be, by the better angels of our nature."[23]

Lincoln hadn't been President for long before people in some of the departments—State, Treasury, War—began to notice "remarkable passages," as one of them put it, "in certain state papers." Who could have written them? In the State Department, admirers of Seward were convinced that he wrote them, but in the Treasury Department the admirers of Secretary Salmon P. Chase had no doubt that their boss was the author. But George Harding, a Philadelphia lawyer who worked in the War Department, thought that Edwin Stanton was

more talented than either Seward or Chase and that he was surely
the cabinet member who had composed such nicely written documents. The next time he ran into Stanton, Harding stopped him, mentioned a state paper that had appeared recently, and announced, "I
know who is the author of that." "Who do you suppose?" Stanton
asked him curiously. "You!" Harding came close to shouting. "Not a
word of it!" responded Stanton emphatically. "Not a word of it. Lincoln wrote it—every word of it. And he is capable of more than that."
Then, recalling how he and some of his associates had originally put
Lincoln down as a second-rater, he exclaimed, "Harding, no men
were ever so deceived as we [were]."[24]

When Vicksburg surrendered to General Grant in July 1863 and
the Mississippi River was open again to Union forces, Lincoln wrote:
"The 'Father of Waters' again goes unvexed to the sea." It is hard to
imagine any other President writing such a stunning sentence, or
composing such masterpieces of prose as the Gettysburg Address
and the first and second inaugural addresses. Thomas Jefferson,
Theodore Roosevelt, and Woodrow Wilson possessed splendid literary skills, but at his best Lincoln towered above them. Charles
Laughton, the highly esteemed British actor who became an American citizen in the mid-twentieth century, made the recitation of the
Gettysburg Address an essential part of his repertoire when he
toured the country and insisted that it was the greatest piece of prose
in the English language. For years, moreover, a copy of a letter written by Lincoln was posted in the Bodleian Library at Oxford with
the inscription: "The most sublime letter written in the English language." Lincoln's plain-spoken sparseness of expression, some commentators believe, shares credit with Mark Twain's prose for moving
American writers away from the effusiveness that was the vogue
among American speakers and writers in the nineteenth century.[25]

Lincoln had a deep feeling for the right use of words, and he em-
ployed them lovingly both in his storytelling and in his letters and
speeches. He was the only President ever to be called a "literary
artist." Literary critic and historian Jacques Barzun, in fact, called him

a "literary genius." "Nothing," wrote John Nicolay and John Hay, who knew Lincoln as members of his staff and published a lengthy biography of him in 1894, "would have more amazed him while he lived than to hear himself called a man of letters; but this age has produced few greater writers." Ralph Waldo Emerson ranked Lincoln with Aesop in his lighter moments, but when it came to serious moments he said this of the Civil War President: "The weight and penetration of many passages in his letters, messages, and speeches, hidden now by the very closeness of their application to the moment, are destined to a wide fame. What pregnant definitions, what unerring common-sense, what foresight, and on great occasions what lofty, and more than national, what human tone! His brief speech at Gettysburg will not easily be surpassed by words on any recorded occasion."[26]

On November 3, 1863, Lincoln, accompanied by his wife and two of his assistants, saw John Wilkes Booth at Ford's Theater in Washington. The play, written by Charles Selby, was entitled *The Marble Heart: or, the Sculptor's Dream,* and centered on Phidias, the ancient Greek sculptor, and Raphael, his reincarnation, with both parts played by Booth. Though the play didn't impress the presidential party, Lincoln was struck by Booth's skillful playing of the two parts and he sent word through the theater's manager that he would like to meet him. Booth, a diehard Confederate, contemptuously rejected the request, sneering that he would "rather have the applause of a Nigger." He also turned down later invitations to meet Lincoln at the White House. It wasn't until April 14, 1865, that he finally sought out the President in Ford's Theater.[27]

☆ ☆ ☆ **17** ☆ ☆ ☆

The Plebeian
Andrew Johnson

Andrew Johnson, the third Vice President to become President, was proud of his lowly origins. Just before taking his oath as Vice President at Abraham Lincoln's inauguration on March 4, 1865, he downed a few swigs of brandy for a cold that was bothering him, and he was feeling no pain when he was sworn in. He felt so good, in fact, after taking the oath, that to everyone's surprise, he launched into a lengthy speech about himself, centering on the belief that the people "are the source of all power" in the American system and that he himself was "one who comes from the ranks of the people."[1]

Johnson's speech was rambling and repetitive, and he soon lost his audience. "Humble as I am," he said proudly, "plebeian as I may be deemed, permit me in the presence of this brilliant assemblage to enunciate the truth that courts and cabinets, the President and his advisers, derive [their] greatness from the people." As he went on, baring his plebeian soul in prolix detail, the audience became restless, and people near him began shushing and pulling at his coattails. But he was not to be stilled. "I, though a plebeian boy," he cried, "am authorized by the principles of Government under which I live to feel proudly conscious that I am a man, and grave dignitaries are but men." When finally, to everybody's relief, he finally ran out of words and sat down, Johnson had convinced many people that he was a boozer as well as a plebeian. But Lincoln reassured his associates. "I have known Andy for many years," he said a few days later. "He made a bad slip the other day, but you need not be scared. Andy ain't a drunkard."[2]

Lincoln was right. Before he received his nomination for a second term in June 1864, he sent General Daniel E. Sickles, a *bon vivant* who knew his way around, to Nashville to see if Johnson, then governor of Tennessee, would be acceptable as a vice-presidential candidate. Sickles spent some time with Johnson and returned to Washington with a favorable report. Secretary of War Edwin M. Stanton also sent a man on his staff—Charles A. Dana—to Nashville to look the governor over. Johnson received Dana hospitably, shared a couple of drinks with him, and, said Dana, talked soberly and intelligently with him at all times. Dana decided that although Johnson drank a bit more than a gentleman should, he was eminently qualified for second place on the Lincoln ticket.[3]

There were other witnesses to Johnson's sobriety. Ben Truman, correspondent for the *Washington Chronicle,* knew Johnson better than either Sickles or Dana did, having spent months in Nashville covering him as governor for his paper. For eighteen months, he reported, he never saw Johnson enter a barroom or drink a cocktail, and though he learned that on occasion he did take "two or three glasses of Tennessee whisky," there were periods "when for days and weeks he would take nothing at all." But what impressed Truman the most was Johnson's almost total indifference to amusements. From time to time Truman invited Johnson to attend the theater with him, but Johnson was always too busy to go. He admitted he had never seen a play, though he once went to a minstrel show and another time went to a circus. When he was young, he explained to Truman, he was too poor to afford entertainments, and when he was older and could afford them he was too busy studying, reading, and working to include them in his schedule. Another reporter, Samuel R. Glenn of the *New York Herald,* was similarly struck by Johnson's asceticism. He was "a model of abstemiousness," he wrote. "He never played cards, for amusement or gain. He never indulged [in liquor] on any single occasion to a greater extent than possibly a clergyman would at a sacrament, and as for the smaller vices, he was free from them all."[4]

Johnson's abstemiousness didn't help him any with his political foes. Whenever he ran for office—as congressman, senator, governor, or Vice President—his enemies liked to toss a whiskey bottle into the race. Sometimes they confused him with his son Robert, who was in fact an alcoholic, but it wouldn't have made any difference if his son had been a teetotaler. Worse than being called a lush, though, was the way his enemies looked down upon him because of his humble background. Johnson started out as a "poor white," whose parents were illiterate, and he "grappled with the gaunt and haggard monster called hunger" when he was a boy. But he was proud of the way he learned to read as a youngster when apprenticed to a tailor and of how, with the help of his wife, Eliza, he learned to write and cipher. Lincoln was able to take slurs on his origins in his stride, but Johnson never could. He was always on the defensive, and sometimes he betrayed his feelings about the situation in public, as he did at Lincoln's inauguration. During the 1864 campaign, the *New York World* lumped Lincoln and Johnson together in an editorial dismissing them as "men of mediocre talents, narrow views, deficient education, and coarse, vulgar manners....A railsplitting buffoon and a boorish tailor, both from the backwoods, both growing up in uncouth ignorance, they afford a grotesque sight for a satiric poet...." Americans like to sentimentalize about the grit and gumption of people who forge ahead in life by their own efforts, but Johnson couldn't help wondering at times whether their real admiration, deep down, was for people born to privilege.[5]

Becoming President upon Lincoln's assassination didn't exempt Johnson from the contempt and condescension of his worst enemies. In 1866, when he made "a swing around the circle"—a visit to ten states—to present his conservative views on Reconstruction of the South after the Civil War, he blew up at times in exchanges with people in the audience, and was of course charged with drunkenness.

"A. Johnson, the 'humble individual,'" sneered the *Chicago Tribune* after one of the President's appearances, "after one or two ineffectual attempts to land in the gutter, was handed or rather lifted into the buggy awaiting his august presence." The *Boston Transcript* also damned him for his egotism, heading a series of reports on his campaign in 1866 with the words, "I, I, I, My, My, My, Me, Me, Me."[6]

For Johnson, life in the White House was quiet and lonely at first. His wife Eliza, never in good health, retired to the family quarters for the duration of his presidency, turning her duties as hostess over to their daughters Martha and Mary. Johnson did almost nothing but work at first. He might play checkers now and then, and sometimes he watched people play baseball on the "White Lot" located on the south grounds of the White House, but it never occurred to him to join in. To William Seward he looked "ill and oppressed," and to Gideon Welles, "pale and languid." Welles, the secretary of the navy, finally persuaded Johnson to take a cruise with him down the Potomac River, and he was convinced it raised the President's spirits. Welles was bothered when he learned that Johnson "took no exercise, and confined himself to his duties," and he tried, without success, to get him to take regular outings on the Potomac. In August 1865, however, things suddenly changed: Two carriages drew up before the White House, and out poured a slew of Johnsons: sons, daughters, in-laws, and grandchildren. As they spread themselves around the White House, the President quickly came alive.[7]

The grandchildren became Johnson's relaxation. He let them have the run of the place, permitted them to interrupt his work, and took them on long rides out into the country. Sometimes he took them to Rock Creek Park, where the children went wading and caught water bugs, while he skipped stones or took little walks by himself, thinking over the problems besetting him as President. When the children couldn't accompany him on the daily rides, he took William Crook, his bodyguard, along as a companion. He also found companionship in Colonel William G. Moore, his private secretary, to whom he recited passages from Thomas Gray's "Elegy on a Country Churchyard" and, surprisingly, from the literary orations of Wendell Phillips, an abolitionist who was very critical of Johnson's reconstruction policies.[8]

In 1868, when the House of Representatives impeached Johnson and the U.S. Senate put him on trial for vetoing their reconstruction legislation, Johnson found his sessions with Colonel Moore indispensable for reducing the stress he endured during the crisis. Once, he brought out his old, battered copy of *The American Speaker* (from which he learned how to read while working as a tailor's apprentice) and asked Moore to read aloud passages from some of the speeches in the book. He also had him read from George Washington's old favorite, Joseph Addison's play *Cato,* and he expatiated on Cato, a man who, he pointed out, would not "compromise with wrong, but being right, died before he would yield." He was thinking of himself, of course, and perhaps he thought too much about himself without learning from his predicament. Johnson was justly acquitted before leaving the White House, but on balance his presidency was a failure. Perhaps if he had been able to understand the plight of the newly freed blacks, more despised than poor whites like himself, he would have had a more fruitful presidency.[9]

☆ ☆ ☆ 18 ☆ ☆ ☆

The Undemonstrative
Ulysses S. Grant

In 1877, Ulysses S. Grant became the first President to try his hand at golf. He was in England with his wife, Julia, shortly after leaving the White House, and the game was just beginning to become popular there, though most Brits still thought there was something silly about mature people chasing a little ball over a piece of land all afternoon with strangely shaped sticks. The Grants were touring the country at the time, and their host stopped his carriage at one side of a golf course so his passengers could see what was going on.

Grant was curious about the game. "That looks like good exercise," he remarked, "but what's the little white ball for?" The golfers invited him to join them and a caddy handed him a wooden club. The former President "looked earnestly at the ball, then at the club," according to one of his friends, "and having measured the distance carefully made a strike, his club going six inches above the ball. Disappointed at this failure, a more careful estimate was made of the length of the club and distance to ball, and another swing was made, the club striking the ground one foot before reaching the ball." Grant tried several more times, but failed to hit the ball even once. Handing the club back to the caddy, he murmured to a gentleman standing beside him, "I have always understood the game of golf was good outdoor exercise and especially for the arms. I fail, however to see what use there is for a ball in the game." He never tried golf again.[1]

Grant never regarded himself as a sportsman, though as a boy on his father's farm in Kentucky he engaged in several sports when not at his chores. "There was no objection to rational enjoyment," he wrote in his memoirs, "such as fishing, going to the creek a mile away to swim in summer, taking a horse and visiting my grandparents in the adjoining county fifteen miles off, skiing on the ice in winter, or taking a horse and sleigh when there was snow on the ground." But he didn't like hunting, one of the most popular sports for young men in those days, because, like Abraham Lincoln, he hated taking the lives of animals. "I could never eat anything that goes on two legs," he once confessed. When he served as a junior officer during the Mexican War, he saw the other officers go out hunting and return triumphantly with the ducks and turkeys they had downed, but he had no desire to join them. Once, though, one of his friends succeeded in persuading him to go on a turkey hunt. "We had scarcely reached the edge of the timber," he wrote later, "when I heard the flutter of wings overhead, and in an instant I saw two or three turkeys flying away. These were soon followed by more, then more, and more, until a flock of twenty or thirty had left from just over my head. All this time I stood watching the turkeys to see where they flew—with my gun on my shoulder, and never once thought of leveling at the birds." He returned to camp realizing he would never become even a mediocre hunter. "Twice in my life," he once reflected, "I killed wild animals, and I have regretted both acts ever since."[2]

Horseback riding was Grant's favorite activity. Like George Washington, Grant was a superb horseman who rode horses for pleasure as well as for work. His love of horses came early, and as a youngster he developed great skill in sensing their moods and figuring out their capacities so he could get them to do the things he wanted them to do. "We do not know how Grant went about 'gentling' difficult and fractious horses, and he may not have known himself," wrote biographer Michael Korda. "He spoke to them softly and calmly, he stroked them, he never resorted to punishment with the whip—but the important thing was that somehow the horses sensed that Grant was their friend, and they trusted him."[3]

When Grant was about eight, he took a shine to a colt owned by a man named Robert Ralston and was eager for his father to acquire the animal. But Ralston asked twenty-five dollars for him and Grant's father refused to pay more than twenty. After Ralston left, young Grant asked for permission to buy the colt at Ralston's price and his father gave his consent, but advised him to offer only twenty at first, and if that didn't work, offer twenty-two and a half; and if Ralston refused that, finally agree to twenty-five dollars. When Grant located Ralston, he told him frankly: "Papa says I may offer you twenty dollars for the colt, but if you won't take that, I am to offer you twenty-two and a half, and if you won't take that, I am to give you twenty-five." Telling the story years later, Grant admitted that it "would not require a Connecticut man to guess the price finally agreed upon," but added: "I certainly showed very plainly that I had come for the colt and meant to have him," which, after all, was the important thing for him. Still, the story of Grant's dealings with Ralston soon got out and the boys around town teased him unmercifully for his simple-mindedness for a long time. But the horse was a good one, Grant knew; he kept him until he was four years old and went blind and then sold him for twenty dollars. A few years later he saw the horse working with other blind horses on the treadmill of the ferryboat at Maysville, Kentucky.[4]

It was a long time before Grant found his place in the sun. His father sent him to West Point, which he didn't particularly like, though he enjoyed reading the novels housed in the Academy's library and showed a real talent for painting in the class devoted to battlefield sketches and military drawings. And he soon won plaudits for his way with horses. "It was as good as any circus to see Grant ride," attested one of the cadets. His jumping feats were especially impressive. In 1843, when he graduated from West Point, he took part in the graduation exercises and produced an amazing jump that thrilled the audience. "The riding master placed a leaping bar higher than a man's head," wrote General J. B. Fry afterward, and then called out: "Cadet Grant!" At once a "clean-faced, slender, blue-eyed young fellow weighing about 120 pounds dashed from the ranks on a powerfully built sorrel and galloped down the opposite side of the hall. As he came into the stretch, the horse increased his pace and, measuring his stride for the great leap before him, bounded into the air and cleared the bar, carrying the rider as if man and beast had been welded together. The spectators were breathless." Serving as a young officer in the war against Mexico a few years later, Grant showed his riding skills again. During the Battle of Monterey he was ordered to retrieve some ammunition for his unit that had been left behind and complied at once. Clinging to the side of his horse, he galloped through enemy fire to an ammunition wagon nearby and procured a fresh supply of powder and bullets for the besieged troops. Though he was cited for bravery and promoted to captain, Grant was by no means an uncritical supporter of the war itself. He looked upon it as an unjust war against the Mexicans, and he developed a real liking for them while stationed in Mexico.[5]

After the war, the tours of duty that took Grant to isolated army posts in the West, far from his wife and family, threatened to destroy him. From Fort Humboldt on the northern California coast he wrote his wife in 1854 that he had no horse of his own at the post, and that "I do nothing but sit in my room and read, and occasionally take a short ride on one of the public horses." He began drinking to assuage his loneliness, and after disgracing himself by driving three horses in tandem at breakneck speed down the street with their buggies careening behind him, he was asked to resign his commission. A civilian once more, he tried farming near St. Louis, peddling firewood, collecting rents, and finally working as a clerk in a leather goods store owned by his brothers in Galena, Illinois.[6]

At the outbreak of the Civil War, Grant volunteered for service, rose rapidly in rank, and ended up as a general who was indispensable for a Union victory. "I cannot spare this man," Lincoln told Grant's crit-ics. "He fights." There were rumors about his drinking, to be sure, and it is a fact that in June 1863, during the Vicksburg campaign, he was drunk for a couple of days while waiting for his siege of Vicks-burg to take effect. But Grant's addiction was smoking, not drinking; he seemed always to have a cigar in his mouth. "He reeked with to-bacco," according to Hamlin Garland. "He was the most appalling smoker of his time.... His cigars were black, rank, poisonous, and he consumed immense quantities of them."[7]

When the war ended, Grant was world-famous, and the presidency came to him as a kind of reward for his services to his country dur-ing the war. He was a mediocre President, and his critics suggested that he understood horses better than he did human beings. But Grant enjoyed being America's Chief Executive, thought he did a good job, all things considered, and didn't mind it at all that he had far more free time on his hands as President than he did when he was supreme commander of U.S. forces during the war. As President, he took little walks after breakfast and longer walks in the afternoon be-fore dinner. After dinner he played cribbage or billiards with friends, all the time puffing his beloved cigars. Given his taciturn nature, Grant was surprisingly accessible to people—Northerners, South-erners, blacks, Indians, beggars—because he thoroughly enjoyed good conversation even if he didn't do much talking himself. "He would sit and *listen and listen,* without saying a word," one visitor de-clared, "having a good time all along, but letting his companion do the talk." He liked young people and frequently watched boys playing ball behind the White House. Sometimes he acted as umpire for them and on occasion joined in on the game. "After playing awhile," according to one of the boys, "he put his hands behind him and strolled away down the avenue. He seemed a kind and fatherly man to us." At his summer home in Long Branch, New Jersey, Grant liked to sit on the porch and read, attend the racetrack with his wife, and play poker with friends into the wee hours on Fridays.[8]

But Grant's favorite recreations involved horses. He liked to drive as well as ride, and he brought a competitive spirit to his driving. He loved to sit on the edge of his seat in a light racing buggy, according to William Crook, his bodyguard, pull the brim of his slouch hat down over his eyes, lean forward until his arms and shoulders were just above the dashboard, and then, speaking a few words to the magnificent trotting horse in front of him, sweep past every other driver on the road. Sometimes people on the streets in Washington thought he had runaway horses on his hands, but of course Grant would never have gotten into that kind of situation. His wife Julia became upset whenever he started driving too fast and always insisted he take her home right away. Once, when he was in a ceremonial procession in New York City, he took the reins from his driver and then challenged the other carriage drivers to a race through Central Park; he didn't win the race himself, but he conceded defeat with a friendly wave of his hat before leaving. Another time, when he was speeding along a street near the White House, a policeman arrested him for driving so fast. When it dawned on the officer that he had arrested the President of the United States, who was plainly and simply dressed, he started apologizing. But Grant interrupted him. "Officer," he cried, "do your duty." So the policeman fined him, took his horse and carriage to the police station, and let Grant walk quietly back to the White House by himself.[9]

As with many of our Presidents, high art, literature, and music held a limited appeal for Grant. The Great Books had little interest for him, even though, in retirement, he wrote one himself: his memoirs, generally regarded as a literary masterpiece. He read books for information, not pleasure, and read newspapers every day mainly to keep up with politics. The theater seems not to have had any charms for him either, although during his early years in the army he once played the part of Desdemona in a production of Shakespeare's *Othello* that the soldiers staged for amusement. He "looked like a girl dressed up," it was reported, but the soldier who played Othello said Grant's Desdemona "did not have much sentiment." Grant was unfortunately too tone-deaf to have much, if any, appreciation for music. At West Point he found it hard to keep in step when his company marched to music. And in Washington, when asked after a concert if he had enjoyed the music, he cried, "How could I? I know only two tunes. One of them is 'Yankee Doodle' and the other isn't." When James Russell Lowell, the U.S. Minister to Spain, took the retired President and his wife to an opera in Madrid, Grant didn't last long there. A few minutes into the singing, he complained that the only noise he could distinguish from any other was the bugle call that was sounded. "Haven't we had enough of this?" he wailed. When it came to fancy balls, he once said that he could dance very well if it weren't for the music.[10]

The Grants turned melancholy when the time came for them to leave the White House. After they boarded the train leaving Washington, Grant heard his wife crying and asked why. "Oh, Ulys," she moaned, "I feel like a waif." Returned Grant: "Is that all? I thought something had happened. You must not forget that I too am a waif." But the Grants weren't exactly waifs when they took a two-year grand tour of the world. Everywhere they went, they received enthusiastic welcomes, as well as countless invitations to "the stateliest houses," and found themselves mingling with some of the highest society around the world. "No man enjoyed ordinary travel, the seeing strange sights and different countries and nations more than Grant," noted Adam Badeau, Grant's former military secretary, who accompanied the couple on their trip, "and no man ever had his extraordinary opportunities. Under these his mind and character grew and enlarged; he received all the benefits of contact with so many minds, of witnessing so many civilizations, of studying so many intellectual and moral varieties of man. He had not in his youth the advantage of what is called a liberal education, but no man ever trod this earth more highly educated than Grant by events and experiences and opportunities…."[11]

Grant insisted the warm receptions he received in Europe, the Middle East, and Asia were "intended more for my country than myself," but he enjoyed the cordiality wherever he went. He also liked having Julia with him most of the time. When they were in Switzerland and "went up from Interlachen to Grindenwald," according to Badeau, Grant and his wife "flirted nearly all the way. They half quarreled as to how they should sit, and wanted always to be by each other's side." Mrs. Grant once changed her position to get a better view of the Wetterhorn and this placed her opposite her husband, "who was a grandfather and nearly sixty years old," and "didn't like it at all." Mrs. Grant realized this, but, said Badeau, "conquettishly refused to return till we arrived at a certain point in the valley; and the hero was uncomfortable until Grindenwald was reached, and he could sit by the side of the mother of his grown-up children. Then he was happy again under the snows and the shadows of the Jungfrau. Neither the compliments of places nor the plaudits of the two continents had lessened his simplicity or his domesticity."[12]

☆ ☆ ☆ **19** ☆ ☆ ☆

The Studious
Rutherford B. Hayes

Rutherford B. Hayes was a lackluster President. Virtue, he learned from Aristotle, "is defined to be *mediocrity,* of which either extreme is vice." But he didn't want to rock the boat in any case. After a fierce electoral dispute, he became President in 1877 as the result of a compromise between the Northern Republicans and the Southern Democrats that ended military reconstruction in the South after the Civil War. Some Democrats were unreconciled; they called Hayes "His Fraudulency" and "Rutherfraud B. Hayes." But most members of the party, including Samuel J. Tilden, the Democratic candidate, accepted the compromise. In the end, Democratic leader Abram Hewitt decided that the Hayes administration was "creditable to all concerned."[1]

Hayes had his fans. One of them was the distinguished novelist and literary critic William Dean Howells, who wrote a campaign biography for him in 1876. "The man fascinates me!" he told one of his friends in the writing world. Hayes, he said, was a "very brave, single-hearted, firm-willed, humorous, unpretentiously self-reliant man." But what he really liked about the President was his love of books and serious interest in good literature.[2]

Howells didn't consider Hayes a "literary man," to be sure, but he did think he was "one of those non-literary men who take a purer and finer delight in literature than is perhaps possible to the professional *littérateur*." In the campaign biography, he had much to say about the Republican candidate's experience in the Union Army during the Civil War and about his achievements as a congressman and then governor of Ohio. But he also devoted several friendly pages to Hayes's appreciation of great books.[3]

Hayes's love of reading came early. As a boy, he read books with his sister Fanny; she read poetry to him and helped him with Shakespeare. Once, they dramatized Sir Walter Scott's "Lady of the Lake" and then acted it out for each other. In addition to the required reading for his courses at Kenyon College in Gambier, Ohio, Hayes did a lot of extracurricular reading. At Harvard Law School, he made an entry in his diary regretting the fact that although he devoted a great deal of time to reading Milton and Shakespeare, he also wasted time reading trashy novels. In Cincinnati, where he set up law practice after leaving Harvard, he joined the Literary Club, a social as well as a literary organization made up of young lawyers, artists, clergymen, and "whoever else loved letters in a city always first in the culture of the west." Members of the club did more than discuss serious books; they debated and orated, and also consumed large quantities of oysters, ham sandwiches, and sour wine. Hayes regarded it as the most educational adventure of his life, and he became one of the club's most energetic members, reciting "Webster's Reply to Hayne" countless times for the delectation of his comrades. "What good times we had!" he once reflected. "Wit, anecdotes, song, feast, wine, and good fellowship—gentlemen and scholars."[4]

In addition to reading and talking about books, Hayes attended lectures by prominent authors sponsored by the Cincinnati Lyceum. When Ralph Waldo Emerson, one of his favorite writers, gave a series of lectures there, Hayes attended every one of them and wrote at length in his diary about the main points Emerson made in each. Howells thought that young lawyer Hayes's reading "was as great as that of most men of literary life," but that unlike men of letters he read to find out what a writer had to say, not to see how he said it.

"Men, character, life, are his study, not art," Howells pointed out, "and it is observable that the books that most interest him are those whose substance is of a greater importance than their form." Still, Hayes had good taste: He devoured the works of Hawthorne, Dickens, Thackeray, Sterne, Cervantes, and Byron. As a congressman, he was for a time chairman of the library committee and enjoyed suggesting books for the Library of Congress to acquire. Like Justice Joseph Story, Howells observed, Hayes seemed "to have always esteemed his love of literature a comparatively guiltless treason to his jealous mistress, the Law; it is the other siren, Politics, that he is always protesting his immovable purpose of having nothing to do with."[5]

But politics came to dominate Hayes's life. His political activity not only cut down drastically on his reading; it also prevented him from having a hobby or taking many breaks from his work. Now and then he took walks for exercise. "This morning I have risen before 6 A.M. and will begin my morning walks," he noted one July day. "I weighed yesterday one hundred and ninety pounds. Warm morning walks will take off during this month at least five or eight pounds. Walked this morning over to the National Cemetery and eastwardly until the clock 7 A.M., when I returned by the President's gate." But there is no reason to believe that morning walks became a regular part of his schedule. When he was younger, Hayes did some sleighing in the winter and some hunting and fishing when visiting friends. As President, though, his routine, judging from his diary, was mostly sedentary. He did climb the Washington Monument one day with William Crook, the White House bodyguard; and he made so many little trips—to attend county and state fairs, to give speeches, to visit kinfolk, and to sightsee—that the *Chicago Times* called him "Rutherford the Rover." Still, Hayes acknowledged that there "is not enough exercise in this way of life."[6]

Music played some part in Hayes's way of life. When courting Lucy, his wife, he wrote her: "With no musical taste or cultivation myself, I am yet so fond of simple airs that I have often thought I never could love a woman who did not sing them." Lucy did sing them; she also played them. When they were living in the White House she frequently went into the Red Room with her husband after dinner, sat down at the piano, gathered the children around her, and began playing and singing hymns and traditional popular songs. A pious Christian, Mrs. Hayes instituted morning prayers in the White House and hosted evening "hymn sings," in which cabinet heads and congressmen joined the Hayeses in singing "Lead, Kindly Light" and "Rock of Ages."[7]

The Hayeses took satisfaction in the fact that the receptions and dinners they sponsored in the White House went off smoothly, if not spectacularly (though there were complaints about their unwillingness to serve alcoholic beverages). Long before Hayes's term of office ended, however, he and his wife began looking forward to retirement. "Lucy and I have had a few minutes' talk on this laborious, anxious slavish life," Hayes confided to his diary in June 1879. "It has many attractions and enjoyments, but she agrees so heartily with me as I say: 'Well, I am heartily tired of this life of bondage, responsibility, and toil. I wish it was at an end.'" Just before leaving office, he wrote his friend Guy M. Bryan that "Nobody ever left the Presidency with less regret, less disappointment, fewer heartburnings, or more general content... than I do. Full of difficulty and trouble at first, I now found myself on smooth waters and under bright skies."[8]

Facing retirement, Hayes asked himself: "How will you pass time? Or that other unwarrantable phrase, how will you kill time?" His guess was that a man with his interests, education, and "sense of duty" to his fellow countrymen would have "more trouble to find time for his work, than to find work to occupy all the time at his command." He was right. Before long, back home on his fine estate, Spiegel Grove, in Fremont, Ohio, he took walks every day; kept up a lively correspondence with friends and acquaintances; joined the fraternal society the Odd Fellows; made speeches for the Grand Army of the Republic (G.A.R.), the Civil War veterans' group; took trips with Lucy; supported the causes of temperance and prison reform; and worried about America's tendency during the Gilded Age to move away from Lincoln's government of, by, and for the people to what he called "government of the rich, by the rich, and for the rich." He also selected books for the local library and, for himself, acquired six thousand volumes of Americana, a collection of biographies, histories, and travel books published in Cincinnati, in which he browsed for "mental improvements—for information—to keep the faculties alert and alive."[9]

But Hayes's greatest interest in retirement was the field of education. "My hobby," he mused, as he left the White House, "more and more is likely to be common school education, or universal education." He was convinced that education would solve most of the problems facing the United States in his time, and he became active in a number of organizations dedicated to furthering public education for both blacks and whites. "The want of public schools in any quarter of the Union," he wrote, "is an injury to the whole Union, as the success of republican institutions rests upon the intelligence & capacity for self government of the whole people & of all the states."[10]

☆ ☆ ☆ **20** ☆ ☆ ☆

The Bookish
James A. Garfield

On November 13, 1874, James A. Garfield, an Ohio congressman at the time, decided to start playing cards. "I am forcing myself to some form of recreation," he wrote in his diary. But he added, "It would please me better to spend the evening in study." Study of course meant books, and books were Garfield's great passion. Still, he took time off to live up to his card pledge by playing euchre with friends in the Lower House; bezique with his wife, Crete; whist with Supreme Court justices; pedro with friends in the Senate; and casino with his children.[1]

For Garfield, cards replaced chess, once his favorite game, but nothing could replace books. When he itched for stimulation, he read books; when he wanted to satisfy his curiosity, he read books; when he hoped to learn something new, he read books; when he was preparing a speech to deliver, he read books; when he was listening to a boring speech, he thought about books; when he wanted to entertain his children, he read to them from books; and when he had a bad cold, he read books and was convinced they restored him to health. He probably took more books out of the Library of Congress than any other congressman. Cleaning the office in his Washington home one day, Garfield wrote his wife that there was a "pile of books three feet high on the floor waiting for the Congr. Library cart. The pile is full of memories of Caesar, Shakespeare, and Tariff."[2]

Love of reading began early with Garfield, and in whatever school he attended—rural schools, Geauga Seminary, the Western Reserve Eclectic Institute in Ohio, or Williams College in Massachusetts—he broadened his interests, increased his inquiries, and sought new books with which to stir up his thinking. He kept a record of his reading in his diary, summarizing the contents of the books he devoured and making a critical evaluation of them. As his tastes became more refined with the passage of time, Garfield gradually discarded his youthful bent for what he called "gush and slush," abandoning the sentimental effusiveness that was so popular when he was a youngster, and developed an honest, forthright, and thoughtful prose style of his own that received much praise. He also came to appreciate fine writing, including the Greek and Roman classics, as well as the great books in English, German, and American literature.[3]

Gore Vidal thought that Garfield's love of literature made him one of the most civilized of all our Presidents, and he was fond of the story novelist William Dean Howells told in his memoirs about his encounter with the Garfields as a young man in June 1870, when he and his father (Garfield's friend) were just back from Boston, where they had met some of the celebrated poets in the area. "As we were sitting with the Garfield family on the veranda that overlooked their lawn," Howells wrote, "I was beginning to speak of the famous poets I knew when Garfield stopped me with 'Just a minute.' He ran down into the grassy space first to one fence and then to the other at the sides and waved a wild arm of invitation to the neighbors who were also sitting on their back porches. 'Come over here,' he shouted. 'He's telling about Holmes and Longfellow, and Lowell, and Whittier.' And at his bidding, dim forms began to mount the fences and follow him up to his veranda. 'Now go on,' he called to me, when we were all seated, and I went on, while the whippoorwills whirled and whistled round, and the hours drew towards midnight."[4]

Garfield always seemed to be reading. "In his later years," recalled his friend Burke A. Hinsdale, "he read everywhere—on the cars, in the omnibus, and after retiring at night. If he was leaving Washington for a few days, and had nothing requiring immediate attention on hand, he would go to the great Library of Congress and say to the librarian, 'Mr. Spofford, give me something that I don't know anything about.' A stray book coming to him in this way would often lead to a special study of the subject." Once, Garfield boarded the train for Pittsburgh and after taking his seat opened his carpetbag to take out Goethe's *Wilhelm Meister.* To his disappointment, he found that by accident he had brought along instead a novel by a Mrs. Holmes entitled *Dora Dean.* After sitting a while regretting his error, he decided to read the book anyway and analyze it the way he would have analyzed the Goethe book. He ended by writing a critical commentary of several pages about the deficiencies of the book in his journal. When he got back to Washington, he went to the Library of Congress and, out of curiosity, looked up Mrs. Holmes in the catalog, and "found, to my disgust that Mrs. Holmes has written eleven novels and is still blazing away."[5]

Born to poverty in a small town in Ohio, Garfield was deprived of access to the institutions of high culture while growing up, but soon after he took up residence in Washington as a member of Congress he developed a liking for both the theater and musical performances. Beginning in the late 1870s he began attending plays regularly with his wife and friends, and he saw a lot of Shakespeare as well as performances in other plays by many of the leading actors and actresses of the day. He liked comedies as well as tragedies, and one night returned home around eleven "with sides sore with laughing." But he was turned off by satirical comedies dealing with corruption in Congress and elsewhere—chiefly, perhaps, because he had been charged, possibly unfairly, with being involved in the Crédit Mobilier railroad scandal. In December 1874, Garfield saw a presentation of *The Gilded Age,* a play based on the novel by Mark

Twain and Charles Dudley Warner, published in 1873, satirizing what they called "lobbyists" in Washington, and denounced it as "a piece of stupidity whose stupidity is only equaled by the brilliant acting of Colonel Sellars. The play is full of malignant insinuations and would lead the hearer to believe that there is no virtue in the world, in public or in private life."[6]

Garfield took in some opera while he was in Congress, but he seems to have enjoyed Gilbert and Sullivan operettas—he saw *H.M.S. Pinafore* four times—much more. There is no analysis of musical shows in his journal; he reacted to music with what one writer called "baffled uncertainty." Reporting on a concert he attended on November 18, 1874, Garfield wrote: "Twenty violins and forty other instruments sounding in harmony make a great volume of melody. There was much in the concert that delighted me, but I do not sufficiently understand the language of music to be able to translate its meaning. Its riddles pique me, and I sometimes wonder whether it has any meaning at all. I wish I could converse with some great master of music and learn something of his mental processes." Like all intelligent people, Garfield was fully aware of the fact that some of his opinions were worth listening to and others weren't.[7]

Garfield's father, an impoverished farmer, was a "man of prodigious strength," it was said, and before he died (when Garfield was only two years old), he had become famous for his skill as a wrestler. Garfield himself, though no wrestler, was a sturdy boy and could take care of himself in fights with the other boys in town. "At fifteen," according to one writer, "he was a large boy, strong and athletic," and "inspired by the traditions of his father's wrestling," he became known as "the fighting boy." When he taught school in his early manhood, he was able to handle unruly pupils, some of them not much younger than he, without difficulty. Once, a sixteen-year-old boy "refused to obey me," he recalled, "and was very saucy. I flogged him severely and told him to take his seat. He caught a billet of wood and came at me and we had a merry time. He vamoosed." As an adult, Garfield never made sports an important part of his life, but he went sleighing in the winter, fished and hunted a bit, and did a little horse-back riding, though he thought it took too much time. He liked to play croquet with his children, go swimming with them, and help them with their lessons. Once, he told his children the story of Iphigenia in Tauris and "was pleased to see how strongly the story touched the hearts of the little ones. J. left the room crying when he thought Iphigenia would be sacrificed. Several other members of the family were shedding tears before the story was completed." After that, he read aloud Charles and Mary Lamb's *Tales from Shakespeare* to them and then took up Audubon, reading them the descriptions of birds and animals, and a little later took them to see the specimens in the Smithsonian Institution.[8]

Garfield was a sociable person and enjoyed good talk, though he made it clear he found "no enjoyment in society where there is no topic of conversation but raising hogs." He could talk interestingly about many things, but avoided discussions of his experiences as an officer in the Union Army during the Civil War unless he was with military professionals. Preparing and delivering speeches also gave him a great deal of pleasure, as did engaging in lively debates in the House of Representatives, where he served seven terms. For vacations, he liked to take trips to other parts of the country with his family and friends; traveling, like books, meant getting to know new people, places, and ideas. Garfield's versatility amazed people. "If he were not in public life," Rutherford B. Hayes declared, "he would be equally eminent as a professor in a college, as a lecturer, as an author, an essayist, or a metaphysician." Massachusetts senator George F. Hoar thought Garfield could have achieved greatness, had he wanted to, as a scientist, mathematician, linguist, orator, or popular leader.[9]

When Garfield was an undergraduate at Williams College, he came under the influence of the school's venerable president, Mark Hopkins, a Congregational minister who taught the course in ethics that all students were required to take. And although as a member of the Disciples of Christ, Garfield could not accept Hopkins's Calvinistic certainties, he found the minister himself an enormously stimulating instructor from whom he was able to learn much. Years later, he met Hopkins again in Washington just after his presidential inauguration, and when his former professor shook hands with him and exclaimed, "I congratulate you, Mr. President," Garfield graciously told him, "You are more President than I." This was on March 4, 1881. On July 2, Garfield was shot by a disappointed office-seeker, and on September 19 he died.[10]

☆ ☆ ☆ **21** ☆ ☆ ☆

The Leisurely
Chester A. Arthur

Chester A. Arthur was an epicure. He liked the good things in life, and he liked the best things even better. He "wanted the best of everything," averred one of the White House guards, "and wanted it served in the best manner." Arthur dressed fashionably, drove the most elegant carriage in Washington, partook of the finest food, cigars, and wines, and hosted state dinners in the White House that thrilled the white-bread crowd in the nation's capital. New York's Chauncey Depew, who dined out frequently with classy people in posh restaurants, declared that "in all the arts and conventionalities of what is known as 'the best society,'" President Arthur "could have taken equal rank" with "the Prince of Wales who afterwards became King Edward VII." Describing her experience as a guest at one of Arthur's dinners, Senator James Blaine's wife wrote that the "dinner was extremely elegant, hardly a trace of the old White House taint being perceptible anywhere, the flowers, the damask, the silver, the attendants, all showing the latest style and an abandon in expense and taste."[1]

To many people, the well-groomed Chester Arthur ("Elegant Arthur") looked pleasingly presidential. But his dignity, graciousness, and sophisticated tastes did not obscure his reputation before becoming President as a "gentleman boss" in the Republican Party in

New York City, whose mastery of the skills of a machine politician led him to be called a "spoilsman's spoilsman." When President Garfield was assassinated by a deranged office-seeker in July 1881, many people were appalled by the thought of Vice President Chester Arthur in the White House. While Garfield was still lingering, a Cincinnati Republican wrote Ohio Senator John Sherman that he had "heard a universal expression of apprehension as to the possibility of Arthur's becoming President with all that would imply." He went on to lament the "fatal mistake" made at the Republican convention in Chicago in the summer of 1880 in nominating Arthur as Vice President. "The prayer for poor Garfield is *universal*," he declared. "There is not a popular confidence in the possible succession...."[2]

Once Arthur became President, however, he confounded his critics. Instead of carrying the shady practices he had learned as a party boss in New York into the White House, he renounced the spoils system once and for all and became a vigorous champion of civil service reform. The *New York Sun* was one of the few observers with confidence in Arthur from the outset. "While Mr. Arthur is not a man who would have entered anybody's mind as a direct candidate for the office," the editors declared, "it is not at all certain that he will not make a successful administration. He is a gentleman in his manners, neither obsequious nor arrogant. His bearing is manly, and such as to prepossess in his favor all whom he meets. Truth in speech and fidelity to his friends and his engagements form a part of his character. He has tact and common sense." For the *New York Times*, Arthur was "a much better and broader man than the majority of those with whom his recent political career has been identified."[3]

Still, Arthur continued to have his critics. His laid-back style led them to think he was all play and no work, and they were convinced that he shirked his grave responsibilities as the nation's chief executive. Arthur was, in fact, bored by much of the routine work that fell to the President in the 1880s, though he tried hard to follow a schedule that included conferences with congressmen, meetings with the cabinet, going through his mail, preparing speeches, attending public functions (including the dedication of the Brooklyn Bridge in 1883) that called for the President's appearance, and, of course, holding the customary receptions and state dinners for the public that gave him so much pleasure. Still, his relaxed sociability and his willingness as a widower (his wife, Ellen, died in January 1880) to accept invitations to dine with people in Washington led critics to doubt that he took his duties as President seriously. To them he was something of a playboy who was always on the town; and although he drank moderately most of the time, they insisted that "his high color, cheery affability, and fondness for genial companionship" revealed a "man inclined to drink and frivolity." As for work, they noted that he was frequently late for appointments, and always arrived with a "property basket" full of official papers in his hand, trying to give people the impression that he had been studying them industriously before coming in late for the scheduled meeting.[4]

One thing is clear: Arthur lived for the most part a sedentary life in the White House. While he sometimes went for a drive or for a horseback ride in the afternoon, more often, if there was no pressing business, he spent the evening drinking and chatting with friends, and then at midnight treated them to a fancy dinner in the private dining room he had designed when renovating the White House at the beginning of his presidency. He also liked to entertain popular actors whose performances in the Washington theater he enjoyed. From time to time he took vacations with his son Alan and daughter Nell, heading for Alexandria Bay on the St. Lawrence River for some fishing, and to Newport, Rhode Island, where he rode to the hounds with his son. But he was no longer the enthusiastic angler he'd been during his years as a party boss in New York City, and he had ceased being active in the Restigouche Salmon Club he had joined in Canada before becoming President. Arthur was far more occupied with his White House entertainments. With the help of his sister, Mary McElroy, who played hostess for him, he brought off fifty state dinners (and numerous private ones), including one in honor of the Grants that served fourteen courses and eight varieties of wine. Former

President Hayes was disgusted. "Nothing like it ever before in the Executive Mansion," he snorted; "liquor, snobbery, and worse." The *Chicago Tribune* doubted that Arthur ever put in a good day's work. "Mr. Arthur's temperament is sluggish," commented the paper. "He is indolent. It requires a great deal for him to get to his desk and begin the dispatch of business. Great questions of public policy bore him. No President was ever so much given to procrastination as he is."[5]

Arthur resented the criticism of his work habits; he was also irked at the inquiries into his private life. Why should newspapers count the days he spent on vacations, he wondered, or inquire into what went on at his midnight suppers? "I may be President of the United States," he told one reporter, "but my private life is my own damned business." He seriously considered asking Congress to devise legislation providing for the separation of the President's workplace (the White House) from his place of residence (a house built nearby where he and his family could live in complete privacy). "You have no idea," he told a reporter, "how depressing and fatiguing it is to live in the same house where you work. The down-town business man in New York would feel quite differently if after the close of his day he were to sit down in the atmosphere of his office to find rest and recreation instead of going uptown to cut loose absolutely from everything connected with the work of the day." In the summer, Arthur loved spending time in the presidential cottage on the grounds of the Soldiers' Home on the outskirts of Washington, where he could sit for hours on the porch with friends, far from the madding crowd, chatting all night.[6]

At times Arthur turned to music for pleasure. He played the banjo himself, and according to one observer he could "make the banjo do some lively humming when so disposed." But he preferred listening to playing, and he liked to provide special music for the guests he entertained at dinner. His favorite guests were the Jubilee Singers, a black chorus from Fisk University, who moved him to tears when they sang for him in the White House. "I never saw a man so deeply moved," said a clergyman who accompanied the singers, "and I shall always believe the President to be a truly good man."[7]

Arthur derived great pleasure from listening to the U.S. Marine Band, too. One evening he asked John Philip Sousa, the director, to play the cachucha so that a young woman among the guests could do a Spanish dance. When Sousa said he didn't have the music with him, Arthur expressed surprise. "Why, Sousa," he exclaimed, "I thought you could play anything. I'm sure you can." One of the bandsmen happened to know the melody, so Sousa succeeded in getting the band to vamp its way through it, and Arthur said pleasedly afterward, "I knew you could play it." Another time, Arthur wanted to know what it was that Sousa played when the people went in for dinner. "Hail to the Chief, Mr. President," Sousa told him. "Do you consider it a suitable air?" Arthur asked him. "No, sir," he answered. "It was selected long ago on account of its name, and not on account of its character. It is a boat song, and lacks modern military character for reception or a parade." "Then change it!" instructed Arthur. So Sousa wrote *Presidential Polonaise* for White House indoor affairs and the *Semper Fidelis March* for review purposes outdoors. The latter became one of Sousa's most popular marches, but "Hail to the Chief" continued to be used anyway.[8]

Despite his White House pleasures, Arthur's health began to decline partway through his presidency, and he became extremely sensitive to questions about it. He wanted the American people to be assured that he was fully capable of handling his problems as President, and that whatever ailments he had were minor and temporary. In October 1882, however, word got out that he had Bright's disease (a kidney affliction almost always fatal in adults) and that only rest and relaxation could reduce the pain that went with it. One of Arthur's friends flatly denied the story "on the authority of the President himself," but reporters covering his public appearances were struck by his feebleness in public. They were also aware of the fact that he threw fewer private parties than in the past, did some fishing, took short walks and horseback rides, and made little trips on the presidential steamer to improve his health.[9]

Before leaving the White House, Arthur took two ambitious vacation trips in 1883, arranged by his friends and associates, designed to allow him to forget the cares of office and to relax and enjoy himself in such a way as to put him back on the road to well-being. First came Florida. After Congress adjourned and the social season ended in 1883, Arthur, pleading a cold, headed south in an elegantly furnished private car provided by the Pennsylvania Railroad Company to visit central Florida for pleasure. He did some fishing (catching five ten-pound speckled trout in one river) and a lot of pleasant sightseeing, but had trouble with his kidneys, got infected with malaria, and spent one night in acute pain after consuming some shrimp salad. The French chef he brought along took a dim view of the whole venture. "Dis is a tretful drip," he told a reporter. Later on: "I vis I vas pack at de Vite House." Arthur was glad to get back, too, but he was upset about the way his illnesses were written up in the newspapers.[10]

The second big trip—to Yellowstone National Park—went better. It featured a 350-mile trip by horseback, taking three weeks, with a lot of camping by streams along the way and plenty of hiking, fishing, and hunting at each stop. The fishing, the fresh air, and the magnificent scenery seem to have done a world of good for Arthur, and when he stopped at Chicago on the way back to Washington, one reporter wrote, "He is looking better even than when he passed through this City en route to the West. His face is tanned, and he says he is invigorated." Arriving back in Washington on September 7, Arthur announced that he was in perfect health. Privately, however, he and his doctor went to work on his swollen legs, a sure sign of Bright's disease.[11]

Shortly before leaving the White House, Arthur gave his last speech at the dedication of the Washington Monument on February 22, 1885, Washington's Birthday, and then held his last reception in the White House, which was jam-packed with well-wishers. Mark Twain, once a critic of New York's gentleman boss, came to think well of him as President. "I am but one in 55,000,000," he wrote; "still, in the opinion of this one-fifty-five millionth of the country's population, it would be hard to better President Arthur's administration. But don't decide until you hear from the rest." Arthur spent his retirement in New York City, suffering increasingly bad health, and just before his death in November 1886, at fifty-six, he had all of his papers and records destroyed.[12]

The Doughty
Grover Cleveland

Grover Cleveland hated exercise. "Bodily movement alone," he once said, "is among the dreary and unsatisfying things of life." Still, he had his hobbies: fishing and hunting. When he became President, some of his critics complained that he spent too much time on fishing trips, but they erred. The conscientious Cleveland put his work first when he was in the White House, and during his first term he frequently stayed up until two or three in the morning, going over official papers or working on speeches and messages to Congress. "It was work, work, work, all the time," according to William H. Crook, his Secret Service guard. "He came about as near earning his salary as any President, if work of that kind is what counts."[1]

But Cleveland was no workaholic. As a young man he comfortably combined work and play while rising steadily in the ranks of the Democratic Party, from assistant district attorney for Erie County, to sheriff, to mayor of Buffalo, New York. He not only fished and hunted whenever he could; he also spent most evenings with his buddies in the saloons and beer gardens of Buffalo, drinking beer, eating sausages and sauerkraut, playing cards, smoking cigars, and talking up a storm. Without exercise, however, he inevitably put on weight, and in 1870, when running for district attorney, Cleveland made an agreement with his opponent to drink only four glasses of lager beer a day during the campaign. It didn't work; they soon redefined a glass of beer as a full tankard. A few years later, when he became governor of New York, Cleveland was known as "the Big One."[2]

In Albany, the "Big One" stayed big. He took his work as governor with the utmost seriousness, and for the first time in his life he cut down on relaxation time so drastically that he probably endangered his health. There were few hunting and fishing trips for the busy governor and no more all-night sessions in restaurants and beer gardens. His life, to be sure, wasn't completely sedentary; he walked to work (about a mile), attended some gubernatorial receptions and dinners (as few as he could), and sometimes played cards with friends on Sunday. Most of his waking time, though, was devoted to his work as governor. "There was not a night last week," observed the *Albany Evening Journal,* with dismay, on March 21, 1883, "when he departed from the new Capitol before one a.m. Such work is killing work."[3]

The *Journal* was extremely displeased by the way New York's governor comported himself. "The visitors who go into the executive chamber are met by the large-headed man," the paper reported, "and he listens patiently to what they have to say. Still there is only a slight glimmer of ideas in response. The words are few and they are listlessly said. The eyes of the large man look glassy, his skin hangs on his cheeks in thick, unhealthy-looking folds, the coat button about his large chest and abdomen looks ready to burst with the confined fat. Plainly he is a man who is not taking enough exercise; he remains within doors constantly, eats and works, eats and works, and works and eats." Cleveland's friends and associates finally persuaded him to take a vacation—to Buffalo, naturally. He received a hearty welcome from his old friends there and spent a few nights with them, drinking noisily and singing loudly, in their old haunts in the city. But his biggest joy was fishing in the Adirondacks. Returning to Albany, he boasted about his "very respectable sunburn" and his wonderful encounters with fish again. He had only one regret: "I had a beautful shot at a deer Saturday and missed him." He refrained from mentioning that he had sneaked in a little work, too, during his vacation.[4]

Cleveland was still the "Big One" when he became President in 1885. "What a Big Man the President is!" exclaimed the *Cleveland Leader,* when the hard-working governor became the hard-working President. "He must weigh nearly three hundred pounds, and a line drawn through the center of his stomach to the small of his back would measure at least two feet. He is six foot tall, has a great width of shoulder, and his flesh, unlike that of most fat men, is solid, not flabby." In the White House, Cleveland found, to his distress, that the chef, picked by President Arthur, served mostly French food. "I must go to dinner," he wrote a friend soon after becoming President. "I wish it were to eat pickled herring, Swiss cheese and a chop of Louis' instead of the French stuff I shall find." One evening, when he was digging into one of the chef's dinners, he recognized a familiar odor coming in through the open windows. "William," he asked the steward, "what is that smell?" "I am very sorry, sir," said the steward, "but that is the smell of the servants' dinner." "What is it," Cleveland wanted to know, "corned beef and cabbage?" "Yes," the servant said, whereupon Cleveland exclaimed: "Well, William, take this dinner down to the servants and bring their dinner to me." When he told the story to a friend, he added that the corned beef and cabbage—he called it *"Boeuf corné au cabeau"*—the steward brought him was "the best dinner I had had for months." Soon afterward he changed chefs.[5]

In Washington, as in Albany, Cleveland slaved away. His friends were concerned by his long hours, his lack of exercise, and his lengthy periods of confinement in the White House. When he wasn't holding receptions and dinners (with his sister Rose serving as hostess), meeting with his cabinet, conferring with congressmen, or working in his office, he seems to have spent whatever free time he had at the White House conservatory, looking at the flowers, instead of venturing forth into the great outside world. After attending a memorial for President Grant in August 1885, however, he decided to zip over to his beloved Adirondacks for a two-week fishing vacation with his doctor and some friends. They had a great time fishing, hunting, and camping out, and when Cleveland got back to Washington, he sighed, "I feel that I am in the treadmill again." But the lonely routine in the White House did not last much longer. On June 2, 1886, he married the attractive young Frances Folsom. He did some fishing during the honeymoon and began a new and happier life as President, with his wife winning kudos from the outset for her appearance as White House hostess. Before the wedding, Cleveland acquired a house in the northern reaches of Washington, which his wife called Oak View, to which he could flee when he needed a change of scenery. He hoped to keep newspapermen away from the retreat ("animals and nuisances," he called them), but he didn't have much luck guarding his privacy.[6]

Cleveland lost his bid for a second term to Benjamin Harrison in 1888, and he moved to New York City with his wife and children to practice law there. He didn't avail himself of much of the city's cultural offerings, for he preferred playing cribbage with his friends (though the *Washington Post* said he didn't attend the theater because he was "too big and fat" to fit into the seats). But he did intersperse his legal work with well-planned trips to the nation's hunting and fishing grounds. In 1891, editor Richard Watson Gilder inveigled Cleveland into a visit to Cape Cod (promising plenty of bluefish and sea bass), and he had such a good time there that he bought some land near Buzzard's Bay, with a cottage on it that he called Gray Gables, as a summer (and fishing) home. The friends Cleveland made in Cape Cod cherished his friendship. "With a few familiar friends," Richard Gilder wrote in his memoirs, "he was the soul of good company, not dominating the conversation, but doing his share of repartee and story-telling, with all the aids of wit, a good memory for detail, and, when necessary, the faculty of mimicry." Actor Joseph Jefferson thought Cleveland could have gone on the stage if he hadn't picked politics as his career. One thing Cleveland's Cape Cod friends soon learned about him: He was as conscientious a fisherman as he was a public servant. Cleveland "will fish when it shines and fish when it rains," Gilder observed; "I have seen him pull bass up in a lively thunderstorm, and refuse to be driven from a Cape Cod pond by the worst hail-storm I ever witnessed or suffered. He will fish through hunger and heat, lightning and tempest....This, I have discovered is the secret of 'Cleveland luck'; it is hard work and no let up."[7]

Gilder thought Cleveland was "immoderate" in only two activities: desk work and fishing. Sometimes he got so absorbed in his fishing that he forgot when it was time to eat. On Cape Cod one day his friends were unable to catch anything and returned to shore. But Cleveland stayed on, and kept changing both his position and the bait until he finally caught a large bass. When he showed it to his friends, he held up the fancy fly he'd used to attract it and cried, "I call this my restaurant fly, because the fish can get anything he likes on it." He had his rules, too, for the sport. When a friend hooked a huge fish and asked for help in bringing it in, Cleveland flatly refused. "No," he said, "every fellow in this boat must pull in his own fish."[8]

The "Cleveland luck" often failed him. Like all fishermen, Cleveland had his frustrations and disappointments when he went out angling. Once, he and his physician, Dr. Joseph Bryant, decided to try using live frogs as bait to catch pickerel in a Cape Cod creek. They got some little brown frogs, hooked them through the skin of their backs, and then hoped the frogs' gyrations in the water would attract the attention of the pickerel. Bryant soon had a strike, catching a nice-sized pickerel, and his luck continued: He caught several more pickerel while Cleveland, puffing away at his cigar, got no bites at all. Suddenly Cleveland noticed a good-looking frog sitting on a tree stump across the creek and decided to grab it and substitute it for the frog on his hook. But as soon as he started reeling in his line, the frog on the stump started struggling, and it dawned on Cleveland that the frog on his hook had somehow made its way over to the stump, hook and all, and taken refuge there, while the pickerel went after Bryant's bait. "I ought to have attended to business," Cleveland chided himself, and he quit fishing that day.[9]

Socially, Cleveland's second, nonconsecutive term as President (he was reelected in 1892) was livelier than his first. He continued to attend diligently to his responsibilities, of course, but he now had Gray

Gables in Cape Cod as a summer place, and he also had a house in Washington called Woodley (near Oak View, which he had sold when he was in New York City), to which he and his wife could escape whenever the White House began to seem oppressive. He enjoyed the White House entertainments this time around, with his popular wife acting as hostess and attracting large crowds eager to get a look at her (some people went through the reception line twice so they could see her again). But he managed to get into a little trouble on one occasion when he took time off from all the entertaining to do some hunting and fishing in North Carolina and told his secretary, Henry T. Thurber, not to reveal where he went. It so happened that in his absence, news came of the death of Russia's Czar Alexander III, and a correspondent for Reuters went to the White House seeking the President's reaction. Cleveland's secretary, following his instructions, told the reporter to wait, went into the President's office as if to tell him the news, walked three times around his desk, and then came out with a sad look on his face and announced: "The President feels that he is inexpressively shocked and grieved by the sad event of which you have just informed him. It was not, perhaps, altogether unexpected, but it was nonetheless prostrating on that account. He thanks you for the thoughtful attention. He would make his acknowledgement in person, but cannot trust himself on this, the first blush of his grief, to see or speak to anyone." The reporter wrote down Thurber's statement and put it on the wire.[10]

While the reporter was recording Thurber's regretful statement in Washington, another reporter, far away, in the mountains of North Carolina, was getting a quite different version of the President's opinions about the death of the czar. This reporter, sent by the Raleigh bureau of the Associated Press to look for the President, finally found him walking along the side of a little stream, wearing an old raincoat, with a rifle and some dead squirrels by his side, smoking a pipe and holding a fishing rod in his hand. Hurrying over to him, the reporter exclaimed: "Mr. President, I am Hawkins of the Associated Press and I wanted to tell you that Czar Alexander of Russia has just died and ask if you have any comment." "Why, no," murmured Cleveland, "I have nothing to say. I didn't know him. I don't believe in public officials making comments about all sorts of situations that they know nothing about." The AP reporter put this story on the wire, and that night, in the city room of the *New York Herald Tribune,* the managing editor wondered what to do with the two reports before him: the dispatch from Washington reporting the President's "prostration" over the czar's death and the one from Raleigh refusing comments. After thinking it over, he put the two reports side by side in parallel columns and added an introductory paragraph: "The grief of President Cleveland over the death of Czar Alexander of Russia was seen to be diminishing tonight." His headline: "Gradually Assuaging."[11]

Cleveland resented charges that he neglected his presidential obligations in order to go fishing almost as much as he did invasion of his privacy by newspapermen. He thought it was contemptible for his enemies to portray the short fishing trips he took to find "relief from the wearing labors and perplexities of official duty" as major derelictions of duty. But he also said he had a kind of "pleasurable contempt" for them because they did not share his love of fishing. "I sadly reflected," he wrote, "how their dispositions might have sweetened and their lives made happier if they had yielded some to the particular type of frivolity which they deplored." So far as "my attachment to outdoor sports may be considered a fault," he declared, "I am...utterly incorrigible and shameless." Cleveland in fact came to regard his fishing and hunting interludes as an indispensable duty, like his work as President, Richard Gilder observed, "for it was only on these little vacations that he was able to obtain the exercise, and release from mental strain, that kept him alive, and made him capable of the application which was a habit as well as a matter of conscience with him. I have heard him say that while on the water he found he could cast his public cares aside, but they would come crushing down upon him the moment he put his foot on dry land."[12]

In retirement, after leaving the White House in 1897, Cleveland settled in Princeton, New Jersey, with his wife and children, and went hunting and fishing as often and as long as he pleased. He also gave numerous speeches, taught a class at Princeton College, exchanged letters with his fishing friends, and wrote articles on his favorite sports for various magazines. In 1906, he published a collection of his articles entitled *Fishing and Shooting Sketches,* which delighted its many readers. In his book, he stressed skill, not profit nor quantity, in duck hunting; recommended a friendly response to fish stories, no matter how preposterous they sounded; expressed tolerance for mild profanity on the part of anglers who had just lost a big one; and reminded people that fishing was "full of strange and wonderful incidents." Above all, he expressed his conviction that "outdoor air and activity, intimacy with nature and acquaintanceship with birds and animals and fish, are essential to physical and mental strength...." The more fishermen, he insisted, the better the country would be. "There can be no doubt," he wrote, "that the promise of industrial peace, of contented labor and of healthful moderation in the pursuit of wealth...would be infinitely improved if a large share of the time which has been devoted to the concoction of trust and business combinations had been spent in fishing."[13]

☆ ☆ ☆ 23 ☆ ☆ ☆

The Austere
Benjamin Harrison

Benjamin Harrison, grandson of William Henry Harrison, the eighth
President, was not very sociable. To most people he seemed cold,
aloof, and a bit supercilious. Even when he took a walk for refreshment in Indianapolis, where he practiced law before becoming President, he kept his head high, preserved the erect military bearing he
had learned as a Civil War soldier, and sometimes passed friends on
the street without noticing them. He was as "cold-blooded as a fish,"
said some people; a "stinking little aristocrat," said others. But his
closest friends begged to differ. "He was a quiet, undemonstrative
man," explained one of them, "and was credited with being cold and
unsympathetic by those who saw him only in his public capacity, and
when acting under the stress and strain of public duty. But to those
who were on terms of personal intimacy with him...Harrison appears in a different light, a genial companion, a tender, great-hearted
man."[1]

But Harrison realized that his austere manner put people off; he
was aware, moreover, of his tendency to get so absorbed in his work
that he neglected to pause even for a moment to look at the roses. He
admitted to Carrie, his wife, that he was "a very poor pleasure and curiosity seeker." Stationed in Washington, D.C., as a brigadier general
at the end of the Civil War, he wrote her that the nation's capital, like

every other city he ever visited, was "a very dull and uninteresting place, except so long as I have business to engage my time." He recalled that earlier in the war he had been stationed near Charleston, South Carolina, for a month, and though he could have visited the city any day, he never got around to doing it. Now, with plenty of time on his hands, he said, he had ridden past the Capitol a dozen times and never bothered to take a look inside. "I shall probably go home," he mused, "without seeing more than its exterior." But if Carrie were with him, he went on to say, he hoped he would push aside his indifference and agree to do some sightseeing with her. "I feel that I have not been generous to you," he told her, "in allowing my selfish habits to keep you away from places of amusement and curiosity." He promised a "great reform" when he got back to Indianapolis.[2]

Harrison did his best to loosen up when he rejoined his wife after the war and resumed his law practice in Indianapolis. But the stern Puritanism he'd absorbed as a boy remained influential. He gave up smoking cigars (his one youthful vice), returned to the teetotalism he had abandoned temporarily when he was in the army, and was still so opposed to dancing that his wife kept it a secret when she and some of the other mothers in their neighborhood acquired an instructor to teach their little girls how to perform the dances then popular. Harrison was a conscientious Sabbatarian, too, as well as a regular churchgoer, carefully refraining from taking even a quick glance at official papers on Sunday. Though he read Scott, Thackeray, and Dickens as a young man, he seems rarely as an adult to have turned to fiction as a means of pleasure, and neither the theater nor music played much of a part in his life, even though Carrie was a fine pianist. Once, though, Carrie persuaded him to attend a production of *Richard III*, which she enjoyed, starring Richard Mansfield. He arrived late; and Mansfield was in the midst of a dramatic scene when the orchestra suddenly started playing "Hail to the Chief." Furious, Mansfield headed toward the orchestra, shaking his fists, and stopped only when an actor ran out of the wings, grabbed him, and pointed to President Harrison taking his seat in one of the boxes.

Mansfield at once paused, smiled, put his right hand on his chest, and gave the president a sweeping bow. Afterward, the two became friends, though Harrison never became much of a theater-goer.[3]

During Harrison's first summer in Indianapolis after leaving the service, he took his family on buggy rides and occasionally went fishing with his son Russell, but his eagerness to rise in his profession and increase his income soon led him to working around the clock despite his wife's efforts to lure him away from his office when she thought he was overdoing it. Once, she succeeded in persuading him to attend a concert with her only to find he had carried the proof sheets of the *Supreme Court Reporter,* of which he was editor, along with him. Harrison's father joined Carrie in remonstrating him. "If I were your physician," he told his son, "I would recommend the relaxation of a year's travel abroad, *with your family*—leaving all business and cares behind. But this I fear you won't do." He was right; Harrison continued putting in long hours. Only after a breakdown in 1867 did he take a vacation in Minnesota, where he did some hunting and fishing in the lake areas. Later on, he acquired a rowing machine— guaranteed to produce healthy men who could "straighten up, throw back the shoulders, and step squarely to the front"—but there is no evidence that he made much use of it.[4]

In the U.S. Senate, to which Harrison was elected in 1880, he continued to work to exhaustion. "I am worn out and disgusted with the Senate...," he complained at one point. "I do not feel as if I could stand it many days longer. I am worn out." When he ran for President against Grover Cleveland in 1888, he pushed himself so hard at first that there were fears he would "utterly collapse before the campaign is half over." An Associated Press reporter who covered the campaign observed that Harrison was "exceedingly sensitive regarding the subject of health and his staying powers, and at times persistently resists his physician, his family, and the Central Committee in their efforts to hold him in check and save his strength." The campaign committee chairman, he noted, "privately thinks the General has not more than one half the vital energy he had the day he was nominated; this loss of strength is largely due to the earnestness with which he does everything, thus employing his nervous as well as his muscular system." Fortunately, Harrison listened to his advisers this time and agreed to suspend his "front-porch" campaign in Indianapolis for a few days of sailing and fishing, and in the end he rode to victory over Cleveland in both good health and spirits.[5]

By the time Harrison became President, he was ready, at long last, to carry out the "great reform" he had promised his wife years before: to play some as well as work hard. He learned to delegate some of his work to people around him, and he insisted on inserting some recreation (including billiards) into his work schedule, even when he was at his busiest, in order to avoid the periodic breakdowns that had punctuated his life for so many years. He took daily walks in Washington, usually late in the afternoon, window-shopping along the way or stopping to chat briefly with passers-by. He also took rides with his wife into Maryland and Virginia, and went on Sunday excursions down the Potomac River on the U.S. naval ship *Dispatch* or on Postmaster-General John Wanamaker's yacht, the *Restless*. Though Harrison usually arranged to have church services held on board the ship during these trips, he received considerable criticism for seeking pleasure on Sunday. "The President," declared one critic, "appears to have come to the conclusion that it is not inconsistent with the Presbyterian idea of keeping holy the Sabbath to go on an excursion of pleasure every other Sunday." Harrison got into even more trouble when Wanamaker and several other well-to-do Philadelphians presented his wife with a cottage at Cape May Point in New Jersey as a retreat for her and her husband during humid summer days in Washington. The "President who takes a bribe," exclaimed the *New York Sun,* "is a lost President." Although Harrison sent Wanamaker a check for ten thousand dollars when he first made the gift, his critics insisted that he made the payment only after he had been exposed as a greedy "gift grabber." In Chicago, a singer who disliked Harrison added an extra verse to a song in one of the Gilbert and Sullivan shows:

> The President said a vacation he'd take;
> Said he to himself, said he,
> Down by the blue sea, where the high breakers break,
> Said he to himself, said he;
> For the place needs the bloom that my presence will bring,
> And my friends who belong to the real-estate ring
> Have promised a cottage, to which I shall cling;
> Said he to himself, said he.[6]

Harrison did a lot of traveling when he was President. An excellent public speaker, he was in much demand for speeches around the country, at conventions, dedications, holiday celebrations, and memorials, and he often worked some recreation—duck hunting, fishing, sightseeing—into his schedule while on the road. He was the first President to travel all the way from Washington to the West Coast, and he ended up doing more traveling while he was President than any of his predecessors. But he made himself accessible in Washington, too, and he dropped the ban on dancing in the White House in order to help make presidential entertainments more lively and pleasurable. If Lew Wallace, the author of *Ben-Hur,* is to be believed, Harrison got into such good physical shape that he was able to overcome an intruder in the White House who was much younger than he. One day, according to Wallace, a young drunk spewing oaths broke into the White House through a window and threatened to kill the President. Two doorkeepers tried in vain to subdue him, but Harrison, hearing the ruckus, rushed down the stairs and wrestled the man down to the floor, "holding his arms down as firmly as if they had been fastened by a vice." Then he asked calmly, "Have you any more of them here?" Assured there were no accomplices, he asked, "And now, what else can I do for you?" The doorkeepers suggested he cut the window cord and use it to tie up the man; it was no sooner said than done. "The President was the coolest, quietest man I ever saw," remarked one of the doorkeepers afterward, "and plucky too."[7]

Wallace's tale appeared in the campaign book he wrote for Harrison during his bid for reelection in 1892. Harrison lost the election to Grover Cleveland; worse still, he lost his wife Carrie to tuberculosis shortly before election day and lost all interest in the campaign. It was hard for him to get back to work after leaving the White House. "I find myself exceedingly lazy," he confessed after settling down in Indianapolis, "unable yet to do much of any work." But he was soon busy with legal cases, speeches and lectures, magazine articles, and charitable work. Harrison avoided politics as much as he could, though he was bothered by the policy of overseas expansion emerging at the end of the nineteenth century, insisting that the United States had "no commission from God to police the world." He spent summers in the Adirondacks, fishing and hunting as well as entertaining his grandchildren. In 1895, he remarried and became more active socially. He even went to concerts with his wife. "I am not devoted to music," he admitted, "but Mrs. Harrison is, and I am devoted to her."[8]

☆ ☆ ☆ 24 ☆ ☆ ☆

The Kindly
William McKinley

William McKinley was not much of a sportsman. Once he attended a football game—Princeton against Yale—with his friend Mark Hanna, a Cleveland industrialist, and didn't have the slightest idea of what was going on down on the field. Time and again he asked Hanna what was happening, but it turned out that Hanna knew as little about football as McKinley did. When they left, McKinley told Hanna that he felt like the country boy who said, "They didn't have no game; they got into a scrap and kept fightin' all the time when they ought to have been playing ball."[1]

As a boy growing up in rural Ohio, McKinley was "serious and rather delicate," according to biographer Margaret Leech, "and he seems never to have taken much interest in sports or games." He was a good soldier, though, serving under Rutherford B. Hayes, a regimental commander, during the Civil War, and he impressed Hayes as "a handsome, bright gallant boy," who was "one of the bravest and finest officers in the army." He became a skilled horseman in the army, but it never occurred to him to make horseback riding one of his recreations after leaving the service. Reared a strict Methodist, he avoided drinking, smoking, and swearing when he was in the service, and when he was studying law in Albany, New York, a few years later, his roommate said young McKinley knew so little about the "pleasures of the flesh" that he hadn't even tasted ice cream before. Handed a plate at a reception for law students, hosted by Judge Amasa J. Parker's wife, he murmured, "Poor Mrs. Parker, do not tell her the custard got frozen."[2]

Years later McKinley began smoking cigars, and they became an important part of his life. He also permitted wine to be served at presidential parties and once in a while took a drink himself. And he tried, without success, to learn something about golf. In 1897, while taking a vacation in Bluffs Point, New York, near Lake Champlain, the Vice President, Garret Hobart, a devoted golfer, persuaded McKinley to try the game, but the President did so poorly that after a few tries he gave up and spent the rest of his vacation sitting under a tree (which came to be called the "McKinley tree") reading books. "The President was not athletically inclined," observed one golf specialist, "and could not obtain much satisfaction in following a golf ball around a meadow." Two years later, however, when McKinley was spending his summer vacation in Hot Springs, Virginia, he decided to try some golf again. This time his aides persuaded him to abandon the idea on the ground that golf was "undignified for a President" and it might offend voters if he was photographed playing the game. There was an election coming up in 1900, with McKinley running for a second term, and the *Boston Evening Record* had recently polled its readers and found that half of them thought the game demeaned both McKinley and the office of the President. It was a few more years before golf became completely respectable for American Presidents to play.[3]

McKinley tried fishing on at least one occasion, but with as little success as with golfing. One day some of his friends persuaded him to go fishing with them, and when they reached the fishing grounds, he stood gamely in their boat, frock coat and all, his line in the stream, hoping for a bite. Suddenly, to everyone's surprise, he hooked a fish, started pulling it in, clumsily unbalanced the boat, and when it sank, he ruined all his clothes. He is not known to have indulged in the piscatorial art again.[4]

William H. Crook, official guard for several Presidents, found little merriment in the White House while McKinley was in office. He found McKinley "a grave, serious-minded man who had been preoccupied with serious affairs for so much of his life that he had never cultivated the lighter side to any appreciable extent." Crook thought "gayety, lightness, music, merriment" were foreign to McKinley's nature. For McKinley, politics was a hobby as well as a profession, and about the only recreation he allowed himself while President was a stroll now and then on the White House grounds. But he did take time off for nonpolitical activities. He brought friends to the White House for informal dinners at which they could eat good food, smoke fine cigars, and exchange amusing stories, including slightly off-color jokes (though McKinley apparently told only one of them during his presidency). He also attended concerts of the U.S. Marine Band whenever he could, and he joined in the choruses at the White House's Sunday-evening "hymn sings," attended by his wife and friends. His favorite hymns were "Nearer, My God, to Thee," "Lead, Kindly Light," and "Jesus, Lover of My Soul."[5]

Except for newspapers, McKinley didn't spend much of his free time reading. "You make me envious," he once told Theodore Roosevelt. "You've been able to get so much out of books." McKinley thought he learned more from practical experience than from books. "I would rather have my political economy founded upon the everyday experience of the puddler or the potter than the learning of the professor." His father had been a pig-iron manufacturer on a small scale, and McKinley did some puddling for him as a boy. Reading for pleasure never became important for him.[6]

McKinley's major preoccupation—it transcended politics—was his wife, Ida. A frail woman, subject to headaches, fainting spells, and epileptic seizures, Mrs. McKinley spent as much time as she could with her husband and depended on his heartfelt loving care for her survival. During his years in Congress, McKinley spent most of his leisure time with her. When they were together, she usually sat in a little rocking chair that she had used as a child, embroidering ties and crocheting bedroom slippers. Because she disliked tobacco,

McKinley got in the habit of going outdoors for his after-dinner smoke, and sometimes he cut his cigar in two and chewed half of it instead of smoking when he was with her. He also chewed tobacco when he was in the House chamber, and, according to James A. Garfield, developed a good aim for the spittoon. Since Mrs. McKinley enjoyed traveling, he took her with him twice when congressional business dictated trips to California.[7]

When McKinley became governor of Ohio, his devotion to his wife became legendary. It was his habit to have breakfast with her every morning, walk across the street to the State Capitol, and before entering the building, stop, turn, and wave to her. At three in the afternoon he stopped his work, opened the window in his office, waved a white handkerchief, and waited for her to wave back. A woman visiting the governor's wife one day was surprised to see the walls of the house covered with pictures of McKinley. She explained why: "He's a dear good man and I love him." While McKinley attended to his official duties, his wife produced several thousand bedroom slippers to use as gifts and turned out black satin neckties, too.[8]

But Mrs. McKinley did more than make bedroom slippers to give to friends. While McKinley was governor of Ohio, he had more leisure time than he had enjoyed as a congressman, and his wife took the opportunity to broaden his interests and introduce him to new ways of enjoying himself when he was not at work. She gave him lessons in cribbage and euchre, making a good card player out of him. She also introduced him to the concert hall and the theater, which she loved, and he began taking her to concerts at the Cleveland Opera House and to the theater to watch the celebrated actor Joseph Jefferson perform Shakespeare. The two of them came to enjoy studying up on Shakespeare's plays before attending Jefferson's performances. She taught her husband to appreciate fine laces and jewelry, too, and after he became President, by filling the White House rooms with flowers, she made a flower enthusiast out of him.[9]

Mrs. McKinley's favorite flower was the rose, but her husband came to prefer pink carnations. A pink carnation in his coat lapel soon became an indispensable part of his attire. He called it his "good-luck charm" and began using it as a little gift to please some of the people with whom he dealt. It got so that whenever he had to refuse someone a request, he took the flower from the buttonhole of his coat and pinned it to the man's lapel, with instructions to give it to his wife with the President's good wishes. One day, a labor leader came by to ask for a favor and when McKinley refused to grant it became offended. McKinley asked if he was married, and when the man answered in the affirmative, took the carnation from his coat and handed it to him, saying, "Give this to your wife with my compliments and best wishes." As the man left, he told McKinley, "I would rather have this flower from you for my wife than the thing I came to get."[10]

When McKinley became President in 1897, his wife resolved to act as White House hostess for him; she wanted to be at his side at receptions and at the table with him at State dinners. This posed problems. Though McKinley minimized his wife's illness as much as he could—she had a headache, he would say, or, she isn't feeling good today—he was fully aware of the fact that she might have a seizure at any time, in private or public, and that he must be fully prepared to respond at once to her plight. At dinner parties he always sat next to her, and whenever he saw a minor seizure coming on, promptly tossed a handkerchief or napkin over her face while continuing to talk with the guests; his wife, once the spell passed, resumed her part in the conversation as if nothing had happened. If he saw that she was on the verge of a major attack, he got her out of a room full of people as quickly and unobtrusively as he could.[11]

But McKinley's measures for handling his wife breached White House etiquette. At presidential receptions, the President's wife was expected to stand next to her husband for hours shaking hands, and Mrs. McKinley simply wasn't up to the task. At State dinners, moreover, the President was supposed to escort the wife of the guest of honor to the dining table and sit next to her, while the guest of honor took the President's wife to a place at the table opposite the President. McKinley perforce changed all that. He arranged for his wife to remain seated at receptions, holding a bouquet so she wouldn't have to shake hands; and he escorted her, not the wife of the guest of honor, to the dining table so she could be next to him in case of a crisis. There was some grumbling about these arrangements by State Department officials and foreign diplomats, but when McKinley exclaimed, "Could it possibly offend anyone for me to have my wife beside me?", Vice President Garret Hobart's wife assured him, "Mr. President, you are Chief Executive. This is your home. It is your power to do as you choose."[12]

The receptions went well with Mrs. McKinley seated, and McKinley himself took great joy in them. "Everyone in that line has a smile and a cheery word," he told his friend Henry L. Stoddard. "They bring no problems with them; only good will. I feel better after that contact." He developed the "McKinley grip" for keeping his hand in good shape despite all the hand-shaking. It involved taking the right hand of a person in the reception line and squeezing it warmly before his own hand got squeezed, and holding the guest's elbow with his left hand and then swiftly pulling him along, so he would be all set for the next person in line. He smiled at each guest, of course, as he produced his handshake.[13]

Both McKinley and his wife enjoyed traveling, and it was one of McKinley's favorite ways of taking a vacation from the busy work of his White House office. One time, though, there was an unexpected crisis when they were visiting the Berkshires and attended a large dinner party in their honor held by John Sloan and his wife in Lenox, Massachusetts. The Sloans had asked their butler to prepare a special surprise for the presidential couple, and when the McKinleys and the other guests entered the great oak-beamed dining room they saw a long table gleaming with silver and brilliant with flowers, with a large object in the center, covered by a big silk American flag. After they sat down, the Episcopal bishop, a friend of the Sloans, said grace, the butler yanked the flag off the table, and they saw a large stuffed American eagle, with outstretched claws, staring at them. Almost at once came the sound of a lock clock whirring, and the bird began to wink and nod toward the McKinleys and flap its wings up to the ceiling. Mrs. McKinley was overwhelmed; she jumped up in panic, and her husband rushed over, took her by the hand, and helped her out of the room. The Sloans, greatly embarrassed, quickly disconnected the butler's patriotic masterpiece, dumped it in the backyard, where it ran down, and resumed the dinner party after McKinley returned with his wife calmed down and feeling sociable again.[14]

On September 6, 1901, President McKinley visited the Pan-American Exposition in Buffalo, New York, and while shaking hands, as he loved to do, that afternoon he was shot by Leon Czolgosz, a radical anarchist. McKinley lingered a few days and then died, at fifty-eight, murmuring, "It is God's way. His will, not ours, be done." One of the doctors who attended him thought the President's sedentary life had so weakened his vitality that he lacked normal healing powers. After his death, Mrs. McKinley was eager to join him as soon as she could, but eventually she decided she wanted to live until the McKinley Mausoleum, erected with federal funds in Canton, Ohio, was completed. She died in May 1907 and was buried in the stately memorial tomb just four days before its dedication.[15]

☆ ☆ ☆ **25** ☆ ☆ ☆

The Energetic
Theodore Roosevelt

It's hard to believe that Theodore Roosevelt, one of our most athletic presidents, was once a weakling. But as a sickly, delicate little boy, near-sighted and suffering from asthma, he was "quite unable to hold my own," he recalled in his memoirs, "when thrown into contact with other boys." One day, when he was about fourteen, some boys he met on a stagecoach began teasing him and he wasn't able to fight back. He resolved, then and there, that he would do whatever he could to build up his strength and never again "be put in such a helpless position." With the hearty approval of his father, who was quite athletic himself, Roosevelt took up boxing. It was two or three years before he was good at it, but boxing came to be one of his favorite sports as an adult. The night before his inauguration as President in March 1905, he invited a heavyweight champion he knew in Washington to drop by the White House for a few lively rounds.[1]

Roosevelt boxed at Harvard when he became a student there in 1876. He also wrestled, ran, rowed, walked, worked out in the gym, and skated. At college, where "it was not considered good form to move at more than a walk," noted one of his classmates, "Roosevelt was always running." He boxed with a trainer five times a week, but, to his disappointment, failed to win the lightweight cup. He didn't win the cup for wrestling, either. He did, though, win admiration for his sportsmanship. In a match witnessed by writer Owen Wister, then a Harvard freshman, time was called on a round, Roosevelt dropped his guard, and his opponent landed a heavy blow to his nose that produced a spurt of blood. There were hoots and hisses in the gallery, Wister remembered, but Roosevelt at once raised his hand to still the crowd. "It's all right," he cried, and then, pointing to the timekeeper, he explained, "He didn't hear him." Walking over to his opponent, he shook hands cordially with him.[2]

Harvard was of course more than an arena for Roosevelt's physical prowess. He took his studies seriously, asked questions in class (to the irritation of some of his professors), and received grades good enough to get into Phi Beta Kappa. He enjoyed history and political economy, but his main interest—an interest he'd acquired as a youngster—was in natural history. He even toyed with the idea of making it his career, though his father warned him against becoming a dilettante and insisted he put forth his very best efforts if he decided to become a scientist. The main trouble for Roosevelt, however, was that science in colleges those days was "purely a science of the laboratory," with no place for "the outdoor naturalist and the observer of nature" like himself. Roosevelt was an avid bird-watcher. With his friend Henry David Minot, he studied the birds in the woods around Cambridge, and at the end of one college year he and Minot headed for the Adirondack Mountains in New York to look for some new species. Out of their observations came Roosevelt's first publication: a pamphlet on the summer birds in the Adirondacks. Later on he published another pamphlet on the various kinds of birds in Oyster Bay, his home on Long Island. But he abandoned his plan to become a scientist.[3]

In 1880, shortly after graduating from Harvard, Roosevelt married Alice Lee, an attractive young woman from Boston, studied law for a time, and then ran successfully for a seat in the New York State Assembly, thus beginning his long career in politics. Whenever he could, however, he worked some bird-watching into his schedule, and he got so good at it that he could tell a bird by its song. Becoming President didn't end his ornithological explorations. In Rock Creek Park in Washington and on the White House grounds, he sought out woodpeckers, mockingbirds, robins, crows, sparrows, and other birds. "No doubt they thought me insane," he once said of people who stopped on the street to watch him gazing up at a tree near the White House. "Yes," said his wife, "and as I was always with him, they no doubt thought I was the nurse that had him in charge." Nothing pleased Roosevelt more than being awakened in the morning by a cardinal singing merrily in a magnolia tree just outside his White House bedroom.[4]

Roosevelt was the most accomplished bird-watcher to occupy the White House; he was also the only real cowboy ever elected President. In 1884, shortly after Alice died after giving birth to a daughter, he headed for some ranches he had acquired in western Dakota, partly to forget his sorrow and partly with the idea of becoming a rancher. He eventually returned to politics and remarried, but his experience living in the West for a time brought an abundance of new interests and skills into his life and transformed him into a professional cowboy. It took time. When Roosevelt first appeared in the Dakota Territory, wearing glasses, speaking with a Harvard accent, and exclaiming "By Godfrey" when he got excited, the Dakota cowboys didn't quite know what to make of him, and they began calling him "Four Eyes." The first time he took part in a roundup, he cried, "Hasten quickly forward there," at one point, and his words became hilariously famous in the Dakota Badlands. But he worked hard, mastered the skills of a good cowboy, and gradually won the respect and admiration of the seasoned hands who came to know him.[5]

Roosevelt had the time of his life in the Dakota Badlands. "You would be amused to see me," he wrote his friend Henry Cabot Lodge in Boston, "in my broad sombrero hat, fringed and beaded buckskin shirt, horse hide chaparajos or riding trousers, and cowboy boots, with braided bridle and silver spurs." But the garb wasn't important; it was what he did as a cowpuncher that counted. He roped horses; branded calves; herded wild horses; hunted buffalo, antelope, and deer; helped get control of cattle stampedes; lassoed skittish steers; and served for a time as a deputy sheriff. In his autobiography, Roosevelt described a confrontation with an aggressive bully in a hotel saloon one night that more than made up for the humiliation he'd experienced as a boy of fourteen. He had spent the day searching for lost horses, he wrote, and stopped in a primitive little hotel looking for a place to spend the night. When he entered the hotel saloon, a "shabby-looking individual in a broad hat with a cocked gun in each hand" hailed him as "Four Eyes" and cried, "Four Eyes is going to treat." Roosevelt ignored him, hoping to avoid trouble, went over to the stove by the bar, and sat down to rest. But the troublemaker walked over, stood leaning over him, a gun in each hand, let loose a flood of profanity, and angrily repeated his command: "Four Eyes is going to treat." "Well," said Roosevelt, "if I've got to, I've got to," and stood up, looking past him. "As I rose," Roosevelt recalled, "I struck quick and hard with my right just to one side of the point of his jaw, hitting him with my left as I straightened out, and then again with my right." As the man fell, his guns went off, and he struck the corner of the bar with his head and landed senseless on the floor. At this point the other men in the saloon began denouncing the bully loudly, and some of them lugged his body out of the hotel and put him in a shed nearby, where, the next morning, he came to and quickly left town. Roosevelt had plenty of reasons to feel elated when he returned to the East. "For good, healthy exercise," he wrote, "I would strongly recommend some of our gilded youth to go West and try a short course of riding bucking ponies and assisting at the branding of a lot of Texas steers."[6]

It wasn't enough for Roosevelt to be a cowboy; he had to be a soldier, too. Time and again in the 1880s and 1890s, whenever the United States clashed with some other country—Britain, Venezuela, Spain—Roosevelt got his hopes up that it would produce a war in which he could participate personally. He finally got his wish in April 1898, when the nation went to war with Spain in a quarrel over Cuban independence, and there was "a chance," as he put it, "to cut my little notch on the stick that stands as a measuring rod in every family." He speedily organized a cavalry regiment made up of cowboys and Ivy Leaguers, soon called the "Rough Riders," and pushed hard to get to Cuba as soon as possible. "It will be awful if we miss the fun," he wailed, and insisted the Rough Riders go with the first expedition, whether properly drilled or not. In Cuba, Roosevelt led his men to victory in a hard-fought battle for Kettle Hill in the San Juan ridges outside Santiago, and he returned to civilian life as a hero when the war ended. He became governor of New York in January 1899, Vice President in March 1901, and, upon the assassination of President McKinley, President of the United States in September 1901.[7]

Roosevelt's critics called him a warmonger who loved war for its own sake and warned that the imperialistic policies he championed posed a serious threat to America's democratic values. Roosevelt never denied that he admired soldierly virtues and gloried in "the strenuous life." Every man, he said, "who has in him any real power of joy in battle knows that he feels it when the wolf begins to rise in his heart; he does not then shrink from blood or sweat or deem that they mar the fight; he revels in them, in the toil, the pain, and the danger, as but setting off the triumph." Still, he contended that he supported only just wars, and that he favored taking measures to prevent wars from breaking out unnecessarily. He also emphasized the importance of people like himself living up to the ideals they proclaim. "One of the commonest taunts directed at men like myself," he said, "is that we are armchair and parlor jingoes who wish to see others do what we only advocate doing. . . . I cannot afford to disregard the fact that my power for good, whatever it may be, would be gone if I didn't try to live up to the doctrines I have tried to preach. Moreover, it seems to me that it would be a good deal more important from the standpoint of the nation as a whole that men like myself should go to war than that we should stay comfortably in offices at home and let others carry on the war we have urged." A man, he once said, "should pay with his body for his beliefs."[8]

Roosevelt's zest for living strenuously, even dangerously, makes it easy to overlook the fact that he derived enormous satisfaction from intellectual endeavors as well as from physical feats. He read as well as boxed at Harvard, and he liked reading books as well as riding horses all his life. His love of books was as great as Thomas Jefferson's, and his ability to read rapidly and absorb what he read equaled that of Bill Clinton years later. Lawrence Abbott, editor of the *Outlook,* who published many of Roosevelt's magazine articles, described him as "a voracious and omnivorous reader" who read all kinds of books, ancient and modern, "with almost unbelievable rapidity."[9]

Roosevelt, Abbott reported, read while waiting for trains and for people trying to keep their appointments, took books with him to conferences and conventions to turn to when things became dull, and sometimes casually picked up a book at a party crowded with friends and got lost in it. In 1910, when he was on a train traveling from Khartoum to Cairo, some of his admirers planned a special dinner in his honor in the private saloon dining car placed at his disposal by the governor-general of the Sudan. When the time came for dinner, and the diner was filled with important officials, Roosevelt was nowhere to be found. After a frantic search, Abbott finally located him in one of the train's lavatories, with its door half open, standing under an electric light and bracing himself between the two walls because of the way the train swayed, devouring Lecky's *History of Rationalism in Europe,* "completely oblivious to time and circumstances."[10]

Roosevelt's tastes were ecumenical; he read for enjoyment as well as enlightenment. He knew the Bible and the classics; he learned from books on science, history, and political economy; he liked travel books and books about explorations; he read novels, adventure stories, and books of humor with zest and enjoyment; and he adored poetry. Combining two of his favorite pleasures, he became an expert on English birds as they appear in English literature. "I know the lark of Shakespeare and Shelley...," he bragged in his autobiography; "I know the nightingale of Milton and Keats; I know Wordsworth's cuckoo...." Once, Roosevelt's sister Corrine took him to a meeting of the Poetry Society of America and was astonished at his familiarity with the work of the poets to whom she introduced him. In one case, he not only knew the poet's work, he was also able to quote the "fifth line of the third verse" of one of the man's poems that he happened to like. Years before, she recalled, young Roosevelt spent a couple of hours boxing, and then proposed teaming up with her to read aloud from Tennyson, and "we became so interested in 'In Memoriam' that it was past one o'clock when we separated."[11]

Roosevelt did a lot of reading when he was President, and after he left the White House, literature—especially poetry—continued to be an integral part of his life. In 1909, shortly before he took off for a big game hunt in Africa, Corrine told him she wanted to give him "a real present" before he left the country. "What do you think you would like?" she asked him. His eyes sparkled as he told her, "I think I should like a pigskin library." "A pigskin library?' she exclaimed. "What is a pigskin library?" He explained. "Of course, I must take a good many books; I couldn't go anywhere, not even into the jungles in Africa, without a good many books. But also, of course, they are not very likely to last in ordinary bindings, and so I want to have them all bound in pigskin, and I would rather have that present than any other." The next day he made a list of the books he wanted to take with him, and among the sixty or so he asked for were the Bible; works by Shakespeare, Homer, Carlyle, Shelley, Emerson, Longfellow, Tennyson, Poe, Keats, Milton, Dante, and Mark Twain, Euripides, Scott, Cooper, Dickens, and Thackeray; and the *Federalist Papers*. Corrine obliged, and so the "famous pigskin library," she wrote later, "carried on the back of 'burros,' followed him into the jungles of Africa, and was his constant companion at the end of long days, during which he had slain the mighty beasts of the tangled forests." But there was no Zola in pigskin; the puritanical Roosevelt was turned off by the French writer's "conscientious description of the unspeakable."[12]

Roosevelt was no pedant. "Personally," he wrote, "the books by which I have profited" the most, were "those in which profit was a by-product of the pleasure; that is, I read them because I enjoyed them, because I liked reading them, and the profit came in as part of the enjoyment." Asked "what books a statesman should read," his answer was poetry and novels, as well as books on history, government, science, and philosophy. The important thing, he thought, was to "know human nature, to know the needs of the human soul; and they will find this nature and these needs set forth as nowhere else by the great imaginative writers, whether of prose or poetry."[13]

There were plenty of books in the White House—some of them in just about every room—when Roosevelt was President. There were also plenty of children, and children, he noted, "are better than books." Roosevelt was a real pal to his kids; he read to them, swam and boated with them, played games with them, and camped and hiked with them. One of their favorite games was the "point-to-point hike," in which they picked an objective to reach and then headed in a straight line toward it, even if it meant climbing walls, going up and down hills, wading through rivers, and pushing through thickets. But Roosevelt liked hiking this way even when he was alone, to the discomfit of the Secret Service men accompanying him, and he also insisted that any adult who joined him for a hike had to follow the point-to-point rule. One day he invited the French ambassador, Jean-Jules Jusserand, for a walk, explained it was a point-to-pointer, and started off. All went well until they came to the bank of a stream, rather wide and too deep to be forded. "I sighed in relief," Jusserand wrote afterward, "because I thought that now we had reached our goal and would rest a moment and catch our breath, before turning homeward. But judge of my horror when I saw the President unbutton his clothes and heard him say, 'We better strip, so as not to wet our things in the Creek.' Then I, too, for the honor of France, removed my apparel, everything except my lavender kid gloves. The President cast an inquiring look at these as if they, too, must come off, but I quickly forestalled any remark by saying, 'With your permission, Mr. President, I will keep these on, otherwise it would be embarrassing if we should meet ladies.' And so we jumped into the water and swam across."[14]

Roosevelt did more than take hikes in a straight line while he was President. He took up tennis early in his presidency, and had a rolled-dirt court installed behind the White House with easy access to his office. When some of his critics in Congress complained about "needless expenditure," he insisted the court was mainly for his children (four boys and two girls). "It surely cannot be meant there is any objection to the president and his children playing tennis," he said, "and of course it is impossible for them to play tennis except on the White House grounds." But it was Roosevelt and his best friends (the so-called "Tennis Cabinet") who used the court the most. Fond of the game because it gave him such a good workout, Roosevelt showed the same bent for fairness when on the court as he did when boxing at Harvard. One day, Archie Butt, his military aide, slammed a ball at him that hit his head, and rushed over to apologize. T.R. waved him away. "If I hit you," he cried, "*I'm* not going to apologize, so just bang at me as much as you like and say nothing in the fray." Roosevelt wasn't sure the American public liked the idea of the President playing tennis. "I never let my friends advertise my tennis," he told William Howard Taft, "and never let a photograph of me in tennis costume appear."[15]

Horseback riding was just as important to Roosevelt as tennis was when he was President. He took brisk gallops on cold days and relaxed canters on hot days in the summer that left his Secret Service guards sweating far behind. Like President Grant, he liked jumping, and when he was riding his favorite horse, Bleistein, a large and strong bay, he sailed over tall fences and jumped hurdles as high as five feet eight inches. Once, when he was out riding with one of the members of his cabinet, the latter jumped over a stone wall and then took a high hurdle, and dared T.R. to do the same. Though he wasn't riding Bleistein at the time, Roosevelt couldn't resist taking the dare, and he succeeded in getting his somewhat jittery horse to perform the same jumps. "I could not let one of my Cabinet give me a lead and not follow," he remarked afterward.[16]

Roosevelt's most dramatic ride occurred when he led the Seventh Cavalry over the Chickamauga battlefield in Georgia early in his presidency. Mounting a spirited army horse at the entrance to the memorial park, he rode onto the battlefield, with the other riders following him in squadron formation. He then asked the colonel in charge to give the order "Forward trot," and, setting the pace himself, saw to it that the trot soon became a canter, and the canter became a gallop. As T.R. rushed along, with the squadron thundering behind him, he suddenly saw a grove of pine trees ahead, but, without any hesitation, plunged into the thicket, lurching this way and that to make his way through, followed by the squadron. About a dozen men were thrown off their horses during the gallop and had to be treated for injuries, but the President came through without a scratch. But it wasn't always that way. In October 1904, Secretary of State John Hay recorded Roosevelt's latest adventure. "The President," he wrote in his diary, "came in this morning badly bunged up about the head and face. His horse fell with him yesterday and gave him a bad fall." A few days later, Hay gave more details: "The President's fall from his horse, ten days ago, might have been very serious. He landed fairly on his head, and his neck and shoulders were severely wrenched. For a few days there seemed to be a possibility of meningitis." Then he added: "The President will, of course, outlive me, but he will not live to be old."[17]

When the weather was such that Roosevelt couldn't take point-to-point walks or go horseback riding, he did some boxing or wrestling in the White House gym. He had begun boxing twice a week with Mike Donovan, one-time middleweight champion, when he was governor of New York, and he continued working out with Donovan after he became President. "Now, Mike," he told his sparring partner the night before his inauguration in 1905, "we must have a good bout this evening. It will brighten me for tomorrow, which will be a trying day." Donovan admired T.R.'s prowess. "Had President Roosevelt come to the prize ring instead of the political arena," he said, "it is my conviction that he would have been successful. The man is a born fighter. It's in his blood." Unfortunately, in a match with an army officer, Roosevelt received a heavy blow to the forehead that caused a hemorrhage and blinded his left eye, and he had to give up boxing. With his usual insouciance, he turned to wrestling, and started working out with Joe Grant, a well-known District of Columbia champion wrestler, in the White House. "I am not the age," he told his son Kermit, "or build one would think to be whirled lightly over an opponent's head and batted down on a mattress without damage." But his wrestling partners were "so skillful," he said, "that I have not been hurt at all." He went on to tell his son that his throat "was a little sore, because once when one of them had a stranglehold I also got hold of his wind-pipe and thought I could perhaps choke him off before he could choke me. However, he got ahead." Wrestling led to jujitsu (he wanted to compare the two), and under the tutelage of two excellent Japanese instructors, he became proficient in the art after two sea-sons. He found time to do some fencing, too, using "single sticks"— long, slender, hard pieces of wood—instead of swords. "Sometimes we hit hard," Roosevelt once told a friend, "and today I have a bump over one eye and a swollen wrist."[18]

There were few sports that Roosevelt neglected to try at least once during his life, but he certainly had his likes and dislikes. He never cared much for sailing; he called it a "lazy man's sport" and rarely made use of the *Mayflower*, a sailing ship placed at the President's dis-posal in 1902. "I supposed it sounds archaic," he said, "but I cannot help thinking that the people with motor boats miss a great deal. If they would only keep to rowboats or canoes, and use oars or paddles themselves, they would get infinitely more benefit than by having their work done for them by gasoline." He liked to row his second wife, Edith, to Cold Springs Harbor for lunch on the beach with no one else around. He once rowed her sixteen miles and felt as fit as a fiddle when he finally put down his oars.[19]

Roosevelt was a good swimmer—he once swam imperturbably in the ocean for a half hour or so with a shark lurking nearby—but swimming was never one of his favorite recreations. Nor was fishing, though he once went devilfishing and landed a big fish, with the help of a friend, off the coast of Florida, using harpoons ("irons") and lances. He played some polo, and regarded it as "infinitely better for vigorous men than tennis or golf," but it also had a low priority. As for golf, he tried it a few times, decided it had no exercise value, and was bored by it. "Golf is for the birds," he was quoted as saying. "The hell with making birdies." Roosevelt's poor eyesight and glasses prevented him from playing baseball, though he liked having his sons take up the game. Once, after seeing his son Quentin play, he wrote, "I like to see Quentin playing baseball. It gives me hope that one of my boys will not take after his father in this respect and be able to play the national game!" When it came to football, he never played the game himself, but gave it his hearty approval. "I greatly admire football," he wrote his son Ted in 1903. To "develop the simple but all-essential traits which go to make up manliness...," he said, "there is no better sport than football." He once said that if any of his sons "would weigh a possible broken bone against the glory of being chosen to play on Harvard's football team I would disinherit him." When he wanted to give young people in America some advice, he chose football lingo: "Don't flinch, don't foul, hit the line hard!" College football in Roosevelt's day was brutal and dangerous; every year there were scores of injuries and even some deaths on the football field, and some colleges contemplated dropping the sport. In 1905, Roosevelt invited athletic directors from some of the leading colleges in the East to a conference at the White House "to make the game of football a rather less homicidal pastime" and thus insure its survival. The following year, representatives from twenty-eight colleges met to adopt new rules making the game safer and more scientific.[20]

Roosevelt probably didn't have a favorite recreation; he threw all his joyous energy into whatever game he was playing. Still, he was particularly energized whenever he was on a hunting trip, and he liked it even better if he could do some nature-watching as well. When he became President, he claimed he was going to curb his desire for hunting, but he never got around to doing so. Before he left the White House, he had gone to the Yazoo delta in Mississippi to hunt bear, to Oklahoma to shoot wolves and rabbits, and to Colorado to hunt mountain lions and cougars. In Roosevelt, as biographer

Henry F. Pringle pointed out, the instincts of the hunter and the naturalist clashed. "The naturalist kept the hunter from being a wanton killer," Pringle wrote. "The hunter caused the naturalist to do strange things." On at least one occasion—Roosevelt's trip to Yellowstone Park with naturalist John Burroughs in the spring of 1903—the naturalist triumphed over the hunter. "I will not fire a gun in the Park," Roosevelt exclaimed beforehand; "then I shall have no explanations to make."[21]

The two naturalists had what Roosevelt would have called a "bully" time during their two weeks in Yellowstone. They camped in tents, went on horseback rides, did some bird-watching, fished for trout, and observed animals, including wild elk, mountain sheep, and black-tailed deer. "Nothing escaped him," Burroughs wrote later, "from bears to mice, from wild geese to chickadees, from elks to red squirrels; he took it all in, and he took it as only an alert, vigorous mind can take it in." Burroughs was fascinated by Roosevelt's endless talk. "What a stream of it poured forth!" he recalled, "and what a varied and picturesque stream!—anecdote, history, science, politics, adventure, literature; bits of his experience as ranchman, hunter, Rough Rider, legislator, civil service commissioner, police commissioner, governor, president—the frankest confessions, the most telling criticisms, happy characterizations of prominent political leaders, or foreign rulers, or members of his own Cabinet; always surprising by his candor, astonishing by his memory, and diverting by his humor." Burroughs admired Roosevelt's courage too. "He can stand calm and unflinching in the path of a charging grizzly, and he can confront with equal coolness and determination the predaceous corporations and money powers of the country." And of course he liked Roosevelt's love of America's natural environment and his determination to safeguard and preserve it for future generations of Americans. "The one passion of his life seemed to be natural history...," Burroughs decided, "and the appearance of a new warbler in his woods—new in the breeding season on Long Island—seemed an event that threw the affairs of state...quite into the background."[22]

But Roosevelt was a President, not a naturalist, and the nation's welfare—not his recreations, indispensable though they were to him—came first. The Roosevelt presidency was one of the liveliest in American history. Time and again Roosevelt took actions that roused the feelings of the American people and made headlines everywhere. He entertained Booker T. Washington, the distinguished black educator, for lunch at the White House; denounced as "nature-fakers" writers who published children's books containing sentimental and inauthentic depictions of dogs, foxes, woodcocks, and other animals; sent a message to Congress that roused a storm because he wrote it in simplified English (which he favored); and sued a newspaper for libel when it portrayed him as a disorderly drunk, and won vindication plus six cents for damages.[23]

White House entertainments hosted by Roosevelt and his wife Edith were by general agreement scintillating affairs. No other President, said William H. Crook, "ever infused into the Executive Mansion such a spirit of joyousness, gayety, and unbounded welcome." Nor did any other President's wife, he noted, give so many private parties, musicales, luncheons, teas, and "at homes" in the White House. At formal receptions Roosevelt was friendly and thoughtful. "He could delight a prince of royal blood who might be dining at his table," according to Crook; "and a few hours later meet on absolutely even ground—man to man!—a group of toilworn, hard-headed and hard-handed laboring men, who had come to Washington to ask his aid in settling a disturbance in which the public was involved."[24]

Roosevelt was a progressive. He was the first President to seriously challenge the social Darwinist philosophy (the struggle for existence and survival of the richest and most powerful) that became so influential during the Gilded Age, and to sponsor legislation to make the United States a safer and fairer country for all Americans. He loved his work. "Perhaps others have lived longer in the place and enjoyed it quite as much," he said, "but none have ever really had more fun out of it than we have." His first big act after leaving the White House was to go on a much-publicized safari in Africa, where for almost a year he hunted big game, followed by a Grand Tour of Europe. He was proud of the number of animals he killed, but he was also pleased that he was able to bring back hundreds of specimens of African wildlife for the Smithsonian Institution to exhibit.[25]

Roosevelt's hunting trip in the wilderness of Brazil a few years later didn't go as well. Roosevelt was ill much of the time, and he never fully recovered his health after returning home. Still, when the United States went to war with Germany in 1917, he was eager to get into the fighting again, and was furious when President Woodrow Wilson refused his request to organize an army division to go to France to fight the "Huns." When he died of a heart attack in January 1919, Vice President Thomas Marshall remarked: "Death had to take him sleeping. For if Roosevelt had been awake, there would have been a fight."[26]

☆ ☆ ☆ 26 ☆ ☆ ☆

The Portly
William Howard Taft

William Howard Taft said he was only a "bumble-puppy" golfer, but he was actually pretty good at the game. He was the first President to take golf seriously—Ulysses Grant and William McKinley had tried it briefly and found it wanting—and his enthusiasm for the sport helped boost its popularity in the United States. "The beauty of the game," Taft said, "is that you cannot play it if you permit yourself to think of anything else. As every man knows who has played the game, it rejuvenates and stretches the span of life."[1]

It was Taft's brother Henry who introduced him to the game years before and made a fan out of him. When Taft ran for President in 1908, Theodore Roosevelt reminded him that golf was considered a rich man's game in the United States and warned him against being seen playing it in public. But Taft ignored his advice, played a lot during the campaign, and rode triumphantly to victory on election day. In a speech in Wolsey, South Dakota, during the campaign, he explained his views: "They said that I have been playing golf this summer, and that it's a rich man's game, and that it indicated that I was out of sympathy with the plain people. I want to state my case before the bar of public opinion on the subject of the game of golf.... It is a game for people who are not active enough for baseball or tennis, or who have too much weight to carry around to play those games; and

yet when a man weighs 295 pounds you have to give him some opportunity to make his legs and muscles move, and golf offers that opportunity." When he moved his 295 pounds (actually 300) into the
White House in March 1909, Taft made the game an essential part of
his schedule. He was also a good dancer—surprisingly graceful for
his size—and took to the ballroom floor with zest at White House
parties. But golf came first in his recreational priorities.[2]

Unfortunately, Taft's great size—he continued to put on weight
while in the White House—produced jokes about his behavior on the
links. "If he put a golf ball where he could hit it," ran a popular joke,
"he couldn't see it. And if he put the golf ball where he could see it,
he couldn't hit it." It is true that Taft had difficulty bending over, and
so asked his caddies to tee balls up for him, and that his enormous
paunch made it hard at times to take swings at the ball, but he did all
right on the whole. His stroke wasn't a "Scotland bonnie swing," according to one reporter. "It is the short swing of the baseball bat." But
he thought Taft's baseball swing was "almost as successful as the
Scottish way." Walter J. Travis, the first world-class U.S. golfer, who
played with Taft, testified that he knew "scores and scores of golfers
who would almost be tempted to sell their immortal souls could they
but put up such a game as he does. The President does play a good
game—a very good one considering if I may be allowed to say so, the
handicap of avoirdupois."[3]

Some people thought Taft had an obsession with golf. He seemed
to be playing it all the time: as many afternoons as he could when he
was in Washington, and just about every day when he was on his
summer vacation in Beverly, Massachusetts. His critics charged that
he neglected his presidential duties in order to play golf. *Hampton's
Magazine* expressed disgust that "the President's celebrated smile
and a large bag of golf sticks" were "conveyed each afternoon to the
Chevy Chase Golf Links," and the *Ohio State Journal* reported sarcas-
tically that the President "hardly gets fairly settled down to golf" than
his presidential duties interrupt the game. One newspaper cartoon
showed Rhode Island senator Nelson W. Aldrich stuffing a high-tariff

bill into the mouth of the GOP elephant while President Taft, pledged to tariff reform, stood in the background calmly playing golf. In the *New York Times,* Mr. Dooley, the famous Irish-American bartending commentator created by Finley Peter Dunne, quoted the President as saying: "Golf is th'thing I like best next to leavin' Washington."[4]

Taft's critics had a point. Taft did in fact put golf ahead of work much of the time. When a State Department official asked about arranging a meeting with the President of Chile, who was visiting Washington, Taft huffily refused to do it. "I'll be damned," he snorted, "if I will give up my game of golf to this fellow." Sometimes, to fool his critics, Taft sneaked out of the White House to play some rounds without telling anybody where he was going, thus producing a crisis when his presence there was required. Taft adored the game, of course, but he also insisted it was good for his health to play it as often as he could. He may have joked now and then about his obesity, but he was not really complacent about it. He realized, as did his wife, his doctor, and his close associates, that it was draining him of his energy, lowering his spirits, and damaging his presidential performance. But he simply couldn't bring himself to cut down on his munching. One evening, after consuming an ample dinner, he sat talking with his table companions. "There was a large bonbon dish of candied fruit before him," Archie Butt, one of his aides, recalled, "and every now and then he would take a piece, apparently unconscious that he was doing it, and before we arose from the table he had eaten every piece there was in the dish." Taft asked his wife to help him curb his appetite, but her efforts to act "as a thorn in my side," he said, proved fruitless.[5]

Taft's weight was fair game for humorists. He was, people said, the politest man in Washington; on streetcars he got up and gave his place to three women. Once, when he was vacationing in Beverly Bay, the story goes, he decided to take a swim, donned one of the largest bathing suits ever produced, and plunged into the water. A few minutes later, one of his neighbors suggested to a friend that they go bathing. "Perhaps we'd better wait," the friend is supposed to have said. "The President is using the ocean." There were jokes, too, about the special bathtub Taft installed in the White House, supposedly the size of a swimming pool, because he got stuck in the old one and it took two men to pull him out of it. But Taft held his own when Chauncey Depew, Republican senator from New York, tried to tease him about his girth. Putting his hand on Taft's big potbelly, he asked, "What are you going to name it when it comes, Mr. President?" "Well," returned Taft, "if it is a boy, I'll call it William; if it's a girl, I'll call it Theodora; but if it turns out to be just wind, I'll call it Chauncey."[6]

Gluttony seemed to produce narcolepsy. Time and again Taft dozed off during conferences, cabinet meetings, White House dinners, and church services, to the embarrassment of his family, friends, and aides, especially when he snored. "He kept his system so filled with undigested food...," wrote James Watson, Republican congressman from Indiana, "that most of the time he simply did not and could not function in alert fashion. Often when I was talking to him after a meal his head would fall over his breast and he would go sound asleep for ten or fifteen minutes." Once, Watson reported, Taft fell asleep in the middle of one of their conversations, but when he awakened, he "laughed heartily" at Watson's crack that Taft was the "largest audience" he ever put to sleep. The President wasn't choosy about where he took his naps; any place would do. He fell asleep attending the command performance of an opera in Washington, during a funeral service at which he sat in the front row, at a White House dinner for the members of his cabinet, and in an open car when he was on a campaign tour in New York. He even dozed off while standing up when his picture was being painted. His wife called him "Sleeping Beauty."[7]

When Taft was unhappy, biographer Judith Icke Anderson pointed out, he had a tendency to overeat. "From his adolescent years," she wrote, his weight "had increased in proportion to his discontents." The fact is that Taft's talents lay in the field of law, not politics, and he simply did not enjoy the White House, with all its responsibilities, the way his friend Roosevelt did. He was a procrastinator, had a poor memory for faces and names, lacked zest in his speechmaking, and felt miserable when under stress. His impulse to escape from the White House came early. During his four years in office, he took more vacations and did more traveling outside Washington than any of his predecessors. He seemed happiest when he was playing golf or was on the road. Taft accepted scores of invitations to minor events out of town, and he saw to it that the special train assigned him for traveling was generously supplied with choice foods. He made two major trips across the country while President, and was warmly welcomed and amply fed wherever he went. Taft, remarked the *New York Times,* "ate his way into the hearts of his countrymen" on these trips. One newspaper carried a cartoon showing the heavy-set President sitting at a huge table shaped like the United States covered with plate after plate of food.[8]

Taft admitted to his brother Horace that he preferred traveling to staying in the White House. Since he was expected to give talks to the people wherever he went, he composed a dozen or so speeches, filled with banalities, which he could use in more than one place. At the end of his first lengthy tour, he acknowledged that after being away from Washington so long, "your conscience begins to prick you and then your duties grow mountain high so that you cannot look over them at all. This is my feeling now. It is a strenuous life to eat and talk and talk and eat, but there are other things…even more burdensome."[9]

In the hope of taking off some pounds, Taft did more than play golf. He tried gymnastics with a trainer in the White House; took walks in Washington with Archie Butt, the military aide he'd inherited from Roosevelt; and sometimes went horseback riding, though he found it increasingly difficult to ride as his weight mounted and he suffered from attacks of gout. The time came when he replaced horses with automobiles. Motorcars were beginning to catch the fancy of Americans in the early twentieth century, and although Theodore Roosevelt looked down scornfully on them the way he did motorboats, Taft became a big fan of the new vehicles. He used them to get around during the campaign of 1908, and once he'd won the election, Congress, at his behest, appropriated twelve thousand dollars to acquire motorcars for the President and his wife and to replace the White House stables with garages. "When the Tafts enter the White House," reported the *Washington Evening Star,* "there will be an automobile administration." President Taft, exulted *Motor Age* after his inauguration, "is an ardent motorist...."[10]

Taft's adoption of motorcars was big news in the United States. "The 'White House Stable' is no more," reported one wire story. "The feed bins have given place to the gasoline tank. From the pegs which formerly supported the harness now hang inner tubes and casings. Exit the coachman, enter the chauffeur. Ring out the 'hay motor,' ring in the steam engine." Taft acquired a chauffeur recommended by the Pierce-Arrow Company, began riding to the Chevy Chase Club for his afternoon golf, and also motored to the ball park to sit in a large chair, specially designed for him, to watch baseball with Archie Butt. In April 1910, he became the first President to throw out the ball at the opening of the baseball season. "I have never seen anyone so keen about motoring as the President," Butt wrote in one of his letters. Theodore Roosevelt's daughter Alice was charmed by Taft's new recreation. "Dear Mr. Taft!" she exclaimed in an interview years later, "I see him now, a great big pink porpoise of a man sitting in the back of an open touring car with his hands on his rotund belly."[11]

Taft used his cars for trips around the country as well as for local transportation, and his joyous jaunts in the fancy cars he acquired as President received coverage in mainline newspapers as well as in the papers and magazines devoted to promoting motor vehicles. He soon became known for his love of speed. In May 1910, the *New York Times* reported a motor ride he took near Pittsburgh during which his car "passed small hamlets, bowled over hills, swept through valleys, rounded sharp curves with the rear wheels sliding, and kept up such a hot speed that he was not recognized at all...." An accompanying editorial chided Taft for his recklessness. When the President goes "immoderately fast," said the editors, he "sets a rather bad example for the people who lack his immunity from arrest." Taft's car slid sideways on a road on one occasion and another time collided with a streetcar, but Taft never confronted the law the way President Grant had years before when driving his carriage at breakneck speed in Washington.[12]

In embracing the automobile, Taft was for once wiser than Roosevelt, whose "intense loyalty to the horse," as one journal put it, led him to take as few motor rides as possible. To Taft, the automobile was a "wonderful development," and in one of his speeches in 1910 he announced: "We live in the Age of the Automobile." He was sure that "the automobile coming in as a toy of the wealthier class is going to prove the most useful of them all to all classes, rich and poor." The American Automobile Association praised the Tafts as "National Autoists," featured them on the cover of its publication *American Motorists* in February 1910, and declared that "President and Mrs. Taft have given a great impetus to motoring in that very large section of officialdom which, even in minor matters, takes its cue from the occupants of the White House."[13]

In 1912, Taft ran for reelection almost as a matter of self-respect, lost the election, and left the White House with a sigh of relief. His years there, his daughter Helen said years later, "were the only unhappy years of his entire life." After attending the inauguration of his successor, Woodrow Wilson, on March 4, 1913, he spent a month playing golf in Savannah, Georgia, and then became a law professor at Yale, where he was much liked and admired. "You don't know how much fun it is to sit back...," he wrote a friend, "and watch the playing of the game down there in Washington, without any responsibility of my own." In 1921, Warren G. Harding, President Wilson's successor, appointed Taft as Chief Justice of the U.S. Supreme Court, and he spent his last years doing what he did best and enjoyed most. He walked to the Court to keep in shape, worked hard on the cases coming before the Court, and lost weight. "The truth is," Taft said, "that in my present life I don't remember that I ever was president."[14]

The Scholarly
Woodrow Wilson

Woodrow Wilson liked to quote what Ulysses Grant said when he first encountered golf in England years before: "What's the ball for?" He had his own definition of the game: "an ineffectual attempt to put an elusive ball into an obscure hole with implements ill-adapted to the purpose." But his frustrated putdown of the game didn't keep him from spending more time on the golf courses than William Howard Taft, the man he beat for the presidency in 1912. He wasn't nearly as good a player as Taft was, but he had just as much fun at the game. One commentator said he was a "fidgety player who addressed the ball as if he would reason with it," and another said he played "reluctantly, joylessly, and most of all terribly." No matter. In 1914 he wrote a friend that "my chief real interest is golf. It seems to put oxigen [*sic*] into my heart."[1]

Some people called Wilson a "crisis golfer." It seemed as if he was always on the links at critical moments in his presidency. On November 6, 1912, as returns were coming in from the presidential election, he was at the eighteenth hole in a game with his physician, Dr. Cary Grayson, when some players asked how he was doing. "Grayson has me three down," he told them, "but I don't care. I am four states up on yesterday's election." In April 1914, when he learned that Mexico had refused to apologize for arresting some American sailors in

Tampico, he left his round at a course in Virginia to write an ultima-
tum threatening military action. On May 7, 1915, Wilson left a golf
course in Maryland when news came that a German submarine had
sunk the *Lusitania,* with the loss of 128 American lives, and hurried
back to the White House for a meeting with his military advisers. In
November 1916, when the results of the election in which he sought
a second term were still in doubt, he played a round of golf in New
Jersey, and one observer said he "seemed as calm as ever, and played
just as poorly." When Dr. Grayson rushed up a little later with the
news that California had gone for Wilson, thus making a second term
a certainty, he just kept playing as calmly, and presumably as poorly,
as ever. In April 1917, a few hours before he addressed a joint session
of Congress to request a declaration of war on Germany, Wilson
played some golf; and the following day, he played again before asking for war with the Austro-Hungarian Empire. In 1918, he was on the
links before deciding to pardon some suffragettes who'd been sent to
jail for picketing the White House to protest his opposition to votes
for women.[2]

Golf wasn't the only sport that Wilson cherished. He liked baseball, too, having played it as a freshman at Davidson College in North
Carolina and become a lifelong fan. When he taught political science
at Princeton University years later, he attended the baseball games
there regularly and became known as the man who "waved his umbrella and cheered." Wilson did more than that; sometimes he got
into arguments with the umpires over their rulings. At one game he
even rushed down onto the field to protest a decision, and it was necessary to halt the game and get him off the field before resuming
play. As President, he happily threw out the opening-day ball for the
baseball season and took in some World Series games.[3]

Wilson became a football fan, too, and he was more involved in the
game than he was in baseball when he taught at Wesleyan College in
Connecticut and at Princeton University in New Jersey, his alma
mater. At Wesleyan he went to the practice field after classes to do
some coaching, and he introduced a series of rotation plays that the

players made good use of in their games. He also boosted their morale. "Go in and win," Wilson told the players before games. "You can lick Yale as well as any other team. Go after their scalps. Don't admit for a moment that they can beat you." At Princeton, Wilson did some coaching, too, and then became chairman of the Committee on Outdoor Sports, organized to improve the university's athletic program as a whole. After he became president of Princeton in 1902, he continued to follow the college's football and baseball games with his usual devotion.[4]

Wilson wasn't in very good physical shape when he became President of the United States in 1913. His life since graduating from Princeton in 1879—as a lawyer, college professor, college president, and governor of New Jersey—was increasingly sedentary, and from time to time he suffered emotional collapses from the stresses of work that forced him to take time off. The vacations were good for him, especially when he took walks, rode his bicycle, and did sightseeing in his beloved British Isles, but he invariably resumed his old work habits upon recovery. When Dr. Grayson took a good look at Wilson shortly after his inauguration, he was convinced that "much sedentary life had been bad for a constitution not naturally vigorous," and that the new President was "below par." Wilson, he decided, was "a clear case for preventative medicine," and he made several recommendations that included walking; horseback riding; trips on the presidential yacht, the *Mayflower;* automobile rides; and, above all, regular games of golf.[5]

Wilson conscientiously followed Dr. Grayson's advice. He took walks in the country, delighting in encounters with people who didn't recognize him; took up riding with a horse named Arisona; enjoyed motor rides, giving his favorite outings special names like "Number One Ride," "Potomac Ride," and "South Maryland Ride"; and tried to fit some golf in every day. "He liked the game," Grayson soon learned, "but he played chiefly from a sense of duty."[6]

Grayson became Wilson's main partner. Wilson never had many partners, because he insisted on playing with people who refrained

from talking politics. "While you are playing," he explained to a
friend, "you cannot worry and be preoccupied with affairs. Each
stroke requires your whole attention and seems the most important
thing in life." In some respects, Wilson had a one-track mind. "He did
one thing at a time," Grayson observed. "When he worked, he
worked to the exclusion of everything from his mind except the matter at hand, and he carried the same spirit into his diversions." The
doctor realized that Wilson's eyes were poor and that he'd taken up
golf too late to become very good at it, but he judged him "a fair
player, due chiefly to his great powers of concentration." Grayson
was being generous. "He's terrible," said a Secret Service man of the
President's performance. "So is Grayson," he added. "Each man," according to one expert, "played a sloppy, train-wreck game of lost balls
and 4-putts." Colonel Edmund Starling, Wilson's personal bodyguard, found it disheartening to watch the two men take a total of
more than two hundred strokes to get around a golf course. "A melancholy prospect," he called his assignment, "following two poor
golfers over a windswept course on a winter's morning." When Wilson played in the winter, he had the golf balls painted red or black so
they could be seen in the snow. But he didn't play any better.[7]

Wilson and Grayson may have been terrible golfers, but they derived a great deal of pleasure from being together on the links during
Wilson's presidency. Wilson, who was good at mimicking people, developed a takeoff on his physician friend that he called "Grayson Approaching a Golf Ball," which the latter enjoyed seeing him perform.
Once, during a vacation in the South, they had occasion to put out a
fire. Returning from a round of golf, they passed a house near the
links and noticed flames on the roof. When they knocked at the door
to warn the owner, a woman came out, spied Wilson, and cried, "Oh,
Mr. President, it's so good of you to call on me. Won't you come into
the parlor and sit down?" "I haven't got time," Wilson replied. "Your
house is on fire!" Then he and Grayson rushed up to the attic, where
they put out a small blaze before the firemen arrived. On another occasion, Wilson's ball narrowly missed hitting another golfer, and the

latter let loose a flood of profanity, stormed over, suddenly realized that his target was the President, and apologized profusely. Afterward, whenever Wilson boarded a streetcar, his friends shouted, "Fore!"[8]

Wilson's first wife, Ellen, who died in August 1914 of Bright's disease, was not a golfer, but his second wife, Edith, whom he married in December 1915, became a member of his "Golf Cabinet" while he was still courting her. Edith made mincemeat out of the old joke that GOLF stood for "Gentlemen Only, Ladies Forbidden" by turning out to be a better golfer than either her husband or his doctor. Time and again she wrote in her diary: "Played golf with W and Grayson. Beat them both." Like Grayson, Edith enjoyed Wilson's playful moods when he was on the links, and she did what she could to contribute to the merriment. Among other things, Wilson liked to tell stories, in a Scotch burr or Irish brogue, using one of his golf clubs for flourishes to underline the points he was making. "Walking along the fairway between shots," Colonel Starling recalled, "the President regaled her with dialect stories and gave impromptu impersonations, one of the best being an interpretation of little Dr. Grayson addressing a ball." One day, Edith laid her niblick across Wilson's shoulders and bent him forward so that it would not slip off. "Immediately," according to Starling, "he changed his stride to imitate the lumbering gait of an ape. When he tired of the funning, he bent forward, let the niblick roll over the top of his head and caught it as it fell." Sometimes the joke was on Wilson. As he was teeing off during one round, Edith recalled, two little boys who were watching them noticed the Secret Service men accompanying them. "Who is them men who don't play?" one of the boys asked. "Why," said the other boy scornfully, "them's his keepers."[9]

Wilson wasn't always in a good mood when he was playing. One humid August day in 1919, Colonel Starling remembered, he had to carry the clubs for the President because there were no caddies available. Wilson "drove about 50 yards for the tee," Starling observed, "and I saw he was in an ugly temper." Wilson usually asked Starling what club to use, but on this occasion he simply said, "Starling, give me my number two iron." As Starling handed him the club, a boy in front of a house on the edge of the course cupped his hands to his mouth and made a series of Indian calls. Wilson stepped to the side, rested on his club, and then said irritably: "That boy must be training to be a Senator. He is always making a noise with his mouth and not saying anything." Having put the Senate (with which he was clashing at the time) in its place, he went on to play better than usual, and "his good humor was restored."[10]

When the United States went to war with Germany in April 1917, the heavy demands on Wilson's time forced him to reduce his golfing drastically and to cut down on the other recreations that Dr. Grayson had recommended at the beginning of his presidency. His wife Edith, concerned for his health, persuaded him to go horseback riding with her, take trips on the *Mayflower,* and try billiards. She even had a billiard room set aside in a section of the ground-floor corridor of the White House, where he could play the game with her and his daughters. But it was not nearly enough. Wilson threw most of his energy into his work as a war President and resumed the largely sedentary life to which he had been accustomed before his election. In November 1918, when the war ended, he was in worse shape than when he began his presidency.[11]

Wilson was the first college professor to become President. He took his doctorate in history at Johns Hopkins University in 1883, and, before entering politics, taught at Bryn Mawr, Wesleyan University, and Princeton, where he became graduate dean and then president. During his academic years he published a series of books that included both scholarly studies like *Congressional Government* (1885) and books directed to the general reader, such as *A History of the American People* (1902). Wilson read a lot both as an academician and a political leader, but he went through books mainly for his work, not for pleasure. Though he claimed that "the very odour of books" from his father's library clung to him all his life, books were never important to him the way they were to Thomas Jefferson and Theodore Roosevelt. According to the White House's chief usher, Irwin ("Ike")

Hoover, Wilson didn't do much reading when he was President; after his first wife died, he sought consolation in conversations with members of his family rather than in books. He did, though, like to read aloud at social gatherings in the White House, and his tastes ran to English literature: the novels of Sir Walter Scott and Jane Austen; the essays of Charles Lamb and Gilbert Chesterton; and the poetry of Keats, Shelley, Tennyson, and Browning. He also liked detective stories, and Edith read so many to him when he was ailing that she became heartily sick of the genre.[12]

In Wilson's younger days he yearned to become a "literary fellow." He tried writing fiction, but finally gave it up when he failed to get any of his short stories published. He tried poetry without any more success. In 1896, he wrote a poem for his wife Ellen that commenced:

> "You were the song I waited for.
> I found in you the vision sweet.
> The grace, the strain of noble sounds,
> The form, the mind, the mien, the heart."

Three days after presenting it to her, however, it dawned on him that the poem really wasn't much good. "No, sweet," he told her, "I am no poet...and those lines written the other day are no poem. The night I wrote them I thought they were. A hot fire was in my brain; my imagination was thronged with every sweet image of love; and, while I wrote, I thought I was writing poetry." In the end, Wilson contented himself with tossing off humorous limericks from time to time and writing essays on literature and history for some of the most respected popular magazines of his day. He wrote the essays, as he did his books, biographer George C. Osborn noted, for "the sheer joy of creative accomplishment."[13]

Wilson had his thespian as well as his poetic side. He liked to mimic people, tell stories in dialect, and perform takeoffs on various kinds of individuals. For his family and friends, he played the part of a befuddled drunk or a heavy-set Brit with monocle and cane; once he donned a feather boa and pretended to be an uppity society woman greeting guests at an afternoon party. "Come on, Nellie," he once said to his youngest daughter, who shared his love of acting, "let's run away and go on the stage. We could do a splendid father and daughter act!" But Wilson's real talent was for singing, not acting. He had a fine tenor voice. When he was a student at Princeton, he sang second tenor in the University Glee Club and was also a member of the College Chapel Choir. Each year he was featured as a soloist at the Grand Princeton Concert and Ball, a big event with which the Glee Club ended its annual tour, and he was acclaimed for the way he held the high note at the end of "The Star-Spangled Banner."[14]

During World War I, some people wanted to shut down the theaters and concert halls in order to concentrate on winning the war, but Wilson vigorously opposed the idea. "The man who disparages music as a luxury and nonessential," he said, "is doing the nation an injury. Music, now more than ever before, is a national need." He felt the same way about movies. In a letter to America's moviegoers in April 1918, he said that a movie theater was "a great democratic meeting place of the people, where within twenty-four hours it is possible to reach eight million citizens of all classes." The government, he went on, "recognizes that a reasonable amount of amusement, especially in war time, is not a luxury but a necessity."[15]

Wilson saw movies himself in the White House, where a screen was set up at one end of the East Room and a projector at the other end. His favorite film was *The Birth of a Nation* (1915), D. W. Griffith's technically innovative epic about the Civil War and Reconstruction, in which the Ku Klux Klan is sympathetically portrayed. Wilson, reared in the South, was deeply moved by the film and said it was like "writing history with lightning." The movie quoted several passages from Wilson's *History of the American People,* including a condemnation of the Republican-dominated Congress after the Civil War for trying to "put the white South under the heel of the black South."[16]

But Wilson was more of a theatergoer than he was a movie fan. His family, it was said, could always get him to go to a play, no matter how tired he was. He went for enjoyment, not instruction, and he was irritated by people who insisted that a drama had to have a message. His preference was for musical comedies and vaudeville, particularly the latter, with its silly jokes and energetic dancing. "I love to see people who have nothing on their minds that they can't express with their heels," he confessed. If a vaudeville act was dull, he said, it was over in a few minutes, but if a dramatic play was dull it went on for three acts. He liked the humorist Will Rogers's performances and enjoyed Gilbert and Sullivan's musical comedies, but despite having read Shakespeare as a student, he took a dim view of dramatic productions. Once, Joseph P. Tumulty, his private secretary, persuaded him to go to New York to see the stage star Laurette Taylor play the lead in *Peg o' My Heart,* a sentimental play much liked by Americans with an Irish background. Tumulty had tears in his eyes when the show was over, but Wilson was turned off by the play's lachrymosity. It was the last play he ever attended. In his last years he confined his stage shows to vaudeville. Colonel Starling enjoyed seeing Wilson "rocking with laughter at a particularly good quip, or humming and tapping his feet while a vaudeville singer gave out with a new song...." Wilson, he realized, "got more genuine recreation from the theatre than he did from anything else....It relaxed his mind....He wanted to laugh at the clowns, admire the pretty legs of the chorus girls—like any normal man he had a deep and sincere appreciation of the female form—and he loved good dancing, being himself an accomplished buck-and-wing artist. He liked to tell dialect stories (English, Scotch and Negro) and he found the stage a rich source of fresh material."[17]

Wilson needed what fun he could get in his later years. The strain of presiding over a war, attending a peace conference, and then touring the country to win support for his beloved League of Nations overwhelmed him. In October 1919 he suffered a major stroke, and for months afterward it took tireless help from his wife Edith to keep his presidency going. Wilson was still weak and unsteady when Warren G. Harding took oath as his successor, but he managed to appear at the inauguration. In retirement his health improved somewhat and he was able to attend vaudeville shows every Saturday night. His wife took him for long drives in the country, joined him evenings for card games, and read books—mainly novels—to him. At one point Wilson decided to write a book on government, but he didn't get past writing the dedication to his wife: "To my incomparable wife, Edith Bolling Wilson, whose gentle benefits to me are beyond all estimation, this book, which is meant to contain what is best in me, is with deep admiration, lovingly dedicated."[18]

The Bloviating
Warren G. Harding

Warren G. Harding liked to bloviate, that is, chat informally with people. He also liked to smoke, drink, play poker and golf, and play wind instruments. He didn't like being President, so he spent as much time as he could bloviating, smoking, drinking, playing poker and golf, and taking part in U.S. Marine Band rehearsals. Historians evaluating our Presidents usually rank Harding, along with Ulysses S. Grant, at rock bottom, labeling him a failure. He accomplished nothing as President, they say, and his administration, like General Grant's, was riddled with corruption. When Harding died of a heart attack in August 1923 while on a trip to Alaska, the *London Times* declared: "President Harding was a happy man—happy in life, happy, we may believe, in death." The *Times* couldn't have been more mistaken. Harding was not happy in the White House; he felt out of place and lonely there. "Oftentimes, as I sit here," he told syndicated writer David Lawrence, "I don't seem to grasp that I am President."[1]

But Harding came alive when he mingled with people. He never forgot that he was a small-town boy from Marion, Ohio, and he took the folksy ways he had learned as a youngster with him to the White House. His wife, Florence, joined him in making the White House accessible to the people. At the reception there following her husband's inauguration, Mrs. Harding saw the servants pulling down the window

shades so people couldn't look in on them, and she quickly intervened. "Let 'em look if they want to!" she cried. "It's their White
House." Harding felt the same way. He saw to it that the lower floors
as well as the grounds were open to visitors, revived the Easter-egg
rolling game for children that had been suspended during World War
I, and, a horn player himself, arranged for the Marine Band to give
regular concerts on the White House lawn. The concerts were so popular that frequently the band had to play "The End of a Perfect Day"
several times before the guests got the point and starting leaving.[2]

While Harding was President he came to be called "the Great
Handshaker." It was one of the things he did well. He held a short reception every day from 12:30 until lunchtime, at which he pumped
the hands of scores of people crowding up to him after receiving a
speedy clearance from the Secret Service. "I love to meet people,"
Harding told his secretary. "It is the most pleasant thing I do; it is
really the only fun I have. It doesn't tax me, and it seems to be a very
great pleasure to them." When he met Henry Ford one day, he said,
"I believe I have shaken hands with at least twenty-five percent of the
American people." Glancing over at his "tin lizzie" (a Model T Ford)
parked nearby, Ford quipped: "And I supposed I have shaken the
bones of about half the population of these United States."[3]

Harding believed the heart of America was its farms, villages, and
small towns, and that it was his responsibility as President to represent them informally as well as formally. At times, though, he was a
bit too folksy for his wife. She explained to him that wienerwurst and
sauerkraut were not suitable for presidential menus, insisted that he
stop chewing tobacco openly in the White House, and tried in vain to
wean him away from toothpicks. Shortly after the Hardings moved
into the White House, the President sent the butler to the kitchen
for some toothpicks. The housekeeper was shocked. "Surely you are
mistaken!" she exclaimed. "No, Ma'am," said the butler, "he asked
me as plain as anything for toothpicks." "Well," she said, "we'll just
forget it." The butler returned to the President and came hurrying

back a minute or two later. "The President asked real forceful-like for those toothpicks," he told the housekeeper.[4]

But Harding had tobacco, toothpicks, wienerwurst, and sauerkraut, if he wanted them, at the little stag parties for a dozen or so of his cronies that he held twice a week at the White House. After dinner came poker games, with plenty of beer and whiskey available, in a room on the second floor near the President's office. One night, Theodore Roosevelt's perky daughter, Alice Roosevelt Longworth, left an official White House reception to go upstairs, and although there was nothing prissy about her, she was genuinely shocked "to see the way President Harding disregarded the Constitution he was sworn to uphold." Prohibition was the law of the land, and although no liquor was served downstairs, there was plenty at Harding's poker party. The air was "heavy with tobacco smoke," Alice observed, "trays with bottles containing every imaginable brand of whisky stood about, cards and poker chips ready at hand—a general atmosphere of waistcoat unbuttoned, feet on the desk, and the spittoon alongside."[5]

Sometimes Mrs. Harding poured the drinks as her husband played poker and took occasional side bets at these parties. Every so often, Harding felt so lonely in the White House that he hurried off to the residences of his cronies to play poker. One night, when Charles Sawyer, the Surgeon General who was the Hardings' physician, was having a party in his suite in the Willard Hotel, the door suddenly swung open and there stood the President. "You fellows can't sneak off and have a party without me," he cried. "I'm here for the evening!" Some of Harding's poker pals held positions in his administration, and he later learned, to his dismay, that they were heavily involved in graft. "My God, this is a hell of a job," he told William Allen White, the editor of the *Emporia Gazette* in Kansas. "I have no trouble with my enemies. I can take care of my enemies all right. But my damn friends, my God-damn friends, White, they're the ones that keep me walking the floor nights."[6]

Harding played golf as well as poker to relax and forget his troubles. On the first Sunday after his inauguration he sneaked off to play golf in the morning, but his wife saw to it that he never did it again. From then on he confined his golfing to weekdays—two or three times a week—except during vacations, when he could play as often as he pleased. Sometimes he used the lawns in back of the White House to hit irons and expected Laddie Boy, his Airedale terrier, to be his retriever. Harding took golf seriously, followed the rules, asked for no "mulligans" or "gimmies," and refused any breaks his golfing friends offered him. "Forget that I'm president of the United States," he urged them. "I'm Warren Harding playing with some friends, and I'm going to beat the hell out of them." If he can "get into the low nineties," George B. Christian, his secretary, reported, "he's tickled to death."[7]

Harding was an amiable partner on the links. Sportswriter Grantland Rice found him "an extremely attractive golf companion, one with dignity minus pretense." Sometimes Harding placed a wager on each swing, and then, Colonel Edmund Starling observed, "he played as if his life depended on every shot. And he made so many bets that sometimes he was betting against himself." Harding also liked a drink now and then while making the rounds. On the private course at the estate of his friend Edward B. McClean, publisher of the *Washington Post,* the butlers served drinks from silver trays, but at the Chevy Chase Country Club, which obeyed the law, he kept a secret cache of bootleg whiskey at hand for his occasional highballs. But he took his game seriously, and gloried in the fact that champion players like Walter Hagen and Gene Sarazen played with him now and then. Harding liked playing with celebrities like Will Rogers, too. When he first met the famous humorist, he told him, "This is the first time I ever got to see you without paying for it." The two got along fine as golf partners for a while, but Harding broke off the friendship when Rogers put on a vaudeville skit in which he did a takeoff on the President at a cabinet meeting jabbering about golf. Harding's encounter with short-story writer and humorist Ring Lardner went better. In one golf game, Lardner sliced the ball and it landed high in a tree near Harding, loosening a branch and sending it crashing down on the President's shoulder. Lardner explained the mishap by joking, "I did all I could to make Coolidge [the Vice President] President." Harding laughed so hard at Lardner's remark that he dropped his club. After the game, the Long Island writer told Harding he wanted to be appointed ambassador to Greece, and when Harding asked why, he said simply, "My wife doesn't like Great Neck."[8]

When Harding wasn't playing cards or making the rounds at the Chevy Chase Country Club, he attended prize fights and baseball games. He took in girlie shows, too, sitting in a special box in Gayety Burlesque that concealed him from the public. Books played no part in Harding's life—Samuel Hopkins Adams said he was "unliterate" rather than "illiterate"—but music meant much to him. Years before, when he was a student at Ohio's Iberia College, he belonged to the Iberia Brass Band and learned to play every instrument but the slide trombone and the E-flat clarinet. As President, he liked to drop in on rehearsals of the U.S. Marine Band, pick up an instrument, and play "just to keep his hand in." In one of his speeches, he confessed, "I love music. We cannot have too much music; we need it; the world needs it; probably more now than ever before." Harding was thinking of popular music, of course, but he once said his big dream was to make Washington a center of music and art, as a means of "developing interest in and taste for good music throughout the nation."[9]

Harding never bragged about his musical skill, but he did consider himself a pretty good writer. He wrote editorials for the *Marion Star,* the newspaper he owned before going into politics, and though he used ghostwriters for some of the speeches he gave as President, he wrote some of them himself. His tastes ran to simile. One of his proudest productions as President might be called the P-passage: "Progression is not proclamation nor palaver. It is not pretense nor play on prejudice. It is not of personal pronouns, nor perennial pronouncement. It is not the perturbation of a people passion-wrought, nor a promise proposed." There is something touching about the fact that unlike most "he-harlots" (as newsman William Allen White called skirt-chasers like Harding), he wrote effusive love letters and poems for his crushes, fun to read today, dripping with heartfelt mush and goo. For one of his beloveds, he wrote an erotic poem which read in part:

> I love your back, I love your breasts,
> Darling to feel, where my face rests,
> I love your skin, so soft and white,
> so dear to feel and sweet to bite,
> I love your knees, their dimples kiss,
> I love your ways of giving bliss,
> Love your poise of perfect thighs,
> when they hold me in paradise.

It is only fair, though, to note that despite all his stylistic infelicities, Harding contributed two good phrases to the American language: "the Founding Fathers" and "Back to Normalcy."[10]

Harding's presidency wasn't any better than his poetry. Not only was it replete with scandals; it also lacked any substantial contribution to the good of the country. Harding's saving grace was his honesty about his incompetency. "Jud, you have a college education, haven't you," he exclaimed one day to a friend who was visiting him in the White House. "I don't know what or where to turn on this taxation matter. Somewhere there must be a book that tells about it, where I could go to straighten it out in my mind. But I don't know where the book is, and maybe I couldn't read it if I found it! There must be a man in this country somewhere who could weigh both sides and know the truth. Probably he is in some college or other. But I don't know where to find him. I don't know who he is, and I don't know how to get him. My God, this is a hell of a place for a man like me to be."[11]

In August 1923, shortly before his death of a stroke, Harding took a trip to Alaska with his wife, partly for his health, partly to make speeches in the West, and partly to get away from Washington, where revelations of the corruption in his administration were the talk of the town. At one point the ship he was on suddenly collided with another, and the captain ordered the passengers to go up on deck. When Harding didn't show up, one of his aides went below to locate him and found him lying on his bed with his face in his hands. When Harding asked what had happened, the aide told him there had been a slight collision and though everyone had been ordered on deck, there wasn't anything seriously wrong. Said Harding quietly: "I hope the boat sinks."[12]

$\star\ \star\ \star$ **29** $\star\ \star\ \star$

The Laconic
Calvin Coolidge

Calvin Coolidge, known as "Silent Cal" for his taciturnity, never had a hobby until he became President of the United States at the age of fifty-two, upon Warren Harding's death in 1923. A few years earlier, when a reporter asked him, "What is your hobby?", he responded frankly: "Holding office." Coolidge became an officeholder soon after taking up law as his profession in Northampton, Massachusetts, joining the city council in 1898, and then moving up rapidly as mayor of Northampton, member of the Massachusetts senate, Vice President with Harding, and then President. Although he did farm chores as a boy growing up in rural Vermont, Coolidge turned out to be one of the least athletic of all our Presidents. Asked once what part he played in sports as a student at Amherst College, he said, "I held the stakes." He added: "I tended to the education of my head, not my legs." Later on, when someone asked him how he got his exercise, he quipped, "Having my picture taken." Coolidge did play a little golf before becoming President, but he was a terrible player, resented the expenses associated with the game, and confessed, "I do not see the sense in chasing a little white ball around a field."[1]

Coolidge was no grind; he believed a man should "do a day's work" and that was that. Lacking the vitality of Presidents like Theodore Roosevelt, he spent his spare time reading and resting. By the time he

became President he was famous for his close-mouthedness, penuriousness, and penchant for long afternoon naps. Walter Lippmann,
columnist for the *New York World,* was fascinated by Coolidge's apparent lassitude. "Mr. Coolidge's genius for inactivity is developed to a
very high point," he wrote in 1926. "It is far from being an indolent inactivity. It is a grim, determined, alert inactivity which keeps Mr. Coolidge occupied constantly. Nobody has worked harder at inactivity,
with such force of character, with such unremitting attention to detail,
with such conscientious devotion to the task." Lippmann linked Coolidge's physical languor to his laissez-faire social philosophy. "Inactivity," he wrote, "is a political philosophy and a party program with Mr.
Coolidge, and nobody should mistake his unflinching adherence to it
for a soft and easy desire to let things slide. Mr. Coolidge's inactivity
is a steady application to the task of neutralizing and thwarting political activity wherever there are signs of life."[2]

Lippmann wasn't being entirely fanciful. Coolidge did, in fact, believe that once the federal government had done all it could to help
the business community, it should refrain from doing much else.
"Four-fifths of our troubles in this life would disappear," he insisted,
"if we would only sit down and keep still." He defended his afternoon
naps by saying that when he was sleeping he wasn't doing anything,
and that was good for the country. Once he woke up from a nice,
long nap and exclaimed merrily: "Is the country still here?" But he
knew he had things to do in the White House. Coolidge concentrated on running the household rather than devising domestic programs to present to Congress or bothering himself with foreign
affairs. Unlike his predecessors, who let their wives supervise the
work of the White House help, he kept a sharp eye on household expenses: checked menus every morning, went into the kitchen to
make suggestions, and encouraged the purchase of supplies from
Piggly Wiggly and other grocery chains in order to save money.
Once he got into an argument with Elizabeth Jaffray, housekeeper
for the Executive Mansion, over the food she ordered for a presidential dinner. "I don't see why we have to have six hams for one dinner,"

he complained. "It seems an awful lot of ham to me." "But, Mr. President," she said, "there will be sixty people here. Virginia hams are small, and we cannot possibly serve more than ten people with one ham and be sure of having enough." "Well," said Coolidge, "six hams look an awful lot to me."[3]

But Coolidge had his playful as well as his fussy side; he enjoyed teasing people. One day, soon after becoming President, he stepped out of his office, pushed an alarm button that roused all the White House guards, and then disappeared into his office before they found out who had sounded the alarm. Another time he pressed the buzzers on his desk for all the members of the White House staff at once and then hid in the closet as people came hurrying to his office from all directions. At dinner one night he suddenly told his wife there was a bug in his food, and when the butlers began anxiously looking into the matter, he said, "Mama, I thought butlers weren't supposed to eavesdrop." Coolidge upset his friends when he allowed himself to be photographed wearing a cowboy outfit presented to him when he was spending the summer of 1927 in South Dakota. "But I don't see why you object," he said. "The people here have sent me this costume, and they wouldn't have sent it unless they expected me to put it on. Why shouldn't I have my picture taken with it on to please them?" When one of his friends explained, "It's making people laugh," Coolidge said: "Well, it's good for people to laugh."[4]

When it came to exercise, Coolidge wasn't as inactive as Lippmann thought. When he became President he got in the habit of taking walks, either alone or with Colonel Edmund Starling, his bodyguard, every morning before breakfast, and sometimes in the evening. He especially enjoyed window-shopping along F Street. "It takes me away from my work," he told an aide, "and rests my mind." Once during the President's evening stroll, a man in a horse-drawn carriage pulled up, lifted his hat, and cried: "Would y'all like to take a ride?" Coolidge beamed and told the aide who was with him, "Let's take a ride." "It'll cost you three dollars," the aide reminded him. "We'll walk," decided Coolidge.[5]

Coolidge wasn't long into his presidency before one of his admirers bestowed upon him a fine electric horse for indoor exercising. The first time he tried it he was wearing a business suit and a hat, and when he pressed the starter, the horse suddenly reared, and Coolidge lost his hat and almost fell off. But he eventually learned how to handle the machine and came to enjoy daily rides. Occasionally, it was said, he whooped it up like a real cowboy when riding his electric steed. In a speech to the Gridiron Club in Washington, Coolidge had the editors and journalists in stitches as he described how he pushed the wrong button on the horse one day and produced paces, trots, and gallops all at the same time and almost broke his neck. He did, though, resent it when newspaper cartoonists teased him about his electric horse-riding.[6]

Despite Coolidge's walks and mechanical rides, Colonel Starling, boss of the Secret Service men assigned the President, was bothered by his failure to have a real hobby. "I was distressed," he wrote in his memoirs, "to find out that he took no other exercise except walking. He did not play golf, ride horseback, fish, hunt, swim, bowl or even play billiards. He had no hobbies, not even stamp collecting. Moreover, he walked with his head thrust forward, his hands clasped behind him." Starling decided to do something about it, but it took time. Not until the summer of 1926, when the Coolidges spent their vacation at White Pine Camp, next to Lake Osgood, in the Adirondacks in New York, did he have any success. When he suggested fishing one morning, Coolidge was doubtful; he had never fished before, not even as a boy, so Starling explained how to handle the rod and reel, bait the hook and cast, and what to do when there was a bite. It all sounded silly to Coolidge, but he decided to try; and when he did, he caught his first fish—a five-pound pike—and fell in love with the sport at once. "He became the most ardent fisherman I have ever known," Starling said later. From then on, Coolidge insisted that Starling accompany him to the lake every day to do some fishing. The news of Coolidge's catch stirred up so much excitement in New York that Governor Al Smith had the fish stuffed. Later on, when Coolidge caught a pickerel, he was featured in a newspaper photograph fully dressed, wearing a tie, a stiff collar, and a Panama hat too small for him, holding the fish as far away from him as he could, with a glum look on his face. But he was proud of being an angler. Fishing with Starling one day on the Brule River in Wisconsin, Coolidge lost a fish he had been playing and exclaimed, "Damn!" Then he looked sheepishly at Starling and said, "Guess I'm a real fisherman now. I cussed."[7]

The Vermont President's fishing was quite Coolidgean. He wore kid gloves when he fished, and he had Secret Service men bait the hook and take the fish he caught off for him. Some of the men complained that every so often he jerked the line as they baited the hook, almost as if he thought that pricking their fingers would add to the fun of the sport. In the summer of 1927, when spending his vacation at the big State Game Lodge in the Black Hills of South Dakota, Coolidge made headlines again with his fishing. When a reporter spied him headed for the lodge carrying five trout on a string, he asked the President if he had used a fly. "No," said Coolidge, "I used a hook and worm." This touched off a storm among the fly-fishermen in the country, who regarded the use of worms as extremely unsportsmanlike. "Worms!" cried the *New York World*. "Words fail. Comment is useless...." Senator William E. Borah of Idaho said he'd never heard of using worms when fishing for trout. Coolidge must have caught catfish, he suggested, "but if they were trout, they must have been imbeciles." Missouri senator James Reed also sounded off. "Any trout that will lie on the bottom of a lake and bite a worm is a degenerate trout," he exclaimed. "As a matter of generosity and common fairness, however, I hope he used a whole worm." Another senator announced that "there's no telling what a man will do who will catch trout with a worm." Coolidge eventually tried fly-fishing, but it took a long time for him to catch on, and Secret Service men had to remove numerous hooks from trees and bushes as well as from his clothes while he was learning.[8]

At Starling's prodding, Coolidge did a little hunting. He went horseback riding a few times, too, though he gave up the latter when he acquired his mechanical horse. His wife, Grace, was a baseball fan, but Coolidge himself had little use for the game. At the insistence of his advisers during his campaign for reelection in 1924, he agreed to attend the opening game of the World Series featuring the Washington Senators and the New York Giants. But when the score was tied at the end of the ninth inning and he got up and started to leave, his wife grabbed his coattails, held tight, and begged him to sit down. He did so resignedly, and watched the rest of the game in boredom. More to his liking were cruises with friends on the presidential yacht, the *Mayflower,* down the Potomac River on weekends, during which he could relax. Sometimes, though, Coolidge could be impenetrable on these jaunts. One evening, when Mrs. Dwight W. Morrow and Mrs. Frank B. Kellogg sat next to him at dinner, they couldn't get him to say a word. The next morning, when his wife joined him in the dining saloon for breakfast, Coolidge asked, "And where are my fair ladies?" "Exhausted by your conversation of last evening!" she told him.[9]

Coolidge was embarrassed by the special honors he received whenever he boarded the yacht. The sailors stood at attention, the band played the national anthem, and the steward ceremoniously handed him his yachting hat. "Personally, I do not like all this attention," he told his aunt on one cruise, "but it is for the President of the United States, and I have great respect for the office." In the White House, however, he mandated a fair amount of formality himself. In the evening, Coolidge and his wife always ate in the State Dining Room and dressed for dinner. They expected their son John to dress formally too. Once the lad told his father that he might be late for dinner and wondered whether he couldn't save time by coming dressed as he was then. "This is the President's House," Coolidge told his son. "You dress for dinner and arrive promptly."

The Coolidges did a lot of entertaining when they were in the White House—far more than many of their predecessors—and the President was usually communicative on these occasions, especially when the guests were celebrities: the Prince of Wales, Queen Marie of Rumania, Charles Lindbergh, and Will Rogers. Just before Rogers met Coolidge for the first time, he supposedly made a bet with some friends that he could make the President smile. And so he did, the story goes, by saying, right after the introduction, "I'm sorry; I didn't get the name." But after Rogers hurt Coolidge's feelings later on by trying to imitate his Vermont twang on his radio show, even though he sent a letter of apology when he learned he had offended the President, the latter never forgave him.[10]

Coolidge was never much of a drinker; even before Prohibition he'd only had a beer or two now and then in his younger days. But he was an incessant smoker; he took to cigars as a young man and became a lifelong addict. As President, he received countless boxes of cigars as gifts from admiring citizens, and he sometimes shared them with members of the White House staff. But he always saw to it that White House workers used to smoking twenty-five-cent cigars received twenty-five-centers and those who smoked ten-cent stogies received ten-centers. He insisted on the very best cigars for himself and tended to be stingy with them. Once, the wealthy engineer John Hays Hammond sent him a box of unusually fine cigars and received a nice thank-you note from the President. The next time he visited Coolidge in the White House, Hammond found him smoking one of the fancy gift cigars. As he sat down, Coolidge opened a drawer in his desk, picked out a box of cigars, and held it out to Hammond. It was an inferior brand, so Hammond smiled and said politely, "No, thank you." At this, Coolidge gave a sheepish grin, went into the desk drawer again and this time came up with Hammond's gift box. "Come to think of it," he murmured, "you sent me these. Try one." Hammond gratefully helped himself.[11]

Good cigars, it must be said, seemed to mean more to Coolidge than good books or good music. His cultural interests—art, music, literature—were surprisingly meager in his maturity. As a young man, he received a good classical education at Amherst College, where he mastered several foreign languages ("he could be silent in four languages," it was said), and he was translating Dante's *Inferno* into English while courting his wife. Shakespeare and Milton, more-over, once meant much to him. But when he was in the White House, he read mostly newspapers and an occasional detective story, and had as little interest in the theater as he did in baseball. It was hard to get him to attend a play, White House usher Ike Hoover observed, and he seemed ill at ease during the performance and happy when it was over. And although his wife played the piano, Coolidge's interest in music seems to have been largely abstract. When he was governor of Massachusetts, his wife recalled, he made a speech about music that contained information about composers and musical composi-tion about which he knew next to nothing. "When he joined us at the conclusion of the ceremony," she wrote in her memoirs, "I burst into laughter in which he quietly joined, a little shamefacedly, as I asked him where he obtained all that information. He did not commit him-self." Still, he agreed to become an honorary member of the Philhar-monic Society of New York and announced that music, as "a peaceful presence that will dispel confusion as light dispels darkness," was "an important national asset."[12]

When the Coolidges returned to Northhampton after Herbert Hoover's inauguration in 1929, Coolidge busied himself working on his autobiography, writing a daily paragraph entitled "Thinking Things Over With Calvin Coolidge" for the McClure Newspaper syn-dicate, and serving on the board of the New York Life Insurance Company. He continued to take vacations, but his health was declin-ing and there wasn't much fishing anymore. "I am comfortable," he told a friend toward the end of his life, "because I am not doing any-thing of real account. But any effort to accomplish something goes hard with me. I am very old for my years."[13]

When the Great Crash of the New York Stock Exchange came in 1929, followed by the Great Depression, there was talk of running Coolidge, instead of Hoover, for President in 1932, but Coolidge firmly rejected the idea. "I have done all I can do," he announced. "Others must now carry on the government." After a campaign speech on Hoover's behalf went poorly, he wrote: "I felt I no longer fit in with these times.... When I read of the new-fangled things that are now so popular, I realize that my time in public affairs is past. I wouldn't know how to handle them if I were called upon to do so." Stage star Otis Skinner's wife was persistent. "Oh, Mr. Coolidge," she exclaimed, "I wish it were you that we were going to vote for in November. It would be the end of this horrible depression." Said Coolidge: "It would be the beginning of mine."[14]

☆ ☆ ☆ **30** ☆ ☆ ☆

The Diligent
Herbert Hoover

Herbert Hoover's motto was "Work is Life." He not only worked hard himself; he thought everyone else should do so, too. And he worked just as hard on Sunday as he did during the week, according to the White House's chief usher, Ike Hoover, "with always a slight frown on his face and a look of worry." President Hoover, he decided, "did not know how to play." Every day Hoover received many visitors in the White House, but "it was only an interlude," Theodore Joslin, his secretary, pointed out. "He never stopped working. He never was too tired, physically or mentally, but that he would take on something else. And he was always disgustingly well, so he got no let up because of sickness." Joslin urged the President to forget work now and then and treat himself to some small talk with people, but Hoover was emphatic: "I have other things to do when the nation is on fire."[1]

During the Great Depression, Hoover got in the habit of wolfing down his food. "The President hardly took enough time to eat," recalled one of the women who worked in the executive mansion, "so anxious was he to get back to work." The White House help began placing bets on how long it took Hoover to get through a meal. "He averaged around nine to ten minutes," she reported, "and he could eat a full-course dinner in eight minutes flat." Only for State dinners did he slacken his pace for the benefit of the guests. He foreswore vacations, too, during the Depression, and cut down on the weekend trips he liked to take to Camp Raridan in the Shenandoah Valley to do a little relaxing. "His hobby," it was said, "is having no hobbies."[2]

One beautiful spring weekend, Hoover yearned to slip away to the camp, but having promised a friend to attend the dedication of the Folger Shakespeare Library in Washington, he absolutely refused when his secretary suggested canceling his engagement and going to Raridan instead for a rest. The result was that he spent that gorgeous Saturday indoors, Joslin recalled, "in the office during the morning and at the library in the afternoon." After the dedication, Joslin suggested he hop in a car and head for the camp. "How can I?" exclaimed Hoover exasperatedly. "Because I had to remain in Washington today, I arranged for four important conferences for tomorrow. I must be here anyway, I have got to straighten out that situation in Congress. Otherwise, this country will keep right going on into a tail spin and crack up." On another occasion, however, Hoover's friends, worried about his overwork, induced him to spend the weekend at Camp Raridan. "You can give your friends in the press a thrill this afternoon," Hoover briefly informed Joslin, "by telling them that I am going to the camp to have a sleep. They won't believe it, but I certainly mean it." He took a long nap after arriving at the camp, and then went fishing.[3]

Fishing saved Hoover from being a stick-in-the-mud. It was a lifelong pleasure for him. He once wrote semi-jocularly that fishing was "the chance to wash one's soul with pure air, with the blue water. It brings meekness and inspiration from the decency of nature, charity toward tackle-makers, patience toward fish, a mockery of profits and egos, a quieting of hate, a rejoicing that you do not have to decide a darned thing until next week. And it is discipline in the equality of men—for all men are equal before fish." As a boy, Hoover had found time for baseball, swimming, and exploring the woods with friends in Cedar Springs, Iowa, where he grew up, but fishing was the only sport he stayed with as an adult. He retained fond memories of fishing as a child. "I—and the other boys—fished with worms," he wrote in his memoirs, "until a generous fisherman gave four of us three artificial flies each. They proved powerfully productive in mountain streams. It never occurred to me that they were perishable. In any event I nursed those three flies and used them until all the feathers were worn off—and still the trout rose to them."[4]

Several years before Hoover entered the White House, he became president of the Izaak Walton League of America, where he gave a speech about fishing at his induction into office that became enormously popular; he used his position to promote legislation for the regulation of America's fishing grounds in the interest of all fishermen. Later on, as secretary of commerce in the Harding and Coolidge administrations, he was in charge of the nation's fisheries, and proposed measures to improve fish hatcheries and check the pollution of rivers and streams around the country. Fishing, Hoover insisted, "is not the rich man's sport"; it provides "recreation and soul satisfaction" for all citizens. Though he had used worms as a youngster, he became a devout fly-fisherman as an adult, and preferred freshwater angling to fishing in the ocean. When he was running for President in 1928, he received a letter from a Kentucky businessman announcing, "I will irrespective of politics vote for you if you fish for trout with the fly. But if you use dirty worms like Cal, goodbye." He enclosed two Scotch "Hare-lug" flies with the letter and promised four more if Hoover wanted to give "our bass" a mouthful. But for some reason he did a turnabout at the end of the letter, promising to vote for Hoover, "fly or worm."[5]

Soon after Hoover won the election, he located a mountain site near a good trout stream in Virginia, about one hundred miles from Washington, and developed it into a hideaway, which he called Camp Raridan, to which he could motor on weekends to rest up and do some fishing. When he received criticism for using the taxpayers' money to build himself a playground, he revealed that he had paid five dollars an acre for the land and contributed fifteen thousand dollars for construction material. The Department of Interior stocked the nearby rivers with trout, and during the first year of his presidency

Hoover spent many weekends at the camp, fishing alone and with friends. He may well have been the most skilled of all the Presidents who were fishermen, and he was something of a snob about fly-fishermen. In an article on "The Class Distinction among Fishermen," he put dry-fly casters at the top of the social order, followed by wet-fly casters and then spin casters. Those who used live bait of course ended at the bottom of the list, and he deplored Calvin Coolidge's failure to move from worms to dry flies while he was in the White House.[6]

When the coming of the Great Depression forced Hoover to stay in Washington most of the time, playing medicine ball replaced fishing as a way of getting some exercise and keeping in shape. The games rarely lasted more than a half hour. But Hoover and his friends—government officials and journalists—met at seven o'clock every morning except Sunday to play "Hooverball" games while he was President and they didn't play their last game until March 4, 1933, the day that Franklin D. Roosevelt took his oath as Hoover's successor. The game involved tossing a ten-pound medicine ball over a ten-foot net on a court laid out on the south side of the White House lawn, like a tennis court, and it was scored the way tennis was. Hoover realized the game required less skill than tennis, but he found it faster and more vigorous, and thought it provided more exercise in a shorter time. His friend Will Irwin said the game was "more strenuous than either boxing, wrestling, or football," but not everyone agreed. Afterward the players had fruit juice, toast, and coffee under an ancient magnolia tree, when the weather was good, before dispersing. By common agreement, they carefully avoided political discussions and kept their conversations on the light side.[7]

Hoover, according to Joslin, put "everything he had into the game. The ball at times may have represented to him a political opponent or a caustic critic. Anyway, he would hurl it viciously across the net. Sometimes the opponents would take it. Sometimes it would be so hot they would duck it. Once in a while they could not get out of the way of it, taking it on the ribs, and for days afterward they were reminded of college football injuries." Was the exercise good for Hoover? "Facts speak for themselves," said Joslin. "He did not have one sick day in the four years of his administration. The grueling tasks tired him. Most of the time he was in need of rest he did not take. But he enjoyed the best of health. The games were a great enjoyment to him, except that he did not like getting up at six o'clock in the morning any better than the next man does. The medicine ball encounters each morning were his only break in a strict routine, except for those intervals when he could go fishing."[8]

There was more than work in the office awaiting Hoover when he finished his medicine-ball game and had his breakfast under the magnolia tree. He had people to meet—plenty of them. Hoover and his wife Lou did an astonishing amount of entertaining during their four years in the White House. They entertained "on so extensive a scale," recalled one White House staffer, "that there was company, company, company, and more company!" It was journalist Anne O'Hare McCormick's belief that Hoover thrived on meeting people. "Next to work," she wrote, "he wants people to talk to." Though he was as taciturn as Calvin Coolidge at times, and almost entirely devoid of small-talk skills, she thought he was the most gregarious President of the United States since Theodore Roosevelt. "He had a very hard time when he was by himself," one of the members of the White House staff noticed. He could put off his loneliness "while in the company of others, but I don't think that otherwise he did." During the Hoovers' first three years in the White House, they were said to have dined alone only three times—to celebrate their wedding anniversary.[9]

But the breakfasts, luncheons, and dinners the Hoovers hosted during the Depression mostly involved work. They were the setting for conferences, discussions, and commission reports dealing with measures to revive the nation's faltering economy. Once, there were no less than twenty-six conferences going on in the White House during a single day. It was not uncommon, moreover, for the Hoovers to plan a meal for five people a few days in advance, and then add enough guests to the guest list during the next few days to turn it into a dinner for thirty people, with the White House cook wondering whether there was enough food to go around. At least once, a new recipe emerged from a White House luncheon crisis. According to Ava Long, housekeeper in the Hoover administration, she went shopping in Washington one morning to purchase food for four guests expected for lunch and ended up buying twelve lamb chops. At 12:30, shortly after she returned to the White House, she learned that the number of guests had been increased to forty and that the luncheon was to be served at one o'clock. Used to emergencies like this, she and the chief cook went through the refrigerators, took out everything they found, added the lamb chops, and ran it all through a food chopper. The result was croquettes, which they garnished with mushroom sauce and a scattering of chopped parsley and served with rice. Not only was there enough for all forty guests; there was also a nice commendation for their concoction. One of the guests— a distinguished foreigner—asked for the recipe. Mrs. Long and the cook hastily listed everything they had put into their masterpiece and sent him a recipe that included ham, beef, lamb, onions, and various condiments. To make it official, she called it "White House Supreme," and it gained a brief fame.[10]

During the Depression, the hard-pressed Hoover hated to waste time. He was irked by an Easter Sunday sermon that he felt went on too long, resented it whenever he had to attend public events at which long-winded congressmen were scheduled to speak, and once, after spending a lot of time greeting a new ambassador from Santo Domingo, remarked testily that the smaller the country, the longer the welcoming ceremony. If he refrained from taking much time off for fishing, why, he wondered, should he interrupt his work for activities that simply didn't interest him? The result was that while he was President, Hoover, in some respects an erudite person, hardly ever took time off for reading, attending a play, or accompanying his wife to the opera. Years before, when the Hoovers lived for a time in London, he had enjoyed an active cultural life, going to the theater regularly, visiting museums, sightseeing, and attending lectures. During this time he wrote a mining textbook that was widely adopted in schools and colleges, and supervised the translation and editing of *De re metallica,* a sixteenth-century treatise in Latin on metallurgy that was published in 1912. In the White House, busy as he was, he would never have dreamed of taking the time to attend plays or recitals.[11]

Hoover did, however, have one pleasurable vice (despite his Quaker background) that he carried into the White House: smoking. When he was President, he was "almost always drawing on a long, thick cigar," according to Joslin, "but occasionally pulling on a favorite pipe in the privacy of his study or when out in the open. Smoking was a pleasure to him." Once he received a letter from a Quaker woman in Pennsylvania who had read about his smoking in a newspaper; she implored him to send her a note, in his own handwriting, assuring her that the report was completely false. When Joslin asked Hoover how he was going to reply, he responded, "I am not going to answer it," and reached for another cigar.[12]

Hoover left the White House in an unhappy frame of mind. He was embittered by the blame he received for failing to pull the economy out of the doldrums, and critical of the New Deal programs that Franklin D. Roosevelt, his successor, sponsored to put the American capitalistic system on its feet again. But after taking some time off to rest up, he was soon busy as ever, and before long people were saying that "work was Hoover's leisure." He wrote books defending his record as President, denouncing the New Deal, and presenting his own conservative social philosophy in some detail. He also made speeches, wrote magazine articles, organized relief efforts after World War II, headed commissions to reorganize and streamline the federal government, and founded a presidential library in Cedar Branch, Iowa, as well as the archival Hoover Institution on War, Revolution, and Peace in Stanford, California. He also did a lot of fishing, of course, and toward the end of his life he published a book on the subject entitled *Fishing for Fun—And to Wash Your Soul* (1963). "Fishing is more than fish," he declared; "it is the vitalizing lure to outdoor life." He also presented his favorite quotation from Izaak Walton: "God never did make a more calm, quiet, innocent recreation than angling." And he told a fish story.[13]

In 1929, according to Hoover's story, there was a minor crisis involving a fish soon after he became President. The Penobscot Salmon Club in Maine had sent the first salmon of the season to the White House, as was its custom, and arranged for photographers to take pictures of the President holding the fish for posting in one of the club rooms. But something went wrong this time. When Hoover learned that the directors of the club had delivered the salmon and were waiting to take pictures, he went looking for the fish and found that his new and inexperienced secretary had sent it to the kitchen and the White House cook had just cut off its head and tail and was preparing to broil it. When the cook learned what had happened, she hastily sewed the head and tail back onto the fish, stuffed it with cotton, and sent it out to the White House lawn for photographs. Hoover's secretary suggested he hold the fish horizontally, since it was very fragile, but when he did so one of the photographers told him there was something wrong with it. Taking a closer look, Hoover found that a large piece of cotton was sticking out of the fish. "A president must be equal to emergencies," he wrote. "I carefully held up the fish with my hand over the spot of cotton. The directors of the fishing club, the fish, and I posed before twenty photographers—and each posed for 'just one more' six times. But the cotton kept oozing out of the fish as was proved by the photographs. The fishing club did not use those later editions."[14]

It wasn't the best fish story ever told, but at least it was true.

☆ ☆ ☆ **31** ☆ ☆ ☆

The Resourceful
Franklin D. Roosevelt

In 1933, when Franklin D. Roosevelt became President, he took with him to the White House a jambalaya of hobbies, major and minor, that he had accumulated while growing up as a country squire in Hyde Park, a little town in southeastern New York on the bank of the Hudson River. He hadn't been there long before one of the maids became convinced that he had more hobbies than any other President in a long time. Roosevelt collected stamps, ship models, rare books, and gewgaws; he played poker, bridge, and double solitaire; he sailed the briny sea with zest and knew a lot about boats, ships, and naval vessels; he was an amateur architect who enjoyed designing buildings; he was good at "bird-listening," that is, identifying birds by their songs; he liked movies, and had the good taste to be a fan of Hollywood's incomparable Myrna Loy; he was an energetic and well-schooled traveler; and he was a good swimmer and a competent fisherman.[1]

FDR's "zeal for activity and change," said one White House observer, "sustained him throughout life." He was a man "who was never boring or bored," averred Grace Tulley, his secretary for seventeen years. "He was interested vitally and actively in people, in places and things. He was the kind of man who accumulated what seemed like strange bits of knowledge, but which often fitted into a pattern for wise judgment. His inquisitiveness was aggressive, and he followed his many interests with dogged thoroughness." It was this inquisitiveness—his interest in geography and in the social and economic conditions of people around the world—that led Roosevelt to stamp collecting. He spent a lot of time with stamps when he was confined to bed after being struck down by polio in August 1921, and in so doing added much to the "large accumulation of intellectual capital" that one of his associates noted he brought to the presidency. Whenever he got interested in a particular stamp, he once told his friends, he sent for an encyclopedia, read all the information it contained about the country that issued the stamp, and sometimes went on to acquire books that gave even more details. By the time he became President he had filled forty albums with 25,000 stamps, and during his presidency he continued adding to his collection and started making suggestions for designing commemorative stamps in this country.[2]

Roosevelt's geographical knowledge was prodigious. Once, at a meeting of his cabinet, he reproduced from memory a map of the China coast while his secretary of the navy was forced to send out for maps to locate the places under discussion. In 1940, while FDR was on a fishing trip down the Potomac with some of his ablest advisers, a dispatch arrived with information about British air strikes on the Italian naval base of Taranto. The President was the only one in the party who had ever heard of the place; beyond that, he knew its distances from Gibraltar and Malta and understood its strategic significance. But stamp collecting was a diversion, not a vocation, for FDR. At times, members of his staff noticed, when something was troubling him, he would wheel himself to his office, get out his stamp album, magnifying glass, scissors, and packages of hinges, and go to work. The President, the White House servants murmured, was "busy stamping out a problem."[3]

Not all of Roosevelt's hobbies were as edifying as his stamp collecting. His penchant for collecting figurines—little dogs and pigs and, of course, Democratic donkeys—was playful, not pedantic, and he covered the desk and mantelpiece in his study with them as well as the table next to his bed. When a visitor spied a miniature elephant, made of muslin and stuffed with cotton, that someone had added to the collection, FDR explained that the Republican pachyderm shrank every time it was dry-cleaned, and that it "has another inch off until you can see that he's just about down to GOP size." More important to him than figurines were the ship models and pictures of ships he acquired; his wife, Eleanor, saw to it that the walls of his office were lined with them. She also included prints and lithographs of the Hudson River that she knew were among his favorites. FDR saved Christmas cards, too, keeping what he regarded as the best among the thousands inundating the White House every December.[4]

Roosevelt also collected books; he was more of a book collector than a bookworm. "He was fascinated by an attractive volume," Jonathan Daniels, one of his chroniclers, pointed out, "the binding, the design, the print and the paper—particularly the rarity." As a student at Harvard, Roosevelt began collecting rare editions of highly esteemed old books and sending them home to become part of the library he was developing at Hyde Park. Later on he began concentrating on naval books, documents, and pamphlets, and he succeeded in assembling perhaps the finest collection of its kind in the country. But he read as well as collected, particularly enjoying books on American political and social history as well as those on naval history. "Most important of all...," Daniels emphasized, "he liked to read for fun."[5] He read popular fiction, including *Gone with the Wind,* and, like so many Presidents, found detective stories a good antidote to the high tension of presidential crises. In November 1943, when he went to Teheran for a wartime conference with Winston Churchill and Joseph Stalin, he took along a box containing more than fifty detective stories selected by the Library of Congress. At his bedside in the presidential cottage at Warm Springs, Georgia, in April 1945 was the book he was reading just before he died: John Dickson Carr's *The Punch and Judy Murders.*[6]

But FDR also read for enlightenment while in the White House.

During the late 1930s, he read several new books on American foreign policy, though he found them too academic and antiwar to give
him much guidance. He also read passages in the earnest books Mrs.
Roosevelt marked for his attention and left by his bed.

As a young man, Roosevelt didn't go in for many sports. He rode
horseback and played a little golf, but his first love was sailing. As a
little boy he read books about ships, wrote about them, and built ship
models; and when he became older he learned to sail on the Hudson
River (even in the winter) and along the coast of New England, and
he contemplated making the navy his career. "For some of us…," he
once reflected as an adult, "the sea persists in remaining romance,
vaguely enticing, dimly alluring, always maintaining its distance."
Long before he became President, he came to excel as a skipper and
a navigator, and there were few things that gave him as much pleasure as piloting a ship. A gifted sculptress once suggested that she
could capture him best in a statue presenting him with his hands on
a wheel, with one hand firm and the other hand almost as flexible as
that of a violinist. "He loved to get out on the water," one of his grandsons recalled. "He was somebody who liked adventure, somebody
who was innovative, somebody who could cope with bad weather
conditions—he could cope and he did it well."[7]

Going to sea was one of Roosevelt's chief sources of recreation
during his twelve years as President. He liked ships so much that he
once called for a cabinet meeting aboard the cruiser *Indianapolis.*
"I'm willing to die for the President," grumbled Harold Ickes, secretary of the interior, "but I won't get seasick for him." Until the war
came, FDR usually spent two weekends a month cruising on the Potomac River. His official yacht was the U.S.S. *Potomac,* a former
Coast Guard patrol boat converted into a presidential vessel. On the
Potomac cruises he liked to explore Chesapeake Bay, do some fishing, and catch up on his mail.[8]

Sometimes the voyages Roosevelt took tested his seamanship. In
June 1933, he sought relaxation on the *Amberjack II,* a schooner be-
longing to a friend that was scheduled to cruise leisurely for eleven

days up the New England coast, from Buzzard's Bay on Cape Cod to the island of Campobello, the Roosevelts' summer resort off the coast of Maine. He got off to a tough start. As he was taking the ship into Nantucket Harbor, a fierce "no'easter" hit the area, making entrance into the harbor enormously difficult. But FDR, thoroughly drenched, insisted on staying at the wheel, and succeeded in taking the ship through the twisting entrance, carefully avoiding the dangerous shoals, with no accidents of any kind. Veteran seamen were impressed. "An ordinary yachtsman wouldn't have done it," one of them declared. Afterward, when FDR was invited ashore to rest up, he said he didn't intend to set foot on dry land for two weeks. In 1938, he took a 5,888-mile trip on the heavy cruiser U.S.S. *Houston,* from San Diego to Pensacola, to collect marine specimens. Among the thirty new species, subspecies, and varieties discovered by ichthyologists during the voyage was a new type of royal palm, which they named *Rooseveltia frankliniana.*[9]

Roosevelt was surely our greatest seafaring President, and his love of the sea, like his love for stamps, helped shape his presidency. He was a President who adored the U.S. Navy. He almost went to Annapolis as a young man; and a few years later only his boss, Secretary of the Navy Josephus Daniels, kept him from resigning his position as assistant secretary of the navy and enlisting in the navy after the United States went to war with Germany in 1917. Even before he became President, Roosevelt had developed a deep affection for admirals, seamen, naval history, and naval hospitals. In his younger days he devoured Captain Alfred T. Mahan's famously influential book *The Influence of Sea Power upon History* (1890), and came to share Mahan's conviction that a nation's strength and well-being rested on sea power, and that without it no nation ever rose to first rank in the world. After he became President, seeking funds from Congress for expanding the navy was as important to him as asking for appropriations to support his New Deal measures. He took special pleasure in boarding the navy's warships for visits; he was even happier when he took cruises on them for a week or more.[10]

Roosevelt's sea voyages almost always included fishing, another longtime hobby of his. He went in mostly for deep-sea fishing and excelled at it. Though polio left his legs paralyzed, the muscles of his arms and shoulders were so strong (partly because of his swimming) that he became a first-rate deep-sea angler who could hold his own with obstreperous sea creatures. Once he landed a 100-pound turtle; another time he hauled in a 250-pound shark after a battle lasting about three hours. Fishing off the Cocos Islands in the Pacific one fine day he hooked a sailfish, and while he was struggling with it, another sailfish hit his line, which formed a knot around the beak of the second fish. The first fish managed to escape, but Roosevelt brought in the second one, had it mounted, and then put it on exhibition in the White House with the line still entangled in its beak. "I love to fish and so do you," a friendly angler wrote him in 1937. "You are physically handicapped and so am I. That puts us in the same boat, so to speak, so let's pull a good oar together."[11]

FDR's inability to walk without braces and someone to lean on forced his hosts on sea voyages to arrange special ways for him to make his way around a ship and to get him in and out of the little fishing boats from which he cast his line. In 1935, cabinet member Harold L. Ickes accompanied him when he boarded the *Houston* to do some fishing, and in his diary he described the way the President fared on the vessel during the trip. "When the *Houston* anchored," Ickes wrote, "a companionway was lowered from the leeside of the ship and the President's fishing launch was brought alongside the little platform at the foot of the companionway. Then two men would carry him sideways down the companionway. They would hand him over to Captain Brown" and another officer, and the two men "would swing him around into his armchair. There he would sit and fish. Especially when the water was rough, as it is sometimes, I was a good deal worried about his transshipment of the President to and from his fishing launch. Any misstep or any sudden lurch of the launch might have caused an accident resulting in serious injury to him. But he never seemed to mind." Ickes marveled at the President's calmness during these maneuvers. "Cheerfully he submitted to being wheeled up and down the special ramps that had been installed on the *Houston* for his use, or to being carried up and down like a helpless child when he went fishing. He was an avid fisherman and, with his strong arms and shoulders, he was able to give a good account of himself if he once got a fish on his hook. Fortunately, he was a lucky fisherman also." FDR liked to insist that the objective of his voyages was not to fish, but to get a perspective on problems at a distance from Washington. He nearly always did some work when he was on vacation, but he usually got in some fishing, too.[12]

Even more important to Roosevelt than fishing was swimming. For FDR, swimming was a therapy as well as a sport. After he was stricken by polio in 1921, he looked to hydrotherapy as a means of rebuilding the muscles of his legs so he could walk again. In 1924, he spent six weeks at a health resort in Warm Springs, Georgia, where the water in a big pool fed by an underground spring was rich in minerals and maintained a temperature of 88 degrees. "Every morning I spend two hours in the most wonderful pool in the world," he wrote a friend, "and it is no exaggeration to say that the muscles in my legs have improved to an extent noticeable every way." He ended up buying the place and developing it into a major center for the relief and cure of victims of paralysis.[13]

FDR never regained the use of his legs, but the swimming he did strengthened his arms, back, and shoulders, and provided a pleasurable way of renewing his energy after a long siege of hard work in Washington. It was also an outlet for his sociability and his sense of fun. "To the people at Warm Springs," Secretary Ickes observed, Roosevelt was "a big jolly brother." He played games in the water with other patients, taught the young ones to swim, invented new swimming strokes (which he impishly called a "floating mare," a "swooning swan," and a "popping porpoise") for patients who couldn't master the standard ones, and even formed a water polo team to take on the medical staff. Like Ickes, Secretary of Labor Frances Perkins was struck by the camaraderie at Warm Springs: "He [FDR] was one of them—he was a big brother—he had been through it—he was smiling—he was courageous—he was feeling fine—he encouraged you to try—he said you could do it. 'I did it, you can do it' was the attitude." Roosevelt eventually learned to walk with the aid of braces and two canes, though for a long time he hoped for more. He spent Thanksgiving at Warm Springs while President, and he turned the train ride down from Washington into a pleasure trip by having the engineers proceed at a moderate speed so he could look at the countryside from the window and observe people along the way.[14]

Shortly after Roosevelt became President, the *New York Daily News* launched a fundraising campaign to construct a pool in the White House for the President's use. It was the first presidential pool. At the dedication in June 1933, FDR sat in a wheelchair on one side of the pool and told the workers that he once built a pool himself, "and when I completed it the pool fell in." This pool, though, he was sure would "stand up," and he added: "I want you men to know that this pool will be a big help to me, and it will be about the only air I can get. It will be one of the greatest pleasures for me during my stay in the White House." FDR used the new pool several times a week when he had the time. He was a good swimmer; he was also a playful one. He couldn't resist ducking a friend if he spied him in the White House pool. Once he took a swim with Robert H. Jackson, the Solicitor-General, whose name he had just sent to the Senate for confirmation as a Supreme Court justice. At one point, Jackson mentioned to FDR that a senator from Utah had announced that "no socialists had done as much harm to the American form of government as Jackson's speeches had." At this, Roosevelt, with his mouth half underwater, responded: "Isn't he an old bastard?" But the last word, Jackson wrote later, "produced a spray that was so funny he tried it again and again, each time producing a considerable spray by saying the word, 'bastard,' under water." As Jackson put it: "We disported like a couple of small boys...."[15]

Roosevelt's sense of humor permeated the White House during much of his presidency. It led him to produce comical nicknames for some of his associates: "Tommy the Cork" for Thomas G. Corcoran,

"Harry the Hop" for Harry Hopkins, "Ickes the Ick" for Harold Ickes. It generated awful puns: "I hope you are having a good dime," to a White House mail clerk buried under tons of coins sent him during one of the annual March of Dimes fundraisers for polio therapy at the executive mansion. It led to practical jokes and enabled him to tell some good stories. FDR was a good storyteller. One of his favorites—he called it "The Hyde Park Cataclysm"—centered on the visit of the king and queen of England to the United States in June 1939 and their entertainment by the Roosevelts for a couple of days at Hyde Park. During dinner the first evening, a rickety table behind a screen suddenly collapsed under the weight of dishes with a bang that took everyone by surprise. "Oh," cried FDR, "this is just an old family custom. Think nothing of it." Dinner over, the guests moved to the library, and the butler approached carrying a huge tray laden with drinks. As he started down the steps leading into the room, he missed his footing, dropped the tray, and bounded after it. When he had cleaned up the mess on the floor and sneaked shamefacedly out of the room, FDR roared with laughter and said to the king: "Well, there's number two! What next? These things usually come in threes!" The following day he invited their Majesties over to Val-Kill Cottage for tea and for a dip in the pool. After his own swim, he sat for a while at the edge of the pool, then decided to move to the lawn. Instead of asking the Secret Service men to carry him, he decided to strike out on his own. He began propelling himself backward by planting his palms downward and raising his own weight toward where he wanted to go. After about five self-starting elevations, he landed *kerplunk* in the middle of a huge tray of assorted delicacies, cold tea, cracked ice, and broken glass. "Say," he cried, "why didn't someone yell?" Then, with a big grin, he looked over at the king and cried: "Didn't I tell you there would be a third? Well, now I can relax; the spell is broken." Telling the Hyde Park story afterward he exclaimed, "It's as funny as a crutch!"[16]

Sometimes there was a touch of cruelty in Roosevelt's humor. When Joseph P. Kennedy told him that he wanted to be the first Irish-American ambassador to England, FDR made him drop his trousers, teased him about his bowleggedness, and reminded him that knee britches and silk stockings were required at the Court of St. James and that he would be a laughingstock wearing them. In the end, he promised to make the appointment only after Kennedy received permission to wear striped pants and a cutaway coat when he appeared in the court. Later on, he played a joke on Francis Biddle, the attorney general, who was a conscientious civil libertarian, by pretending he wanted him to help draft a proclamation abrogating all freedom of speech and information in the United States for the duration of World War II. Astonished, Biddle made such an impassioned argument against such action that it was several minutes before he realized that the President was pulling his leg. FDR also took on Winston Churchill on one occasion. At the Big Three conference in Teheran in 1943, he teased Churchill unmercifully at one session in order to get a smile out of Joseph Stalin, and finally succeeded in eliciting one. But at least he had warned his friend Winston ahead of time about what he planned to do.[17]

Despite his merry ways, Roosevelt was deadly serious about his responsibilities as President. "Roosevelt always impressed me by his intense application to the work of his office," wrote U.S. Supreme Court justice Robert Jackson after FDR's death. "But it was not labor; it seemed to be his delight. He often worked at his breakfast in bed, frequently seeing Cabinet members or other aides at that time. He was immersed in work nights, holidays, on weekend cruises, and on vacations." In his 1944 book *What Manner of Man?* journalist Noel Busch singled out Roosevelt as one of those fortunate persons who was able to fulfill himself completely in his job. That job required dealing with all kinds of people, and "there was nothing Roosevelt liked better." His interests, and thus recreations, were manifold: He fished, swam, traveled, played cards, saw baseball games, attended plays, watched movies in the White House, read books, and, of course, entertained countless numbers of people as "America's Number One Host" in the White House, in a friendly and informal but dignified manner.[18]

While Roosevelt was in the White House, he made a ritual out of the cocktail hour. It became an informal little gathering just before dinner at which he could relax and enjoy chatting with his guests and forget his work for a half hour or so. "The cocktail hour was the pleasantest of the day," recalled Grace Tully, "especially if the group was small. Those of us who dined at the White House tried not to discuss any serious business at cocktail time." FDR was the host and made the drinks—usually martinis—and if he thought he had come up with an especially good cocktail, he would take a sip and exclaim, "Yummy, that's good." Two drinks were his limit; he was a heavy cigarette smoker, but was moderate in his drinking. His wife, Eleanor, usually came late; she hated to waste time and took only one drink. Once she violated the unspoken rule against work by bringing some papers with her, handing them to her husband and saying, "Now Franklin, I want to talk to you about this." FDR pushed the work over to his daughter Anna, who was visiting at the time, and cried: "Sis, you handle these tomorrow morning." He resumed his small talk and his wife got into a conversation with one of the guests.[19]

Roosevelt's health began deteriorating during the last year of his presidency, and he was forced to cut down drastically on his activities. The cocktail hour was one of the first to go. But he got to perform the ritual once more toward the end of his life when he went to Yalta in February 1945 for another Big Three conference with Churchill and Stalin. When it came time for cocktails before the first dinner attended by the Big Three and their staffs, FDR was invited to host. He made a pitcher of martinis, and as he passed a glass to Stalin, he had his interpreter tell him that a good martini really needed a twist of lemon. At six the next morning, Robert Hopkins, an American cameraman covering the conference, went to the main entrance hall where the leaders were meeting, and to his astonishment he found just outside the door to the anteroom a huge lemon tree, with some two hundred pieces of fruit on it. Stalin had ordered it flown in from his native Georgia "so the President could serve his martinis with a twist." Stalin wasn't always so obliging.[20]

☆ ☆ ☆ **32** ☆ ☆ ☆

The Plain-Speaking
Harry S. Truman

Harry S. Truman, the plain-spoken man from Independence, Missouri, was a great music lover. He was also a fine pianist. But most Americans didn't know this until one day in 1945, when he was Vice President, he started playing the grand piano in the National Press Club in Washington. The attractive young movie actress Lauren Bacall, then at the start of her career, jumped atop the piano, in a kind of publicity stunt, and sat there dangling her legs over the side while looking mischievously over at Truman as he continued playing. A photographer caught the scene, and the picture soon appeared everywhere. Mrs. Truman was extremely upset; she told her husband she thought "it was time for him to quit playing the piano." He didn't quit, of course, but he was careful about photographers after that.[1]

Truman had undoubted musical talent and, despite rumors, he could play much more than the "Missouri Waltz." The song, in fact, left him cold. "I don't give a damn about it," he once exploded. "But I can't say that out loud because it is the song of Missouri. It's as bad as The Star-Spangled Banner so far as music is concerned." It was serious music that Truman loved, and he showed so much promise as a boy that his mother saw to it that he took piano lessons, eventually locating a teacher in Kansas City who was a professional, trained by some of the best European masters. Young Harry got in the habit of rising at five every morning and practicing the piano for two hours before going off to school. When Ignace Paderewski, the famous Polish composer and pianist, appeared in a concert in Kansas City, Harry's teacher took him to meet the celebrated musician afterward and receive some pointers on playing the "turn" in Paderewski's popular "Minuet in G." Truman mastered many compositions of the nineteenth-century romantic composers Beethoven, Mozart, Chopin, and Liszt, and for a time he contemplated a career as a concert pianist. His teacher always featured him in her student recitals, and both she and his mother were eager for him to go on to advanced training. But at seventeen Truman couldn't afford the expense, and he also knew enough about the piano by this time to realize he wasn't really up to such a career. "I missed being a musician," he said later on, "and the real and only reason I missed being one was because I wasn't good enough." After he got into politics, he liked to put it this way: "My choice early in life was either to be a piano player in a whorehouse or a politician—and to tell the truth there's hardly a difference."[2]

But music continued to be one of Truman's greatest delights after he entered politics, and he was both pianist and politician the rest of his life. No matter where he lived, as county judge, senator, Vice President, or President, he always had a piano at hand, either to play for relaxation or to entertain his friends. In the White House, the three Trumans—Harry, his wife Bess, and daughter Margaret— were "a perfect team at the piano," recalled one of the household workers; "one played, one sang, and one applauded." There was a Steinway in the East Room when the family moved into the White House, but Truman acquired a Baldwin for the other end of the room, insisting there should be an American-made piano there, too. He didn't realize that the Steinway had been made by the American firm of Steinway & Company, not by the German firm, which made the "Hamburg" Steinway piano.[3]

Truman attended concerts with his wife as often as he could, and he became a fan of Josef Lhevinne, the much-acclaimed Russian concert pianist. When he wanted Margaret to take up the piano, too, he acquired a baby grand to give her as a Christmas present. On Christmas morning he tiptoed to her bedroom, woke her up, and said, "Wait until you see what you've got." She rushed off to the parlor and stood there uncertainly. "Well, there it is," he said. "Where?" she wanted to know. "Right in front of you," he cried, and pointed to the piano. Instead of being pleasantly surprised, she was hugely disappointed. "But I wanted a train," she exclaimed, and started crying. Eventually Truman taught his daughter how the play the piano, but she decided to concentrate on singing, not playing.[4]

In July 1945, when Truman went to Potsdam shortly after becoming President for a Big Three conference with Winston Churchill and Joseph Stalin, music became a major part of the entertainment provided for the three leaders and their staffs in the evening after all their hours of hard work during the day. Truman was the first to host a party, and he asked the young American concert pianist Eugene List, then an army sergeant, to put on a recital for the occasion. First, at Stalin's request, Truman played some of Paderewski's "Minuet in G," and then List put on a performance of piano music, mainly Chopin, that thrilled the President. Churchill was bored stiff; his taste in music ran to popular songs and music-hall favorites like "Ta-ra-ra-boom-der-ay." Stalin, however, liked Chopin, and seems to have enjoyed List's performance as much as Truman did. The Russian leader's turn to entertain came next. For his evening, he had two male pianists and two immensely talented female violinists present a lengthy program of classical music that Truman enjoyed but that only prolonged Churchill's agony. For the British prime minister, Stalin's program seemed endless. Finally he got up, went over to Truman, and whispered, "When are you going home?" "What's the matter?" Truman asked. "This is excellent music and I'm having a fine time. I'm going to stay until our host indicates the entertainment is over." "Well," growled Churchill, "I'm bored to tears. I do not like the music. I'm going home." But he stayed to the end anyway and vowed to "get even" with Truman and Stalin. A few days later, when it was his turn to play host, Churchill had the full orchestra of the British Royal Air

Force play noisily throughout the dinner and afterward, "with puckish malice," according to Admiral William Leahy, and he saw to it that his musicians went on until two A.M.[5]

When Truman hosted dinner a second time, he asked List to give another performance and requested Chopin's "Waltz in A Major," one of his favorites, for the program. It so happened that the waltz was not in List's repertoire, so Truman arranged to have the music flown in from Paris, and the young pianist spent an entire day practicing. When the time came for him to play, however, he confessed that he had not had time "to memorize, so if someone in the party would be kind enough to turn the pages for me I would be grateful." A young American officer offered to help, but admitted he couldn't read music. "Just at that point," List wrote later, "the President rose, and with a marvelously sweeping gesture said, 'No, I'll turn the pages myself.'" And he did. "Just imagine!" List told his wife later. "Well, you could have knocked me over with a toothpick! Imagine having the President of the United States turn pages for you!" He added: "That's the kind of man the President is." Truman was pleased that Stalin, if not Churchill, enjoyed List's performance. "The old man loves music," he told his wife afterward. Then he added proudly: "Our boy was good."[6]

Truman loved books as well as music. "Harry Truman's recreation," wrote one of his admirers, "was a stack of books." When he was a boy, his mother gave him a four-volume set of Charles Francis Horne's *Great Men and Famous Women,* which he read and reread, and he came to believe that reading biographies was one of the best ways to learn about the past. In high school he studied Latin and world history, and upon graduation he began making extensive use of the Independence Public Library. "I read everything I could get my hands on—," he said later, "histories and encyclopedias and everything else."[7]

Truman's special interest was military history, beginning with the ancient Greeks, and the factual knowledge he mastered impressed people who knew something about the subject themselves. "When I

first became an aide," George Elsey remembered, "I must confess I
was a little condescending about the President's supposed expertise
in history. After all, I had majored in history at Princeton and Harvard. I soon found out that he was one of the most thoroughly informed men, historically, that I have ever met. When I made a
historical reference or comparison, he not only agreed with me, but
his comments very quickly made it clear that he was familiar with all
the details." When a newspaper compared Henry Wallace (who ran
against Truman in 1948 as a Progressive) to Alcibiades, a Greek demagogue, Truman insisted he was more like Aeschines, another Greek
leader, and gave his reasons. When people quoted the well-known (in
those days) Latin statement *Carthago delenda est* (Carthage must
be destroyed), he enjoyed setting them straight: "*Ceterum censeo
Carthagines esse delendam* (In my opinion Carthage must be destroyed)." One of Truman's favorite books was Marcus Aurelius's
Meditations; he filled his copy with marginal comments and heartily
approved of the Stoic philosopher's belief that the four greatest
virtues were moderation, wisdom, justice, and fortitude.[8]

Truman's view of history was in tune with his times. "Men make
history," he asserted. "History does not make the man." He had no
interest in the social history that was developing in the United States
during his lifetime nor in women's history, despite Horne's section on
"Famous Women" in his biographical collection. For Truman, history
was indispensable to statesmen; it taught lessons. He insisted that he
looked to the past for knowledge to guide him when he had important decisions to make, particularly in the field of foreign affairs.
"Readers of good books, particularly books of biography and history," he once wrote, "are preparing themselves for leadership. Not
all readers become leaders. But all leaders must be readers." Truman
rarely went in for light reading, but when he did it was usually "who-
dunits." Erle Stanley Gardner, creator of the character Perry Mason,
always sent Truman (as he did FDR) autographed copies of his latest
detective novel.[9]

Truman didn't go in much for sports. When he was a boy, his eyesight was so bad that he had to wear expensive thick glasses that pre-

vented him from playing baseball and football and from roughhous-
ing with the other boys in town. Once in a while he acted as umpire
for their baseball games, but mainly he "just smiled his way along,"
one of his grade-school teachers recalled. As a young man he joined
the Kansas City Athletic Club and learned to swim, using a special
sidestroke that enabled him to keep his head—and his glasses—
out of the water. He went fishing now and then but his heart wasn't
in it—partly, his friends thought, because he didn't like to eat fish.
Once, when he was Vice President, Speaker of the House Sam Ray-
burn lured him into some fishing in a little lake in eastern Maryland,
but they hadn't been at it very long before Truman fell out of the boat
into the lake's icy waters and spent the rest of the trip wrapped in
blankets and shivering at one end of the boat. "You just go on and
catch the fish, Sam," he sighed, "and I'll do the swimming." His wife
Bess was a good angler, though, and one day, when the *Kansas City
Star*'s Brent Fraser offered to take her fishing, Truman decided to go
along. After she caught several trout, she handed the fishing rod to
her husband, but he declined to make use of it. Still, when Fraser decided to take a picture, Truman grabbed the fish out of Bess's hands
and posed triumphantly with them. "We all had to laugh about that
one," Fraser said afterward. "He was a politician. He knew how to get
those votes."[10]

Truman's chief exercise was walking. He began taking daily walks
when he was a county judge in Missouri, kept them up when he was
a senator and Vice President, and hewed closely to the walking routine as President. "Well, you know," he once explained, "when you're
on a job where you have to sit down all day, the best thing you can
possibly do is to walk, especially after you're forty years old, because
that exercises all the muscles of the body, a walk does. Legs were put
on us to use. The present-day youngsters, and most people, will get
in a car to go a block. They'd be much better off if they'd walk."
When he was President, he usually rose at five A.M., read the newspapers, shaved, dressed, and then took a brisk two-mile walk, accompanied by his Secret Service guards, at the pace he learned in the
army during World War I: 120 steps a minute.[11]

At first Truman took his fitness walks without being noticed, but when newspapers began running stories about his outings, reporters and photographers, as well as curious sightseers, started showing up and trailing along, as best they could, while he moved at a rapid clip down the streets. For a while Truman tried changing his route frequently, but that didn't help. Finally he arranged for the presidential limousine to pick him up in the morning and take him to different places on the outskirts of Washington where he could do his walking in peace and quiet. One of his admirers sent him a pedometer labeled "For President Truman and his steps forward." Truman thanked him. "The very next morning after I received it," he told the donor, "I rung up two and a half miles on it. I appreciate your sending it to me because now I can keep track of just how far I go." Sometimes when Truman finished his walk, he took a short swim in the White House pool before joining his wife and daughter for breakfast and then heading for his office. Truman's physician, Dr. Wallace Graham, was convinced that the Missourian was in better condition when he left the White House than when he entered it, "and, in my opinion, walking had a lot to do with it."[12]

There were other diversions. Truman arranged for the construction of a horseshoe pit—the very first one—on the White House grounds, and after being presented with horseshoes plated with bronze and chromium, he invited friends to join him in trying to pitch ringers. He also did some bowling on the two lanes that the people of Missouri paid to have installed in the basement of the West Wing. But for relaxation, Truman much preferred playing poker with his buddies. He played for small stakes and didn't seem to care whether he won or lost; it was the companionship and the breezy talk of the poker sessions that appealed to him. Sometimes he invited people he was considering for appointments to play in order to size them up and see how they stood up to the kidding that went on.[13]

At first the games took place in the White House, but when Truman's enemies began moaning about the immorality of having poker games there, he shifted them to the *Williamsburg,* the presidential yacht on which he liked to take cruises, and to Key West, where he spent his vacations. One of the regular players was Chief Justice Fred M. Vinson, an old Missouri friend whom Truman appointed to the U.S. Supreme Court in 1946. Unlike Truman, Vinson took the game seriously, and once, when they were playing, Truman dealt him a card that upset him so much that he burst out, "You son of a bitch!" He was instantly repentant. "Oh, Mr. President, Mr. President...!" he wailed, while everyone in the room exploded in laughter. Truman teased him about lèse majesty for a long time after that.[14]

Dean Acheson, secretary of state from 1949 until 1953, was impressed with Truman's capacity for hard work and also by the way he went to sleep "as soon as his head touched the pillow, never worrying, because he couldn't stay awake long enough to do so." On normal days he was in his office at seven A.M. and, with time out for lunch followed by a short nap, stayed until five or six in the afternoon. Dinner with his family came at seven. If he didn't have paperwork to do after dinner, he spent the evening with his family, chatting, listening to music, or taking in a movie, usually a musical picked by Margaret. Before dinner, however, came cocktails. FDR had his martinis; the Trumans had their old-fashioneds. It took a while, though, before they got what they wanted in the White House. The first few times the drinks were too sweet for their tastes, and it wasn't until Mrs. Truman complained that "they make the worst old-fashioneds here I've ever tasted" that the butler began serving the big splashes of bourbon over ice the way they liked. At dinner, the family tended to kid around a lot at the table before Truman returned to his office for more work, and at one dinner they reduced the White House butler to helpless laughter when they got into a friendly little watermelon-seed fight after dessert was served.[15]

Truman's easy informality made him popular with the White House help. He never talked down to them, treated them with respect and consideration, and always introduced them to his guests—sometimes eminent personages—when they happened to be in the same room. The Trumans, according to Lillian Rogers Park, daughter of one of the White House employees, were "the most informal of any of the First Families I have known or heard Mama talk about. They did nothing for show; they simply behaved naturally."

But Truman wasn't always in an amiable mood; he had a short temper, and he couldn't help blowing up when he thought people criticized his policies unfairly. He was even more touchy about attacks on members of his family, for Bess and Margaret were, at heart, his whole life. After Republican congresswoman Clare Boothe Luce of Connecticut took some cracks at Mrs. Truman in a speech in Congress, he omitted her from the guest list when entertaining congressional members at the White House, even though her husband, Henry R. Luce, the founder of *Time, Life,* and *Fortune,* begged him to relent. He was even angrier when the *Washington Post* music critic wrote a harsh review of Margaret's singing recital in Washington in 1951. His letter to the critic, widely publicized, became one of the most famous he ever wrote: "You sound like a frustrated old man who never made a success, an eight-ulcer man on a four-ulcer job and all four ulcers working. I never met you, but if I do you'll need a new nose and a supporter below. Westbrook Pegler, a guttersnipe, is a gentleman compared to you. You can take that as more of an insult than a reflection on your ancestry." The first draft, Truman later revealed, was even angrier than the letter he sent. Fortunately for everybody concerned, he put most of his stormy letters in his files rather than in the mailbox.[16]

In 1953, after leaving the "Great White Jail," as the Trumans liked to call it, Truman returned to Independence. His health continued good, and he kept himself busy writing his memoirs, dictating letters (almost forty a day), giving speeches, and, of course, taking daily walks. During a trip to Europe with his wife in 1956, he had the exquisite pleasure of visiting Salzburg, Austria, the birthplace of Mozart, and playing some Mozart himself on the ancient organ in the Salzburg Cathedral, visiting the composer's home and playing his pianoforte, and then attending a concert of Mozart's music in his honor.

"I've never attended a happier or more pleasing music event," he wrote afterward.[17]

While Truman was in Europe, he had another happy experience: He visited Bernard Berenson, the distinguished art critic, when he was in Italy. Truman didn't pretend to be an expert on painting. He was familiar with the art museum in Kansas City and had spent time in the National Gallery in Washington, however, and he knew what he liked: Holbein, Rubens, Leonardo da Vinci, and his favorite painting, Charles Keck's *Stonewall Jackson* in Charlottesville, Virginia. He also knew what he disliked: modern art. "Any kid," he said scornfully, "can take an egg and a piece of ham and make more understandable pictures." His preference, he said, was for "beautiful pictures, landscapes, and portraits that look like people. We see enough squalor. I think art is intended to uplift the ideals of the people, not pull them down." But when he met Berenson, he listened carefully when the lively old man, then ninety-one, "explained to us what to look for in painting," and he acknowledged that it was a big help "when we got to those museums in Florence and elsewhere."[18]

Berenson was impressed by the former President. "Harry and his wife lunched yesterday," he wrote in his diary for May 28, 1956. "Came at one and stayed till three. Both as natural, as unspoiled by high office as if he had gone no further than alderman of Independence, Missouri. In my long life I have never met an individual with whom I felt so instantly at home. He talked as if he had always known me, openly, easily, with no reserve (so far as I could judge). Ready to touch on any subject, no matter how personal. I always felt what a solid and sensible basis there is in the British stock of the U.S.A. if it can produce a man like Truman. Now I feel more assured about America than in a long time. If the Truman miracle can still occur, we need not fear even the McCarthys."[19]

☆ ☆ ☆ 33 ☆ ☆ ☆

The Golf-Playing
Dwight D. Eisenhower

Dwight D. Eisenhower loved to play golf and go fishing, and he was good at both. He also enjoyed playing bridge in his spare time and reading westerns. But he never neglected his work to do any of these things. At heart, Eisenhower was a duty-centered person; he felt obliged to do the best he could when he was in the army as well as when he was President. One day, when he was a young officer, he had to leave home suddenly on an assignment, shortly after marrying. He explained to his wife, Mamie, "My country comes first. You come second."[1]

Eisenhower put his country before himself, too. He vowed "to perform every duty given to me to the best of my ability—no matter what its nature." In a thorough examination of Eisenhower's health while he was President, writer Robert E. Gilbert went so far as to say that Ike's "drive to do his duty was so obsessive as to be compulsive." In the army, he put in such long hours at times that his commanders had to order him to take vacations; and in the presidency, the demands on his energies frequently strained his health so much that he was forced to take vacations. Despite his heavy smoking (which he gave up, on doctor's orders, in 1949) and his "Type A" personality, he kept in fairly good shape until the end of World War II.[2]

Eisenhower was a natural athlete. He took to sports readily and did well at whatever he tried. "It would be difficult," he once said, "to overemphasize the importance that I attached to participation in sports." When he was a little boy growing up in Abilene, Kansas, he once got to talking with a buddy about what they wanted to do when they grew up. "I told him that I wanted to be a real major league baseball player, a genuine professional, like Honus Wagner. My friend said he'd like to be president of the United States." The upshot: "Neither of us got our wish." At his high school in Abilene, Ike, it was said, became the baseball team's best hitter and the football team's best tackler. At West Point, he went out for boxing and track as well as for baseball and football, did well at all four sports, and came to be called the "Kansas Cyclone." But his major sport was football; he hadn't played in many games for Army before a *New York Times* sportswriter singled him out as "one of the most promising backs in Eastern football." Unfortunately, Eisenhower injured his left knee so badly in one of the games that he was forced to give up playing. His disappointment was overwhelming. He plunged into gloom for a while, started smoking cigarettes and playing poker for stakes (both forbidden by the academy), and even contemplated leaving West Point. But he finally came to terms with the situation and began filling in for cheerleaders at the games, giving speeches at pep rallies, and serving as coach for the junior varsity squad.[3]

Eisenhower remained a loyal Army fan the rest of his life. There was only one problem: When he became President and attended the Army–Navy game, he was expected to be neutral, so he arranged to sit with the midshipmen on the Navy side of the stadium for the first half of the game and then, at half time, walk across the field to sit with the cadets for the second half. Just before the Army–Navy game in 1958, he sent a telegram to the Navy team offering his "best personal wishes," and then a telegram to the Army squad mentioning what he had told the Navy, adding: "The requirements of neutrality are thus scrupulously observed. But over a span of almost half a century, on the day of the Game, I have only one thought and only one song: 'On, brave old Army team.'"[4]

Eisenhower's knee injury forced him to give up baseball, at which he had been quite good, as well as football, but he maintained his interest in the sports and enjoyed attending baseball as well as football games after leaving West Point. In 1953, however, shortly after his first inauguration as President, he decided to skip the opening game of the baseball season in Washington so he could spend a golfing holiday in Augusta, Georgia. His decision produced a great deal of disappointment among baseball fans, who had expected Eisenhower, like his predecessors in the White House, to throw out the first ball of the season. "The major leagues had counted on Ike to throw out the first ball," wrote Dan Daniel in *The Sporting News*. "They have long regarded the presence of the Chief Executive at the Griffith Stadium inaugural as a boost for the entire game, marking White House approval of our National Pastime." Fortunately for Eisenhower, the opening game was cancelled because of rain, so after playing golf in Augusta that day he returned to Washington in order to throw out the first ball of the rescheduled game.[5]

Golf came first with Eisenhower when he was President; it was clearly his favorite sport. But he was a latecomer. He didn't start golfing until 1927, when he was in his thirties, attending the Fort Leavenworth Command School in Kansas, and although he continued to play in the 1930s, when he was stationed in Washington and in the Philippines, and during World War II, when he was Supreme Allied Commander in Europe, he didn't get hooked on the game until he was back in Washington after the war as Army Chief of Staff. Eisenhower was in his fifties by then, but, encouraged by his wife, who knew it helped reduce stress, he took lessons, practiced regularly, and worked hard to become a good player. When he ran for President in 1952, he got in as many games as he could during the campaign, and, his supporters claimed, there was a big golf-playing voter turnout on his behalf. Right after his election, Eisenhower flew to Augusta for a ten-day vacation that included golf every day at the Augusta National Golf Club. "I enjoy and need the exercise from occasional golf practice," he once said, "and this makes it easy for me to step out a half hour or so whenever I find the time."[6]

Eisenhower found the time—plenty of it—in the interstices of his work schedule. Soon after he became President, he went out to the White House's south lawn to practice chipping balls, and to his dismay, crowds gathered at the fence in front to watch him. He felt impelled to either duck into the police shack nearby and wait until they were gone or go down to the little gymnasium on the ground floor of the West Wing to hit balls into a special net he had set up there. "You know," he mused, "once in a while I get to the point, with everyone staring at me, where I want to go way back indoors and pull down the curtain." In 1954, however, the U.S. Golf Association installed a putting green, with a small sand trap on one side, in a less exposed area on the lawn, just outside the President's office, where he could practice late afternoons during the week with no gawkers around. But there were squirrels. Before long, the little creatures decided the new green was a handy storage area for their acorns, and they began digging holes all over the place. Eisenhower asked the Secret Service men to shoot them, but they informed him they weren't authorized to do so. He then instructed the White House gardeners to set traps to catch them. At this point, Congress intervened. In the Senate, Richard L. Neuberger pleaded with the President to tolerate "a few scratches and bumps on your private putting green in order to continue a fine and colorful heritage of White House squirrels." A few Democrats organized a "Save the White House Squirrels Fund" to pay for an aluminum fence to ring the green, and Eisenhower's aides announced they would stop trapping the squirrels.[7]

Eisenhower's favorite course was Augusta National, where the club members built a large, fancy "cabin" for the President and his wife to stay in when they vacationed there. He also played twice a week at the Burning Tree Country Club near Washington, and just about every day when he went to the presidential hideaway in the Catoctin Mountains of Maryland, which FDR had called Shangri-la but which Eisenhower renamed Camp David. Some of his critics complained that he spent too much time on golf, but his physician, Major-General Howard Synder, vigorously defended him. "Golf is a tonic for the president," he pointed out. "It is good for his nerves and muscle tone, and it takes his mind off the anxieties that confront him daily. I say he should play whenever he gets the chance." Eisenhower usually forgot his troubles when he was on the links, but every so often, he admitted, he found himself thinking about the affairs of state "right in the middle of my backswing." James Hagerty, his press secretary, acknowledged that Eisenhower couldn't always keep his mind on the ball. "You can see it," he said. "He'll be going along playing really well—par, par, bogey, par, bogey. All of the sudden his mind comes off golf. Suddenly he's thinking about Quemoy or Lebanon or Berlin. Then it's triple bogey, double bogey and we all might as well go home. It isn't going to be any more fun that day."[8]

Eisenhower usually shot in the middle 80s, and he was elated when he made the low 80s and miserable if he went up to the 90s. He kept his scores secret when he was President because he thought it would spoil the fun if the public was following his every move on the golf course. His partners were businessmen, government officials, and sometimes foreign dignitaries. It was Eisenhower's belief that a friendly round of golf with an official from abroad was sometimes more helpful than a formal conference was in developing fruitful relations with other countries. He played with celebrities, too, including Bob Hope, as well as professional golfers like Bobby Jones and Arnold Palmer. "The President is companionable," said Ben Hogan, "good fun to play with. He has the trick of making you feel at ease. He convinces you, without saying so, that he likes the game as much as you do."[9]

But Eisenhower didn't like to lose. "He gets pretty steamed up when he misses a shot," revealed one partner, "and he curses a little under his breath." Sometimes, said another partner, he uses "five-star profanity—but softly." Still, he had a nice sense of humor about his playing. After he recovered from a heart attack in 1955 and went back to the links, his doctors ordered him not to play so intently, and he began telling partners: "You're going to hear a heck of a lot of laughter today. My doctor has given me orders that if I don't start laughing instead of cussing when I miss those shots, he's going to stop me from playing golf. So every time I miss a shot you're going to hear a haw-haw-haw."[10]

Eisenhower did much for the advancement of golf in the United States after World War II. In a letter he issued to "golfers and fellow duffers," early in his first administration, he wrote: "While I know that I speak with the partisanship of an enthusiast, golf obviously provides one of our best forms of healthful exercise accompanied by good fellowship and companionship. It is a sport in which the whole American family can participate—fathers and mothers, sons and daughters alike. It offers healthy respite from daily toil, refreshment of body and mind." During his eight years in the White House, Eisenhower played nearly eight hundred rounds of golf, and in so doing inspired millions of Americans to take up the game. "People like to follow the leader," the manager of the public golf courses in Washington pointed out. "The papers keep talking golf. People start talking golf and then start playing it. I tell you, the President really has given the game a shot in the arm....Ever since he went into the White House, all you hear is golf, golf, golf." In 1953, when Eisenhower became President, there were some 3.2 million golf players in the country; in 1961, when he left the White House, there were twice that many.[11]

Eisenhower didn't do nearly as much for fishing, the world's oldest sport, as he did for golf, but anglers throughout the country followed his piscatorial peregrinations as President with zest, sending him letters of commentary and commendation and showering him with gifts: rods, reels, spinners, and flies; recipes for "Trout Eisenhower"; and even fish. Eisenhower fished mostly in Maine, South Dakota, Maryland, Georgia, and Wisconsin, and, to his discomfiture, sometimes attracted crowds of curious spectators. Once, when he and former President Herbert Hoover went on a fishing expedition in Colorado, a flock of reporters showed up for the fun, and Hoover was as irritated as Eisenhower was. "I used to believe," he murmured, "there were only two occasions in which the American people had regard for the privacy of the president—in prayer and in fishing. I now detect you have lost the second part."[12]

Eisenhower was a fly-fisherman who liked to tie his own flies; he also used a bamboo rod and reel that had to be wound by hand. "I used a bamboo rod when I started to fish as a kid," he explained, "and I just got used to it. I prefer the old-fashioned reel because I like to play my fish—wind the line myself. As for the dry fly, I feel it's a more natural way to fish for trout." One day, the members of his cabinet presented him with an assortment of colorful flies to show their affection for him. Enormously pleased, he couldn't wait to try them out, so he tied one to a line and made a gentle cast across the room. Sad to say, the hook got caught in the seat of press secretary Jim Hagerty's pants, and no one was able to detach it. The President finally cut the line with a pocket knife, and Hagerty, it was said, left the room resignedly with the fly still attached to his trousers.[13]

Eisenhower didn't like losing fish any more than he liked losing at golf. When one of his fishing companions was asked if the President ever lost a fish, he exclaimed, "You betcha he does. Just like anybody else." "What then?" he was asked. "Well, let's put it this way," said the friend. "If Ike loses a fish, he has more than a few well-chosen words at his command to express his disappointment. After all, he was in the army for forty-odd years." Still, Eisenhower knew, as Herbert Hoover and most other fishermen did, that catching fish wasn't all there was to fishing. In June 1955, when he went fishing with Judge Milford R. Smith in Vermont, they didn't have much luck with the trout, but they had a wonderful time enjoying the great outdoors. Afterward, the judge pronounced the President a real fisherman. "Every detail of the setting in which he fished registered itself upon his senses and received its commentary; a stand of birches gleaming in their whiteness against the dark of the evergreens, a hawk circling in the hot sky, even the caddis nymphs dislodged from their rock homes by boot-shod feet." The judge was convinced Eisenhower enjoyed himself even though he caught no fish; after all, when they parted, he said it was "the most relaxing time he has had in many long months." What was it like fishing with a President? Fishing with Ike, the judge declared, was like "fishing with your best friend, taking it for granted that this friend of yours is as fine an angler, sportsman and gentleman as you ever knew."[14]

Eisenhower had his favorite indoor indulgences as well as his enjoyable activities outdoors, and the one he liked best was card-playing. He took up poker when he was at West Point, played it during his years in the army, and supplemented his army pay for years with his poker earnings. He finally gave up the game in middle age, partly, he joked, because his fellow officers were losing more than they could afford, and turned to bridge. Eisenhower's bridge game, General Mark Clark said, was like everything else he did: "He had to excel. He always had to excel." General Andrew J. Goodpaster, one of Eisenhower's longtime aides, said that he played bridge "very much in poker style" and that he was "a tremendous man for analyzing the other fellow, and what line he can best take to capitalize on or exploit the possibilities, having figured the options open to the other man." When he became President, Eisenhower played with Democrats, if they were good players, as well as with Republicans, and he liked to get a foursome together to play either Saturday evening or Sunday afternoon while Mamie and her friends were playing canasta. Back in the 1950s, Ely Culbertson, the bridge expert, said he thought the President was one of the best players in America.[15]

Eisenhower was good at cooking, too. He learned it from his mother when he was a kid, making vegetable soup, baking potatoes, broiling steaks, and even turning out decent peach, apple, and cherry pies. At his first army post, Fort Sam Houston, he volunteered for the Cooks and Bakers School, and though he didn't absorb enough to qualify as a cook, he did learn how to feed large groups of army men. After leaving the service, he enjoyed taking over as cook when he and Mamie (who never learned to cook) were entertaining their friends. When he was president of Columbia University (1948–1950), he received as much attention from the press for his chicken soup recipe as for public statements he made as a university president. When he was in the White House, Eisenhower liked to putter around in the kitchen, or, better still, to invite some close friends to dinner and take them to the solarium on the White House roof to broil steaks and roast corn in the husks on a portable charcoal grill. Exclaimed the United Press's Merriman Smith: "The man is a walking recipe book!" The President became famous for his vegetable soup, charcoal-broiled steaks, and cornmeal pancakes, and newspapers and magazines featured shots of him broiling fish or steaks over a fire. Cooking, he confessed in his memoirs, "gave me a creative feeling."[16]

Eisenhower felt creative about painting, too. He came late to the art. In 1945, when Thomas E. Stephen, a New York artist, began doing a portrait of Mamie, Ike sat and watched one session; then, when his wife and Stephens stepped out of the room for a short break, he decided to do a little painting of his own on another canvas. The next thing he knew he was making a copy of Stephens's unfinished portrait of Mamie; it was, he said later, "my first grand venture into 'art.'" Instead of making fun of it on his return, Stephens asked to have Eisenhower's handiwork as a souvenir, encouraged him to do more painting, and a few days later sent him a package containing everything he needed, "except ability," to start painting. Eisenhower held back for a week or so, and then plunged in with a will and a way, and found "the attempt to paint absorbing." At Columbia, he used the penthouse of the building where he and Mamie lived as his studio, and in the White House, he arranged for a little room off the elevator on the second floor to be his place to paint. He also did some painting at his farm in Gettysburg, Pennsylvania, which he and his wife bought for retirement. After a while, he tried landscapes and still life, but, "with magnificent audacity," as he put it, "I have tried more portraits than anything else."[17]

Eisenhower deprecated his achievements. "I attempt only simple compositions," he wrote in one of his books. "My frustration is complete when I try for anything delicate. Even yet I refuse to refer to my productions as paintings. They are daubs, born of my love of color and in my pleasure at experimenting, nothing else. I destroy two out of each three I start. One of the real satisfactions is finding out how closely I come to depicting what I have in mind...." But he was serious about his work, and he regretted having so little time for it in his busy schedule. One evening in 1954, Robert Kutler, one of his aides, came by to discuss an urgent piece of business that needed immediate action, and he found the President dressed in sport shirt, slacks, and a white linen cap, going from one of his paintings to another, trying out different kinds of retouching varnish. "Hello, Bobby," said Eisenhower, "which one of these do you think is best?" Then, without looking up, he started doing some work on a portrait he was doing of Mamie's sister, and all he talked about for the next few minutes was painting. Finally he looked up and asked, "What did you come over for?" When Kutler explained the problem, Eisenhower went over it in some detail for the next half hour or so, his eyes on the canvas all the time, and then gave his aide exact instructions on what to do.[18]

Eisenhower eventually did portraits of all the members of his family, including grandchildren, and also of people he admired, including George Washington, Abraham Lincoln, and Winston Churchill. Beginning in 1954 he began using reproductions of his portraits on Christmas cards; Washington appeared on the first one, and his own painting of St. Louis Creek, his favorite trout stream in the Rockies, was on the next. For Eisenhower, painting had only one "defect": It provided no exercise. "I've often thought what a wonderful thing it would be," he said, "to install a compact painting outfit on a golf cart."[19]

Music and the theater played a small part in Eisenhower's life, and he was never much of a movie buff. But he arranged to have current movies shown in the White House. His preference was for westerns, though he liked war pictures and sports films, too. "Providing Mr. Eisenhower with enough Westerns became a major task for the Usher's office," recalled J. B. West, chief usher for the White House when Eisenhower was President, "because he had seen them all, per-haps three or four times." When the Russian leader Nikita Khrushchev visited the United States in 1959, Eisenhower told him about his af-fection for western movies. "I know they don't have any substance to them," he said, "and don't require any thought to appreciate, but they always have a lot of fancy tricks. Also, I like horses." One of his fa-vorites was *High Noon* (1952); he saw it three times. Eisenhower had his dislikes as well as likes when it came to movies. He didn't think highly of films starring Audie Murphy (the actor who was the most decorated American soldier during World War II) because he thought Murphy was too small "to beat up the big guys" in his westerns. He didn't like Robert Mitchum either, because the actor was once ar-rested for taking drugs. One night he started watching a movie, but as soon as Mitchum appeared on the screen, he got up and left.[20]

When it came to television, the Eisenhowers enjoyed some of the popular shows of the 1950s, such as *I Love Lucy,* and sometimes watched the evening news while eating dinner on TV trays. As for music, Mamie was an amateur pianist (she played by ear), and oc-casionally played for songfests at the White House, all the time ad-monishing, "Don't screech, Ike!" The Eisenhowers entertained such serious musicians as pianist Artur Rubenstein, violinist Isaac Stern, and conductor and composer Leonard Bernstein at the White House, but their tastes ran to bandleaders like Fred Waring and Lawrence Welk and to Broadway show tunes. One night, when Welk played for a White House party, Eisenhower tapped his foot vigorously to the music of "I've Got Spurs That Jingle, Jangle, Jingle," and then asked whether Welk knew "The Yellow Rose of Texas." "Well," said Welk, "if we don't, we can certainly make it up." He and his band went on to do just that. No one recognized the tune; this time Eisenhower re-frained from tapping his foot. In any case, his favorite White House entertainments were the little stag dinners he initiated shortly after his inauguration, which included some artists, writers, scientists, and labor leaders, but mainly businessmen, with whom he could have in-formal chats about everything under the sun, important and trivial, until eleven or so at night. When women complained about being excluded from the parties, he began holding special breakfasts for women over which he quietly presided.[21]

Eisenhower didn't do much reading for pleasure when he was in the White House. Painting may well have replaced reading for him in his maturity. Once an avid reader of serious books, his extracurricular reading as President was mostly limited to western novels in paperback. As a youngster, though, he always had his nose in a book. He read so much, in fact, that his mother once took away his books and locked them in a closet. But he found the key, buried himself in his books whenever his mother was away, and, like Harry Truman, amassed a great deal of information about the ancient world in his youth. "Since those early years," he wrote years later, "history of all kinds, and certainly political and military, has always intrigued me mightily." Eisenhower's love for history produced an entry in his high school's yearbook describing him as "our best historian and mathematician," and predicting that someday he would be a professor of history at Yale. West Point stifled his interest in history; it was taught, he recalled, "as an out-and-out memory course." Later on, when he was stationed at Camp Gaillard, he encountered a learned general named Fox Conner, who took a liking to him and revived his love of history by suggesting books for him to read and spending hours discussing them with him. For three years, Eisenhower said, "life with General Conner was a sort of graduate school in military affairs and the humanities."[22]

Reading history, Eisenhower insisted, "was an end in itself, not a search for lessons to guide us in the present or to prepare me for the future." It was a labor of love. "I read history for history's sake," he said, "for myself alone." Gradually he expanded his interest in ancient and European history to include American history, with special emphasis on Abraham Lincoln and the Civil War. When he was President, he read Bruce Catton's books on the subject and filled the bookcases in his office with the works of Thomas Jefferson and Abraham Lincoln so he could dip into them whenever he had a little spare time. He urged members of his cabinet to read Lincoln for political insights. His favorite passage by Lincoln had to do with government: "The legitimate object of government, is to do for a community of people, whatever they need to have done, but can not do at all, or can not so well do, for themselves—in their separate, and individual capacities. In all that the people can individually do as well for themselves, government ought not to interfere."[23]

☆ ☆ ☆ **34** ☆ ☆ ☆

The Dashing Young
John F. Kennedy

John F. Kennedy was a great sports-lover. As a youngster he dreamed
of becoming a famous quarterback someday, and as President he followed college and professional football with as much eagerness as he
had when he was growing up. He also listened to major boxing
matches on the radio, and on one occasion arrived late at a special
White House cultural event because he couldn't bring himself to
leave the radio until the final knockout. Kennedy was a baseball fan,
too. He befriended Boston Red Sox great Ted Williams and St. Louis
Cardinals legend Stan Musial, depended on his friend Dave Powers—his so-called "Undersecretary of Baseball"—for baseball information, and once kept a foreign prince waiting in the White House
while he stayed to the end of a game he was attending in a new Washington ballpark.[1]

When it came to baseball, Kennedy was regarded as a "great open-
ing President." On April 10, 1961, shortly after his inauguration, he
threw what was regarded as the longest and hardest first ball ever
tossed by a President, and it ended up in the hands of the White
Sox's Manuel Joseph ("Jungle Jim") Rivera. Rivera walked over to the
President's box to get the ball signed, as was the custom, but when
Kennedy carelessly scribbled his name on it, Rivera cried playfully:
"What kind of garbage college is that Harvard, where they didn't

even teach you to write? What kind of garbage writing is this? What is this garbage autograph? Do you think I can go into any tavern in Chicago's South Side and really say the president of the United States signed this baseball for me? I'd be run off." Then he moved closer to Kennedy and exclaimed: "Take this thing back and give me something besides your garbage autograph." Kennedy was highly amused by Rivera's kidding, and he promptly took the ball and signed it carefully this time. "You know," said Rivera, "you're all right." *Sports Illustrated* called Kennedy "The Man Who Loved Sports."[2]

Kennedy took a special interest in health and fitness when he was President, insisting that a strong nation required citizens who were physically fit. "Our growing softness," he warned, "our increasing lack of physical fitness, is a menace to our security." To his delight, early in his presidency he had an opportunity to promote fitness in the country. It so happened that David M. Shoup, commandant of the U.S. Marine Corps, came across an order issued by Theodore Roosevelt in 1908 requiring junior officers to show that they could march fifty miles in three days while carrying twenty-four pounds of equipment, and he turned it over to Kennedy, knowing that he would like the idea. "It would be interesting," Kennedy said, "to know how well our present-day officers could perform the tests specified by President Roosevelt." Shortly afterward, Shoup ordered a group of Marines at Camp Lejeune, North Carolina, to take the fifty-mile hike, and they proved to his satisfaction they were as fit as the Marines in Roosevelt's day. Soon Marines at other bases took the test, the Boy Scouts followed suit, and around the country high school kids, college students, politicians, and businessmen joined in. In Seattle, some youngsters even tried it on roller skates. Some of Kennedy's White House staff members and military aides went hiking, too, though they reduced the mileage. But Kennedy's brother Robert, the Attorney General, set out at dawn one wintry morning and completed the three-day hike successfully, though the three aides who went with him had to drop out along the way. "For good or bad," commented a San Francisco newspaper, "one of President Kennedy's campaign promises had come true. He's surely got the country moving again."[3]

Jack Kennedy was on the move himself from almost the beginning. When he was a boy, his father saw to it that all the Kennedy children mastered the major sports, strove to excel at them, and refused to settle for second place in any contest. The Kennedys, according to a family friend, were "the most competitive family I've ever seen." Young Jack named his first sailboat *Victura*, because it had to do with "something about winning." If any member of the family triumphed at some game, Jack's sister Eunice recalled, her father "got terribly enthusiastic. Daddy was always very competitive. He always kept telling us that coming in second was just no good." People marrying into the Kennedy family were obliged to show their mettle, too—at baseball, touch football, tennis, bicycling, and, in general, by their high-spiritedness—if they wanted to be accepted as equals. The same was true of the family guests. For the fun of it, one friend who took part in the boisterous Kennedy games at Hyannis Port on Cape Cod in Massachusetts composed "A Guest's Rules for Visiting the Kennedys," based on first-hand experience. "Prepare yourself," he advised, "by reading the Congressional Record, U.S. News and World Report, Time, Newsweek, Fortune, The Nation, How to Play Sneaky Tennis, and the Democratic Digest. Memorize at least three good jokes. Anticipate that each Kennedy will ask you what you think of another Kennedy's a. dress, b. hairdo, c. backhand, d. latest public achievement. Be sure to answer 'Terrific.' This should get you through dinner. Now for the football field. It's *touch* but it's murder. If you don't want to play, don't come. If you do come, play, or you'll be fed in the kitchen and nobody will speak to you. Don't let the girls fool you. Even pregnant, they can make you look silly. If Harvard played touch, they'd be on the varsity. Above all, don't suggest plays, even if you played quarterback at school. The Kennedys have the signal, called department, sewed up, and all of them have A-pluses in leadership. If one of them makes a mistake, keep still. But don't stand still. Run madly on every play, and make a lot of noise. Don't appear to be having too much fun, though. They'll accuse you of not taking the game seriously enough. Don't criticize the other team, either. It's bound to be full of Kennedys, too, and the Kennedys don't like that sort of thing. To become really popular, you must show raw guts. To show raw guts, fall on your face now and then. Smash into the house once in a while, going after a pass. Laugh off a twisted ankle, or a big hole torn in your best suit. They like this. It shows you take the game as seriously as they do. But remember, don't be too good. Let Jack run around you now and then. He's their boy."[4]

Jack Kennedy had "raw guts" all right; he needed them if he was to survive. Despite his love of sports, the fact is that he was frail and sickly as a boy and suffered major illnesses as an adult. His brother Robert once said that "at least one half of the days that he spent on this earth were days of intense physical pain." He had a bad back, which surgery could not correct, and he suffered from Addison's disease, which produced failure of the immune system. Kennedy concealed his pain—and, indeed, the illnesses themselves—from the public, and to most of his contemporaries he appeared to be the handsomest, healthiest, most athletic, and liveliest President ever to hold office. He had his good interludes, to be sure, when he could engage in touch football, play golf, and do some fishing, but time and again he was bedridden with life-threatening illnesses, and on two occasions the last rites were administered to him in the hospital. Mused his mother: "Almost all of his life, it seemed, he had to battle against misfortunes of health."[5]

But Kennedy never complained. "The marvel was that he could make jokes about his own pain," recalled his friend Charles Spalding. "He'd turn everything into a funny remark, sometimes at the expense of the doctor or the nurse or himself or the hospital or science or everything." He was resigned to the fact that whenever he took a trip, he was forced to take with him "more pills, potions, poultices, and other paraphernalia," according to Ted Sorensen, one of Kennedy's White House advisers, "than would be found in a small dispensary." But poor health didn't hold him back; his stoic endurance enabled him to live an active and productive life despite his disabilities. During World War II, his father pulled strings to get him in the navy despite his poor health, and he saw action in the South Pacific as the skipper of a torpedo boat. Recovering from back surgery at the end of the war, Kennedy served in the House of Representatives for three terms and then as senator from Massachusetts before becoming President in 1961. Making the rounds during his campaigns for office produced a great deal of physical pain, but he wore a back brace, slept on firm mattresses with a heavy board underneath to provide support, and, in private, utilized crutches to get around. Both as senator and then as President he sat in rocking chairs, designed for his use, to relieve the pressure on his back.[6]

Kennedy thought that being President was "a damned good job"; he found its challenges enormously stimulating. "His work and his hobby are one," declared Jim Bishop, who spent a day with him at the White House. "He shows no sign of wear....He works at being President as though he had spent many years preparing for it. There is no procrastination, no hesitation. He makes his decisions quickly and precisely." Keeping in shape, however, formed an important part of Kennedy's daily schedule. It was his habit to swim for a half hour before lunch, with the White House pool heated to 90 degrees, and to return to the pool late in the afternoon for another half-hour dip before dinner. Sometimes he worked calisthenics into his routine to strengthen his back muscles, and he always took several restful hot baths during the day. He liked having Dave Powers join him in the pool ("All you have to do," Powers told reporters, "is keep your head above water so you can talk"), and he made it a habit to play with his two children during the late-afternoon swim.[7]

Whenever he felt up to it, Kennedy played golf with family members and friends. He was quite good, often scoring in the high 70s and low 80s. "Jack never fusses," said one golf pro. "He just walks up and hits the ball." Despite his back ailment, he had "a fluid, graceful swing," according to one expert, "drove the ball impressive distances off the tee, possessed a polished short game and had the perfect attitude for golf: he truly enjoyed the game." His friend Ben Bradlee (later editor of the *Washington Post*) thought Kennedy was "fun to play golf with, once you get out of sight of the sightseers, primarily because he doesn't take the game seriously and keeps up a running conversation." But Kennedy insisted on privacy; he carefully avoided being photographed while playing the game. He didn't want to become the target of golf jokes the way Dwight Eisenhower ("Golfer-in-Chief") was while in the White House. He was anxious, of course, to demonstrate that he was physically fit when he ran for President in 1960, but he emphasized swimming, sailing, and touch football instead of golf.[8]

Kennedy didn't even want to make a hole-in-one if it meant publicity. In July 1960, just before the Democratic convention met, when he was playing golf in California, his ball landed on the green and rolled straight toward the hole, on its way, it seemed, into the cup. While his friend Paul B. ("Red") Fay, Jr., yelled, "Go in! Go in!", JFK looked frightened; but when the ball stopped just six inches from the hole, he breathed a sigh of relief and told Fay, "You're yelling for that damn ball to go in the hole and I'm watching a promising political career coming to an end. If that ball had gone into the hole, in less than an hour the word would be out to the nation that another golfer was trying to get into the White House." A few days later he received the Democratic nomination for President, and he went on to defeat Richard Nixon in November. After the election, Pierre Salinger, his press secretary, told reporters that the President-elect "does not plan to play golf after he enters the White House unless he's on an out-and-out vacation." Shortly before his inauguration, however, he sneaked off for a game or two. "If the word leaks out," he warned his aides, "I can just see some eager reporter writing, 'The new President couldn't even wait until the snow was off the ground before engaging in the first game of golf as President. At this rate President Kennedy could devote more time to the golf links than his predecessor.'" An article in *Sports Illustrated* explained that the only difference between Eisenhower's golf and Kennedy's golf was that Kennedy's was a "secret vice."[9]

But Kennedy's golfing days were soon over. In May 1961 he strained his back so badly while shoveling dirt during a tree-planting ceremony in Ottawa, Canada, that his doctors ordered him to give up the game. It wasn't until the summer of 1963 that he ventured to play a few holes again, with his wife, Jacqueline, at Hyannis Port, and it turned out to be his last game.[10]

Sports clearly meant a great deal to Kennedy, despite the limits to his participation in them, but books meant even more to him. He was the only Kennedy who might be called a bookworm, partly because of his natural curiosity and partly because he was frequently confined to the sickbed and had plenty of time to read. His mother said he "gobbled books." As a boy, he read the novels of Sir Walter Scott, Robert Louis Stevenson, and Rudyard Kipling. As an adult he came to prefer history and biography to fiction, focusing on the role that heroic individuals played in shaping historical events. His favorite book, he told journalist Hugh Sidey, who was doing an article on the President's reading habits for *Life*, was Lord Cecil David's *Melbourne* (1939), a biography of Lord Melbourne, Queen Victoria's prime minister and political adviser in the early nineteenth century. "It was the story about the young aristocrats of Britain…," Kennedy said, "who gave their lives in military campaigns, who held the ideal of empire and national honor above all else. But on the weekends, when they went to their country estates, it was broken-field running through the bedrooms. I mean they swapped wives, they slept with others. But the code of the period was nobody talked about it. And you didn't get divorced; otherwise you were disgraced." Sidey was struck by Kennedy's explanation for his interest in the book, and said thoughtfully, "*Melbourne* tells me more about you than anything else." Kennedy laughed. "Well," he said, "I'm fascinated with it. It was an interesting period in history." From then on, Sidey wrote later, he and Kennedy had a "shared secret."[11]

Kennedy was a speed-reader—twelve hundred words a minute, compared to the average two hundred and fifty words for most people—and, like Theodore Roosevelt, he read all the time: while sitting in a hot tub, putting his clothes on, eating meals, and sometimes while walking to the Oval Office. He went through a flock of newspapers the first thing in the morning, kept up with the major newsweeklies and little journals of opinion, and sometimes snitched magazines from other people if they attracted his curiosity. Pierre Salinger said that when JFK "came into my office and saw one he hadn't read on my desk, he would inevitably walk out with it. No one on the staff was safe from his shoplifting." Kennedy read for information and insight, of course, but he also delighted in elegant prose, and for years kept a little notebook in which he jotted down quotations he came across in books and newspapers that he thought he might want to use someday in a speech or piece of writing. He helped make British writer Ian Fleming's novels about secret service agent James Bond famous in the United States by revealing his liking for them, though he was more apt to be reading biographies of American political leaders— Daniel Webster, Henry Clay, John Quincy Adams, John C. Calhoun— than books about the perilous peregrinations of Agent 007.[12]

Kennedy saw Bond movies, starring Sean Connery, too, for although he was never a real movie buff, he enjoyed having movies shown on the White House's 35-millimeter projector every so often. His favorite old-time films were *Red River,* a 1948 Western in which young Montgomery Clift challenged John Wayne, his overbearing stepfather, for control of a cattle drive; *Bad Day at Black Rock* (1955), centering on the way an FBI agent (Spencer Tracy) deals with a racist murder in an unfriendly Western town; and *Casablanca* (1942), the World War II classic about war-torn Morocco, in which Rick (Humphrey Bogart), a cynical nightclub owner, gradually sees the light and decides to join the anti-fascist cause. Another film Kennedy liked was *Spartacus* (1960), the story of a rebellious slave, played by Kirk Douglas, who leads a crusade for freedom in the Roman Empire. He wasn't able to see it in the White House because the projector there couldn't handle wide-screen 70-millimeter films, so he headed for a downtown theater in Washington with one of his friends (and some Secret Service agents), sneaked in when the lights dimmed, and when he sat down spotted Orville Freeman, his secretary of agriculture, in the row of seats ahead of him. With a big grin

on his face, he whispered: "This is a hell of a way to write a farm program." Afterward, Kennedy told the manager of the theater that it
was the best film he had ever seen. His comment boosted the movie
the way he had boosted the Bond books.[13]

Kennedy's cultural tastes were mostly simple. "He had no interest
in opera," Ted Sorensen declared, and "dozed off at symphony concerts and was bored by ballet." His wife teased him by saying that the
only music he appreciated was "Hail to the Chief." Unlike Jackie, his
preference was for country-and-western music, Irish songs, tunes
from Broadway and Hollywood musicals, and rock and roll. "Pablo
Casals?" he once exclaimed to a friend. "I didn't know what the hell
he played—someone had to tell me." But Jackie saw to it that the
great cellist performed in the White House, and that violinist Isaac
Stern and composer Igor Stravinsky made their appearances, too, at
the elegant dinners hosted by the Kennedys. Under her prodding,
and with her husband's approval, the Kennedy administration became known for its high culture. Metropolitan Opera stars were on
the guest list, as were Shakespearean actors, gifted writers, prominent scientists, renowned artists, and famous stage and screen performers and directors. "Not since Thomas Jefferson occupied what
was then known as the President's Palace," observed a *New York
Times* writer, "has culture had such good friends in the White
House." Exclaimed novelist John Steinbeck: "What a joy that literacy
is no longer prima facie evidence of treason." Art critic Lewis Mum-
ford hailed Kennedy as "the first American President to give art, literature and music a place of dignity and honor in our national life."[14]

Kennedy never pretended to be one of the cultural elite. His tastes
ran to playing backgammon with friends while cruising on the presidential yacht, the *Honey Fitz;* taking vacations at Hyannis Port, Camp
David, and Palm Beach (where he could read, swim, fish, and sometimes play golf); and exchanging quips and witticisms with guests
after dinner while smoking a cigar or two. One afternoon, when he
was showing off the White House to some of Jackie's friends who
were interested in her renovations, he came across some paintings of
Renoir and Cézanne, and his friend "Red" Fay asked impishly, "Who

are they?" Jack and Jackie were stunned. "My God," Kennedy whispered, "if you have to ask a question like that, do it in a whisper or wait till we get outside. We're trying to give this administration a semblance of class." Kennedy, to be sure, had no objection to his wife's chamber music, poetry readings, and operatic arias; they just weren't his style. More to his liking was the party thrown for his forty-fifth birthday on May 19, 1962, in New York's Madison Square Garden. A Democratic fundraising salute to the President, it was attended by more than fifteen thousand people, including "a glittering array of show people," according to the *New York Times*, with appearances by Jack Benny, Maria Callas, Harry Belafonte, Ella Fitzgerald, Henry Fonda, Greer Garson, Bobby Darin, Jimmy Durante, Mike Nichols, and Elaine May. "The amazing thing to me," announced comedian Benny, one of the masters of ceremony, "is how a man in a rocking chair can have such a young wife." Returned Kennedy (aware that the sixty-eight-year-old Benny always claimed he was thirty-nine), "I'm very glad you could come to a birthday party for an older man." He went on to assure his audience that his businessman father's remark that "all businessmen are S.O.B.'s" didn't apply to show business. During the three-hour program, he was relaxed and happy, smoking his cigar and clapping his hands in time to the music when Belafonte sang "Michael Rowed the Boat." The show ended with a bang: Marilyn Monroe appeared on the stage, swept the furs from her shoulders revealing that she was wearing a skintight, flesh-toned gown, and, in what *Time* called "a sincere Campfire Girl voice" (but which other observers regarded as seductively lascivious), sang:

> Happy birthday to you,
> Happy birthday to you,
> Happy birthday
> Dear Mr. President—
> Happy birthday to you!

"I can now retire from politics," responded Kennedy, "after having had *Happy Birthday* sung to me in such a sweet, wholesome way."[15]

In May 1963 Kennedy celebrated his last birthday. In November he took a political trip to Texas to heal a dispute in the state's Democratic party and to raise money for his campaign for reelection in 1964. On November 22, as he was riding with his wife in an open car through Dallas, he was shot and killed by a lone assassin standing at a window on the sixth floor of the Texas Book Depository overlooking Dealey Plaza. In their grief at the tragedy, some Americans looked back on his presidency as a kind of romantic "Camelot." But Kennedy, who once said he was an "idealist without illusions," would have been amused by the notion.[16]

☆ ☆ ☆ **35** ☆ ☆ ☆

The Frenetic
Lyndon B. Johnson

Lyndon B. Johnson was eager to learn what people thought about the issues when he was President, and he sought enlightenment as well as entertainment when he hosted dinners at the White House. Sometimes, in fact, he came close to treating his guests as if they were students in a classroom with himself as the teacher. On such occasions, he saw to it the guests were well fed, and then passed a basket around containing slips of paper marked either "Speaker" or "Writer"; when everyone had drawn a slip, he announced that the "Speakers" were expected to tell him what was on their minds that evening and the "Writers" were to sound off in letters to him in the near future, to which he promised to respond. He then proceeded to call on the "Speakers" from each table, listened quietly to what they had to say about various issues—the economy, education, civil rights, medical programs—and then led the applause when they finished.[1]

At one such dinner, however, a business executive ventured a bit of criticism. "Mr. President," he said, "we've heard these briefings and we've seen these people in your cabinet. They are very talented, very bright, very wise people. But they all look very tired. Mr. President, in business at our company we require that our top executives each go away and take at least a month of vacation a year. I suggest you insist on that for your top people." Johnson's face darkened as the executive was talking; when the man finished, the room remained still, and Johnson simply motioned for the next speaker. Johnson didn't like to be lectured; he was also sensitive about the charge that he overworked his subordinates. He worked extremely hard himself, and he saw no reason why his staff shouldn't do the same. Zephyr Wright, the Johnson cook, once put it plainly to him: "Anybody who works for you for a long time has to love you, because you kill yourself and everybody else too."[2]

In November 1963, when Johnson became President after John F. Kennedy's assassination, reporters preparing stories about him for their newspapers found it almost impossible to dig up anything about his hobbies. Johnson "has no daily routine of relaxation," concluded the Associated Press, "but at the end of the day he likes to sit and talk." He did, to be sure, take time off now and then to board the presidential yacht, the *Honey Fitz*, with his wife and friends, and cruise down the Potomac to Mount Vernon and back; and he liked spending vacations at the Johnson Ranch in Texas. But his work was usually on his mind when he was supposed to be relaxing. He talked politics while playing golf, and when he went to a baseball game presidential problems were so much on his mind that he hardly noticed the plays. "On such days," recalled George Reedy, one of his press secretaries, "I sat at home praying that television cameras would not catch him with his back turned to the field in deep conversation about a tax bill or an upcoming election while a triple play was in process or when a cleanup hitter had just knocked a home run with the bases loaded."[3]

One of Johnson's friends summed it all up: "Sports, entertainment, movies—he couldn't have cared less." Until his heart attack in 1955, just after becoming the youngest Senate majority leader in American history, his habits were those of a "Type A" personality: He smoked three or four packs of cigarettes a day, gulped down his food, and was always in a big hurry. Once, his aides persuaded him to see someone in the Oval Office for a "brief moment," and when the visitor ended up staying twenty minutes, Johnson was furious. "Hell," he stormed afterward, "by the time a man scratches his ass, clears his throat, and

tells me how smart he is, we've already wasted fifteen minutes!"
Johnson gave up smoking after his heart attack, and slowed down his
pace for a while after he got on his feet again, but he was soon back
to his breakneck speed and lengthy workdays.[4]

LBJ, said Reedy, "knew of no innocent form of recreation....The
only sanctified activity was hard work to achieve clearly defined
goals; the only recreation was frenetic activity that made one forget
the problems of the day; and the only true happiness was the oblivion
he could find in Scotch or in sleep. The concept of reading for the
sake of contemplation, of community activity for the sake of sharing
joy, of conversation for the sake of human contact was totally foreign
to his psyche. He did understand dimly that other people had some
interests outside of their direct work but he thought of such interests
as weakness and, if they included classical music or drama, mere
snobbery practiced by 'the Eastern establishment.'" Politics was, as
Reedy observed, LBJ's main interest in life; it was close to being an
obsession.[5]

But Johnson was no couch potato. He did some swimming, in the
White House pool and in the outdoor pool on his ranch in Texas,
though he almost always had at least one person with him so he
could do a little bloviating. He enjoyed horseback riding on his ranch,
too, but of course he was doing his job as a ranch owner when he
made the rounds to see that all was well. Above all, Johnson liked to
dance—he was a good dancer—and there is no reason to believe
that he talked only politics with his partners on the dance floor. "He
had a good sense of the rhythm," observed one social columnist,
"and did a smooth fox trot." He was " a marvelous dancer, a strong
lead," said singer Edie Adams, who had been at one of the presidential parties. "You don't find dancers like that anymore. Usually they're
sort of Milquetoast fellows, but he knew exactly where he was
going....I thought, 'Gee, that's good. This is a strong man we've got
up here running the country. I like that.'" Blues singer Sarah
Vaughan also danced with him in the White House, and afterward
Mrs. Johnson's social secretary found her crying in the dressing

room. When she asked what was the matter, the black artist said that nothing was the matter, but that it was "just 20 years ago when I came to Washington, I couldn't even get a hotel room, and tonight I sang for the President of the United States in the White House—and then, he asked me to dance with him. It is more than I can stand."[6]

When Johnson was a senator he did a little golfing, but he didn't take the sport seriously. He was a devotee, it was said, of the "hit-till-you're-happy school of golf." He had a swing that looked like he was chopping wood or trying to kill a rattlesnake, and he always hit as many shots as he wanted to until he made one he liked. One observer said he played by his own rules: He "flattered, cajoled, needled, scolded, belittled, and sweet-talked the golf balls" the way he did his colleagues in the Senate. In the spring of 1964, a few months after LBJ became President, Jack Valenti suggested taking a little time off from work to play some golf with him. Johnson hadn't played in a long time and he was reluctant to interrupt his work for a game he'd never taken the trouble to learn to play decently. But when Valenti proposed inviting some senators to join him, his eyes lit up. "That's a helluva idea," he cried. "This can be a new forum for me to browbeat these guys." When a newspaper reported that LBJ liked golf because he had a "zest for walking," Valenti insisted it was "a zest for politicking." People teased Johnson about his golfing, but he didn't seem to mind. "I don't have a handicap," he once said. "I'm all handicap." One golf pro said Johnson "didn't play very well, but he had a hell of a good time. He would josh around, kidding whoever was with him. He'd make comments to the other players—of a personal nature."[7]

Johnson didn't play much golf when he was President. As the Vietnam War became increasingly unpopular, he decided to give up the game, telling his aides that if people saw him on the golf links while American boys were dying in Asia, they would "eat me alive." Then, in the late summer of his last year in office, he announced playfully at a White House dinner that he was planning to give up alcohol and return to golf. "This is alarming, if true," wrote James Reston mischievously in his *New York Times* column, "for in the present state of the world and the Presidency it really should be the other way around." Golf, Reston went on to say, was a form of self-torment, invented by the Scots, along with whiskey, to make people suffer. "To substitute golf for 'whiskey's old prophetic aid' is a puzzle and could be a calamity. And to do it as an escape from agony is the worst miscalculation since the start of the Vietnam War. Golf is not an escape from agony. It is itself an agony."[8]

Golfing was never an "agony" for Johnson, but it was not a major pleasure, either. Swimming and dancing were also minor indulgences. His greatest enjoyment was his 410-acre ranch outside Johnson City in south Texas. He liked to go boating on the Pedernales River, which ran in front of his ranch house, and sometimes even went fishing for bass and catfish in the ponds and lakes in the surrounding area. More fun for him, though, was taking people—friends, reporters, White House aides—on tours of his ranch. Like Johnson himself, the tours were fast-paced, a bit rowdy, and at times challenging. They usually included a trip to the ramshackle cabin that he claimed was his humble birthplace (like Lincoln's), even though he knew it wasn't. He also liked to show off the horses and cattle they encountered as he careened around the place, sometimes at ninety miles per hour. Once, when he had a carful of reporters with him, he came across a big sow surrounded by a bunch of piglets. Stopping the car abruptly, he offered to pose for pictures if any of the reporters was able to catch one of the little pigs. When a couple of photographers jumped out of the car and started chasing the piglets around, the sow became angry, as Johnson knew it would, and began charging furiously after them. As the reporters scrambled to get out of the way, Johnson hooted gleefully, honked the horn of the car, and yelled: "Whooee! Whooee!" Finally one of the reporters managed to catch one of the piglets, and Johnson posed for a picture with a big grin on his face. "Mr. President," acknowledged one of the reporters afterward, "you're fun."[9]

Johnson liked to have fun on the ranch with people on his staff, too, and with people he was considering for a position in his administration. In July 1965, he invited Joseph H. Califano, Jr., whom he expected to make his adviser on domestic affairs, for a visit so he could size the man up. First came a swim. After breakfast, Johnson asked Califano to join him in the pool, and as the latter got in the water Johnson asked solemnly, "Are you ready to come help your President?" Replied Califano with equal solemnity, "It would be an honor and a privilege." There was more talking than swimming after that, but Califano seems to have held his own with LBJ. Next came a drive around the ranch followed by a car and a station wagon containing Secret Service agents. While LBJ drove and talked, he helped himself generously to Cutty Sark, ice, and soda in a large white plastic foam cup, and whenever he wanted a refill, he slowed down, held his left hand out the car window, and started shaking the cup with the ice in it. Califano was impressed by the way one of the Secret Service men rushed up, took the cup, ran back to the station wagon, asked another agent to refill it, and then took it back to Johnson as the car continued moving slowly along.[10]

The afternoon activities were more vigorous. Johnson persuaded the aide-to-be to do some water-skiing on a nearby lake; his main objective, as he began driving his speedboat up and down the lake, seemed to be to propel Califano off the skis into the water. "He drove faster and faster," Califano recalled, "zigging and zagging around the lake and between the concrete pillars. The faster he drove and twisted, the more I was determined to stay up. He threw me once. He was going so fast that I thought I'd split apart when I flew off the skis and hit the water. Determined to prove myself, I got back up and managed not to fall off again."[11]

But Johnson wasn't through with Califano. The real test came in the evening. This time Johnson took Califano for a ride around the lake in a small blue car, with his secretary, Vicky McCammon, sitting next to him in front and Califano in the backseat. At one point the car reached a steep incline at the edge of the lake and started rolling down toward the water. "The brakes don't work!" Johnson yelled frantically. "The brakes won't hold! We're going under!" The car then splashed into the lake and Califano started to get out. Just then the car leveled, and he realized they were in an amphibious car, and in no danger at all. As they putted along the lake, Johnson started teasing him. "Vicky," he said, "did you see what Joe did? He didn't give a damn about the President. He just wanted to save his own skin and get out of the car." It turned out that Johnson was fond of playing this trick on visitors. He especially enjoyed trying it out on young married couples to see whether the husband would try to save his own life before helping his wife survive. It wasn't a nice prank; but, then, Johnson's sense of humor wasn't always very nice.[12]

But there was work as well as play for Johnson during the Califano visit. He spent time talking about "his hopes for America and for its poor people" as they drove around the ranch, and when they happened to pass a man, half-drunk, stumbling along the road, "unshaven, dirty, and red-eyed," Johnson turned to Califano, held his right thumb and forefinger closely together and said, "Don't ever forget that the difference between him and me and him and you is that much." When they got back to Washington, he gave Califano his kind of provisional approval. "They tell me you're pretty smart, way up in your class at Harvard. Well, let me tell you something. What you learned on the streets of Brooklyn will be a damn sight more helpful to your President than anything you learned at Harvard."[13]

The Great Society programs that Johnson discussed with Califano were mostly practical and down-to-earth: civil rights, Medicare and Medicaid, the war on poverty, and environmental protection. But, to the surprise of people who regarded LBJ as "a Texas hill philistine," he sponsored federal aid to the arts and humanities as well. The "desire for beauty," he declared in a speech on the Great Society in May 1964, was as important as "the needs of the body." He may well have believed this—he loved the countryside where his ranch was located—but art and literature played a small part in his life. He never read novels or poems, had as little interest in opera, ballet, or symphonic music, knew little about painting and sculpture, and wasn't much of a playgoer or movie fan. Yet Abe Fortas, one of his closest advisors (who played the violin), insisted that Johnson had an "extraordinary aesthetic sensibility," and though it was "untrained as far as music and art are concerned," it gave him "a kind of natural appreciation" of good art.[14]

It was the art of the American West that Johnson appreciated the most. S. Dillon Ripley, the secretary of the Smithsonian Institution, was impressed with the President's "friendly and genuine interest in the art with which he had grown up in the West.... He loved Western pictures that reminded him of the past, pictures of cowboys, Remington's pictures, local artists who painted around Fredericksburg, Texas, who transmitted some of the spirit of derring-do." Western music—"Wagon Wheels," "Navajo Trail," "The Yellow Rose of Texas"—appealed to Johnson, too. In one of his speeches, Johnson called art America's "most precious heritage," and he did what he could to further it by sponsoring the establishment of the National Council on the Arts and the National Endowment for the Arts and the Humanities. In the summer of 1965, moreover, he and his wife, Lady Bird, hosted a Festival of the Arts at the White House, attended by scores of artists and writers, which presented poetry readings, dance recitals, art exhibitions, and film screenings. Johnson's enjoyment of the festival was spoiled by the criticism he received of his Vietnam policy by some of the participants. In November 1968, however, when the Johnsons entertained members of the National Council on the Arts for dinner at the White House, there was only praise. "President Johnson," announced theatrical producer Roger Stevens, head of the organization, "has done more for the arts than any other President in the history of the United States."[15]

The Sports-Loving
Richard M. Nixon

When it came to sports, Richard M. Nixon was a better spectator than he was a participant. "I was not a good athlete," he acknowledged in his memoirs. As a student in California's Whittier College, in the early 1930s, he went out for football, basketball, baseball, and track, "and never made a letter." Still, he thought he learned a lot from the football coach: how to win, how to lose, and, most important of all, how to make a comeback. "You know who a good loser is?" he mused. "It's somebody who hates to lose and who gets up and comes back and fights again." Knowing this, he said, was crucial for him when he went into politics after serving in the U.S. Navy during World War II. But sports themselves—in fact, any kind of regular exercise—played a minor part in his life as he moved from congressman in 1946, to senator in 1950, to Vice President in 1952, and then to President in 1968, in a remarkable comeback after losing to John F. Kennedy in 1960.[1]

In 1953, soon after Nixon became Vice President, President Eisenhower, in an effort to get to know him better, took him fishing, and tried to teach him how to cast for trout. "It was a disaster," Nixon remembered. After hooking a nearby tree limb three times, he caught Eisenhower's shirt on his fourth try. "The lesson ended abruptly" at that point, and Eisenhower was deeply disappointed, because he loved fishing himself and couldn't understand why Nixon didn't take to it the way he did.[2]

A few weeks later, however, Eisenhower gave Nixon a second chance. This time it involved golf, another Eisenhower passion, but a game that Nixon had tried only a few times before becoming Vice President. The second encounter with Ike went no better than the first. For some reason, when he joined Eisenhower for a game at the Burning Tree Club in Washington, Nixon gave him the impression he was a better player than he actually was, so Ike made him a partner in a game on which he placed some bets. Nixon's clumsy playing insured defeat, and in the end Eisenhower had to pay off the bet. "Look here," he told Nixon, disappointedly, "you're young, you're strong, and you can do a lot better than that." As Nixon remembered it, he "talked to me like a Dutch uncle."[3]

But Nixon took Eisenhower's advice seriously; he decided to do what he could to improve his game. "I had learned from the Navy," he wrote afterwards, "that when your superior officer makes a suggestion, you should take it as a command." He asked Max Elbin, the club professional at Burning Tree, to teach him the basics of the game. "I don't want any of that top-drawer stuff," he told him. "I just want to know how to play the game." After working with Elbin forty-five minutes or so, he was eager to play a few holes. "Mr. Vice President," warned Elbin, "you aren't ready for that yet," but Nixon headed for the course anyway and hit three or four balls, all of which landed in the parking lot. Still, Elbin admitted later on, Nixon took his game seriously and "improved as rapidly as anybody I saw."[4]

At first, though, Nixon received a fair amount of ridicule for his performance on the course. People were amused by the way he dressed for the game: golf shirts buttoned all the way up to the top, even on hot days; golf pants pulled up so high it looked as if they reached his armpits; and a cap that was much too large for his head. As for his swing, it was "herky-jerky," people said; he looked as though he was trying to beat the dust out of a floor rug. Nixon's golf balls, said one caddie, "spent more time in the trees than most squirrels." Nixon "was terrible," in the opinion of Senator George A. Smathers. "You wondered," when playing with him, "whether you were playing golf or out hunting balls." Even after Nixon became President, the teasing continued. "Not since Calvin Coolidge," wrote *New York Times* columnist James Reston, "have we had a more awkward uncoordinated locker-room character in the White House than Richard Nixon." According to a popular joke circulating in golf circles, President Nixon announces proudly, "I scored 128 today." Henry Kissinger exclaims, "Your golf game is getting better," and Nixon snaps, "I was *bowling*, Henry." Nixon was not amused by the story.[5]

Young Pat Buchanan, then a caddy, was aware of Nixon's deficiencies on the course. "You did not need to be Ben Hogan," he said, "to see that the Vice President of the United States was uncoordinated." But Buchanan (later to become Nixon's speechwriter) realized that Nixon "was obviously enjoying himself hugely. Banging the ball around in that summer sun, he seemed genuinely happy, laughing heartily at the men's jokes and wisecracks." In contrast, George P. Shultz, a lawyer who was to join Nixon's cabinet in later years, was impressed by his deadly seriousness about the game. Shultz thought Nixon's approach to golf was similar to the way he handled politics. "Nixon was an intense personality," he pointed out, "and he was a tough competitor. And in golf, I would say, he maximized his potential. He got everything out of himself that he could get. And I think in a lot of ways his political life was the same way—you could see a man who was very determined and worked hard at it but wasn't a natural at schmoozing with people. Golf didn't come naturally to him. And neither did politics."[6]

When Nixon became President, he had golf balls made with the Presidential seal and his signature on them, which he gave to his golfing partners and to members of the clubs where he played. He kept his scores secret and refused to have his picture taken when he was playing. The time came when he shot a hole-in-one—"the biggest thrill I had playing golf"—and received a congratulatory letter from former President Eisenhower. Later on, he broke 80, and found doing so "an even greater thrill" than getting the hole-in-one. "I must admit it was on a relatively easy course in San Clemente," he said, "but for me it was like climbing Mount Everest." Golf was important to him, he once wrote, because it "combines exercise, stimulating competition, and warm companionship." He also enjoyed the beauty of the courses where he played in various parts of the country. But the Watergate crisis during his second term led him to abandon the game, and it wasn't until he resigned office in August 1974 and recovered from a serious illness that he took it up again. Golf, he said, "became my life saver" after leaving the White House, and for a while he played just about every day with a friend who was a pro. It would have been unthinkable for him to spend that much time on the course while he was President.[7]

"Recreation," Nixon once wrote, "is a means to an end, not the end in itself. You don't want to be President so that you can have fun. You want to have fun so that you can be a better President." But Nixon's fun was grudging much of the time. Despite his golf—and some swimming and bowling—he was reluctant to take time off from his presidential activities in order to relax. In December 1968, a few weeks after he defeated Hubert Humphrey for President, he flew to Key Biscayne in Florida for a little rest before his inauguration in January. The staff members who went with him wondered how they could get his mind off work for a few days. "What do we do with him?" H. R. Haldeman, his chief of staff, wrote in his diary. "He knows he needs to relax, so he comes down to Florida. He likes to swim, so he swims for ten minutes. Then that's over. He doesn't paint, he doesn't horseback-ride, he doesn't have a hobby. His best relaxation is talking shop, but he knows he should not be doing that, because that doesn't seem to be relaxing. So what do we do with him? It's a problem." They ended up talking shop with him.[8]

But Nixon, Haldeman soon learned, could do more than talk politics. He was an avid sports fan and loved to talk football and baseball. Following professional games, as Stephen A. Ambrose noted, was the "perfect relaxation" for Nixon when he was in the White House. He devoured the sports pages in newspapers and magazines, traveled around the country to take in major sports events, attended testimonial dinners for sports celebrities and delivered congratulatory addresses, watched football and baseball games on television, and entertained top people in the sports world at the White House to show his respect and admiration for them. "Like many who never made the team," he told some all-star baseball players, "I am awed by those who made it. I'm proud to be in your company." Nixon's knowledge of the records and history of baseball in America was prodigious. While he was President he received a trophy as "Baseball's Number 1 Fan," and was asked to name his "all-time baseball team." The "dream teams" he came up with for several different periods in baseball history received much acclaim from the experts. "This man knows baseball," exclaimed the sportswriter for the *New York Daily News*.[9]

Nixon's absorption in professional sports was so great that he wondered at times whether he would have been happier as a sportswriter than as a politician. "I like the job I have now," he once said, "but if I had my life to live over again, I'd like to have ended up as a sportswriter." He once told a sports reporter for the *Washington Post* that "my favorite vacation, if I had an opportunity to take a week off at the right time, would be to travel with a baseball club. The dugout chatter and, particularly, the conversation on the train or plane between cities would be a welcome relief from some of the heavy discussions in which I participate in my office!" He added: "I think you have one of the best jobs possible. If I could only write, I would trade places with you today...." Nixon was proud of his knowledge about professional sports and liked to use sports language when he was explaining his views on governmental matters.[10]

Nixon was interested in music as well as sports. When he was a little boy, his mother heard him picking out tunes on the piano and arranged for him to take piano and violin lessons from professionally trained teachers. He took to the piano at once and gradually developed into a competent pianist who liked to play popular music for his family and friends, and sometimes for himself when he felt discouraged and lonely. He never mastered the classics the way President Truman did, but he was good at ballads and popular songs. His best-known performance as President, however—at a Gridiron Club dinner in Washington on March 14, 1970—was a comedy act, not a recital. The Gridiron dinner, made up of journalists and publishers, "roasted" the President, as was the custom, by teasing him about his "Southern strategy" to lure Southern whites, traditionally Democrats, into the Republican Party. The program began with a series of songs and skits spoofing the President's strategy, and then Nixon and his Vice President, Spiro Agnew, a Marylander, went up to the stage, sat down before two little black pianos, and when Nixon asked, "What about this 'southern strategy' we hear so often?" Agnew responded, "Yes, suh," in a heavy Southern accent, "Ah agree with you completely on yoah southern strategy." After a few more exchanges, Nixon started the piano duet by playing FDR's "favorite" song ("Home on the Range"), Truman's ("The Missouri Waltz"), and then LBJ's ("The Eyes of Texas Are Upon You"), with Agnew banging out "Dixie" at the same time through all of them. "The crowd ate it up," noted Roy Wilkins, a black civil rights worker, disappointedly. "They roared." Nixon ended the skit playing his own favorites, "God Bless America" and "Auld Lang Syne," with Agnew playing it straight this time.[11]

"Playing the piano," Nixon wrote in his memoirs, "is a way of expressing oneself that is perhaps even more fulfilling than writing or speaking. In fact, I have always had two great—and still unfulfilled—ambitions: to direct a symphony orchestra and to play an organ in a cathedral. I think that to create great music is one of the highest aspirations man can set for himself." But music was not a major diversion for Nixon when he was President. He sometimes listened to LP records containing musical comedy scores as well as symphonies and concertos, he attended symphonic concerts now and then with his wife, Pat, and once in a while he played the piano in public to amuse people. When he wanted to relax, however, he was more likely to watch movies than play the piano.[12]

Nixon saw more movies in the White House, as well as in his fa-
vorite vacation places—Camp David, Key Biscayne in Florida, and
San Clemente in California—than any other President up to his time.
The movies he liked best were historical epics, westerns, musicals,
war movies, and romantic comedies. His favorite actor was John
Wayne, but he also liked Clint Eastwood. One of his favorite films was
Patton (1970), the splendid Oscar-winning screen biography of World
War II's temperamental General George Patton, played by George C.
Scott. Nixon saw it several times, according to Herb Klein, his direc-
tor of communications, and he admired Patton as a leader. But his favorite film was *Around the World in Eighty Days* (1956), a fast-moving
comedy based on the Jules Verne novel, which included more than
forty cameo appearances by popular movie stars. In 1971, he had
it screened at Camp David to celebrate Texas Democrat-turned-
Republican John Connally's birthday, and he chortled throughout.
"He was hysterical through it," reported Haldeman, "as each scene
was coming up, he'd say, 'you're going to love this particular part' or
'the scenery is just great, now watch this closely'....He obviously has
seen it time after time and knows the whole thing practically by
heart."[13]

Nixon saw few foreign films. "I like my movies 'Made in Hollywood,'" he once said. He saw many fine Hollywood productions: classics like *The Grapes of Wrath* (1940) and *Citizen Kane* (1941), as well
as *War and Peace* (1956) and *The Brothers Karamazov* (1958). He had
a special liking for *A Man for All Seasons* (1966), a film centered on
Sir Thomas More's conflict with King Henry VIII over his loyalty to
the Catholic Church. But Nixon also saw a fair number of clinkers.
His daughter Julie told writer William Safire that "No matter how terrible the first reel is, he always thinks it will get better. 'Give it a
chance,' he'll say. Oh, we sat through some real lemons. Bebe [Re-
bozo] would fall asleep. Mother and Tricia would tiptoe out, but
Daddy would stick with it. 'Wait,' he'd say. 'Wait—it'll get better.'" He
did walk out on one film—*West Side Story*, a brilliant musical about
youth gangs in New York in the late 1950s—because, said Halde-

man, he "couldn't stand the propaganda." But to the surprise of some of his associates, he took a liking to *Doctor Zhivago,* an epic about the fortunes of a Russian poet and doctor during World War I and the Bolshevik Revolution. One of his guests walked out in protest during the screening of the film, and Haldeman himself was also upset. "Strange," he confided to his diary, "to sit in a room with the leader of the Free World and Commander in Chief of Armed Forces and the pictures of the Russian Revolution, Army overthrown, etc. We all had the same thought."[14]

Nixon preferred movies to television for entertainment. Though he is said to have watched the popular program *Kojak* on Sunday nights, he depended on TV mainly for the news. Even so, he regarded newspapers and magazines as far more reliable sources of information about what was going on in the world. He tended, in fact, to be hostile to television. It stressed appearance over substance, he pointed out, and it killed the ancient art of conversation, contributed to the decline of newspapers, and, in general, replaced reading for many Americans. "I must admit to a lifetime personal prejudice for reading," he wrote in one of his books. "My mother taught me to read before I went to school. I was fortunate to have had outstanding teachers who inspired me to love books. Except when my favorite teams are playing, I always prefer reading to TV."[15]

At Whittier College, Nixon took courses in British and American civilization, acquired a love for history and biography, and learned that history could be "a tool of analysis and criticism" as well as a chronicle of past events. He came to appreciate novels, too. At the end of his junior year, one of his professors told him that his "education would not be complete" until he read some of the nineteenth-century Russian masters. That summer he plunged into the novels of Tolstoy and Dostoevsky, and was tremendously impressed by Tolstoy's sympathy for the downtrodden masses, hatred of war, and perception of spiritual elements in all aspects of life. For a while, he recalled, "I became a Tolstoyan." Though his reading as an adult was mainly in American history and biography, he never forgot the impact of the great Russian novels on his understanding of the world. In his 1990 memoir *In the Arena,* Nixon declared that one "could learn more about the revolutionary forces that convulsed Russia in the nineteenth century from Tolstoy and Dostoevski than from the turgid scholarly histories of the period. And some of the better current novels," he added, "are a more accurate portrayal of real life than most of the narrow and biased tomes emanating from the ivory towers of academia." He may well have been correct, but he neglected to mention any of the "turgid scholarly histories" or "better current novels" with which he was acquainted. The fact is that he seems rarely to have turned to fiction for surcease from work while in the White House.[16]

Nixon's bedtime reading when he was President was usually American history and biography, but eventually he began reading in the field of political philosophy as well. "Philosophy," he exclaimed in an interview about his reading habits toward the end of his life. "I don't always understand it, but it's worth reading for the great questions: what is the best form of government? what is the state of nature for man?" He talked knowledgeably about Plato, Aristotle, Hobbes, Rousseau, Machiavelli, Burke, Marx, and Nietzsche, but he was particularly interested in the natural-rights philosophy of John Locke, which (along with the Scottish common-sense philosophy) played a major role in shaping the thought of America's Founding Fathers. Still, he told Monica Crowley in an interview, "just because Locke was right about natural rights doesn't mean that democracy is for everybody. We have to face up to the fact that many states just don't have the traditions and institutions to make democracy work....We can endorse freedom and human rights around the world, but we should never be in the position of imposing our values on others. It's not right, and it doesn't work."[17]

In 1965, when Nixon visited Australia, Prime Minister Robert Menzies told him that he always set aside a half hour each day, and an hour on weekends, to read for pleasure, and he suggested that Nixon do the same. "I have never received better advice," Nixon reflected. "A President should never be so burdened by what he has to read that he does not have some time for what he wants to read." Nixon acknowledged that reading for pleasure might be regarded as "purely escapist" and that Presidents shouldn't waste time on it. "But no one," he insisted, "would disagree that a leader needs some relief from the heavy burdens of his office, and reading is one of the best ways to get it. Watching movies or television can also serve this purpose, but both are passive forms of entertainment. Reading is active. It engages, exercises and expands the mind." Nixon admired Theodore Roosevelt for his reading habits as well as his athleticism. He recalled that T.R. once said that he would never go anywhere, "not even to the jungles of Africa," without books to read, and added: "I did the same thing in the jungles of Washington."[18]

Sometimes people asked Nixon, "Was it *fun* to be president? Were you *happy?*" He considered the questions silly. "Leaders take on the office," he said, "to accomplish something, not to be happy or to have fun." Still, there is no doubt that he enjoyed being top dog in Washington for a few years when he was able to accomplish something— opening up relations with the People's Republic of China, and achieving an arms-control treaty with the Soviet Union—for his country. But the Watergate scandal in effect ended Nixon's presidency. Charged with obstruction of justice and abuse of presidential power, he was forced to resign his office in August 1974 in order to avoid almost certain impeachment by the House of Representatives.[19]

In retirement, Nixon wrote his memoirs (in which he dismissed his crimes as blunders), as well as a series of books dealing with the leading issues of the day. He also read a lot; he called it "exercising the brain." His favorite field was now philosophy. "This is heavy stuff," he told Monica Crowley, as he picked up a copy of one of Aristotle's works. "There are so many books left to read, and time is running out." He included Nietzsche in his heavy reading. He liked the German philosopher's view that "struggle makes life," and that "growth takes place only when you struggle." He took to heart, too, Nietzsche's warning against "the last man," which he defined as "a creature completely obsessed with material security and comfort and incapable of giving himself to a higher cause."[20]

In his last years, Nixon got physical as well as mental exercise. "Sometimes I am asked what a 78-year-old former president does for exercise," he wrote in one of his last books. "Again, I do not set a very good example. I have never gone hunting or fishing, just isn't my bag....I do not ski or play tennis....I quit golf ten years ago....In 1969 I asked President Eisenhower what he did for exercise. He told me he believed that walking was the best thing a leader could do for mental, physical, and emotional health. I now follow his advice and walk four miles a day." Years before, Nixon fished with Eisenhower and played golf with him as best he could. But he never got to walk with him.[21]

☆ ☆ ☆ 𝟯𝟳 ☆ ☆ ☆

The Agile
Gerald R. Ford

Gerald R. Ford, who became President upon Richard Nixon's resignation in August 1974, was one of the healthiest and most physically fit of all America's Chief Executives. He swam, played tennis, skied, and golfed, and he was almost never sick. He was, in fact, practically weaned on sports. When he was a little boy, his stepfather played ball with him and took him fishing. His dad "loved sports," Ford attested. "He believed sports taught you how to live, how to compete but always by the rules, how to be part of a team, how to win, how to lose and come back to try again."[1]

Football was young Ford's favorite sport. He did so well at the game when attending South High in Grand Rapids, Michigan, where he grew up, that when he was a senior he was named all-state center and captain of the all-state team. "Jerry was one of the hardest working kids who ever played football for me," the high school coach declared, "and totally dependable in every game." Ford adored the coach; from him, he said, he learned that "[y]ou play to win. You give it everything you've got, but you always play within the rules." Football was Ford's "ticket to college," as he put it, and at the University of Michigan, where he enrolled in 1931 on a scholarship, he performed so ably on the college team that he was voted the most valuable player and received bids from the Green Bay Packers and the

Detroit Lions to play professional football. The University of Michigan yearbook for 1935 elevated him to its Hall of Fame for the following reasons: "because the football team chose him as their most valuable player; because he was a good student and got better grades than anyone else on the squad; because he put the DKE House back on a paying basis; because he never smokes, drinks, swears, or tells dirty stories...and because he's not a bit fraudulent and we can't find anything really nasty to say about him."[2]

Upon graduation, Ford accepted a position at Yale University as assistant football coach under the popular Ducky Pond and agreed to coach the boxing team as well. Since he had never boxed before, he took lessons during the summer and arrived at Yale in the fall of 1935 ready to do creditable work at both jobs. He went on to get a law degree from Yale, serve in the navy during World War II, and begin his long service as a Michigan congressman in 1948. He no longer played football, but he busied himself with other sports in his free time: baseball, skiing, golf, and swimming. His successor as President, Jimmy Carter, no couch potato himself, averred that Ford was "the best athlete who ever lived in the White House."[3]

Ford's brief presidency—it lasted only two and a half years—was, he thought, a "time to heal" the wounds inflicted on the nation by the agitation over the Vietnam War and the Watergate crisis, and to move on to a more tranquil and harmonious era. He ended intervention in the Vietnam civil war (albeit reluctantly), sought better relations between the President and Congress, and met with Soviet leaders in Vladivostok to discuss a new arms-limitation agreement. But there was no peace and harmony in the nation. A month after Ford became President, he granted Nixon a "full, free and absolute pardon" for his offenses, but instead of putting Watergate on the shelf, as he'd hoped, his action angered many Americans who had been shocked by Nixon's recklessness and led them to take a hostile view of his administration from almost the outset. "Gerald Ford is an awfully nice man," the *New Republic* decided, "who isn't up to the presidency." The media—television, newspapers, and magazines—began portraying him as a mumbling, bumbling, rumbling, and stumbling kind of guy who could hardly make his way around the world without bumping into things. Ford's critics picked up the crack Lyndon Johnson had made years before, in a dispute with Ford, that the Michigander had played center on the University of Michigan football team without a helmet, and that he couldn't walk and chew gum at the same time. It was extraordinary: The most athletic of all our Presidents came to be regarded as a clumsy stumblebum.[4]

Like so many important developments in politics, the denigration of President Ford began with a trivial incident. On May 3, 1975, Ford flew to Salzburg, Austria, from Spain, for a meeting with Egyptian president Anwar Sadat. "The weather in Spain had been fair," Ford related in his memoirs; "rain clouds hung low over the Salzburg airport, however, and when the airplane taxied to a stop, I tumbled down the ramp, literally. What happened is this: Betty and I were descending the steps. I had my right arm around her waist to help her, and I was carrying an umbrella in my left hand. Two or three steps from the bottom of the ramp the heel of my shoe caught on something. I had no free hand to grab the rail, so I took a tumble to the tarmac." He got up at once, with no harm done, and proceeded on his way with his wife, only to be told by Ron Nessen, his press secretary, a little later that reporters covering the trip were showering him with questions about the President's "missteps." Ford told him not to worry about it, but later the same day he slipped twice on the long, rain-slick staircase at the Residenz Palace in Salzburg where he was to have the conference with Sadat. From that point on, for most reporters, the big news of the day was that America's new President was a klutz. One reporter even wrote that Ford had "toppled over and, for a moment, lay spread-eagled at the bottom of the airline ramp" when he first arrived in Salzburg.[5]

Ford refused to take the reporters' stories seriously. "I'm an activist," he told Nessen. "Activists are more prone to stumble than anyone else. If you don't let their questions get under your skin, they'll realize that they're just wasting time, and they'll start to focus on something else." He was wrong. After Salzburg, he learned to his dismay that "every time I stumbled or bumped my head or fell in the snow, reporters zeroed in on that to the exclusion of almost everything else." Any little mishap of Ford's made the news: bumping his head on a helicopter door; taking a fall while skiing; getting tangled in his dogs' leashes while playing with them. If there were no mishaps, that was news, too. CBS's Bob Sheiffer reported that one of Ford's campaign trips was "remarkably free of gaffes." But an Oklahoma reporter, doing a story on the President, lamented the eventlessness: "I kept wishing the president would bump his head or skin his shins or suffer some small mishap for me to peg a paragraph on."[6]

The de-athleticizing of President Ford proceeded apace. *New York* magazine depicted him as Bozo the Clown on one of its covers; a *Washington Post* columnist referred to him as "The Great Flub-Dub" and entitled his piece "Our Top Fall-Down Comic;" a *Denver Post* cartoon showed him skiing backwards down a mountain; and there was said to be a "Jerry Ford doll," which, when wound up, lurched into things. There was even a *Jerry Ford Jokebook* making fun of his efforts to win reelection in 1976. "During the 1976 primary in frigid New Hampshire," went one joke, "Mr. Ford in his absent-minded way kissed a snowball and threw a baby." Ford did, of course, have his defenders. *Washington Star* social columnist Betty Beale wrote that Ford was the most graceful of all the Presidents she had danced with, and *Sports Illustrated* insisted, "The irony is that no president has come close to Ford in athletic ability." But the ribbing was unrelenting. "Ford's continuing problem in the White House...," Nessen pointed out, "was the portrayal of him in the media as a bumbler. This false image was perpetuated by news reports, photographs, and TV film clips that magnified every presidential stumble. Alleged physical clumsiness was subtly translated into suggestions of mental ineptitude. Such ridicule in the press and on television undermined public respect for Ford as a leader and damaged his chances in the 1976 election. After all, no one wants a clown for president."[7]

At first Ford took the ribbing in good humor. After being teased for a fall he took while skiing in Colorado, he told Nessen that many of the young reporters who were making fun of him got most of their exercise on barstools and were too far out of shape to make it down the beginner's slope in Vail. "Most of the critics...," he said in a *Washington Post* interview, "have never played in a ball game, never skied. I don't know whether it is a self-defense mechanism in themselves or what, but I'm kind of amused at that. It doesn't bother me at all." The following day, though, talking to some reporters in the Oval Office, he said, "Some of the things you read or hear or see, you know, it kind of hurts your pride a little bit because you know it isn't true. You have to be a little thick-skinned, and I think that comes from some experience." But the President's advisers persuaded him to cut down on public appearances at holiday celebrations or sports events that might provide openings for reportorial mirth.[8]

One of Ford's tormenters was comedian Chevy Chase on TV's *Saturday Night Live*. Chase's takeoff on Ford became a regular feature of the program during his presidency, with Chase/Ford tripping over furniture, falling on the floor, bumping into things, and making inane remarks, week after week, for the delectation of a sizeable television audience. Ford's advisers finally decided to take the sting out of the *Saturday Night Live* program by having the President himself do a takeoff on Chase/Ford in public, thereby showing that he was a good sport who didn't take himself too seriously and could laugh about his missteps. In March 1976, at the annual dinner of the Radio and Television Correspondents Association in Washington, Chase, by prearrangement, put on his act, with the Fords sitting at the head table to watch him, as the band played "Hail to the Chief": He stumbled across the ballroom, bumped his head on the rostrum, and cried, "I have asked the Secret Service to move the salad fork embedded in my left hand." Ford puffing his pipe, laughed heartily with everyone else, and when Chase finished his spoof, it was his turn to put on a little act of his own that he had carefully rehearsed in the White

House. As he stood up, he pretended to get tangled up in the table-cloth, pulled a cup and some silverware off the table, stumbled over to the podium, put the pages of a speech on the podium, and then spilled them all over the floor. "I'm Jerry Ford, and you're not," he burbled. "Mr. Chevy Chase, you are a very, very funny suburb." The audience warmly applauded his shenanigans, and some of the guests thought he had beat Chase at his own game. But the President's act didn't stop the ribbing, and the false image the media created for him undoubtedly contributed to his defeat for reelection when he ran against Jimmy Carter in November. The confused answer he gave to a question in one of the televised debates with Carter—giving the impression he didn't think the Soviet Union dominated the nations of Eastern Europe—also hurt him badly.[9]

Media teasing didn't keep Ford from engaging in his favorite recreations—skiing and golfing—as often as he could while he was President. In 1975, when he took his family to Vail, Colorado, where he owned a condominium downtown, for some skiing, he took some work with him, since, as *Time* put it, he was "acutely conscious of some press complaints that he shouldn't be schussing downhill while the nation's economy was slipping in the same direction." But he also arrived in Vail carefully prepared for skiing. "At 61," *Time* reported "the most celebrated former college football center in the history of the sport is still a man who craves exercise, and he had trained for his annual assault on Vail like the seasoned athlete he is." For two months Ford had followed a diet-and-exercise prescribed by Dr. William Lukash, the White House physician, for losing weight. Every day he strapped fifty pounds of weights on one leg, raised it twenty-five times, and then repeated the exercise with the other leg. He then pedaled on a stationary bicycle for fifteen minutes and after that did twenty-five sit-ups. He succeeded in reducing his weight from 206 to 195 pounds, and was eager to get going when he arrived in Vail. Every time he set out on a run there, he was accompanied by an entourage of family members, friends, and Secret Service men chosen for their skiing skills. "He's fast," said a ski instructor who went along

one day. "He isn't in the professional class, but he's an advanced inter-
mediate." Just before he left for Washington at the end of his vacation, one of the local residents told him, "We're really proud to have
you here in Vail." Returned Ford exuberantly: "You make me justice
of the peace, and I'll quit!"[10]

Ford was a golf nut as well as a ski bum. Two days after becoming
President, he headed for the links. Asked why he was in such a hurry
to play, he explained that with "all of the hectic publicity about
Nixon's resignation and my taking over, I thought I needed a little
breather." Ford's hope was that if he played a round of golf, it would
send a message to the American people that it was time to return to
"our normal lives, and try to have a little fun." Ford was a good golfer.
He began as a caddie when he was a boy, played as often as he could
through the years, and had developed a respectable game by the
time he became President. He was "a good putter and chipper," declared a pro at one of the clubs where he played, "sort of sweet and
smooth, like his personality." After he became President, he refused
to pull rank with the other golfers, and when they started calling him
"Mr. President," he said, "Out here, I'm just Jerry Ford." None of
them stopped using the formal title, but they appreciated the simple,
natural, and unpretentious way he behaved with them. Whenever
Ford arrived at the club, according to one player, he acted "like any
other member and picked up a game with anyone who's ready to go.
He just goes out there and has a hell of a good time." He refused to
accept any breaks or special favors—"mulligans" and "gimmes"—
from other players.[11]

Ford was deeply devoted to the game. "I've seen him play in snow
and rain, with a cold, and he wouldn't quit," said a Wall Street executive who played with him many times. "His knees were hurting, but
he'd go into deep traps and then go on to the next hole, putting it all
behind him. You're talking about a man who absolutely loves the
game." Ford was a pleasant companion most of the time, but when he
was behind, people noticed, even the Secret Service agents kept their
distance. "Sometimes the air is blue when he gets mad at himself on

the golf course," said one player. "But the anger is directed at himself—and most of the time he is in control of his temper." To the delight of reporters, Ford came up with wild tee shots from time to time, sending the ball into the ranks of spectators, thus enabling them to jazz up their coverage of his game. The *New York Times* once compared him to former golfing Vice President Spiro Agnew in an eye-catching headline: "Ford, Teeing Off Like Agnew, Hits Spectator In Head With Golf Ball." Exaggeration of his errant shots was inevitable. Comedian Bob Hope, with whom he played many a game, couldn't resist exaggerating the accidents and teasing him in his comedy routines:

"Jerry Ford has made golf a contact sport. He's the most dangerous driver since Ben Hur."

"Ford doesn't really have to keep score; he can just look back and count the wounded."

"One of my most prized possessions is the Purple Heart I received for all the golf I've played with him."

"You can recognize him on the course because his golf cart has a red cross painted at the top."

"The Russians used to say that if we were really serious about disarmament, we'd dismantle his golf clubs."

"Ford, the first president to use a lethal weapon—a golf club."

Ford once good-naturedly told Hope: "Although you have taken some license in ridiculing my golf game before large audiences, I am nevertheless proud that you treat me in a manner equal to that of other Presidents you have known, such as Teddy Roosevelt, James Polk, and Andy Jackson."[12]

When Ford retired, he moved from the White House, people said, to the golf links. He played so often that a golf magazine pointed out that he might end his first year out of office playing in more events than Jack Nicklaus himself. Eventually he settled down with his wife, Betty, in Rancho Mirage, near Palm Springs, California; built a house on the golf course; and, according to experts, started playing the best golf of his life. He also continued to spend vacations in Vail, where he could ski as well as play golf, and founded a program called the Jerry Ford Invitational to promote golf there. When he reached eighty, Ford began to reduce his schedule, but he was chosen an honorary lifetime member of the Professional Golfers' Association for his contributions to the advancement of the sport. Asked why golf had become the favorite game of American Presidents in recent years, he said, "I think it's the camaraderie. You make friends and you expand friendships when you play golf. There is a downside—it takes a lot of time. It's a good atmosphere for relaxation and escape." Then he added: The game "is competitive. And I think most Presidents are competitive or they wouldn't be there."[13]

The Nature-Loving
Jimmy Carter

Jimmy Carter was a great outdoorsman. When he was President, he fished, hunted, skied, jogged, hiked, and went canoeing, and he kept these activities up for years after leaving the White House. The pleasure, moreover, of simply being "in the woods and fields, or along a stream" was essential to his well-being. "During the most critical moments of my life," he wrote in his *Outdoors Journal* (1988), "I have been renewed in spirit by the special feelings that came from the solitude and beauty of the out-of-doors." In the great outdoors, he confessed, "my concentration is so intense that for long periods the rest of the world is almost forgotten." To deepen his understanding of the natural world, he devoured books on plants, insects, birds, fishes, and mammals, without forgetting that "books and articles must be supplemented continually by personal experiences...."[1]

Carter's experiences in the natural world stemmed in great part from fishing. His father took him fishing when he was a little boy, and he never forgot the trips they made together to the ponds and streams around Plains, his hometown, and to places farther away in southern Georgia. "Many of the most highly publicized events of my presidency," he said years later, "are not nearly as memorable or significant in my life as fishing with my daddy...when I was a boy. Certainly almost none of them was as enjoyable." He continued fishing,

as often as he could, when he was in the navy and after entering politics. In 1973, however, Carter made a major change in his fishing
habits: He converted to fly-fishing. From then on, fishing became an
art and a science for him, as well as an endlessly fascinating recreation from which he learned something on just about every trip he
took.[2]

Carter worked hard at it. He steeped himself in information about
fishes, fishing rounds, and fishing techniques, held a conference of
fly-fishermen at Camp David, the presidential retreat in Maryland,
went fishing with expert anglers, and experimented with wet and dry
flies of his own making when casting his lines. Fly-fishing "opened
up...a new panorama of challenges," he explained in an interview,
"because you had to learn the intricacies of streams, of currents, of
water temperature, of different kinds of fly hatches, how to tie your
own flies, which wouldn't ordinarily do in other kinds of fishing, and
then try to match whatever fly is hatching off and experiment. It's a
matter of kind of stalking, a great element of patience, because the
consummate fly-fishers really spend a lot of time observing a pool or
a stream or current run before they ever put a fly in the water." Carter
came to be the most knowledgeable and sophisticated of all our piscatorial Presidents.[3]

Carter belonged to the catch-and-release school of fly-fishermen.
He found the pleasure of landing a difficult fish to count as much as,
if not more than, the pleasure of devouring it afterward, and he
couldn't help regarding the spunky fish as a worthy adversary rather
than a helpless victim. Some of the fish he caught ended up on the
dinner table, to be sure, but more of them were returned to the waters after he had succeeded in locating them, attracting their attention with his special flies, and then bringing them in successfully by
utilizing the techniques he had mastered through years of discipline
and hard work. Carter's wife, Rosalynn, was a constant companion
on his fishing trips, and in time she came to approximate the skills
he had developed. When they were living in the White House, the
couple liked to take short fishing vacations in Camp David, where

there was a stream nearby stocked with trout. But the presence of reporters spoiled the fun for them, so when they could manage it they
sneaked off to Spruce Creek in Pennsylvania, where they had more
privacy, to fish with their farmer-fisherman friend Wayne Harpster.
"President Carter was a stickler," Harpster observed, "and when he
decided to do something, he worked at it until he got it done. I think
he enjoyed the whole action of going into the stream and casting and
trying to catch fish. It was a good way to clear his mind." Harpster
soon learned that Carter enjoyed using dry flies the most, and sometimes, "when the dry flies weren't doing well, I would try to get him
to do nymphs and streamers, and he would sometimes. But he would
almost prefer to go out and catch nothing on dry flies to catching fish
other ways." Carter was known for his stubborn streak.[4]

During and after his presidency, Carter fished all over the world—
in Canada, Britain, Switzerland, the Virgin Islands, China, Japan, Australia, and New Zealand—and did well wherever he went. But his
biggest triumph came in Alaska, in 1985, when he was fishing for
rainbow trout in the Copper River about two hundred miles south of
Anchorage. His luck was poor at first, but one afternoon, when he decided to try a yellow stonefly nymph given him by a friend, he quickly
made a connection. "Suddenly there was a tremendous whirl in the
water," he recalled, "and the rod was almost pulled from my hands.
At first the trout moved upstream, near the bottom; through the vi-
brating line I could feel its head shaking. As I carefully shifted my
feet around to move toward the fish and into shallower water, he
leaped into the air—the biggest trout I had ever seen." The trout
turned out to be thirty inches long and nineteen inches around its
midsection, weighing twelve pounds. Afterward, when Carter was
asked how he wanted it mounted, he said, "I'd rather the fish were
alive in the Copper River." So measurements were made and photographs taken, and an experienced taxidermist created a mounted trophy for the former President, along with a plaque on which an official
guide vouched for his accomplishment. Carter knew that the fish he
returned to the river "was probably the largest trout I would ever
catch in a lifetime of fishing."[5]

Carter enjoyed hunting as well as fishing with his father when he was growing up in Plains, and he continued hunting as an adult. During his first Christmas vacation in Plains after becoming President he went quail hunting with one of his sons, and they saw to it that the family had a nice quail supper that night. The hunting trip soon made the news, and when he headed for church the following Sunday, Carter was astonished to encounter angry demonstrators on the sidewalk protesting his "murderous habits" as a hunter. Though he continued to go hunting a few times each year—for doves, ducks, and turkeys, as well as quail—he became defensive about it. "The effortless taking of game," he admitted, "is not hunting—it is slaughter." If the hunt centered on skill, not food, he said, there must be rules limiting the size of the catch, as well as measures to protect depleted game and programs to increase the population of declining species. "As governor and President," he said, "I have always worked very closely with game biologists responsible for prescribing and enforcing strict game laws. Whenever possible I like to visit nesting areas myself to listen to the specialists explain what was being done to maintain the waterfowl population at a maximum level." But he continued to take pleasure in testing his skills at hunting as well as fishing, while carefully avoiding what he called "slaughter."[6]

Whenever Carter went fishing or hunting, he managed to work some hiking and mountain-climbing—usually with his wife—into his schedule. He was always keenly aware of the natural setting in which he was acting, and it intensified the pleasure he received from engaging in his favorite recreations. In Alaska, he wrote, the "abundant wildlife"—bears, caribou, otters, moose, and eagles—"provided almost constant excitement," and once, while he was fishing, "a light-gray wolf came across the tundra, lay down on the cliff above me to watch for a while, and then quietly loped away." While fishing in Turniptown in northern Georgia, Carter saw black bears, ruffed grouse, and a white-tailed deer pass by, and one evening, when he and Rosalynn opened the cabin door, they saw a flock of wild turkeys "calmly walk just in front of us, not thirty feet away, cross the water, and disappear up the mountain." In Canada, when the couple were fishing one day, they saw "a pair of eagles circling overhead, building their nests and giving the high-pitched cries of love, excitement, or warning," and a day or so later, while on the way to the river, "we stopped to watch a gray whale moving slowly along the coast, only a few yards offshore, spouting regularly."[7]

Carter once remarked that he had never been a very good athlete, but his aspirations were high, he strove hard to excel, and he ended up as an extremely versatile sportsman. In addition to fishing and hunting, he liked to play softball, bowl, ski, and swim (he was a crack diver), and he played a lot of tennis during the early years of his presidency. In 1978 he took up jogging, and "in his usual fashion," said Dr. William Lukash, the White House physician, "he went at it intensely." Carter started running short distances on the White House driveway on weekdays and longer ones at Camp David on weekends. "I start looking forward to it almost from the moment I get up," he confessed. "If I don't run, I don't feel exactly right." Soon he was good enough to enter some ten-kilometer (6.2 miles) races in a park near Camp David. In his first four races, his best time was fifty minutes, and in September 1979, when he raced for the fifth time, he was bent on reducing it by four minutes. But it was not to be. As he neared the four-mile mark at the top of a hill he began to slow down, became wobbly, and started to fall. A Secret Service agent got hold of him and took him back to his quarters, where, after some tests, his doctor determined that he had been felled by heat exhaustion, not a heart attack, and treated him accordingly. After an hour Carter was on his feet again, and a little later, at an awards picnic, he handed out trophies to the winners and mentioned his mishap during the run. "They had to drag me off," he told people with a big smile. "I didn't want to stop." And he added: "The main thing for those of us who are senior citizens and joggers is to keep on."[8]

Carter did keep on, with jogging, fishing, hunting, and skiing, when he could spare the time, but he also spent as much time as he could with music, for it was one of his greatest delights. He and his wife liked both popular and classical music, which they listened to both on records and at live performances. Carter was "obsessed" with classical music when he was in the navy, he once confessed, but started listening to Bob Dylan's music "primarily because of my sons," and soon became a fan of Dylan, Paul Simon, and the Allman Brothers. He liked gospel music, too, and sponsored an "Old Fashioned Gospel Singin'" festival at the White House. Most gospel programs were, he knew, "24-hour sings," but he kept the festival to three hours. "Gospel music is really rural music," he told the audience. "It has both black and white derivations; it's not a racial kind of music....It's a music of pain, a music of longing, a music of faith."⁹

Carter's appreciation of classical music resembled President Truman's, though it included opera as well as symphonic music. Rosalynn recalled that the two of them liked listening to recordings of Richard Wagner's *Tristan and Isolde* as well as of Rachmaninoff piano concertos. One night, at the end of a diplomatic reception at which the Juilliard Quartet played, the guests had all left and the musicians were about to disperse when the Carters asked if they would play a little longer for them. "The Carters sat down," first violinist Robert Mann wrote later, "and we played the hymn-like slow movement from Haydn's op. 20, no. 1. We fully expected them to get up in the middle and excuse themselves gracefully. But they sat and listened, really listened—after thirty years of performing, one can sense the kind of quietness that implies deep concentration. There was a silent pause after we finished, a quite wonderful moment, and the President said, 'You know, this is the kind of music that brings tears to your eyes.'" When the Carters could manage it, they sat in on the rehearsals for the concerts that they had arranged for their White House evenings. "They loved the programs so much," said social secretary Gretchen Poston, "we couldn't keep them away. I think the presence of the president and first lady beforehand made the artists more relaxed during the evening's performance. They are often very nervous."¹⁰

The Carters were movie fans as well as music-lovers. Paul Fisher, the White House projectionist since 1953, thought Carter was the "biggest film buff" of all the Presidents since Eisenhower. "He loved good movies," Fisher noted, "everything from news films to the classics." The first movie screened for him, two days after his inauguration, was *All the President's Men* (1976), centered on the Watergate scandal. Carter had said he and his wife wanted only pictures rated G and PG, but Fisher told him if "that's all they wanted to see, they wouldn't have much of a choice." Soon he was including R-rated films, such as *The Godfather* (1972), *Chinatown* (1975), and *Blazing Saddles* (1975), in his screenings without any complaints from the Carters. During his four years in the White House, Carter had 465 screenings.[11]

Books were indispensable to Carter in or out of the White House. He had been an avid reader since his earliest years. As a youngster, he went through the Tarzan books in his father's library, as well as the Tom Swift series. His parents encouraged his reading habits and didn't mind it a bit if he brought a book to the table to read while he was eating. Julia Coleman, one of Carter's high school teachers, got him reading books on a higher level, including books of poetry, and at the same time helped him develop an appreciation of classical music. When he was only thirteen, she urged him to read Tolstoy's *War and Peace;* he was somewhat confounded when he checked it out of the library, expecting a book about cowboys and Indians, only to find it was a lengthy tome about the Napoleonic Wars and the invasion of Russia in the early nineteenth century. When he was older, he reread it a couple of times and came to cite it as an inspiration for his populistic view of human development. Tolstoy, Carter declared, believed that "the course of human events—even the great historical events—is determined ultimately not by the leaders, but by the common ordinary people. Their hopes and dreams, their doubts and fears, their courage and tenacity, their quiet commitments to determine the destiny of the world."[12]

A lot of Carter's reading was practical; he read to gather information that he could put to immediate use. Both he and his wife took courses in speed-reading so they wouldn't have to tarry too long over some of the books they felt impelled to read. But Carter came to appreciate the poetry of Dylan Thomas, found pleasure in books devoted to American history and biography, and read extensively in the fields of religion and philosophy, dipping into the works of Dietrich Bonhoeffer, Martin Buber, Karl Barth, Reinhold Niebuhr (one of his favorites), Hans Küng, Paul Tillich, and Søren Kierkegaard. Although he was exceedingly well-read when he became President, he wasn't exactly an intellectual. Some of his critics, in fact, doubted that he fully penetrated to the fundament underlying the ideas of the philosophers and poets whom he liked to quote. "He is a smart man," attested James Fallows, one of his speechwriters, "but not an intellectual in the sense of liking the play of ideas, of pushing concepts to their limits to examine their implications." Carter's sister Ruth regarded him as "a very logical, methodical, punctual, well-programmed man with a mind like a steel trap. I would not say that he's particularly creative or innovative."[13]

In retirement, though, Carter entered into one of the most creative periods of his life. A year or so after leaving the White House, he wrote his memoirs, explaining and defending his presidency (as most former Presidents did in the twentieth century), and the book received good reviews. Then, just for the fun of it, he proceeded to write a book about his childhood in Plains, Georgia, and another about his hunting and fishing excursions around the world, and both of them did so well that he began to look to writing as a major source of pleasure. He even ventured into poetry, publishing a collection of poems called *Always a Reckoning* in 1995 that became a bestseller. Poetry, Carter came to believe, was a "more deeply self-revelatory experience" than other kinds of writing. "I had always written as an engineer," he told an interviewer, "as briefly and concisely and clearly as possible, and I was never interested in anything but the most simple words. With poetry I experience kind of a mind expander, as I search for the most appropriate word, study the derivation of words and learn what their original meanings might have been." In 2004, at seventy-nine, he published his first novel, *The Hornet's Nest*, dealing with the American Revolution in Georgia. Carter was the first President to

publish a novel, and when asked to grade it, he suggested: "A tenta-
tive B-plus." By this time, with eighteen books to his credit, he thought
of himself—with a great deal of pride—as a professional writer, whose
major source of income came from writing.[14]

Carter derived enormous satisfaction from writing books for the
general public, but he was anxious to do more in his retirement
years. He was especially eager to do what he could, in his position as
a former President, to promote peace, democracy, and human rights
around the world. When plans were being made for the customary
presidential library in his honor, he wanted it to be more than a depository for his papers and records. After thinking about it for some
time, he woke up one night with an idea. "I know what we can do with
the library," he told his wife. "We can develop a place to help people
resolve disputes." The Carter Center, founded in 1986 and associated
with the Carter Library in Atlanta, Georgia, did more than that.
Under Carter's leadership, it monitored elections and fought disease
as well as mediated disputes around the world.[15]

Carter soon became a "globe-trotting missionary." He "circles the
globe at 30,000 feet," wrote Stanley W. Cloud in *Time* magazine,
"seeking opportunities to do good." And "you get the feeling," he
added, "that maybe this is what he thought the presidency would be
like—all good works—when he set out from Plains many years ago,
naively determined, against the odds, to make a difference." With the
exception of bringing Israel and Egypt together, Carter's presidency
had failed to achieve any of his goals, and he seemed determined
as former President to make up for lost time. Working through the
Carter Center, he helped mediate disputes in Asia and Africa, monitored elections in many Latin American and African countries to see
that they weren't rigged, and worked to eradicate Guinea worm disease in Africa and river blindness in South America. He and Rosalynn
also did some carpentry work for Habitat for Humanity, an organization dedicated to building homes for the poor. Periodically, according
to an article in *Time*, "they don their carpenter's aprons, pack up their
hammers, saws and chisels, and travel to the South Bronx or Phila-

delphia, or Tijuana." Carter was a good carpenter, in fact, and one of his hobbies was woodworking.[16]

Carter, who won a Nobel peace prize in 2002, was at his best when he was engaged in worthwhile activities that he thoroughly enjoyed doing. In retirement, he received the kind of acclaim that was notably lacking when he was President. The *New Yorker*'s Hendrik Hertzberg, one of Carter's former speech consultants, called him "the most imaginative, the most exemplary, the most useful to his country, in short, the most presidential of the ex-presidents." He was "not a great president," wrote *Washington Post* columnist Richard Cohen, "but he is indisputably a great ex-president." *Time* agreed. The "consensus view," said the newsweekly, is that "he has been a superb ex-President."[17]

The Movie-Struck
Ronald Reagan

Ronald Reagan, the first actor to become the nation's Chief Executive, thoroughly enjoyed the ceremonial side of the President's life. He liked hearing "Hail to the Chief" played whenever he appeared in public, got a big kick out of saluting military officers even though as President he was a civilian and not in uniform, and looked forward to throwing out the first ball for the opening of the baseball season. A few months after his inauguration in January 1981, he was scheduled to be the "Presidential opener" for the season but had to cancel because of the serious injuries he incurred during an attempt on his life in March. The season started without him, but there was a moment of silence in his honor before the first game commenced. When he finally recovered from the assault, Reagan was eager to make the friendly gesture to the sport that so many of his predecessors in the White House had made, and he was delighted when asked to perform the ceremony at Memorial Stadium, home of the Baltimore Orioles, in 1984.[1]

When Reagan appeared at the stadium that day, the crowd roared its approval, and Rick Dempsey, the Orioles' catcher, gave him a hearty welcome on the foul line between home plate and first base. After handing the President the ball, Dempsey suggested that he take up a position halfway between the pitcher's mound and the plate. After all, a throw from the mound to home plate was about sixty feet—"a tad long," Michael Deaver, one of Reagan's aides, observed, "for your average septuagenarian"—and Dempsey didn't want the President to make a wayward throw. But after Reagan took the ball, he listened politely to Dempsey's instructions, all the while quietly backing up toward the mound, and when the catcher realized what was happening, he gave in and took his position behind the plate. At that point, Reagan, according to Deaver, "wound up and dealt a dead strike." It was, Deaver thought, "one of the happiest times I have seen Reagan have." Reagan had, in fact, spent the previous six or seven weeks practicing the throw whenever he and his wife, Nancy, visited Camp David for a short vacation. As a professional actor, he knew what he had to do in order to give a good performance. And, as he had hoped, he performed superbly that day.[2]

Though Reagan liked baseball, he wasn't much of a player himself. When he was a student at Eureka College, near Peoria, Illinois, he went out for football rather than baseball because of his nearsightedness. "I never cared for baseball because I was ball-shy at batting," he once explained. "When I stood at the plate, the ball appeared out of nowhere about two feet in front of me. I was always the last chosen for a side in any game. Then I discovered football: no little invisible ball—just another guy to grab or knock down, and it didn't matter if his face was blurred." But baseball became important to him. After graduating from college, he took a job at station WHO in Des Moines, Illinois, covering the Chicago Cubs. To prepare himself for the position, Reagan watched some games in Chicago and received instructions in telegraphic re-creation before reporting for work. At WHO, he covered the Cubs' games by taking the brief reports of each pitch and play that an operator handed him and transmuting them into lively narratives that delighted radio audiences. One day, the wire went dead in the middle of a game, and he improvised his coverage for six or seven minutes so skillfully that his listeners were unaware of what had happened. Soon *The Sporting News* was calling him "an Iowa Air Ace" and reporting that he had "a thorough knowledge of the game, a gift for narrative and a pleasant voice."[3]

Success as a radio announcer wasn't enough for Reagan; he was eager to get into the movies. He had acted in plays for his high school in Dixon, Illinois, and at Eureka College, and the award he received for the part he played in a college production of Edna St. Vincent Millay's *Aria da Capo* whetted his appetite. The day he received the acting award, he said later, "was the day the acting bug really bit me, although I think it was probably orbiting pretty close to me for a long time before that...." In 1937, Reagan accompanied the Chicago Cubs to Catalina Island, not far from Hollywood, to cover their spring training, and managed to get a screen test at Warner Bros. that won him a contract. "He's the greatest find since Robert Taylor—," exclaimed the woman in charge of his takes, "if he'll just get rid of those glasses and do something about that awful haircut." Reagan discarded his glasses for contact lenses and let the makeup people take care of his hair.[4]

Reagan became a competent professional in Hollywood. He was always on time, knew his lines, gave no trouble on the set, and was soon much liked by the public for his amiable presence in scores of low-budget movies and, later on, in several major productions. One of his favorites was *Knute Rockne—All-American* (1940), in which he played the part of the dying halfback George Gipp, whose plea, "Win just one for the Gipper," was carried over into his presidency. In *Kings Row* (1942), he played the part of a man whose legs were amputated by a sadistic surgeon and who asked, after the operation, "Where's the rest of me?" He regarded it as his best performance, and years later, when he wrote his memoirs, he used the line as the title of the book. In *The Winning Team* (1952), he starred as Grover Cleveland Alexander, the Hall of Fame pitcher, and derived a great deal of pleasure from playing the part. Bob Lemon, the great Cleveland Indians pitcher, was Reagan's adviser and double during the making of the picture, and the two worked splendidly together. Reagan, Lemon found, "was very graceful and easy to teach. I had this little quirk in my own motion where I did a little hop after I released the ball so I would be in a position to field a ball hit back at me. By the time they started shooting the movie, Reagan was doing exactly the same thing." At one point, the script called for Alexander to hit a catcher's mitt nailed to the side of a barn. "Piece of cake," said Lemon, who was going to double for Reagan in the scene. For some reason, though, Lemon was not in good form at the time, and he proceeded to hit everything but the mitt. "Mind if I try?" Reagan finally asked, and when he did, Lemon said later, it was "[o]ne pitch, smack in the middle of that mitt. I've never been so embarrassed in all my life." It was Reagan's finest hour when it came to playing baseball.[5]

Movies helped shape Reagan's presidency. He brought the style, manners, gestures, attitudes, and even ideas he'd learned in movie-making to his work as President. In his speeches he liked to quote from movie dialogue, referred to episodes in films that he believed taught lessons, and sometimes discussed some of the events portrayed in movies as if they had actually happened. Movies, moreover, became one of the chief sources of entertainment for Reagan and his wife Nancy (who had made films, too, including one in which the two appeared together), when they spent their evenings together. The Reagans were both avowed film addicts. At Camp David on weekends, and sometimes during evenings at the White House, they watched movies, mostly "golden oldies," and consumed popcorn before retiring for the night. Reagan's preference was for science fiction, westerns, and war movies, while his wife liked romantic comedies. They rarely picked films made after the 1960s, because they regarded the newer ones as vulgar and too sexually explicit. "I have always thought it was more suggestive," Reagan told Deaver, "to see a hand reach out and hang the 'Do Not Disturb' sign on the door."[6]

Movies were on Reagan's mind much of the time that he was in the White House. Once, James Baker, his chief of staff, gave him a briefing book to review before presiding over an important conference of industrialized nations in Williamsburg, Virginia, and Reagan never got around to opening the book. "Well, Jim," he explained jauntily,

"*The Sound of Music* was on last night." On another occasion, he watched *War Games* (1983) at Camp David one night, and its tale of a computer whiz-kid who taps into the government's early warning system and almost sets off World War III fascinated him so much that a couple of days later when he met some congressmen to discuss arms control, all he could talk about was the movie. "I don't understand these computers very well," he told the congressmen, "but this young man obviously did. He had tied into NORAD [the early warning system]." He went on to tell the chairman of the Joint Chiefs of Staff how mean and slovenly the general in the movie had been, leaving the real-life general bewildered and uncomfortable.[7]

Sometimes Reagan got ideas from movies that he actually tried to promote as President. One of his own movies, *Murder in the Air* (1940), centering on the invention of a ray gun that could shoot down distant enemy aircraft, may well have inspired the strategic defense program ("Star Wars") that he began promoting during his second term in office. Another movie, *The Day the Earth Stood Still* (1951), about a dignified alien who visits the earth to warn people to "join us and live in peace" or be wiped out, seems to have promoted his desire to share strategic defense technology with the Soviet Union after Mikhail Gorbachev became the Soviet leader. During one of Reagan's meetings with Gorbachev, he gave him a video copy of *Friendly Persuasion* (1956), a movie about Quakers, because he said it showed not only the tragedy of war, but also "the problems of pacifism, the nobility of patriotism, as well as the love of peace."[8]

Reagan's movie memory was at times tricky. Sometimes he thought that scenes in some of the movies he liked were actual occurrences: the black messman cradling a machine gun at Pearl Harbor on December 7, 1941, and firing away at Japanese planes (*Air Force*, 1943); and a B-17 navy torpedo bomber pilot who went down with a wounded gunner instead of using his parachute and letting him die alone (*A Wing and a Prayer*, 1944). When confronted with his imaginings, he took the view that some stories are so inspirational that their authenticity was really beside the point. A reporter who had grown up in Lexington, Virginia, once told Reagan that as a boy he had been thrilled to see him years before on location in his hometown filming a story about the cadets at Virginia Military Institute called *Brother Rat* (1938). It was, he said, a "marvelous moment in a small boy's life." Reagan was enormously pleased to be regarded so highly, but he felt obliged to tell the reporter that his role in the picture hadn't required him to accompany the other performers to Lexington and he "simply wasn't there." The reporter was astonished. "Mr. President, how can that be? I've known it all my life. I've told it so many times." Reagan then asked him how many times he had seen the movie, and when the reporter said five or six times, Reagan told him: "That implanted in your head that I was there. You believed it because you wanted to believe it. There's nothing wrong with that. I do it all the time."[9]

Important as movies were for Reagan, they weren't his only indoor diversion. Some evenings he read books instead of watching movies. He wasn't exactly a "voracious reader," as he liked to call himself, but he read a lot when he was a boy and did a fair amount of reading for pleasure as an adult. "My idea of 'hell,'" he once said, "is I find myself in a hotel room without a book to read." In 1977, the director of the public library in Mobile, Alabama, asked one hundred notables, including former California governor Reagan, to name the five books that influenced them the most as young adults. Reagan was forthright. "I must confess your letter gave me some moments of mixed emotions," he wrote the director. "There must be a little snob in each of us, because my first reaction was to try to think of examples of classic literature I could list as my favorites in my younger years. None were forthcoming so I decided to 'come clean.'" His favorites, he said, were the King Arthur stories; *Northern Trails*, a book about animal life in Newfoundland and Labrador; the Tarzan books by Edgar Rice Burroughs (as well as his science-fiction books); *Frank Merriwell at Yale;* and Harold Bell Wright's novel *The Printer of Udell*, published in 1903 and subtitled "A Story of the Middle West." Reagan said Wright's book made "a lasting impression on him," mainly because of "the goodness of the principal character." It was about a young man, Dick Falkner, whose father (like Reagan's) was an alcoholic, who got a job as a printer with a publisher named George Udell, went to night school, rose rapidly in life, rescued a woman from prostitution and married her, got interested in community betterment, and ended up as a congressman bent on doing good in the world. Reagan didn't mention the other books that captured his interest as a youngster: Zane Grey's westerns, Arthur Conan Doyle's Sherlock Holmes stories, and Mark Twain's books about Tom Sawyer and Huckleberry Finn. "All in all," he told the librarian, "as I look back I realize that all my reading left an abiding belief in the triumph of good over evil. There were heroes who lived by standards of morality and fair play." The wry, ironic bent of the Twain books seems to have escaped him.[10]

Like most Presidents, Reagan went through a great deal of official documents and papers during the day, and he didn't find much time to read for pleasure. He did insist on seeing three newspapers every morning—the *Washington Post*, the *New York Times*, and the *Los Angeles Times* (his "hometown paper")—and he never missed reading the "funnies." He was also a devout reader of two conservative magazines: *Human Events* and the *National Review*. Always on the lookout for useable quotations from conservative sources, he once complained that when he cut out an appealing passage from a page in *Human Events*, he was likely to lose a good quote on the other side of the page. One of his aides suggested getting two subscriptions to the magazine, but he never bothered to do that.[11]

The books that Reagan got around to reading during vacations and just before bedtime in the White House often dealt with politics and economics from a conservative perspective. He liked to read anticommunist books, too, and regarded former communist Whitaker Chambers's *Witness* (1952), an account of his disillusioning experiences in the American Communist Party, as one of the best. For pleasure he turned to the novels of Louis L'Amour, Tom Clancy, and Allen Drury. Early in his presidency, when Drury sent him a copy of his latest novel about Washington politics, Reagan wrote to thank him for the gift but reminded him of how little time he had to read for sheer enjoyment. Drury's book, he wrote, "will go on the shelf in the White House library, but it took me a while to read it because most of my personal reading is limited to that last brief period before the lights go out after I've done all the 'homework' I bring home with me. Sometimes I've had to force myself to turn off the light. I enjoyed that book so much. You know, when I read all the others I was, of course, an outsider in Washington. It was quite something to read this one here in the White House where I have the problems faced by the principal in your book. Nancy is now going to get a chance to read it, but I told her I had to read it first because I was learning how to be president. I very much feel you have come close to the truth as to what perhaps my problems will be."[12]

Reagan collected jokes as well as quotes that he could use in speeches, interviews, and daily chitchat, and during his second term as President he went on a quest for Soviet jokes. "You know, I have a recent hobby," he remarked in a speech on economic matters he gave in August 1987. "I have been collecting stories that I can tell, or prove are being told by the citizens of the Soviet Union among themselves, which display not only a sense of humor but their feeling about the system." He proceeded to tell one of his favorites, dealing with a Russian who wants to buy a car. The Russian goes to the official agency, puts down his money, and is told that he can take delivery of the automobile in exactly ten years. "Morning or afternoon?" he asks. "Ten years from now, what difference does it make?" exclaims the clerk. "Well," says the car buyer, "the plumber is coming in the morning." Another one Reagan treasured was about the American who tells a Russian that the United States is so free he can stand in front of the White House and yell, "To hell with Ronald Reagan!" "That's nothing," retorts the Russian. "I can stand in front of the Kremlin and yell, 'To hell with Ronald Reagan!' too."[13]

Reagan received many contributions to his Soviet joke collection from friends, associates, the CIA, foreign visitors, and from a Soviet émigré who became a popular comedian in Los Angeles nightclubs. For Reagan, accumulating Soviet jokes was "a fun thing to do"; it gave him "a way of pointing up the differences between Russian and American society," noted one of his aides, "but without a hard edge." Sometimes, though, he overused his material. Reporters covering one of his speech-making tours got heartily sick of hearing an old joke about the Soviet potato farm day after day. In this tale, a party official asks a farmer how things are going and when the farmer says the harvest is so bountiful that the potatoes would "reach the foot of God" if piled on top of one another, the party official exclaims: "But this is the Soviet Union. There is no God here." "That's all right," says the farmer, "there are no potatoes either." But Reagan eventually abandoned his Soviet-joke hobby. When Gorbachev decided to open up Soviet society, tried to improve its economy, and sought an accommodation with the United States, Reagan responded hopefully, and there was the beginning of a thaw in the Cold War.[14]

If Reagan took time off from work every day to relax and have a little fun, he also reserved time for keeping in good physical shape. After being wounded by the would-be assassin in March 1981, he arranged to have a small gymnasium installed in the family quarters on the second floor of the White House where he could work out, with the help of a professional trainer, a half hour every day. A friend advised acquiring a punching bag on which to put pictures of his political foes to punch vigorously after a hard day, but he stuck to a stationary bicycle, a treadmill (from which he could watch the news on television), and hand weights. When he finally recovered from his injuries, the doctors told him he was in better physical shape than when he entered the White House. Despite surgery for colon cancer in 1985 and prostate surgery in 1987, Reagan continued to be physically strong and energetic until he left office.[15]

In addition to his daily workouts, Reagan did some swimming—in the White House pool and the pool at Camp David—when he was President, but he may well have spent more time bragging about the seventy-seven people he rescued as a youthful lifeguard in Dixon, Illinois, than doing any actual swimming. As President he was similarly neglectful of golf, another sport he had enjoyed during his movie-making years. "As an actor for Warner Brothers," he recalled, "I was always occupied making one picture after another, and golf was a relaxing way to spend a weekend afternoon." He even appeared in a short film, *Shoot Yourself Some Golf,* with long-hitter Jimmy Thomson. After leaving Hollywood and becoming a host for *General Electric Theater,* he seems to have reached his peak as a golfer. One pro who played with Reagan at that time testified that he had "a powerful, if somewhat wristy swing, and the prettiest set of Tommy Armour clubs you could ever imagine." When Reagan became governor of California, however, the game was "all downhill," he said, and when he became President, his game, he admitted, "took a dramatic nose-dive." He carried one golf lesson, though, with him into the White House. One day when he lost his temper, threw a pencil across the room, and then walked over to retrieve it, he said apologetically, "I learned a long time ago that if you're going to throw a club in anger, throw it in front of you so you won't have to go back and pick it up."[16]

By the time Reagan became President, his favorite sport was horseback riding. He quit tennis, he joked, "because I can't get the horse on the court." He began riding when he was a youthful lifeguard at Lowell Park and liked it so much that he joined the Fourteenth Cavalry Reserves as a second lieutenant in order to receive expert training and unlimited use of the regiment's horses in Des Moines. "A lot of people don't realize what good exercise horseback rising is," he said. "You just don't get on a horse and sit there as if you are in a deck chair. When that horse takes its first step, every muscle in your body reacts and moves with it. And the faster the horse moves, the more your muscles react." Horseback riding, Reagan insisted, not only helped keep people physically fit; it also stimulated their thinking. "Once you're up there on that horse," he said, "you get a different perspective on life itself. It's a tonic, really refreshing." In his acting days, some of his favorite movies were those dealing with horses and shot on location. In *Stallion Road* (1947), he did all the riding and jumping himself, and novelist William Faulkner, who helped write the screenplay, told a friend upon its release, "If you're a horse, you'll like the picture." In *The Last Outpost* (1951), filmed in Arizona, Reagan played the part of a Civil War cavalryman and proudly used Tarbaby, his own horse, during the filming.[17]

When Reagan took rides as President, he made use of the trails at the Quantico Marine Base in northeastern Virginia during the week, and on weekends did his riding at Camp David. But the place he liked best was Rancho del Cielo, his "ranch in the sky," the 688-acre ranch in the Santa Ynez Mountains northwest of Santa Barbara that he had acquired in 1974. There he could do ranch chores as well as take rides during vacations away from Washington. The chores included taking care of the horses by saddling them and cleaning their hooves and making the rounds of the ranch, cleaning brush from the trails, chopping wood, pruning trees, and repairing fences. It was "good, solid work," Reagan declared, and it gave him a feeling of having done something worthwhile during the day. One summer, after he succeeded in building four hundred feet of fence out of some old telephone poles, with the help of a ranch hand, he admitted that it was "tiring, heavy work," but added that "the exertion felt good, and we ended up with a handsome fence as well."[18]

Some of Reagan's staffers thought he spent too much time at his ranch and called it "Rancho del Lazio." But when Michael Deaver once suggested that to avoid media criticism he postpone or shorten one of the long vacations he planned there, Reagan was offended. "Look, Mike," he cried, "you can tell me to do a lot of things, but you're not going to tell me when to go to the ranch. I'm seventy years old and I figure that ranch is going to add some years onto my life, and I'm going to enjoy it." By the time he left the White House he had spent a total of 345 days—almost a complete year—at his ranch. But there wasn't any real "lazio." Reagan's "form of relaxation is hard physical labor," sighed one of his aides who on occasion did ranch chores with him. "That's what puts color in his cheeks." In December 1983, *Parade* magazine carried an article on fitness by Reagan

that concluded: "Why don't you get out there and enjoy some exercise yourself? If all of us do, America will be in better shape, too. I'll
be thinking of you." One day, when a reporter who was talking to
the President at the ranch realized he was eager to get back to his
chores, he ended the interview abruptly by referring to *King's Row:*
"Well, don't cut your leg off." And Nancy Reagan impishly quoted
Reagan's line in the movie: "Where's the rest of me?"[19]

In June 1987, Reagan received a letter from an old friend asking
him whether he was "still jumping hurdles" as he did the last time
she saw him, back in the 1950s. Reagan responded that he didn't take
horses over fences anymore because he wanted to avoid accidents
while he was in the White House. "We still ride," he told her, "but
since we only get to the ranch a few times a year and my long time favorite 'Little Man' has gone to horse heaven, I've decided it wouldn't
be fair to the job I have. I used to feel that way when I was doing
movies. While I was making one I wouldn't jump. It is a sport where
accidents can happen to the best of riders and while I miss it I have
to feel it wouldn't be right to have to cancel a summit meeting or such
while bones mended."

After retiring in January 1989, Reagan spent all the time he could
riding and doing chores at his "heavenly ranch" in California. In July,
however, he ran into some bad luck. While riding on a rocky trail at
the private ranch of a friend in Mexico, his horse suddenly "bucked
wildly several times," stumbled, and sent him flying down fifteen feet
onto the ground, where he slammed his head on a rock. Flown to the
Mayo Clinic in Rochester, Minnesota, he underwent an operation
that included puncturing his forehead to drain fluid off his brain. He
recovered after a few weeks, and took a light view of the accident.
"The riding incident was actually a miracle," he wrote afterward. "I
landed on my back from a height of about fifteen feet on a hard surface covered with rocks and all I suffered were some bruises." But
his wife and some of his friends came to believe that the accident
touched off the Alzheimer's disease that destroyed his mind a few
years later.[20]

Reagan was bored by some of the work he was expected to do in the White House, but on the whole he enjoyed being President for eight years. When playwright Clare Boothe Luce, introducing him at a dinner, quoted the laments of some of his predecessors about how tough it was being President, Reagan exclaimed: "Well, Clare, I must be doing something wrong. I'm kind of enjoying myself." He liked attending ceremonial events, entertaining celebrities at the White House, welcoming foreign dignitaries to the United States, reviewing the troops, passing on jokes to his aides and friends, and delivering speeches containing moralistic asides to the American people in person and on television. Asked by ABC's David Brinkley what effect his career as an actor had on his presidentiality, he mused, "There have been times in this office when I've wondered how you could do the job if you hadn't been an actor." Pressed to expand on this remark years later by biographer Lou Cannon, Reagan said that acting taught him to understand the feelings of other people, prepared him to face cameras and answer questions from the press, and enabled him to perform on the spot at public gatherings. Acting, in short, helped prepare him for "new roles, new challenges, and new performances" in the big world outside the movie studios.[21]

Not all Americans were enchanted by their Actor-President's performances. For progressives, it was the message (right-wing simplicisms), not the medium (television), that turned them off. Others disliked the medium, which Reagan used so adroitly, because they thought it turned politics into show business. Reagan, said *New Yorker* film critic Anthony Lane, "took gestures that he had refined on the screen...and floated them into the methodology of a canny public servant." *The New Republic*'s theater specialist, Robert Brustein, called Reagan a "Super TV Salesman" who "sells a product—or at best...acts the role of someone selling a product," the way he did when he was a host for *General Electric Theater*, before getting into politics. And film critic David Thompson said that Reagan "made it" in a "nationwide series in which, for eight years, he played *Mr. President?—That's Me!*, amassing more camera time than anyone else in the Actors' Guild and deftly feeding the lines and situations of Warner Brothers in the 1940s back into world affairs."[22]

Reagan, our oldest President, was willing to tease about his age and about charges that he didn't work hard enough, but when it came to his acting, he was more sensitive to criticism. People "struck a live nerve," he confessed, when they said he was a mediocre performer during his movie years. He resented it even more when critics like Thompson dismissed his whole presidency as an enormously successful piece of acting without any real substance behind it. If he put on such a good act as President, he couldn't help thinking, why shouldn't he receive compliments instead of putdowns for his dramatic skills? "Now that I am something else besides an actor, everybody is saying that I am an actor," he told his aides. Then he added, no doubt ruefully, "I'll probably be the only fellow who will get an Oscar posthumously."[23]

The Fast-Paced
George Herbert Walker Bush

There was nothing bookish about George H. W. Bush. When he became President in 1989, sports, not books, had long been his passion. In an interview during the 1988 campaign, Garry Wills asked Bush what books he read as a boy, and he became confused. He mentioned J. D. Salinger's *Catcher in the Rye* (1951), a bestseller that didn't appear until he was a grown man, and then trailed off: "But I can't—Garry, I don't read that much." Had he been quizzed about boyhood sports, however, he could have gone on endlessly about baseball, soccer, tennis, fishing, hunting, boating, and swimming. Both his parents were good athletes, and they saw to it that young "Poppy" (his boyhood nickname) was physically adroit, too. One of his boyhood friends swore that Bush had "the fastest eye-hand cordination of any person I have ever known," and at Yale, where he played baseball, one of his teammates recalled that "the key thing about Poppy—as everyone called him—was that he was so sure-gloved. All the infielders knew that if they threw the ball anywhere near him, he was going to pull it in."[1]

No President was as absorbed in sports as Bush was when he entered the White House. It was his opinion that "competition, whether it's in the political spectrum or athletically, teaches you some pretty good lessons," according to his son Marvin. "You learn how to lose

and how to be part of a team. You learn that life isn't a straight shot
north." After he was elected President, Bush took time out to pick a
cabinet and work on his inaugural address, but "mostly," reported the
New York Times's Maureen Dowd, "he kept up a grueling schedule of
shooting, casting, jogging, putting, pitching, lobbing, boating, diving
and body surfing." Bush made no secret of his intention to continue
the sporting life when he became President. In an interview in Kennebunkport, Maine, a longtime summer spot for the Bushes, he told
a reporter about his plans for recreation after his inauguration. "I'll
play a good deal of golf here," he said, "a good deal of tennis, a good
deal of horseshoes, a good deal of fishing, a good deal of running...."
Then he added with a smile, "and some reading." He explained: "I
have to throw that in for the intellectuals out there."[2]

One of those sports—horseshoes—was a fairly recent addition to
his recreational repertoire. When he was Vice President in the Reagan administration, the Secret Service men assigned to Bush taught
him how to play the game, and he became such an enthusiast that
after his inauguration as President he installed a regulation horseshoe pit on the White House's south lawn; another pit at Camp David,
the presidential retreat; and a third one at his summer home in Kennebunkport. Not only did he play numerous games with his family,
the White House press corps, Secret Service men, and members of
the cabinet; he also joined the National Horseshoe Pitchers Association, subscribed to the *Horseshoe News Digest*, and invited some of
the country's best horseshoe pitchers to the White House for exhibitions. At Walker's Point in Kennebunkport, the "Agent Busters"
(the Bush family) took on the "Bush Whackers" (the Secret Service
agents) at parties, and the head of the Whacker team said of Bush,
"He's a good loser, but he's a much better winner." In June 1990,
when Mikhail Gorbachev visited Camp David, Bush invited him to
play the game and was astonished when the Soviet leader made a
wing ringer with the first shoe he threw. When writer George Plimpton pitched horseshoes with Bush shortly before his inauguration, he
was impressed by the seriousness with which the President-elect

took the game and even more by the enormous pleasure he derived from playing it. Periodically, as they played, Bush exclaimed: "Isn't this game great? Have you ever had a better time? Isn't this just *great!*" When he won the game, he flung his arms up in triumph. But Plimpton realized that Bush's joy came as much from playing the game as from winning. Bush seemed to feel that way about all his sports.[3]

Horseshoes, of course, was only one of Bush's presidential recreations. His four years in the White House turned out to be what one observer called "an aerobic Presidency." He got as much golf, fishing, tennis, hunting, swimming, horseshoes, jogging, and boating into his schedule as he could without shirking his official responsibilities. "Mr. Bush works so hard at playing," commented the *New York Times*, that "he may not notice the difference when he returns to work in the White House." Frequently he squeezed two or more sports into one day. When he was on a vacation in Kennebunkport, he liked to inform the media that he was undertaking a "quintathlon," which might consist of a two-mile jog, two sets of tennis, a high-speed ride in his speedboat *Fidelity*, eighteen holes of golf, and fishing for striped bass in the Kennebunkport River. When visiting Florida, he liked to fish from a seventeen-foot skiff for a few hours and then rush off to work some other sports into his aerobic day. "Eight hours he spends out there," exclaimed a local guide who sometimes fished with him, "and when he gets back he'll have a game of tennis with Ted Williams and a couple of others. Then after that he goes jogging." Whenever the guide came back from fishing with Bush, he felt "pooped enough to go to bed!"[4]

Bush went from one sport to another in retirement, too. In his wife Barbara's book of reminiscences about their doings after leaving the White House, there are scores of references to his crowded days. On one occasion, he challenged and beat George P., one of his grandsons, in two close games of tennis. "It was the first time George had played singles in forty or fifty years," Mrs. Bush pointed out. "He was dead tired—and should have been—as he fished all morning, raced in and beat George P., and then rushed out to play eighteen holes of golf after lunch."[5]

When Bush rushed off to play golf that day, he probably hurried through that game, too. To golf he brought the same kind of frenetic energy he displayed when navigating his speedboat around the waters off the coast of Maine. His golf partners had various nicknames for the kind of golf he played: "power golf," "aerobic golf," "speed golf." Bush himself called it "cart polo"; he liked to careen around the green in his golf cart. One of his main objectives in golf was to play a round as rapidly as he could. "He plays twice as fast as the normal player," remarked a golf pro who often played with him. Once, Bush finished eighteen holes in one hour and twenty-five minutes; the average player took over four hours. "I play golf fast because I don't like to stand around and wait," he once explained. "Like a lot of other golfers, I get cold when I wait. Besides that, there are lots of other things to do. So get it on, play fast, go on to the next event." Rushing past a foursome one day, he yelled: "We may not be good, but we're fast!"[6]

Despite his haste on the course, Bush seemed to find the kind of relaxation from his presidential work that he was seeking when playing golf. "I guess there's no other job like the American presidency," he once mused. "It's hard to leave it, hard to get away from it, hard to relax. Golf helps an awful lot. It's a wonderful way to concentrate on a game and, thus, avoid some of the frustrations of the job." His partners almost invariably enjoyed his company; they found him lighthearted and outgoing during games. "He liked to have a good time out there," said one pro who knew and liked him, "so he'll be talking and joking when he's hitting. I know he wants to improve; he's told me so. But he just doesn't have the touch, or the seriousness to develop this finesse." Dan Jenkins, a popular sportswriter and novelist, played some games with Bush and was entranced. "If it's a fact that a man reveals his true character on a golf course," he wrote in *Golf Digest*, "I can only attest that the President was easier to be around than any captain of industry I've ever been paired with in a pro-am....He was the friendliest and most relaxed person...on every fairway."

According to golf pro Paul Marchand, Bush was "a great competitor and a great partner. He loves to kid and be kidded, and is a super cheerleader for your side. Whenever you make a birdie he'll yell, 'We did it.'" Still, some of Bush's partners regretted the speed he insisted on so much of the time. "He plays so fast he doesn't have time to concentrate," said Ken Raynor, the professional at the Cape Arundel Golf Club. "There's definitely no deliberation over a shot."[7]

Bush's precipitateness led the Secret Service to call him "The Mexican Jumping Bean," and he didn't seem to mind. Sometimes, though, he pushed himself too hard. In January 1992, he made a twelve-day trip with his wife, Barbara, through the Western Pacific, promoting the cause of American business, and when the couple arrived in Tokyo, the last stop, he was thoroughly exhausted. But the next day, feeling queasy, he faced a crowded schedule. In the morning he and Barbara paid a courtesy call on the emperor, exchanged gifts with him, and then did some shopping and sightseeing in the city. In the afternoon, Bush joined the American ambassador in a vigorous tennis game with the emperor and the crown prince, which he and the ambassador lost. By this time Bush felt so ill that he consulted his personal physician, learned that he had intestinal flu, and was advised to rest in his quarters until the next day.[8]

Despite his doctor's advice, Bush insisted on hurrying over to the Japanese prime minister's residence, where there was a state dinner in his honor that night. "We stood in a receiving line for quite a while," Mrs. Bush wrote in her memoirs, "and then George asked to be excused. I thought he had been called to the phone. Not true. He had been violently sick to his stomach." After a trip to the men's room, Bush felt a little better, and he and Barbara took their places at the dining room table. But Bush was worse off than he realized. As he finished the first course, he suddenly turned pale, threw up on the prime minister seated next to him, as well as on himself, and passed out. Barbara rushed over to hold a napkin to his mouth while a Secret Service man leaped over the table to lower him gently to the floor. Bush soon regained consciousness, however, got up, forced a smile as the crowd applauded, and then left for his quarters wearing an overcoat provided by the Secret Service to cover up his soiled clothes.[9]

This time Bush slowed himself down. He cancelled all his engagements for the following day, and he was well on the road to recovery by the time he and his wife boarded the plane for Washington. But films of his collapse in Tokyo began appearing on television in the United States and attracted a great deal of attention. His campaign managers—he was running for reelection in 1992—were extremely upset. The "collapsing and falling under the table in full view," said one of his aides wryly, "was never a political plus for a President." But Bush minimized the incident. "I don't think there is any political downside," he said gamely. After all, even "Democrats get the flu." As for the Japanese, they felt sorry for their honored guest's mishap, but they also used his name to coin a new Japanese verb: *bushu-suru* ("to do a Bush"), meaning "to throw up."[10]

Asked to name his favorite sport in an interview just before his inauguration, Bush was briefly tongue-tied. "I like 'em all," he finally said. "I like exercise. I think maybe fishing is my favorite. But then there's tennis." He was good at both but spent more time fishing. The *New York Times*'s Howell Raines, who fished with him, called Bush "a deeply snake-bit fisherman." He fished in many places in the United States, but he particularly liked angling for bluefish off the coast of Maine and for bonefish in the Florida Keys. When he was in Kennebunkport, he enjoyed maneuvering his twenty-eight-foot cigarette boat around the coves and inlets near the shore and then racing across the ocean at high speed, with the Secret Service men trying to keep up with him in their chase boats. "When he's got a rod in one hand, the steering wheel in the other and everything under control," said one of his fishing companions, "there's not a happier man anywhere."[11]

Bush did not regard himself as a good fly-fisherman, but after leaving the White House he began working hard to become one. In an interview with Bill Mares, chronicler of presidential fishing, he explained his great love for the sport. "It totally, totally clears your mind," he said. "You relax. It's not just catching the fish; it's the background, the environment, the beauty of it all. You can get mesmerized by these waves and this clear surf. So I get a kick out of not just catching or trying to catch a fish but from being in this setting...." The appeal of tennis, the other sport he mentioned in his pre-inaugural interview, was quite different from that of fishing. Bush was convinced that tennis had practical as well as recreational value. He played it about twice a week in good weather, and he used the game to size up people he was considering for positions in his administration. "Subconsciously at least," according to Marlin Fitzwater, his press secretary, "the president judges people by their competitive attitude on the court. He likes people who are competitive as well as fun."[12]

Keeping on the move, George Plimpton decided, was a "near obsession" with Bush. If he wasn't on a golf outing, taking a fishing trip, or playing tennis, he might be out hunting with his friends. In the winter he liked to spend time on the ranch of a business friend, south of Houston, hunting quail and turkey. He preferred stalking quail to catching turkey. "He'll walk for hours behind the dogs," said the rancher, "but waiting down in the creek beds for a turkey, that is a little confining." There was time for jogging, too, in Bush's aerobic world, three miles a day in nice weather; in bad weather he worked out on a stationary bike and treadmill in the little White House gym. "Unlike many who say they've never seen a happy jogger, I really enjoy it," he told people. "It gives me time to reflect, to clear the head."[13]

Baseball, Bush's favorite sport in college, continued to be a major interest of his as President. He attended games as often as he could, and took pride and pleasure in throwing out the first ceremonial ball of the season. "Throw it high," Nolan Ryan, his pitcher friend, advised him, "because amateurs get out there and throw it in the dirt. But if you heave it over the catcher's head, the crowd goes 'Oooh' and 'Aaah.'" Bush wasn't always able to follow Ryan's advice. On the opening day in Baltimore in 1992, his toss bounced in the dirt and he threw his hands over his head in embarrassment. "That was the worst toss I've ever seen in my life," groaned Oriole catcher Chris Hoiles. Bush vowed to do better the next time, but after losing his bid for reelection that fall, he never had another chance.[14]

Bush's frantic aerobic activities inevitably got him in trouble with the American public. Some people charged that it was all play and no work with the Yankee Texan and that he was neglecting his presidential responsibilities. During the Gulf War, moreover, his critics insisted that it was unseemly for him to play golf and zip around in his gas-guzzling speedboat in Maine while American boys were fighting in the Middle East. Victory in the war restored his popularity, but a turndown in the economy soon after revived the criticism. It got so that when he attended baseball games he was as likely to be booed as cheered. At one game, when he learned that two children were scheduled to go out on the field before he did, he offered to walk out with them, figuring no one would boo the kids. "It was a little defensive on my part," he admitted later. "But it worked."[15]

Bush attended plays as well as baseball games when he was President, but they were never a priority. He and his wife liked traditional musicals, but they tiptoed out of the theater after sitting through the first act of Stephen Sondheim's innovative musical play *A Little Night Music*. Bush's musical tastes, he once confessed, ran to country and western; they certainly didn't extend to classical music. After hearing Fort Worth pianist Van Cliburn perform for some Latin American presidents who were attending a conference in the United States, he told the Mexican president at breakfast the next day that he wanted "to commend the Mexican delegation for staying awake through the piano music." Bush wasn't much of a TV-watcher, except for the news and sporting events, but he did like Angela Lansbury's *Murder, She Wrote*. His favorite movies were action pictures, and his favorite actors during his Washington years were Clint Eastwood, Chuck Norris, Sylvester Stallone, and Arnold Schwarzenegger. In the movies of his younger days, he liked Clark Gable and Greer Garson.[16]

Reading for pleasure was never much of an option for Bush. Most of the reading he did was related to his work. Before going to China to represent the United States in Beijing in 1969, he and his wife diligently went through books on the country's history and culture and even learned a little Chinese. But Bush got more fun out of bicycling around China than reading books about it. "Instead of getting into a big limo, I'd arrive at a diplomatic function on a bike," he boasted. "It didn't surprise the Chinese, though sometimes they were startled to see my mother, who was in her seventies, arrive with me." Bush, his friend James Baker once remarked, "never learned to sit still," and some people doubted that he could sit still enough to do much reading. There are indications, however, that he enjoyed Tom Clancy's suspense novels and that from time to time he read books on American history and biography.[17]

In retirement, Bush retained his good health and continued with his favorite sports. But he found excitement in a new endeavor: parachuting. He was the only President ever to jump from a plane, and he did it three times. The first time, to be sure, was in the line of duty when he was in harm's way. It took place in 1944, during World War II, when the Japanese shot down the torpedo bomber he was piloting in the Pacific, forcing him to parachute into the ocean, where, after floating on a rubber raft for a couple of hours, he was finally rescued by an American submarine. Looking back on the event years later, he decided that it was perhaps the most important experience in his life up to that point. Since he had injured himself as he left the plane, he told friends before leaving the navy that he wanted to make another parachute jump someday and do it exactly right.[18]

Bush's second jump didn't come until 1997, when he was seventy-two. With his "hip-hip-hip hooray enthusiasm about life still undiminished," reported the *New York Times*, he parachuted from a plane circling 12,500 feet above the army base in Yuma, Arizona, plunged toward the earth in a headlong free fall, pulled the rip cord at 4,500 feet, and floated down into a soft landing below. "Unbelievable," he exclaimed afterward. "I know I made a few little mistakes. But it was wonderful. I'm a new man. I go home exhilarated." In 2004, when he was almost eighty, Bush made another jump, this time in Texas. He did it for the thrill, of course, but he also did it as part of a fundraising program to help pay for the construction of his presidential library at Texas A&M University in Bryan, Texas.[19]

☆ ☆ ☆ 41 ☆ ☆ ☆

The Unflappable
Bill Clinton

Bill Clinton was the only President ever to conduct a symphony orchestra while he was in Washington. During Clinton's second term in
office, Leonard Slatkin, conductor of the Washington National Symphony, called one day to invite him to direct the orchestra in the playing of Sousa's famous march, "The Stars and Stripes Forever," at the
Kennedy Center. He added that all the President actually had to do
was wave the baton more or less in time and the musicians would do
the rest. He even offered to give him a baton and said he would be
happy to show him how to hold it. To Slatkin's surprise, Clinton not
only said he would be delighted to do the conducting; he also asked
Slatkin to send the score of the Sousa march to the White House so
he could look it over beforehand. "When I stood before the orchestra," Clinton said later, "I was nervous, but we got into it, and away we
went. I hope Sousa would have been pleased." As a member of a school
band in his younger days, Clinton had already done some conducting.[1]

Music, not sports, was Clinton's biggest passion when he was
growing up in Hot Springs, Arkansas. He learned to play the clarinet
in fourth grade, shifted to the tenor saxophone ("because the band
needed one"), attended junior high school band rehearsals faithfully
every day, won some medals for his performances, and began attending the band camps held every summer at the University of Arkansas
in Fayetteville. The summer camps, where he studied for seven years,

"proved to be one of the most important experiences in my growing up," Clinton wrote in his memoirs. "First, I played and played. And I got better. Some days I would play for twelve hours until my lips were so sore I could hardly move them. I also listened to and learned from older, better musicians." He marched with the high school band at football games and in Christmas parades, played in a dance band (the "Stardusters"), and attended the regional and state band festivals at which judges rated the bands and awarded prizes for solo and ensemble performances. "It was in high school that I really fell in love with music," he recalled. "Classical, jazz, and band music joined rock and roll, swing, and gospel, as my idea of pure joy. For some reason, I didn't get into country and western until I was in my twenties, when Hank Williams and Patsy Cline reached down to me from heaven." In a jazz band competition in Camden, Arkansas, he won a prize for the "best sweet soloist," and at state band festivals he won medals for solos and ensembles and for student conducting. In college he played in a jazz trio, the "3 Kings," with a pianist and a drummer for a time, but he gave it up in order to concentrate on his studies at Georgetown University.[2]

Though Clinton liked classical music, especially Bach, his forte was popular music. His hero in the 1950s was Elvis Presley. He saw all of the singer's movies—his favorite was the first, *Love Me Tender* (1952)—and watched his famous appearance on the *Ed Sullivan Show*, with adoration but also with amusement over the way the camera carefully cut off Presley's lower body movements. "I loved Elvis," he said. "I could sing all his songs." He acknowledged that Presley's later movies were mediocre, but he continued to admire him so much that when he ran for President in 1992 some of his campaign workers called him "Elvis." After the election, when he appointed Kim Wardlaw of Louisiana a federal judge, she sent him a scarf Elvis had worn and signed for her at one of his concerts years before, which gave him much pleasure.[3]

While Clinton was President, he took in concerts in Washington, with his wife, Hillary; invited musicians—classical, jazz, blues, Broadway, and gospel—to the White House to perform; and sometimes

played the saxophone himself at parties. In January 1994, when he
visited Václav Havel, president of the Czech Republic, in Prague,
Havel took him to one of the jazz clubs that had supported his
"Velvet Revolution" (which transformed Communist Czechoslovakia
peacefully into a democratic country in 1989). After the band played
some tunes, he introduced Clinton to the players, presented him with
a fine new saxophone, and asked him to play with the band. Clinton
readily agreed; he tried out his new sax while the band performed
Gershwin's "Summertime" and a popular number sung by Frank
Sinatra, "My Funny Valentine," with Havel playing the tambourine.
Playing the saxophone, Clinton once said, gave him "the opportunity
to create something that was beautiful, something that I could channel my sensitivity, my feelings into."[4]

Clinton grew up loving books as well as music, and by the time he
became President he owned so many books that he had a problem
finding space for them in the White House. "It is truly one of the
things that distinguishes him from most active politicians," said Bet-
sey Wright, his chief of staff when he was governor of Arkansas, "that
he *never stops reading!* Most politicians don't have the time for it and
furthermore convince themselves that they pretty much know what
they have to know. And he never knew enough! He always had three
or four books going—*always!* From trash to economic treatises!" For
fun, Clinton breezed through mysteries and thrillers, but his main interest was in serious literature and nonfiction, and he loved talking
with other people about his reading.[5]

In 1993, when Tony Blair, the British prime minister, met President Clinton for the first time, the latter mentioned James Madison,
Shakespeare, and W. H. Auden during the first few minutes of their
conversation, and went on to stress the importance of knowing what
people read in order to understand their outlook on life. "It is difficult
to imagine Jefferson, for example, without John Locke before him,"
Clinton told Blair; "difficult to imagine Lincoln without knowing that
he read Shakespeare and Bunyan on the frontier." Several years later,
Harold Evans, former president of Random House, had a similar ex-

perience with the bookish President. When he interviewed Clinton shortly before he left the White House in 2001, he happened to notice a copy of David Hackett Fischer's *Albion's Seed* on the table, asked about it, and received a lively report on "our murderous Anglo-Saxon forbears." Evans mentioned some "dark deeds" committed by the Brits discussed in Simon Schama's *History of Britain*, and Clinton expressed eagerness to read the book. When Evans asked Clinton about the way the U.S. Supreme Court overruled actions of various states, Clinton mentioned a new book about John Marshall that "showed me how as chief justice in *Marbury* v. *Madison* (1803) he built the case for the American nation, and that's one of the most important things in American history." He elaborated on his point by citing "that wonderful book about the Gettysburg Address by Garry Wills." Evans concluded that when it came to books, Clinton was "an omnivore more than a collector."[6]

As a boy, Clinton devoured books on Native Americans; he read children's biographies of Geronimo, the great Apache; Crazy Horse, the Lakota Sioux who killed General George Custer and destroyed his troops at Little Bighorn; Chief Joseph of the Nez Percés; and the great Seminole chief Osceola. In high school he came to admire Shakespeare, and, like Abraham Lincoln, he liked to quote him and to expound on scenes from his favorite plays. At Georgetown and then at Oxford as a Rhodes scholar, he became familiar with many of the great thinkers in Western civilization: Montaigne, Hobbes, Rousseau, Hegel, Nietzsche, and Kierkegaard. But he was also reading books of his choice—sometimes, in fact, when he should have been studying the books assigned him in his classes. When he wasn't able to sleep at night, he turned on the lights and read. "I wish," he once mused, "I could wake up and read in the middle of the night every night." But he didn't linger over books. "He was very quick," according to Don Pogue, one of his Oxford housemates. "I would love to know how fast he could read. He would get through more in an hour of concentrated effort than just about anybody I've ever seen." After Clinton had been President for a while, he decided to "unclutter [his] day" by setting aside two hours in the middle of most days to "read, think, rest, and make phone calls. It would make a big difference."[7]

Clinton had his favorites: fiction, history, biography, and books on current events. As a young man, he was fascinated by George Orwell's *Animal Farm*, the allegorical tale about a totalitarian society, and he went on to read more of Orwell later on. He liked Southern writers—William Faulkner, Flannery O'Connor, and Carson McCullers—and made a point of introducing their novels to his friends in the North and in Britain. Dylan Thomas, the lyrical Welsh poet, meant a lot to him, and Clinton regretted not getting around to making a pilgrimage to his birthplace while he was in Britain. Before taking a trip to Spain with a fellow Rhodes scholar, he read Orwell's *Homage to Catalonia*, André Malraux's *Man's Hope*, Ernest Hemingway's *The Sun Also Rises*, Franz Borkenou's *The Spanish Cockpit*, and Hugh Thomas's *The Spanish Civil War*. He also became familiar with Russian literature, including the works of Tolstoy, Dostoevsky, and Turgenev. Once, when he was supposed to be studying procedures at Yale Law School, his friends found him reading a novel, Proust's *Remembrance of Things Past*. During the impeachment crisis of his second term as President—a government investigation into his private life charged that he had lied under oath—Clinton turned for solace to the Bible, Thomas à Kempis's *The Imitation of Christ,* and Marcus Aurelius's *Meditations*. He was eventually acquitted, but there wasn't much he could accomplish as president in his remaining months in office. He continued to read novels as well as books on current events. In his memoirs, he singled out Gabriel García Márquez's *One Hundred Years of Solitude*—a comic novel about the rise and fall of the mythical town of Macondo—as the greatest novel in any language since Faulkner died, and called García Márquez, whom he got to know, "my literary hero." The Colombian writer enjoyed pointing out that he was the only man who was friends with both Fidel Castro and Bill Clinton.[8]

In 1968, when Clinton was a senior at Georgetown and decided to apply for a Rhodes scholarship for study at Oxford, he was afraid that his failure to excel at any sport might work against him. Though he played touch football, his main skill, his friends joked, was his ability to win arguments over whether someone in the game had been touched. He was a mediocre basketball player, too, "lumbering," it was said, with his feet "seemingly glued to the gym floor." Clinton was a fairly good bowler, but bowling itself was not regarded as "Rhodish." The same was true of jogging. Clinton took up running when he was at Georgetown, but the reason may have been as much appetitive as athletic. "The running is a good deal," a friend told him. "You can run for 30 minutes or so and then eat all you want and put on no weight." Clinton eventually became notorious for his ability to combine running fast with eating fast.[9]

Just before interviews for the Rhodes scholarships commenced, Clinton became chairman of the Student Athletic Commission at Georgetown in the hope that it might be of some help to him. In the end, though, it was his high intelligence, amiable articulateness, and likable personality, not athletic achievements, that counted with the Rhodes interviewers. At the Southern regional interviews in New Orleans, Clinton talked affectionately about Arkansas and made it clear that he planned to return to his beloved state after finishing his education and devote his life to public service. His sociability also impressed the Brits he met at Oxford after winning a two-year scholarship. The younger English students "were in constant fascination with Bill and he with them," according to one of Clinton's classmates. "They were so verbally facile. It was expected that you would not just eat and run but eat and talk and debate the great issues of the day until you were thrown out of the dining room. Bill was always in the thick of it."

Clinton went out for rugby soon after arriving in Oxford and was thrilled when he scored his first touchdown for the university's team. It was "a big thing for a former band boy," he recalled. "I liked rugby. I was bigger than most English boys and could normally make an acceptable contribution by running to the ball and getting in the opposition's way...." One of the British students said that Clinton "wasn't

very good" at rugby, "but it didn't matter because what he contributed was wonderfully American enthusiasm. Actually, a bit much
enthusiasm. He flattened a guy in the first lineup who didn't have the
ball. When the ref said you don't have to do that I had to explain,
'Sorry, he's from America, where you can flatten anyone.'"[10]

When Clinton became President, he made running a regular part
of his daily schedule. Five days a week he got up at six A.M, donned
blue shorts, a red T-shirt, a blue baseball cap, and running shoes with
the words "Mr. President" inscribed on the sides, and took a three-
mile run in Haines Park, or along the Mall to Capitol Hill, or down
Pennsylvania Avenue to Georgetown. He always had plenty of company: senators, congressmen, governors, mayors, students, doctors,
TV and movie stars. "Jogging with the President," remarked one
White House official, "is bigger than an audience in the Oval Office."
A fundraising campaign by his admirers produced thirty thousand
dollars to build a running track on the South Grounds for his use, and
when it came under criticism, a White House spokesman insisted
that it was "perfectly acceptable that the president have a place to run
without leaving the grounds." Most of the time, though, he ran outside the White House, so he could indulge in one of his greatest pleasures: chatting informally with the people.[11]

If Clinton liked to jabber while jogging, he was even more sociable
while playing golf. "He's like a great big jovial host," said one of the
White House staffers who played with him. "His golf game is an ex-
tension of him in the sense that he makes people enjoy being with
him when he's out there." He liked leisurely games; a Clinton round
took five or more hours to complete. "What I like about golf," he once
remarked, "is what other people dislike—it takes so long to play. I
like the time it takes. Sometimes it takes me five or six holes to get
into the game." Clinton's style was "public links," some golfers said,
not "tony country club." He dressed casually, sometimes chomped on
an unlit cigar, talked to the golf balls—"Come on, baby!", "Come to
daddy!"—and gave his partners gratuitous advice: "You've got to turn
your ass!" But he asked for advice, too, before swings. And as the

game proceeded, he told stories and jokes, tossed out compliments for his partners' good shots and regrets for bad ones, discussed golf equipment, and talked about his experiences playing golf with Arnold Palmer and Jack Nicklaus. Politics was strictly off limits. One day, while he was playing with two Democratic senators, nature suddenly called when he was at the third hole, and since the nearest rest room was four holes away, one of the senators drove his cart over to a woman standing nearby in front of her house and asked if the President could use her bathroom. She readily assented, and afterward, as the President left, exclaimed to her husband: "God, this is a great country. Can you believe it? The President of the United States uses our bathroom and, Ernie, you didn't even vote for him!"[12]

When Clinton was governor of Arkansas he played golf about once a month, but once he was President he liked to get in some golf once a week. He insisted on going out to play even when the weather was poor. According to Sharon Farmer, the director of White House photography, "We've had rain golf, snow golf, mud golf. Other than reading and music, he'd rather be playing golf than anything." Golf "is an escape for Bill," said one friend. "He'll call and say, 'I can get away. Can you?' It's a chance to laugh and tell stories. For the first few holes, he's just warming up. Then he'll go around the turn and really start bearing down on you. A real good athlete. A really good attitude." President Eisenhower's putting green, plowed under during Nixon's presidency, was restored after Clinton became President, and he used it four or five times a week. "It's a think tank," said George Stephanopoulos, one of his aides. "It's quiet. It's quiet, there are no phones, and he can use the game to distract part of his mind and let the other part do its work."[13]

At a press conference on August 19, 1994, Clinton's birthday, a reporter asked him what he would choose if he were granted three wishes. His first wish, he replied, was the passage by Congress of a crime bill he was sponsoring; the second was a request for more civility in Washington; and the third involved golf. "I still have dreams of breaking 80 on the golf course," he said, "before I'm fifty." Two years later, at the Coronado Golf Course in California, he told the press corps on Air Force One that he had finally broken 80. When he saw that no one believed him, however, he exclaimed, "Heck, even a blind pig finds an acorn sometimes." Then he added triumphantly: "No freebies, no second drives, no nothin'." But Clinton was known for his mulligans (second shots) on the course; he called them a "presidential right." Where golfers usually got one do-over shot a round, Clinton often took several, and his critics called them "Billigans."[14]

Clinton, said one of his friends, "treats himself to lots of mulligans and gimmes. He likes to say he grants presidential pardons to the bad balls." The friend insisted he never saw Clinton "shoot a legitimate round in the 80s. Without all the mulligans and gimmes, he'd be in the 90s—okay, maybe the low 90s." The experts rated him "passable" as a golfer, but they gave him high marks for his enthusiasm and love of the game. "I love it—," Clinton told an interviewer, "it really is a lot like life. There is a lot of skill to it, but it's mostly a head game once you reach whatever level you are swinging. If you don't concentrate or get upset or you do all the stuff I did, you make mistakes and you pay for them. The other thing I like about it is, to some extent, it's an art, not a science. You do get breaks, both ways. You get some bad breaks, like when I hit the tree. And you get some great breaks—I hit another tree, and it went on the green. It's just a lot like life. I love it."[15]

On February 15, 1995, President Clinton joined former Presidents Gerald Ford and George H. W. Bush at the Indian Wells Country Club in California to play golf in the thirty-sixth annual Bob Hope Chrysler Classic, and the event attracted considerable media attention throughout the country. "We are as nervous as cats," Clinton told Dick Enberg, the NBC sportscaster, beforehand. "We were just talking about it. We're just as nervous as can be." Bush said his main goal was "just to get it in the air." Ford said presciently: "I would advise people they should stay behind us." When the game commenced, each of the Presidents displayed his own particular golfing style.

Clinton talked a lot, worked the crowd, and played at a relaxed rate. Bush, known for his fast pace, tried to keep things moving and sometimes putted out before the other players reached the green. Ford, famous for shots that struck spectators, lived up to his reputation by hitting a woman on the hand when he took his second shot on the eighth hole. But when it came to hitting spectators, Bush nudged Ford aside this time. On his first hole, he stroked a ball that veered off course, ricocheted off a tree, and hit a seventy-one-year-old woman named Norma Earley on the head. "I'm sorry I got in the way of your shot," she said, when Bush went over to apologize. It took several stitches to close a cut at the bridge of her nose, but she remained a loyal Bushie. Later on, Bush stroked again. "How's the wounded?" he asked a spectator when his ball hit him in the back of his thigh. "No blood, no problem," exclaimed the man, as Bush kindly autographed the ball for him. Bush won the match with a score of 92; Clinton's score was 93, and Ford's 100. Clinton couldn't resist making a populist point in his interview with Enberg that day. Golf, he said, was no longer the preserve of elites. "All kinds of people, all these new courses coming up, public courses, people are able to play who never could have played 10, 20 years ago. And that's very rewarding, because it's a sport that you can play throughout your life and at all different skill levels. It's really a perfect sport for our people."[16]

Like most Presidents, Clinton played games in the White House as well as outdoors. Shortly after becoming President, he arranged for the solarium on the third floor to be turned into a family room where family members and guests could sit and chat, watch television, and play cards (hearts and pinochle), as well as Trivial Pursuit and a new card game called "Oh Hell!" He liked doing crossword puzzles there, at high speed, using pens, not pencils, because he was so good at it. More important to him, though, were movies, having grown up at a time when thousands of Americans took in at least one movie every week. As a boy he'd feasted on *Flash Gordon* and *Rocket Man* serials, *Bugs Bunny* cartoons, and western features, and when he was older he took to biblical epics like *Samson and Delilah* (1949), *The Robe* (1953), and *Ben-Hur* (1959). He especially liked Cecil B. De Mille's *Ten Commandments* (1956), in which Charlton Heston played the part of Moses; he sat through it twice. Years later, when he invited Heston, then head of the National Rifle Association, to the White House as a Kennedy Center honoree, he told the audience that as a sponsor of gun control legislation he liked the former movie star better as Moses than as NRA head.[17]

The Clintons liked to see a movie every weekend when they were in town. "They read the entertainment pages like everyone else," according to a White House press aide, and chose the "hottest first run films," though avoiding movies containing "gratuitous violence." They liked the classics (*Casablanca*, 1942), comedies (the *Naked Gun* series starring Leslie Nielsen), idealistic fantasies (*Field of Dreams*, 1989), and current films like *Sling Blade* (1996), written and directed by and starring Billy Bob Thornton, a fellow Arkansan. But Clinton's all-time favorite was *High Noon* (1952), the classic western starring Gary Cooper and Grace Kelly. He saw it a half dozen times when it first came out and screened it more than a dozen times more when he was in the White House. "It's still my favorite movie," he wrote in his memoirs, "because it's not your typical macho western. I loved the movie because from start to finish, Gary Cooper is scared to death but does the right thing anyway."[18]

When Clinton told Dan Rather that *High Noon* was his favorite movie, the news reached Fred Zinneman, its director, nearly ninety and living in London, and he was so pleased with the President's comments that he sent him a copy of his annotated script for the movie as well as an autographed picture of himself with Cooper and Kelly on the *High Noon* set. In his memoirs years later, Clinton repeated what he had said in his interview with Rather: "Over the long years since I first saw *High Noon*, when I faced my own showdowns, I often thought of the look in Gary Cooper's eyes as he stares into the face of almost certain defeat, and how he keeps walking through his fears toward his duty. It works pretty well in real life too." As he prepared to leave the White House at the end of his second term, he said he would recommend the movie to his successor. And a few years later, when he established his presidential library in Fayetteville, Arkansas, he arranged one of the exhibits to display a scene from *High Noon* that he had drawn in crayon as a youngster after seeing the movie for the first time.[19]

☆ ☆ ☆ **42** ☆ ☆ ☆

The Physically Fit
George W. Bush

George W. Bush had one thing—and only one—in common with
Franklin D. Roosevelt: He liked to bestow nicknames on the people
he worked with when he was President. His nicknaming, which far
exceeded FDR's, was partly for the fun of it and partly to show people
who was boss. It would have been unthinkable in the American political system for presidential aides to respond in kind.

In an amusing takeoff on Bush's penchant for tossing off pet
names entitled "Yo, Sparky. Yeah, You Know Who You Are," writer
Bruce McCall described what he called the "first crisis" in the Bush
administration soon after the inaugural festivities in January 2001.
"Internal communications are in turmoil," wails a Bush staffer known
as "Frenchy" (though he doesn't know why). "The president says get
me Knuckles on the line, or here's the Esquimo, or let Bones and
uptown handle this, and nobody has a clue as to who he is talking
about." When the President orders that Bullets be sent to represent
him at a forthcoming conference on farm subsidies, according to Mc-
Call, one of Bush's aides assumes he meant General Colin Powell,
only to find out that the nickname referred to the secretary of agriculture. When Bush hears about the error, he exclaims: "Why for
heck's sake would I send Balloonfoot to do Bullet's job?" Later, when
reporters quiz the President about plans for developing a White

House nickname hotline to simplify things, he expresses surprise and confesses that he doesn't know anything about it. "For that," he says, "you'd have to talk to Stilts." McCall quotes *Newsweek* as saying of the new President: "He's our nicknamer in chief."[1]

But Bush himself also received nicknames—not, to be sure, from his associates, but from reporters, Op-Ed writers, columnists, and commentators who were eager to distinguish him from his father, former President George H. W. Bush. Sometimes they called him "Junior"; other times they reduced him to his pronunciation of his middle initial, "Dubya," or simply "W"; and now and then they turned to presidential chronology, designating him as "43" and his father as "41." (Rumor had it that George and his dad greeted each other numerically on occasion.) More colorful, though, were the nicknames referring to Bush's athletic endeavors: "Gym Rat"; "Biker-in-Chief"; "Baseball Fanatic-in-Chief"; "Sub-Seven Miler"; "Fastest President." The media got it right. If nicknames were an essential part of the Bush style, so were athletics. It was clear from the outset that George W. intended to keep as fit as a fiddle while he was in Washington despite the unavoidable distractions of presidential business. Newspaper headlines told the story: "A President Leaves No Doubt About Being Fit To Run The Country"; "Bush Is Known For His Commitment To Fitness"; "Bush Gets Clean Bill of Health"; "Doctors Say Bush Lost 8 Pounds And Is In 'Excellent Health.'"[2]

The "Fittest President" nickname is probably accurate. In his periodic checkups as President, doctors rated Bush in the top two percent of men his age for cardiovascular fitness, and in a book entitled the *White House Workout*, health specialists recommended that the American people adopt his "four pillars" of good health: daily physical activity, proper nutrition, basic screenings, and healthy lifestyle choices. Bush found it great fun keeping in good shape. "I like to be fit," he told some reporters and aides after giving them a rather rigorous tour of his ranch in Crawford, Texas. "My personality is such that I like to drive myself; I like to work hard." The doctors did, however, "caution President Bush about his posture," announced comedian Jay Leno. "They noticed when he starts, he tends to lean way to the right."[3]

Basic to Bush's fitness was the exercise room he set up on the top floor of the White House, which he visited at least once a day while in Washington. It contained a treadmill, an elliptical trainer, and some weights for strengthening his muscles. Arkansas governor Mike Huckabee was the Bushes' guest one night, and he joined the President for a workout the next morning. Bush, he concluded, was "an incredibly disciplined person who works out every day and is in terrific shape." Sometimes, when Bush planned a flight to some distant place, he had the treadmill placed in the conference room on *Air Force One* to make use of en route.[4]

For Bush, though, using the treadmill was not nearly as invigorating as running outdoors. He took up running in 1972, and for a long time it was his favorite sport. "For me," he told interviewers from *Runner's World*, "the psychological benefit is enormous. It helps me to clear my mind." And "over time," he added, "I'm convinced that running helped me quit drinking and smoking....If you're drinking too much, and you're running to cure a hangover, pretty soon you have to make a choice. Do you want to keep getting a hangover or do you want to feel the way you do after a run? Running is a way to heal people." When he became President, he continued his daily running and, in June 2002, also became "the poster president for working out," as one writer put it, by joining four hundred White House workers in a three-mile run around the parade ground at the army's Fort McNair in southwestern Washington. Wearing blue shorts and a white T-shirt bearing the message "Healthier U.S. Government," he finished twenty-sixth under a hot morning sun, taking only twenty minutes and twenty-nine seconds. At his ranch in Crawford, Texas, where Bush always ran when on vacation there, he formed a "100 Degrees Club," made up of staff members and Secret Service agents who were able to keep up with him on hilly three-mile runs when it was 100 degrees out. Unfortunately, sore knees eventually forced him to give up running. But he soon turned to a new sport: bicycling.[5]

Bush enjoyed being America's "Biker-in-Chief" even more than he did being its "Runner-in-Chief," and from the outset he was an aggressive cyclist. "That goddam bicycle riding he's doing is crazy," said a family friend. "He's got all this energy he's got to burn up." Bush biked everywhere: in Washington, at Camp David, on his Crawford ranch, and in foreign countries if he could arrange it. Though he flew over his handlebars, scraping his face and hands, on one occasion, and another time crashed into a police officer in Scotland, he reassured people, "I am a safe mountain biker." He was proud of his prowess. He scheduled tough ninety-minute races over a course containing steep hills around Camp David for his healthiest friends to enter, and often left them in the dust as he sped along in his Trek mountain bike. In August 2005, he invited Lance Armstrong, a fellow Texan and a seven-time Tour de France winner, to take a seventeen-mile ride with him on his ranch. After the two-hour midmorning ride, Bush presented Armstrong with a red, white, and blue "Tour de Crawford" T-shirt along with some cycling socks with the presidential seal on the ankles. Armstrong, twenty-five years his junior, later said the President was "one competitive dude," but he was critical of his war in Iraq. A cancer survivor, Armstrong insisted that the "biggest downside to a war in Iraq is what you could do with that money. What does a war in Iraq cost a week? A billion? Maybe a billion a day? The budget for the National Cancer Institute is $4 billion. That has to change. It needs to become a priority again."[6]

Biking wasn't Bush's only sport after he gave up running. He liked to fish and hunt when he was vacationing in Crawford, but when he visited his parents at their summer home in Kennebunkport, Maine, he was apt to take on his father in a few rounds of golf. Like his dad, George W. was a player in a hurry, though he never approached the record of eighteen holes in one hour and twenty-four minutes that his father and Ken Raynor once made. Raynor, a pro at Cape Arundel Golf Club, said that George W. had two priorities: "to excel as an athlete and to play quickly." Nobody, he went on to say, "plays as fast as the Bushes like to play." In August 2002, Bush was set to play one afternoon when news came through of the suicide bombing of a bus in Israel that killed nine people. With his driver in his left gloved hand, Bush exclaimed to reporters standing nearby: "I call upon all nations to do everything they can to stop these terrorist killings." Then, without a pause, he went on to say, "Thank you. Now watch this drive." He hit his first ball into the rough, took a mulligan, and then teed off nicely. "Hard this early in the morning to loosen up," he remarked to the reporters.[7]

Crawford, with his beloved 1,600-acre ranch, was Bush's favorite vacation place. He went fishing as well as biking there, catching bass in the nine-acre lake near the ranch house he had helped design, build, and stock before he became President. "He catches a fish every time he goes there," according to a Bush confidant. "This is his favorite outdoor pursuit." A state senator who fished there with him found him extremely focused and competitive when trying to reel in a big fish. "He fishes hard," he said. "It's like his arm is moving all the time, casting, casting, casting." Bush once joked that his "best moment" as President "was when I caught a 7½-pound largemouth bass on my lake." He hunted as well as fished when he was in Crawford. "I love to get in the pickup truck with my dogs as the sun is setting," he told reporters, and "go look for game." He exulted in the fact that the Secret Service let him drive his own car on the ranch, something he couldn't do in Washington. In his hunting excursions he shot doves, but not turkeys. "I don't want to shoot the turkeys," he explained. "I like turkeys."[8]

Bush spent a lot of time clearing cedar away from the oak trees on his ranch, utilizing a chain saw and a brush-thinning tool called an anker biter. "I'm able to clear my mind, and it helps me put it all in perspective," he told a reporter one day as his pickup bumped its way across a field, country music pouring forth from the radio. "Problems don't go away when we're here, but you can see them in a different light." The cedar problem was serious enough, he thought, but it was a welcome respite from the problems he faced in Washington. One afternoon, a reporter for the *Fort Worth Star-Telegram* watched the dirty and sweaty but exuberant Texas President haul freshly cut cedar to a burn pile. "We're lifting weights," he exulted with a big log on each shoulder, and then, throwing them onto the pile, he cried: "Oh, baby!" Occasionally there was an accident. During his Christmas vacation in Crawford in 2005, Bush turned up at the Brooke Army Medical Center in San Antonio and told reporters: "As you can possibly see, I have an injury myself—not here at the hospital, but in combat with a cedar. I eventually won. The cedar gave me a little scratch. As a matter of fact, the colonel asked if I needed first aid when she first saw me. I was able to avoid any major surgical operations here, but thanks for your compassion, colonel."[9] Not all Texans accepted Bush as an honest-to-goodness rancher. "He doesn't know dirt," harrumphed Fred Mattlage, a Crawford landowner. "All of Bush's brush-clearing," he insisted, was "for show. It's not necessary." Still, critics like Mattlage didn't deny that the President was a competent sportsman.[10]

Bush was an avid sports fan as well as an enthusiastic sportsman. In September 2001, only a few months after he became President, he tossed a coin in the White House to open the National Football League season, "an act," according to a *New York Times* reporter, "that will further burnish the president's credentials as the nation's First Fan." Formerly part-owner of the Texas Rangers, Bush followed the custom of throwing out the first baseball of the season, as other Presidents had done, but he was the first President to launch the professional football season. The President's coin toss appeared on huge scoreboards in ten stadiums around the country (where the home teams had picked heads or tails) and determined which team got the football first. "The man adores sports," the *Times* writer reminded his readers.[11]

Bush adored baseball even more than he did football. He had a T-ball baseball diamond installed on the South Lawn of the White House and spent "a fair amount of time" each day reading the box scores. It was, he said, "one way to take your mind off your job." Reporters soon learned that he preferred "chatting about balls and strikes to the fuzzy math of the federal budget." During his first few months in office, *Time* magazine reported, "Dubya's been promoting the game nationwide," and went on to list the baseball events on his schedule during his first four months as President: called Ted Williams in a New York City hospital to wish him well after open heart surgery (January 25); hosted a White House dinner for Yankees manager Joe Torre and other baseball people (February 7); discussed baseball in an interview with sports commentator Bob Costas (February 21); was host at a lunch for Hall of Famers such as Yogi Berra, Stan Musial, and Nolan Ryan (March 30); invited the widows of Mickey Mantle and Roger Maris to the screening of actor Billy Crystal's HBO baseball movie (April 9); and attended a White House correspondents' dinner at which *Saturday Night Live*'s Darrell Hammond presented him with a baseball glove, saying he had always wanted to play catch with the President (April 28). In November 2001, two months after the terrorist attacks on New York City and Washington, D.C., Bush's pitch to open the third game of the World Series in Yankee Stadium was, according to Florida's *Orlando Sentinel*, "nothing short of brilliant. It was a public relations home run as well as an act of stupendous courage...." When Bush entered the field to toss a pitch, he "put his manhood on the line. Could he do it? He did. He did it perfectly. Bush knows how to wind up, how to aim, how to coordinate hand and eye, how to follow through, how to hit the target, how to accept victory with grace and humility." Concluded the *Sentinel*'s sportswriter: "George, you da man, and Osama wears skirts."[12]

Bush's interest in sports far exceeded his interest in books, movies, and music, and he seemed happiest when he was on a "working" vacation in Crawford. "One of the things I find to be, you know, helpful, is to get outdoors," he told reporters one day there, just before teeing off at the Ridgewood Country Club nearby. "Washington, D.C., is a fine place, and I'm honored to be working in the Oval Office, staying in the compound there. But I'm the kind of person that needs to get outdoors. I like to be outdoors, I like to work outdoors.

It keeps my mind whole, it keeps my spirits up." Being outdoors at Crawford meant jogging, at first, and then biking, as well as fishing, hunting, hiking, and golfing—with, of course, time off for "liberating" the oak trees from cedar brush. "You're always the president—," Bush admitted, "no president can fully escape the job, nor should they want to—but you can put yourself in a different environment. When I'm out fishing, I think about issues a lot but in a way that's unique to Crawford, and certainly different from Washington."[13]

One day, after going on a seventeen-mile bike ride near Crawford, with reporters and photographers trailing along in cars, Bush outlined his plans for the rest of the day: "I'm going to have lunch with Secretary of State [Condoleeza] Rice, talk a little business; Mrs. Bush, talk a little business; we've got a friend from South Texas here, named Katharine Armstrong; take a little nap. I'm reading a little Elmore Leonard book right now, knock off a little Elmore Leonard this afternoon; go fishing with my man Barney; a light dinner and head to the ballgame. I get to bed around 9:30 P.M., wake up about 5 A.M. So it's a perfect day." Some days there were also "endless shots of him strutting around in his cowboy hat, blue jeans, [and] short-sleeved work shirts," noted one observer, with "question-and-answer sessions in which he's leaning on a fence rail."[14]

Some people thought Bush overdid the "working vacations." In August 2005, when he left Washington for a five-week vacation in Crawford, a *Washington Post* article pointed out that it was the forty-ninth trip to his cherished ranch since becoming President, and his 319th day—almost a year—in Crawford. "W., who has spent nearly 20 percent of his presidency at his ranch," wrote *New York Times* columnist Maureen Dowd, "is burrowed into his five-week vacation and two-hour daily workouts. He may be in great shape, but Iraq sure isn't." Two weeks later, when Bush left Crawford to spend a couple of days at the Tamarack Resort in the Idaho mountains, she wrote that "W. vacationed so hard in Texas he got bushed. He needed a vacation from his vacation." When reformer Ralph Nader, a critic of Bush's policies, was asked if he saw any redeeming qualities in President

Bush's administration, he exclaimed, "Yes, physical fitness." Comedian Jon Stewart, host of *The Daily Show,* couldn't resist teasing the President about his health consciousness. "A recent checkup," he said, showed that "Bush is arguably the healthiest Chief Executive ever. His secret? Daily exercise and a near total disengagement with reality."[15]

Acknowledgments

I am grateful to Bill Mares for permission to quote from *Fishing with the Presidents* (Mechanicsburg, Pa.: Stackpole Books, 1999), p. 84, and to James McGregor Burns for permission to make use of the wonderful "Rules for Visiting the Kennedys," appearing in his biography *John Kennedy: A Political Profile* (New York: Harcourt, Brace, 1959, 1960), pp. 129–130.

I want also to thank literary agent Gerry McCauley for all the help and encouragement he has given me through the years, as well as Jeff Barnard, my good friend in St. Louis, for his suggestions to improve the manuscript, and Sara Crowley, a graduate student in history at TCU, for putting my manuscript into "computer language," as I like to put it. The input of my editors at Harcourt, especially Andrea Schulz, was indispensable.

Notes

Preface

1. Richard H. Rovere, "The Loneliest Place in the World," *American Heritage,* August 1964, p. 32; February 21, 1779, *The Book of Abigail and John: Selected Letters of the Adams Family, 1762–1784* (Cambridge, Mass.: Harvard University Press, 1975), p. 239.

2. Morris K. Udall, "Choosing the President," Colorado Springs, Colo., March 15, 1974, *Proceedings of the Sixteenth Air Force Academy,* p. 12.

3. Rovere, "Loneliest Place," p. 32.

4. Shepherd Campbell and Peter Landau, *Presidential Lies: The Illustrated History of White House Golf* (New York: Macmillan, 1996), p. 3.

Chapter 1. The Dignified George Washington

1. Douglas Southall Freeman, *George Washington: A Biography* (abridgement to one volume by Richard Harwell, New York: Scribner's, 1968), p. 516.

2. James Parton, *The Life of Thomas Jefferson* (Boston: James R. Osgood & Co., 1874), p. 369.

3. Robert Norton Smith, *Patriarch: George Washington and the New American Nation* (Boston: Houghton Mifflin, 1993), p. 25; John Adams to Thomas Jefferson, July 1813, *The Writings of Thomas Jefferson,* 20 vols., ed. Albert Ellergy Bergh (Washington, D.C.: Thomas Jefferson Memorial Association, 1904–1905), vol. 8, p. 301.

4. Kevin L. Cope, *George Washington in and as Culture* (New York: AMS Press, 2001), p. 267.

5. Edmund Lindop and Joseph Jares, *White House Sportsmen* (Boston: Houghton Mifflin, 1964), p. 23.

6. Paul Leicester Ford, *The True George Washington* (Philadelphia: J. P. Lippincott, 1899), pp. 183–84.

7. Ibid., p. 184; Foster Rhea Dulles, *America Learns to Play* (New York: D. Appleton Century Company, 1940), p. 61.

8. Cope, *Washington in and as Culture,* p. 264.

9. James Thomas Flexner, *George Washington and the New Nation, 1783–1793* (Boston: Little, Brown & Co., 1969), p. 269.

10. Ibid.; Ford, *True Washington,* p. 198; Smith, *Patriarch,* p. 3.

11. Flexner, *Washington and New Nation,* pp. 269, 289.

12. Ford, *True Washington,* p. 163.

13. Ibid., p. 179.

14. Ibid., p. 163.

15. "After-Dinner Anecdotes of James Madison," *Virginia Magazine of History and Biography,* vol. 60 (1952), pp. 257–58.

16. Ford, *True Washington,* pp. 173–74.

17. Ibid., p. 174.

18. Smith, *Patriarch,* p. 28.

19. Edna M. Colman, *Seventy-Five Years of White House Gossip* (New York: Doubleday, Page & Co., 1925), p. 17.

20. *The Diary of William Maclay and Other Notes on Senate Debates,* ed. Kenneth R. Bowling and Henry E. Veit (Baltimore: Johns Hopkins University Press, 1988), p. 138.

21. Ford, *True Washington,* p. 171; Smith, *Patriarch,* p. 28.

22. Ford, *True Washington,* pp. 174, 178.

23. Paul Leicester Ford, *Washington and the Theater* (New York: Benjamin Bloom, 1899, 1967), p. 36.

24. Doron K. Antrim, "Our Musical Presidents," *Etude,* vol. 58 (May 1946), p. 337; Mel Peacock, "Music in the White House," *Etude* (January 1954), p. 54.

25. Elise K. Kirk, *Music at the White House* (Urbana: University of Illinois Press, 1986), pp. 7–14.

26. James Thomas Flexnor, *George Washington: Anguish and Farewell, 1793–1799* (Boston: Little, Brown & Co., 1969), p. 369n.

27. Ibid., p. 370.

28. Flexnor, *George Washington,* p. 357; Ford, *True Washington,* p. 189.

29. Flexnor, *George Washington,* p. 205; Ford, *True Washington,* p. 291.

30. *The Works of Thomas Jefferson,* 12 vols., ed. Paul Leicester Ford (New York: G. P. Putnam, 1905), vol. 1, p. 254; Flexnor, *Washington, Anguish and Farewell,* p. 67.

31. Ford, *True Washington,* p. 208.

32. John Bernard, *Retrospections of America, 1792–1811* (New York: Harper's, 1887), pp. 86–87; Paul Leland Haworth, *George Washington: Country Gentleman* (Indianapolis: Bobbs Merrill, 1915, 1925), pp. 311–12; Charles

W. Stetson, *Washington and His Neighbors* (Richmond, Va.: Garrett and Massie Incorporated, 1956), pp. 293–94. Some historians have doubted the veracity of Bernard's account of his encounter with Washington.

33. Bernard, *Retrospections,* p. 87.

34. Ibid., p. 89.

Chapter 2. The Conscientious John Adams

1. To Abigail Adams, Hague, July 25, 1782, L. H. Butterfield, ed., *The Book of Abigail and John: Selected Letters of the Adams Family, 1762–1784* (Cambridge, Mass.: Harvard University Pres, 1975), p. 320.

2. Ibid., pp. 320–21.

3. John Ferling, *John Adams: A Life* (Knoxville: University of Tennessee Press, 1992), p. 16.

4. Ibid.

5. Ibid., p. 17.

6. Ibid., p. 18.

7. L. H. Butterfield, ed., *Diary and Autobiography of John Adams,* 4 vols. (Cambridge, Mass.: Harvard University Press, 1961), vol. 1, pp. 115, 131, 168.

8. Ibid., 73; John Durant, *The Sports of Our Presidents* (New York: Hastings House, 1964), p. 23.

9. To Abigail Adams, August 14, 1776, *Book of Abigail and John,* p. 156.

10. Ferling, *John Adams,* p. 75.

11. To Abigail Adams, Passy, April 12, 1778, *Book of Abigail and John,* p. 210.

12. Ibid.

13. To Abigail Adams, Passy, February 21, 1779, *Book of Abigail and John,* p. 240.

14. To Abigail Adams, Passy, February 26, 1779, *Book of Abigail and John,* pp. 240–41.

15. Ibid.

16. To my dear Portia, Paris, May 12, 1780, *Book of Abigail and John,* p. 260.

17. Ibid.

18. Ibid.

19. To Abigail Adams, the Hague, August 15, 1782, *Book of Abigail and John,* p. 321; August 31, 1782, ibid., p. 322.

20. To Abigail Adams, Passy, February 21, 1779, ibid., p. 239.

21. Plymouth, May 1772, ibid., p. 53.

22. Spring 1759, *Diary and Autobiography of Adams,* vol. 1, p. 86.

23. Zoltán Haraszti, *John Adams and the Prophets of Progress* (Cambridge, Mass.: Harvard University Press, 1952).

24. Page Smith, *John Adams,* 2 vols. (Garden City, N.Y.: Doubleday, 1962), vol. 2, pp. 803–804.

25. June 15, 1760, *Diary and Autobiography of Adams,* vol. 1, p. 135.

26. Paul Wilstach, *Patriots Off Their Pedestals* (Indianapolis: Bobbs-Merrill, 1927), p. 101; Lester J. Capon, ed., *The Adams-Jefferson Letters,* 2 vols. (Chapel Hill: University of North Carolina Press, 1959), vol. 2, p. 542; Worthington C. Ford, ed., *Statesman and Friend: Correspondence of John Adams and Benjamin Waterhouse* (Boston: Little, Brown & Co., 1983), p. 77.

27. Smith, *Adams,* vol. 1, p. 589.

28. Frank Donovan, ed., *The John Adams Papers* (New York: Dodd, Mead, 1965), p. 209.

29. David McCullough, *John Adams* (New York: Simon & Schuster, 2001), p. 589.

Chapter 3. The Gifted Thomas Jefferson

1. Henry S. Randall, *The Life of Thomas Jefferson,* 3 vols. (New York: Derby & Jackson, 1858), vol. 3, p. 345; "Writings, Thomas Jefferson," *American Heritage* (February/March 1998), p. 32.

2. To John Garland Jefferson, New York, June 11, 1790, *The Works of Thomas Jefferson,* ed. Paul Leicester Ford (New York: G. P. Putnam, 1905), vol. 5, pp. 180–81; to Peter Carr, Paris, August 19, 1785, ibid., vol. 5, pp. 85–96; Bernard Mayo, *Jefferson Himself* (Boston: Houghton Mifflin, 1942), p. 18.

3. Welles Lobb, "Founding Father of Fitness," *Runner's World,* June 1993, p. 10.

4. William Mead and Paul Dickson, *Baseball: The President's Game* (Washington, D.C.: Farragut Publishing Co., 1997), p. 8.

5. Edmund Lindop and Joseph Jares, *White House Sportsmen* (Boston: Houghton Mifflin, 1964), p. 56.

6. Mayo, *Jefferson Himself,* p. 18.

7. Edna M. Colman, *Seventy-Five Years of White House Gossip* (New York: Doubleday, 1925), pp. 84–85; Lindop and Jares, *White House Sportsmen,* pp. 116–17.

8. *Time,* November 30, 1953, p. 6; Willard Sterne Randall, "Thomas Jefferson Takes a Vacation," *American Heritage,* July/August 1996, p. 77.

9. Randall, "Thomas Jefferson," pp. 76–83; Dumas Malone, *Jefferson and the Rights of Man* (Boston: Little, Brown & Co., 1951), pp. 359–61.

10. Malone, *Jefferson,* p. 361; Diane Ackerman, "America's First Gardener," *Parade Magazine,* July 15, 2001, p. 17; Eleanor Davidson Berman, *Thomas Jefferson among the Arts* (New York: Philosophical Library, 1947), p. 155.

11. Ibid., p. 150; Ackerman, "America's First Gardener," p. 17.

12. Berman, *Jefferson among the Arts,* p. 114; Douglas L. Wilson, "Thomas Jefferson and the Character Issue," *Atlantic Monthly,* November 1992, p. 66.

13. Edwin T. Martin, *Thomas Jefferson: Scientist* (New York: Henry Schuman, 1952), p. 104.

14. Dumas Malone, *Jefferson the President, Second Term, 1805–1808* (Boston: Little, Brown & Co., 1974), p. 19; "Those Clever Levers," *U.S. News and World Report,* February 1, 1993, p. 59; Wilson, "Jefferson and Character Issue," p. 65; Martin, *Jefferson: Scientist,* pp. 69, 73, 74, 78, 85, 86, 90, 104.

15. Berman, *Jefferson among the Arts,* p. 266; J. Bernard Cohen, *Science and the Founding Fathers* (New York: W. W. Norton, 1995), pp. 61–68.

16. "Founding Fathers," *U.S. News and World Report,* February 1, 1993, pp. 58–59; Dumas Malone, *Jefferson and the Ordeal of Liberty* (Boston: Little, Brown & Co., 1962), p. 345; Harlow Shapely, "Notes on Thomas Jefferson as a Natural Philosopher," Proceedings, *American Philosophical Society,* vol. 87 (1944), pp. 234, 237.

17. Mayo, *Jefferson Himself,* p. 31; Helen Cripe, *Thomas Jefferson and Music* (Charlottesville: University Press of Virginia, 1974), pp. 2, 3, 14, 20, 44, 89, 92; Elise K. Kirk, *Music at the White House* (Urbana: University of Illinois Press, 1981), pp. 25–27; Dumas Malone, *Jefferson the Virginian* (Boston: Little, Brown & Co., 1948), pp. 78–79; Doron K. Antrim, "Our Musical Presidents," *Etude,* vol. 58 (May 1946), p. 299.

18. Antrim, ibid.; Berman, *Jefferson among the Arts,* p. 182.

19. Ona Griffin Jeffries, *In and Out of the White House* (New York: W. Funk, 1960), pp. 41–42.

20. Jean Hanvey Hazelton, "Thomas Jefferson, Gourmet," *American Heritage,* October 1964, p. 21; Jeffries, *White House,* pp. 41–42, 52; John Adams to Benjamin Rush, December 25, 1811, in Charles Francis Adams, ed., *The Works of John Adams,* 10 vols. (Boston: 1850–1856), vol. 10, p. 11.

21. Charles B. Sanford, *Thomas Jefferson and His Library* (Hamden, Conn.: Archon Books, 1977), p. 42; Jefferson to John Adams, Monticello, June 10, 1815, *The Adams-Jefferson Letters,* ed. Lester J. Capon (Chapel Hill: University of North Carolina Press, 1959), p. 443; *Three Presidents and Their Books* (Urbana: University of Illinois Press, 1955), pp. 2–3.

22. Arthur Bestor *et al., Three Presidents and Their Books* (Urbana: University of Illinois Press, 1955), p. 8; Mayo, *Jefferson Himself,* p. 18.

23. John Adams to Thomas Jefferson, July 12, 1822, *Adams-Jefferson Letters,* p. 582; Jefferson to Adams, April 8, 1816, ibid., p. 467.

24. Jefferson to Roger C. Weightman, June 24, 1826, *The Works of Thomas Jefferson,* 12 vols., ed. Paul Leicester Ford (New York: G. P. Putnam, 1905), vol. 12, p. 477.

Chapter 4. The Learned James Madison

1. Ralph Ketcham, *James Madison: A Biography* (New York: Macmillan, 1971), p. 407.

2. Calvin Dill Wilson, "Our Presidents Out of Doors," *The Century Magazine* (March 1909), p. 703.

3. Gordon S. Wood, "Impartiality in America," *The New Republic* (December 6, 1999), pp. 52–56.

4. Ketcham, *Madison,* p. 107.

5. Margaret Bayard Smith, *The First Forty Years of Washington Society,* ed. Gaillard Hunt (New York: Fisher Unwin, 1906), pp. 27–29.

6. Ketcham, *Madison,* p. 407.

7. Irving Brant, *James Madison: Secretary of State, 1801–1809* (Indianapolis: Bobbs-Merrill, 1953), p. 47.

8. Irving Brant, *James Madison: The Virginia Revolutionist* (Indianapolis: Bobbs-Merrill, 1941), p. 87; Ketcham, *Madison,* p. 36; Frank Cormier, *Presidents Are People Too* (Washington, D.C.: Public Affairs, 1966), pp. 157–59.

9. Ketcham, *Madison,* p. 36.

10. Ketcham, *Madison,* p. 35; Brant, *Virginia Revolutionist,* p. 40.

11. Smith, *First Forty Years,* p. 63.

12. Ibid., p. 62.

13. "Dolley Madison," *American National Biography,* ed. John Garraty and Mark C. Carnes (New York: Oxford University Press, 1999), vol. 14, p. 303.

14. Ketcham, *Madison,* p. 620; Smith, *First Forty Years,* pp. 232–37.

15. Irving Brant, *James Madison: Commander in Chief, 1812–1816* (Indianapolis: Bobbs-Merrill, 1961), pp. 421–22.

16. James C. Clark, *Faded Glory: Presidents Out of Power* (New York: Praeger, 1985), p. 22.

17. Homer F. Cunningham, *The Presidents' Last Years* (Jefferson, N.C.: McFarland, 1989), p. 35.

Chapter 5. The Unpretentious James Monroe

1. George Morgan, *The Life of James Monroe* (Boston: Small, Maynard & Co., 1921), p. 438.

2. Ibid.; Harry Ammon, *James Monroe: The Quest for National Identity* (New York: McGraw Hill, 1971), pp. 543–44.

3. Ibid., pp. 368–69.

4. W. P. Cresson, *James Monroe* (Chapel Hill: University of North Carolina Press, 1946), p. 370; Ammon, *Monroe,* p. 403.

5. Cresson, *Monroe,* pp. 369–70.

6. Cresson, *Monroe,* pp. 364–65.

7. Morgan, *Life of James Monroe,* p. 419; Daniel C. Gilman, *James Monroe* (Boston: Houghton Mifflin, 1898), p. 221.

8. Ona Griffin Jeffries, *In and Out of the White House: From Washington to the Eisenhowers* (New York: W. Funk, 1960), p. 72.

9. Gilman, *Monroe,* p. 215.

10. Cresson, *Monroe,* p. 470.

11. Homer F. Cunningham, *The Presidents' Last Years* (Jefferson, N.C.: MacFarland, 1989), p. 40.

12. Gilman, *James Monroe,* pp. 225–26.

Chapter 6. The Aquatic John Quincy Adams

1. Thurlow Weed, *Autobiography,* 2 vols. (New York: Da Capo Press, 1970), vol. 1, p. 179.

2. Charles Francis Adams, ed., *Memoirs of John Quincy Adams,* 12 vols. (Philadelphia: J. B. Lippincott, 1874–77), vol. 7, pp. 27–29.

3. Edna M. Coleman, *Seventy-Five Years of White House Gossip* (Garden City, N.Y.: Doubleday, Page & Co., 1925), pp. 140–42; James E. Pollard, *The Presidents and the Press* (Washington, D.C.: Public Affairs Press, 1964), p. 139.

4. Robert Remini, *Andrew Jackson and the Course of American Freedom* (New York: Harper & Row, 1981), p. 134.

5. Jack Shepherd, *Cannibals of the Heart: A Personal Biography of Louisa Adams and John Quincy Adams* (New York: McGraw Hill, 1980), pp. 345–346n.

6. Paul C. Nagel, *John Quincy Adams: A Public Life, A Private Life* (New York: Alfred A. Knopf, 1997), p. 76.

7. Ibid., pp. x, 61; Robert A. East, *John Quincy Adams: The Critical Years, 1785–1794* (New York: Bookman Associates, 1962), p. 54.

8. Nagel, *John Quincy Adams,* pp. 20–37.

9. Elise K. Kirk, *Music at the White House* (Urbana: University of Illinois Press, 1986), p. 42.

10. Ibid.; John T. Morse, *John Quincy Adams* (Boston and New York: Houghton Mifflin, 1898), p. 73.

11. Lynn Hudson Parso, *John Quincy Adams* (Madison, Wisc.: Madison House, 1998), p. 267.

12. Leonard Falkner, *The President Who Wouldn't Retire* (New York: Coward-McCann, 1967), pp. 299–399.

Chapter 7. The Two-Fisted Andrew Jackson

1. Cyrus Townshend Brady, *The True Andrew Jackson* (Philadelphia: J. B. Lippincott, 1906), p. 63.

2. James Parton, *Life of Andrew Jackson,* 3 vols. (New York: Mason Brothers, 1861), vol. 1, p. 64; Brady, *True Jackson,* pp. 208–209.

3. Brady, *True Jackson,* pp. 59, 140; Parton, *Jackson,* vol. 1, pp. 107–108.

4. Brady, *True Jackson,* p. 60.

5. Ibid., p. 61.

6. Ibid., p. 61; Parton, *Jackson,* vol. 1, pp. 104, 108–109.

7. Edmund Lindop and Joseph Jares, *White House Sportsmen* (Boston: Houghton-Mifflin, 1964), p. 121.

8. Ibid., pp. 122–23.

9. Ibid., p. 123.

10. Parton, *Jackson,* vol. 3, p. 489; Brady, *True Jackson,* p. 166.

11. Parton, *Jackson,* vol. 3, pp. 244–45.

12. Brady, *True Jackson,* pp. 203–205.

13. John Spencer Bassett, *The Life of Andrew Jackson* (New York: Macmillan, 1916), p. 9.

14. John T. Morse, *John Quincy Adams* (Boston: Houghton Mifflin, 1882), p. 73.

15. Ona Griffin Jeffries, *In and Out of the White House* (New York: W. Funk, 1960), pp. 99–100; Edna M. Colman, *Seventy-Five Years of White House Gossip* (New York: Doubleday, 1925), pp. 169–70; Robert V. Remini, *The Life of Andrew Jackson* (New York: Harper & Row, 1984), pp. 322–23.

16. Colman, *Seventy-Five Years,* pp. 170–71.

Chapter 8. The High-Toned Martin Van Buren

1. Denis Tilden Lynch, *An Epoch and a Man: Martin Van Buren and His Times* (New York: Horace Liveright, 1929), p. 299; Holmes Alexander, *The American Talleyrand: The Career and Contemporaries of Martin Van Buren* (New York: Russell and Russell, 1935), p. 8.

2. Ibid., p. 20.

3. Ibid., pp. 51, 314–15; Lynch, *Epoch and a Man,* p. 364.

4. Alexander, *American Talleyrand,* pp. 281, 284; *The Complete Works of Washington Irving,* vol. 3, Letters: 1823–1838 (Boston: Twayne Publishers, 1979), pp. 673, 680, 684, 696.

5. Alexander, *American Talleyrand,* p. 295.

6. Ibid., p. 352.

7. Edna M. Colman, *Seventy-Five Years of White House Gossip* (New York: Doubleday, Page & Co., 1925), pp. 174–75, 179; Alexander, *American Talleyrand,* p. 354.

8. Charles Ogle, *The Regal Splendor of the President's Palace,* April 18, 1840, House of Representatives, pp. 3–7, 9, 26; Robert Gray Gunderson, "Ogle's Omnibus of Lies," *Pennsylvania Magazine of History and Biography,* vol. 80 (October 1956), pp. 443–51.

9. Meade Minnigerode, *Presidential Years, 1789–1865* (New York: G. P. Putnam, 1928), p. 205.

10. Lynch, *Epoch and a Man,* pp. 470–74.

11. Alexander, *American Talleyrand,* pp. 407–408.

12. Edward M. Shepard, *Martin Van Buren* (Boston: Houghton Mifflin, 1916), p. 455.

Chapter 9. The Amiable William Henry Harrison

1. Mrs. E. F. Ellet, *The Court Circles of the Republic* (Hartford, Conn.: Hartford Publishing, 1869), p. 287; Dorothy Burns Goebel, *William Henry Harrison: A Political Biography* (Indianapolis: Indiana Library and Historical Department, 1926), p. 370.

2. Freeman Cleaves, *Old Tippecanoe: William Henry Harrison and His Times* (New York: Scribner's, 1939), p. 305.

3. Allan Nevins, ed., *The Diary of Philip Hone, 1821–1851,* 2 vols. (New York: Dodd, Mead, 1927), vol. 2, p. 529.

4. Cleaves, *Old Tippecanoe,* p. 337.

5. Nathan Sargent, *Public Men and Events* (Philadelphia: J. B. Lippincott, 1875), p. 114.

6. Nevins, *Diary,* vol. 2, p. 531; Cleaves, *Old Tippecanoe,* pp. 337–38.

7. Ellet, *Court Circles,* p. 289.

8. Goebel, *Harrison,* p. 377; Nevins, *Diary,* vol. 2, pp. 536–37.

9. Geoffrey C. Ward, "Presidents, Imperial or Otherwise," *American Heritage,* May/June 1987, p. 20; Cleaves, *Old Tippecanoe,* p. 280.

Chapter 10. The Hospitable John Tyler

1. Oliver Perry Chitwood, *John Tyler: Champion of the Old South* (New York: D. Appleton-Century Co., 1939), p. 20; Lyon G. Tyler, *The Letters and Times of the Tylers,* 2 vols. (New York: Da Capo Press, 1970), vol. 1, p. 230.

2. Ona Griffin Jefferies, *In and Out of the White House: From Washington to the Eisenhowers* (New York: W. Funk, 1960), p. 122; Carl S. Anthony, *First Ladies* (New York: William Morrow, 1990), p. 129; Chitwood, *John Tyler,* p. 147.

3. Tyler, *Letters and Times,* vol. 1, p. 544n; Chitwood, *John Tyler,* pp. 253, 388.

4. Chitwood, *John Tyler,* pp. 386–87.

5. Jeffries, *In and Out of the White House,* p. 116.

6. Elise K. Kirk, *Music at the White House* (Urbana: University of Illinois Press, 1981), p. 59.

7. Chitwood, *John Tyler,* p. 145; Tyler, *Letters and Times,* vol. 1, pp. 200–201, 288, 546, 549, 551–52.

8. Robert Seager II, *And Tyler Too: A Biography of John and Julia Gardiner Tyler* (New York: McGraw Hill, 1963), pp. 261–64.

Chapter 11. The Assiduous James K. Polk

1. Eugene Irving McCormac, *James K. Polk: A Political Biography* (Berkeley: University of California Press, 1922), p. 140.

2. Ibid., p. 349n.

3. John R. Bumgarner, *The Health of the Presidents* (Jefferson, N.C.: Mc-Farland and Company, 1994), pp. 67–71, on Polk's health.

4. January 28, 1847, *Polk: Diary of a President, 1845–1849,* ed. Allan Nevins (New York: Longman, Green & Co., 1929), p. 194; December 29, 1848, Diary, p. 360.

5. March 20, 1846, *Polk: Diary,* p. 63; April 1, 1846, ibid., p. 69; April 7, 1846, ibid., p. 70.

6. June 1, 1846, *Polk: Diary,* p. 108; August 15, 1846, ibid., p. 140; December 25, 1846, ibid., p. 179; January 1, 1847, ibid., p. 180.

7. January 1, 1849, *Polk: Diary,* p. 362.

8. Charles Grier Sellers, *James K. Polk, Jacksonian, 1795–1843* (Princeton, N.J.: Princeton University Press, 1957), p. 460.

9. Ibid., p. 211.

10. February 13, 1849, *Polk: Diary,* p. 374.

Chapter 12. The Unpretentious Zachary Taylor

1. Brainerd Dyer, *Zachary Taylor* (Baton Rouge: Louisiana State University Press, 1946), p. 302; Laura Carter Holloway, *Ladies of the White House* (New York: United States Publishing Co., 1870), p. 492.

2. Silas Bent McKinley and Silas Bent, *Old Rough and Ready: The Life and Times of Zachary Taylor* (New York: Vanguard Press, 1946), p. 32; Holman Hamilton, *Zachary Taylor: Soldier of the Republic* (Indianapolis: Bobbs-Merrill, 1941), p. 20.

3. McKinley and Bent, *Old Rough and Ready,* p. 32; Homan Hamilton, *Zachary Taylor: Soldier in the White House* (Indianapolis: Bobbs-Merrill, 1951), p. 23; Homer Cunningham, *The President's Last Years* (Jefferson, N.C.: MacFarland, 1989), p. 85.

4. Dyer, *Zachary Taylor,* p. 184.

5. Ibid., p. 186.

6. Hamilton, *Soldier of the Republic,* p. 135.

7. Dyer, *Zachary Taylor,* pp. 398–99.

8. Hamilton, *Soldier in the White House,* p. 323.

9. Dyer, *Zachary Taylor,* p. 401; Elise K. Kirk, *Music at the White House* (Urbana: University of Illinois Press, 1986), p. 64; McKinley and Bent, *Old Rough and Ready,* pp. 264–65.

10. McKinley and Bent, *Old Rough and Ready,* pp. 285, 288; Hamilton, *Soldier in the White House,* p. 398; Dyer, *Zachary Taylor,* p. 406.

Chapter 13. The Earnest Millard Fillmore

1. Robert J. Scarry, *Millard Fillmore* (Jefferson, N.C.: McFarland & Co., 2001), pp. 16, 27; Frank H. Severence, ed., *Millard Fillmore Papers,* 2 vols. (Buffalo, N.Y.: Buffalo Historical Society, 1959), vol. 2, p. 483.

2. Scarry, *Millard Fillmore,* p. 16.

3. Ibid.

4. Ibid., pp. 39–40, 87.

5. "President Fillmore's Bathtub," in Paul F. Boller, Jr., *Not So! Popular Myths About America from Columbus to Clinton* (New York: Oxford University Press, 1995), pp. 61–62.

6. Scarry, *Millard Fillmore,* pp. 188–89; Edna M. Colman, *Seventy-Five Years of White House Gossip* (New York: Doubleday, Page & Co., 1925), p. 232.

7. Elise K. Kirk, *Music at the White House* (Urbana: University of Illinois Press, 1986), pp. 69–70.

8. *New York Times,* October 11, 1991, p. 19; *Fort Worth Star-Telegram,* June 19, 1991, p. B4.

Chapter 14. The Convivial Franklin Pierce

1. Roy Franklin Nichols, *Franklin Pierce: Young Hickory of Granite Hills* (Philadelphia: University of Pennsylvania Press, 1931, 1958), pp. 224–25; Larry Gara, *The Presidency of Franklin Pierce* (Lawrence: University Press of Kansas, 1991), p. 44.

2. Nichols, *Franklin Pierce,* pp. 16, 21, 25.

3. Ibid., pp. 71, 72, 73, 81, 86–87.

4. Ibid., pp. 71, 110, 123, 129, 215; Ona Griffin Jeffries, *In and Out of the White House: From Washington to the Eisenhowers* (New York: W. Funk, 1960), p. 144.

5. Nichols, *Franklin Pierce,* pp. 234, 241.

6. Ibid., p. 313.

7. Ibid., pp. 283–84.

8. Nichols, *Franklin Pierce,* p. 509; Harry Barnard, *Rutherford B. Hayes and His America* (Indianapolis: Bobbs-Merrill, 1954), p. 503; Brenda Wineapple, *Hawthorne: A Life* (New York: Alfred A. Knopf, 2003), p. 359.

Chapter 15. The Fastidious James Buchanan

1. Philip Shriver Klein, *President James Buchanan* (University Park, Pennsylvania: Penn State University Press, 1962), p. 6.

2. Ibid., pp. 9–12.

3. Ibid., pp. 14, 120.

4. Ibid., pp. 96, 246.

5. Ibid., pp. 211, 275.

6. John Whitcomb and Claire Whitcomb, *Real Life at the White House* (New York: Routledge, 2000), p. 126; Ona Griffin Jeffries, *In and Out of the White House: From Washington to the Eisenhowers* (New York: W. Funk, 1960), p. 158.

7. Edna M. Colman, *Seventy-Five Years of White House Gossip* (New York: Doubleday, Page & Co., 1925), p. 258; Jeffries, *In and Out of White House,* p. 149; Klein, *President James Buchanan,* p. 350.

8. Philip Shriver Klein, *The Story of Wheatland* (Lancaster, Pa.: Junior League of Lancaster, Inc., January 1936), p. 48.

Chapter 16. The Mirthful and Melancholy Abraham Lincoln

1. Paul Selby, ed., *Stories and Speeches of Abraham Lincoln* (Chicago: Thompson and Thomas, 1900), pp. 188–89, 204, 212–13; Salmon P. Chase, *Chase Diary,* Annual Report, American Historical Association (Washington, D.C., 1902, vol. 2), pp. 87–89; Charles C. Coffin, *Abraham Lincoln* (New York: Harper & Bros., 1892), pp. 342–46; Keith W. Jennison, *The Humorous Mr. Lincoln* (New York: Crowell, 1965), pp. 99–100.
2. Ibid.
3. Carl Sandburg, *Abraham Lincoln: The Prairie Years* (New York: Harcourt, Brace, 1926), vol. 1, p. vii; Albert J. Beveridge, *Abraham Lincoln, 1809–1858* (Boston: Houghton Mifflin, 1928), vol. 1, p. 531; A. K. McClure, ed., *Lincoln's Yarns and Stories* (Chicago: John C. Winston, n.d.), p. 261.
4. Jennison, *Humorous Mr. Lincoln,* p. 38; Ona Griffin Jeffries, *In and Out of the White House* (New York: W. Funk, 1960), p. 179.
5. Sandburg, *Lincoln: Prairie Years,* vol. 2, p. 243; Richard Hanser, "The Laughing Lincoln," *Saturday Review,* February 8, 1958, pp. 11–38.
6. J. G. Randall, *Lincoln the President: Midstream* (New York: Dodd, Mead & Co., 1952), p. 7; Tyler Dennett, ed., *Lincoln and the Civil War in the Diaries and Letters of John Hay* (New York: Dodd, Mead & Co., 1939), p. 179; Paul M. Angle, *The Lincoln Reader* (New Brunswick, N.J.: Rutgers University Press, 1947), p. 437.
7. Richard Hanser, "The Lincoln Who Lives in Anecdotes," *Reader's Digest,* February 1959, p. 253; Paul M. Angle, ed., *Abraham Lincoln by Some Men Who Knew Him* (Freeport, N.Y.: Books for Libraries Press, 1969), p. 51.
8. J. G. Randall, "The Unpopular Mr. Lincoln," *Abraham Lincoln Quarterly,* vol. 2, June 1943, p. 275.
9. Dennett, *Lincoln in Diaries of Hay,* p. 233; Kenneth A. Bernard, *Lincoln and the Music of the Civil War* (Caldwell, Id.: Caxton Printers, 1966), pp. 253–54; McClure, *Lincoln's Yarns and Stories,* pp. 160–62.
10. Ward Hill Lamon, *Recollections of Abraham Lincoln* (Chicago: McClurg, 1911), pp. 141–46.
11. Mel Peacock, "Music in the White House," *Etude,* January 1954, p. 54; Elise K. Kirk, *Music at the White House* (Urbana: University of Illinois Press, 1986), pp. 78, 80; Bernard, *Lincoln and Music of Civil War,* pp. xvii, 31, 112–13.
12. Kirk, *Music at White House,* pp. 80–89.
13. Carl Sandburg, *Abraham Lincoln: The War Years* (New York: Harcourt, Brace, 1939), vol. 3, pp. 301, 311.
14. Allen Thorndike Rice, ed., *Reminiscences of Abraham Lincoln* (New York: Harper, 1909), pp. 236–37.

15. Roy Basler, *The Lincoln Legend* (Boston: Houghton Mifflin, 1935), pp. 53–54; David Donald, *Lincoln's Herndon* (New York: Alfred A. Knopf, 1948), p. 158; Robert S. Harper, *Lincoln and the Press* (New York: McGraw-Hill, 1951), passim.; McClure, *Lincoln's Yarns and Stories,* p. 176; Sandburg, *Lincoln: Prairie Years,* vol. 2, pp. 355, 381; Sandburg, *Lincoln: War Years,* vol.1, pp. 119, 182, 556, 557, 614; Dixon Wecter, *The Hero in America* (New York: Scribner, 1941), p. 243.

16. Wecter, *Hero in America,* p. 255; Richard Hofstadter, *The American Political Tradition* (New York: Alfred A. Knopf, 1948), p. 136.

17. Doris Kerns Goodwin, "The Master of the Game," *Time,* July 4, 2005, p. 54; Basler, *Lincoln Legend,* p. 60; Thomas A. Bogar, *American Presidents Attend the Theatre* (Jefferson, N.C.: McFarland & Co., 2006), p. 98.

18. Arthur Bestor *et al., Three Presidents and Their Books* (Urbana: University of Illinois Press, 1955), pp. 72, 80.

19. Emily Todd Helm, "Mary Todd Lincoln," *McClure's Magazine* (September 1898), p. 479; Carlos W. Goltz, *Incidents in the Life of Mary Todd Lincoln* (Sioux City, Iowa: 1928), pp. 15–16.

20. *Three Presidents and Their Books,* pp. 46–83; Frank J. Sulloway, "He Almost Scooped Darwin," *New York Review of Books,* June 2, 2004, p. 34; Richard Hanser, "Lincoln and the Poets," in Henry B. Kranz, ed., *Abraham Lincoln: A New Portrait* (New York: G. P. Putnam's Sons, 1959), pp. 111, 114.

21. Hanser, "Lincoln and the Poets," pp. 109, 111, 112.

22. William E. Wilson, "There I Grew Up," *American Heritage,* October 1966, p. 100; *Parade Magazine,* October 22, 1989, p. 9.

23. Frederick W. Seward, *Seward at Washington* (New York: Derby and Miller, 1891), pp. 512–13.

24. William Lee Miller, *Lincoln's Virtues: An Ethical Biography* (New York: Alfred A. Knopf, 2000).

25. Bruce Catton, *U.S. Grant and the Military Tradition* (Boston: Little, Brown, 1954), p. 108; Jules C. Ladenheim, "Lincoln Didn't Lack for Erudition," letter, *New York Times,* February 15, 1996, p. A14.

26. Jacques Barzun, "Lincoln, the Literary Genius," *Saturday Evening Post,* February 14, 1959, pp. 30–64; John G. Nicolay and John Hay, *Abraham Lincoln: A History* (New York: Century, 1914), pp. x, 351.

27. Bogar, *Presidents Attend Theatre,* p. 100; Stanley Kimmel, *Mr. Lincoln's Washington* (New York: Coward-McCann, 1957), p. 392.

Chapter 17. The Plebeian Andrew Johnson

1. Benjamin Perley Poore, *Perley's Reminiscences of Sixty Years in the National Metropolis* (New York: W. A. Houghton, 1886), vol. 1, p. 437; Carl Sandburg, *Abraham Lincoln: The War Years* (New York: Harcourt, Brace, 1939), vol. 4, p. 89.

2. Sandburg, *Lincoln: War Years,* vol. 4, pp. 90, 91.

3. Lately Thomas, *The First President Johnson* (New York: William Morrow, 1968), pp. 269, 270.

4. Ibid., p. 269.

5. Sandburg, *Lincoln: War Years,* vol. 3, p. 271.

6. Thomas, *First President Johnson,* pp. 494, 507.

7. Ibid., pp. 353, 354.

8. Ibid., pp. 356, 361, 529; W. H. Crook, *Memories of the White House* (Boston: Little, Brown, 1911), p. 61.

9. Thomas, *First President Johnson,* pp. 581, 595.

Chapter 18. The Undemonstrative Ulysses S. Grant

1. *New York Times,* May 9, 2003, p. B42; Don Van Natta, Jr., *First Off the Tee: Presidential Hackers, Duffers and Cheaters from Taft to Bush* (New York: Public Affairs, 2003), p. 114; Shepherd Campbell and Peter Landau, *Presidential Lies: The Illustrated History of White House Golf* (New York: Macmillan, 1996), p. i.

2. William S. McFeely, *Grant: A Biography* (New York: W. W. Norton, 1981), p. 29; Edmund Lindop and Joseph Jares, *White House Sportsmen* (Boston: Houghton Mifflin, 1964), p. 58.

3. Michael Korda, *Ulysses S. Grant: The Unlikely Hero* (New York: Harper-Collins, 2004), reviewed in *Wilson Quarterly,* Winter 2005, p. 11.

4. McFeely, *Grant,* pp. 10–11.

5. Lindop and Jares, *White House Sportsmen,* pp. 114–15; George Sullivan, *Presidents at Play* (New York: Walker & Co., 1995), p. 106; Mark Perry, *Grant and Twain: The Story of Friendship That Changed America* (New York: Random House, 2004), p. 21.

6. McFeely, *Grant,* p. 52.

7. Ibid., pp. 132–35; Hamlin Garland, *Ulysses S. Grant: His Life and Character* (New York: Macmillan, 1920), p. 403.

8. Garland, *Ulysses S. Grant,* p. 402.

9. John Durant, *The Sports of the Presidents* (New York: Hastings House, 1964), p. 64; W. H. Crook, *Memories of the White House* (Boston: Little, Brown & Co., 1911).

10. McFeely, *Grant,* p. 29; Adam Badeau, *Grant in Peace* (Freeport, N.Y.: Books for Libraries Press, 1887, 1971), p. 305.

11. James C. Clark, *Faded Glory: Presidents Out of Power* (New York: Praeger, 1985), p. 74; Badeau, *Grant in Peace,* p. 314; Garland, *Ulysses S. Grant,* p. 456.

12. Badeau, *Grant in Peace,* p. 309.

Chapter 19. The Studious Rutherford B. Hayes

1. Charles Richard Williams, ed., *Diary and Letters of Rutherford B. Hayes,* 5 vols. (Columbus: Ohio State Archaeological and Historical Society, 1924),

vol. 1, p. 130; Allan Nevins, ed., *Selected Writings of Abram Hewitt* (Port Washington, N.Y.: Kennikat Press, 1937, 1964), p. 381.

2. Harry Barnard, *Rutherford B. Hayes and His America* (Indianapolis: Bobbs-Merrill, 1954), p. 283; W. D. Howells, *Selected Letters* (Boston: Twayne Publishers, 1979), vol. 2, pp. 139–40.

3. William D. Howells, *Sketch of the Life and Character of Rutherford B. Hayes* (Boston: Hurd and Houghton, 1876), pp. 34–36.

4. Barnard, *Rutherford B. Hayes,* pp. 171–72; Howells, *Sketch of Life and Character,* pp. 12, 25.

5. Howells, *Sketch of Life and Character,* pp. 35, 36.

6. July 8, 1880, Williams, *Diary and Letters,* pp. 607–608.

7. W. H. Crook, *Memories of the White House* (Boston: Little, Brown & Co., 1911), p. 116; Ona Griffin Jeffries, *In and Out of the White House* (New York: W. Funk, 1960), p. 212; Elise K. Kirk, *Music at the White House* (Urbana: University of Illinois Press, 1986), pp. 113–15.

8. June 6, 1880, Williams, *Diary and Letters,* pp. 557, 633; Barnard, *Rutherford B. Hayes,* pp. 488, 500.

9. H. J. Eckenrode, *Rutherford B. Hayes: Statesman of Reunion* (New York: Dodd, Mead & Co., 1930), pp. 327–29, 336.

10. Williams, *Diary and Letters,* vol. 3, p. 619; Hayes, *The Diary of a President, 1875–1881,* ed. T. Harry Williams (New York: David McKay Co., 1964), p. 292.

Chapter 20. The Bookish James A. Garfield

1. Theodore Clarke Smith, *The Life and Letters of James Abram Garfield,* 2 vols. (New Haven, Conn.: Yale University Press, 1925), vol. 2, p. 902.

2. Ibid., vol. 2, pp. 752–53.

3. Ibid., vol. 1, p. 49.

4. Gore Vidal, *United States: Essays, 1952–1992* (New York: Random House, 1993), pp. 212–13.

5. Smith, *Life and Letters of Garfield,* vol. 2, pp. 747–48.

6. Ibid., vol. 2, p. 752; December 30, 1874, *The Diary of James A. Garfield* (ed. Harry James Brown and Frederick D. Williams, East Lansing, Michigan State University Press, 1967), vol. 2, p. 412; Thomas A. Bogar, *American Presidents Attend Theatre* (Jefferson, N.C.: McFarland & Co., 2006), p. 127.

7. Smith, *Life and Letters of Garfield,* vol. 2, pp. 751–52.

8. John M. Taylor, *Garfield of Ohio: The Available Man* (New York: W. W. Norton, 1970), p. 36; Smith, *Life and Letters of Garfield,* vol. 1, pp. 6, 13; vol. 2, p. 924.

9. Charles Richard Williams, *The Life of Rutherford B. Hayes,* 2 vols. (Columbus: Ohio State Archaeological and Historical Society, 1928), vol. 2, p. 239; George F. Hoar, *Autobiography of Seventy Years,* 2 vols. (New York: Charles Scribner's Sons, 1906), vol. 2, p. 17.

10. Smith, vol. 2, *Life and Letters of Garfield,* p. 1097.

Chapter 21. The Leisurely Chester A. Arthur

1. Thomas C. Reeves, *Gentleman Ross: The Life of Chester A. Arthur* (New York: Knopf, 1975), p. 270; George Frederick Howe, *Chester A. Arthur: A Quarter Century of Machine Politics* (New York: Dodd, Mead & Co., 1934), pp. 15, 176; *Letters of Mrs. James G. Blaine,* ed. Harriet S. Blaine (Beale, New York: Duffield & Co., 1908), vol. 2, pp. 4–5.

2. John Whitcomb and Claire Whitcomb, *Real Life in the White House* (New York: Routledge, 2000), p. 182; Howe, *Chester A. Arthur,* p. 151.

3. Howe, *Chester A. Arthur,* p. 156; Reeves, *Gentleman Boss,* p. 249.

4. Howe, *Chester A. Arthur,* p. 174.

5. Reeves, *Gentleman Boss,* p. 275.

6. Ona Griffin Jeffries, *In and Out of the White House* (New York: W. Funk, 1960), p. 230; Reeves, *Gentleman Boss,* pp. 274–75.

7. Elise K. Kirk, *Music at the White House* (Urbana: University of Illinois Press, 1986), p. 136.

8. John Philip Sousa, *Marching Along: Recollections of Men, Women, and Music* (Boston: Hale, Cushman, and Flint, 1941), pp. 79–80, 85.

9. Reeves, *Gentleman Boss,* p. 317.

10. Howe, *Chester A. Arthur,* p. 116; Reeves, *Gentleman Boss,* p. 356.

11. Reeves, *Gentleman Boss,* pp. 366–67.

12. Howe, *Chester A. Arthur,* p. 254.

Chapter 22. The Doughty Grover Cleveland

1. Grover Cleveland, *Fishing and Shooting Sketches* (New York: The Outing Publishing Co., 1907), pp. 198–99; W. H. Crook, *Memories of the White House* (Boston: Little, Brown, 1911), p. 14.

2. H. Paul Jeffers, *An Honest President: The Life and Presidencies of Grover Cleveland* (New York: William Morrow, 2000), p. 2; Frank Cormier, *Presidents Are People Too* (Washington, D.C.: Public Affairs, 1966), p. 120; Gerald R. Ford, *Humor and the Presidency* (New York, 1987), p. 31.

3. Jeffers, *Honest President,* p. 71.

4. Ibid., pp. 79, 81.

5. Robert McElroy, *Grover Cleveland: The Man and the Statesmen,* 2 vols. (New York: Harper & Brothers, 1923), vol. 1, p. 112; Denis Tilden Lynch, *Grover Cleveland: A Man Four-Square* (New York: Horace Liveright, 1932), p. 321; John Whitcomb and Claire Whitcomb, *Real Life in the White House* (New York: Routledge, 2000), p. 321.

6. Jeffers, *Honest President,* pp. 133, 155, 180.

7. Richard Watson Gilder, *Cleveland: A Record of Friendship* (New York: Century Co., 1910), pp. 60–61; Jeffers, *Honest President,* p. 238; Edmund Lindop and Joseph Jares, *White House Sportsmen* (Boston: Houghton-Mifflin, 1964), p. 75.

8. Lindop and Jares, *White House Sportsmen,* pp. 75–76.

9. Ibid., pp. 76–77; Jeffers, *Honest President,* pp. 153–54.

10. Henry Cabot Lodge, *The Storm Has Many Eyes* (New York: W. W. Norton, 1973), pp. 34–36; William J. Miller, "I Am a Jelly-Filled Doughnut," *New York Times,* April 30, 1988, p. 15.

11. Ibid.

12. Cleveland, *Fishing and Shooting Sketches,* p. 4; Lindop and Jares, *White House Sportsmen,* p. 85.

13. Cleveland, *Fishing and Shooting Sketches,* pp. 9, 20–21.

Chapter 23. The Austere Benjamin Harrison

1. Harry J. Sievers, *Benjamin Harrison: Hoosier Statesman, 1865–1888* (New York: University Publishers Incorporated, 1959), pp. 56, 63.

2. Harry J. Sievers, *Benjamin Harrison: Hoosier Warrior, 1833–1865* (Chicago: Henry Regnery Co., 1952), pp. 309–10.

3. Sievers, *Harrison: Hoosier Statesman,* p. 65; Thomas A. Bogar, *American Presidents Attend Theatre* (Jefferson, N.C.: McFarland & Co., 2006), p. 163.

4. Ibid., pp. 52, 143; Frank Cormier, *Presidents Are People Too* (Washington, D.C.: Public Affairs, 1966), p. 119.

5. Sievers, *Harrison: Hoosier Statesman,* pp. 294, 373.

6. Homer E. Socolofsky and Allan B. Spetter, *The Presidency of Benjamin Harrison* (Lawrence: University Press of Kansas, 1987), p. 163.

7. Lew Wallace, *Life and Public Services of Hon. Benjamin Harrison* (Edgewood Publishing Co., n.p., 1892), pp. 455–56.

8. Sievers, *Benjamin Harrison: Hoosier President* (Indianapolis: Bobbs-Merrill, 1968), p. 268.

Chapter 24. The Kindly William McKinley

1. *Mark Hanna—His Book* (Boston: Chapple, 1904), pp. 66–67.

2. Margaret Leech, *In the Days of McKinley* (New York: Harper & Brothers, 1959), pp. 5, 10.

3. Don Van Natta, Jr., *First Off the Tee: Presidential Hackers, Duffers and Cheaters from Taft to Bush* (New York: Public Affairs, 2003), pp. 115–16.

4. H. Wayne Morgan, *William McKinley and His America* (Syracuse, N.Y.: Syracuse University Press, 1963), p. 319.

5. W. H. Crook, *Memories of the White House* (Boston: Little, Brown & Co., 1911), 246–47; Ona Griffin Jeffries, *In and Out of the White House* (New York: W. Funk, 1960), p. 266.

6. Morgan, *William McKinley,* p. 323; Leech, *In the Days of McKinley,* p. 24.

7. Leech, *In the Days of McKinley,* pp. 22–23.

8. Hugh Baillie, *High Tension* (New York: Harper, 1959), p. 29; Morgan, *William McKinley,* p. 82.

9. Leech, *In the Days of McKinley,* pp. 30, 239, 437; Jeffries, *In and Out of White House,* p. 267.

10. H. H. Kohlstaat, *From McKinley to Harding* (New York: Scribner's, 1923), p. 5.

11. Paul F. Boller, Jr., *Presidential Wives* (New York: Oxford University Press, 1988), p. 188.

12. Leech, *In the Days of McKinley,* p. 445.

13. Morgan, *William McKinley,* p. 318; Lewis L. Gould, *The Presidency of William McKinley* (Lawrence: Regents Press of Kansas, 1980), p. 37.

14. James Barnes, *From Then Till Now* (New York: D. Appleton Century, 1934), pp. 219–22.

15. Homer F. Cunningham, *The Presidents' Last Years* (Jefferson, N.C.: McFarland, 1989), p. 177.

Chapter 25. The Energetic Theodore Roosevelt

1. Theodore Roosevelt, *An Autobiography* (New York: Charles Scribner's Sons, 1913, 1920), pp. 27–28.

2. Henry F. Pringle, *Theodore Roosevelt* (New York: Harcourt Brace, 1931), p. 33; Owen Wister, *Roosevelt: Story of a Friendship* (New York: Macmillan, 1930), pp. 4–5.

3. Roosevelt, *Autobiography,* p. 25; John Burroughs, *Camping and Tramping with Roosevelt* (Boston: Houghton Mifflin, 1907), pp. 41, 99; Kathleen Dalton, *Theodore Roosevelt: A Strenuous Life* (New York: Alfred A. Knopf, 2002), p. 68; Nathan Miller, *Theodore Roosevelt: A Life* (New York: William Morrow, 1992), p. 73.

4. Burroughs, *Camping with Roosevelt,* p. 84.

5. Pringle, *Theodore Roosevelt,* p. 97.

6. Roosevelt, *Autobiography,* pp. 122–123; Pringle, *Theodore Roosevelt,* pp. 97, 101; Burroughs, *Camping with Roosevelt,* pp. 55–56.

7. Frank Cormier, *Presidents Are People Too* (Washington, D.C.: Public Affairs, 1966), p. 38.

8. Edward Wagenknecht, *The Seven Worlds of Theodore Roosevelt* (New York: Longmans, Green, 1958), p. 249; letter to William Sturgis Bigelow, March 29, 1898, *The Letters of Theodore Roosevelt,* 8 vols., ed. Elting Morison *et al.* (Cambridge, Mass.: Harvard University Press, 1951–1954), vol. 2, p. 803; *Time,* July 3, 2006, p. 60.

9. Lawrence F. Abbott, *Impressions of Theodore Roosevelt* (Garden City, N.Y.: Doubleday, Page & Co., 1920), p. 183.

10. Ibid., p. 185.

11. Roosevelt, *Autobiography,* p. 322; Corrine Roosevelt Robinson, *My Brother Theodore Roosevelt* (New York: Charles Scribner's Sons, 1921), pp. 103, 324–25.

12. Robinson, *Brother Theodore,* pp. 251–53; Anthony Lane, "Politicians and Their Books," *New York Review of Books,* October 16 and 23, 2000, p. 178.

13. Roosevelt, *Autobiography,* pp. 332–33, 334.

14. Robinson, *Brother Theodore,* p. 212; Roosevelt, *Autobiography,* p. 45; James E. Amos, *Theodore Roosevelt: Hero to His Valet* (New York: John Day Co., 1927), pp. 81–83.

15. Edmund Lindop and Joseph Jares, *White House Sportsmen* (Boston: Houghton-Mifflin, 1964), pp. 160–61; George Sullivan, *Presidents at Play* (New York: Walker and Co., 1995), pp. 57–58; Frank Cormier, *Presidents Are People Too* (Washington, D.C.: Public Affairs, 1966), pp. 113–14.

16. Lindop and Jares, *White House Sportsmen,* pp. 105–106.

17. Sullivan, *Presidents at Play,* p. 103; Lindop and Jares, *White House Sportsmen,* pp. 106–107.

18. W. H. Crook, *Memories of the White House* (Boston: Little, Brown and Co., 1911), pp. 302–303; Lindop and Jares, *White House Sportsmen,* pp. 49, 160; Sullivan, *Presidents at Play,* p. 30.

19. Roosevelt, *Autobiography,* p. 30; Lindop and Jares, *White House Sportsmen,* p. 153.

20. Shepherd Campbell and Peter Landau, *Presidential Lies: The Illustrated History of White House Golf* (New York: Macmillan, 1996), p. 12; Lindop and Jares, *White House Sportsmen,* pp. 1–4; Sullivan, *Presidents at Play,* pp. 131–32.

21. Pringle, *Theodore Roosevelt,* p. 17; Burroughs, *Camping with Roosevelt,* p. 6.

22. Burroughs, *Camping with Roosevelt,* pp. 52, 59, 81.

23. Pringle, *Theodore Roosevelt,* pp. 248–50, 467–68; Cormier, *Presidents Are People Too,* pp. 94–95; Charles Willis Thompson, *Presidents I've Known* (Indianapolis: Bobbs-Merrill, 1929), pp. 188–97.

24. Crook, *Memories of the White House,* pp. 280, 282.

25. Ibid., p. 30.

26. Homer F. Cunningham, *The Presidents' Last Years* (Jefferson, N.C.: McFarland, 1989), p. 188.

Chapter 26. The Portly William Howard Taft

1. Don Van Natta, *First Off the Tee: Presidential Hackers, Duffers and Cheaters from Taft to Bush* (New York: Public Affairs, 2003), p. 125; Shepherd Campbell and Peter Landau, *Presidential Lies: The Illustrated History of White House Golf* (New York: Macmillan, 1963), pp. 18, 19; Ron Hutcheson, "Gang of Fore," *Fort Worth Star-Telegram,* June 11, 1997, p. 17.

2. Campbell and Landau, *Presidential Lies,* p. 23; Van Natta, *First Off the Tee,* 17; George Sullivan, *Presidents at Play* (New York: Walker & Co., 1995), p. 47.

3. Campbell and Landau, *Presidential Lies,* pp. 17, 19, 20.

4. Judith Icke Anderson, *William Howard Taft: An Intimate History* (New York: Walker & Co., 1981), pp. 32–33; Campbell and Landau, *Presidential Lies,* p. 30.

5. Maureen Dowd, "The Hootie Doctrine," *New York Times,* April 13, 2003, p. 13; Campbell and Landau, *Presidential Lies,* p. 25; Van Natta, *First Off the Tee,* p. 130; Anderson, *William Howard Taft,* p. 33; *Taft and Roosevelt: The Intimate Letters of Archie Butt, Military Aide* (Garden City, N.Y.: Doubleday, Doran & Co., 1930), p. 37.

6. Anderson, *William Howard Taft,* p. 28.

7. Ibid., pp. 29, 31; Van Natta, *First Off the Tee,* p. 125.

8. Anderson, *William Howard Taft,* pp. 27, 34.

9. Ibid., p. 35.

10. Michael L. Bromley, *William Howard Taft and the First Motoring Presidency, 1909–1913* (Jefferson, N.C.: McFarland & Co., 2003), p. 95.

11. Ibid., pp. 133–34; Bromley, *William Howard Taft,* p. 97; Michael Teague, *Mrs. Longworth: Conversations with Alice Roosevelt Longworth* (Garden City, N.Y.: Doubleday & Co., 1931), p. 139.

12. Bromley, *William Howard Taft,* p. 202.

13. Ibid., pp. 21, 221, 223.

14. James C. Clarke, *Faded Glory: Presidents Out of Power* (New York: Praeger, 1985), p. 114.

Chapter 27. The Scholarly Woodrow Wilson

1. Ray Stannard Baker, *Woodrow Wilson, Life and Letters: Youth, 1856–1890* (Garden City, N.Y.: Doubleday, Page & Co., 1927), vol. 2, p. 51; Don Van Natta, Jr., *First Off the Tee: Presidential Hackers, Duffers and Cheaters from Taft to Bush* (New York: Public Affairs, 2003), pp. 136, 138, 139; Shepherd Campbell and Peter Landau, *Presidential Lies: The Illustrated History of White House Golf* (New York: Macmillan, 1996), pp. 38, 40.

2. Alden Hatch, *Edith Bolling Wilson: First Lady Extraordinary* (New York: Dodd, Mead & Co., 1961), p. 88; Van Natta, *First Off the Tee,* pp. 148–49; Campbell and Landau, *Presidential Lies,* pp. 35–37.

3. William Mead and Paul Dickson, *Baseball: The Presidents' Game* (New York: Farragut Publishers, 1997), p. 36; Bernard A. Weisberger, "Our Sporting Presidents," *American Heritage,* September 1992, p. 22.

4. George Sullivan, *Presidents at Play* (New York: Walker, 1995), 129; Edmund Lindop and Joseph Jares, *White House Sportsmen* (Boston: Houghton-Mifflin, 1964), p. 7.

5. Cary T. Grayson, *Woodrow Wilson: An Intimate Memoir* (New York: Holt, Rinehart and Winston, 1960), p. 81.

6. Ibid., p. 46; Irwin Hood Hoover, *Forty-Two Years in the White House* (Boston: Houghton Mifflin, 1934), p. 61.

7. Edmund W. Starling, *Starling of the White House* (New York: Simon & Schuster, 1946), p. 34; Van Natta, *First Off the Tee,* pp. 137–39; Campbell and Landau, *Presidential Lies,* p. 40.

8. Grayson, *Woodrow Wilson,* p. 31; Campbell and Landau, *Presidential Lies,* p. 43.

9. Starling, *Starling of the White House,* p. 66; Hatch, *Edith Bolling Wilson,* p. 61; Van Natta, *First Off the Tee,* pp. 146, 149; Campbell and Landau, *Presidential Lies,* pp. 42, 46.

10. *Starling of the White House,* p. 113.

11. Lindop and Jares, *White House Sportsmen,* p. 163; Van Natta, *First Off the Tee,* pp. 148–49.

12. Baker, *Woodrow Wilson,* p. 30.

13. Henry Wilkinson Bragdon, *Woodrow Wilson: The Academic Years* (Cambridge, Mass.: Harvard University Press, 1967), p. 229; George C. Osborn, *Woodrow Wilson: The Early Years* (Baton Rouge: Louisiana University Press, 1968), p. 299.

14. Ruth Cranston, *The Story of Woodrow Wilson* (New York: Simon & Schuster, 1945), p. 66; Harold Garnet Black, *The True Woodrow Wilson: Crusader for Democracy* (New York: Fleming H. Revel, 1946), pp. 134, 137; Elise K. Kirk, *Music at the White House* (Urbana: University of Illinois Press, 1986), pp. 192–93.

15. Doran K. Antrim, "Our Musical Presidents," *Etude,* May 1946, p. 300; David Nasaw, "Learning To Go To the Movies," *American Heritage,* November 1993, p. 92.

16. Peter C. Rollins and John E. O'Connor, *Hollywood's History: The American President in Film and History* (Lexington: University Press of Kentucky, 2003), p. 116.

17. Charles Willis Thompson, *Presidents I've Known* (Indianapolis: Bobbs-Merrill, 1929), p. 319; *Starling of the White House,* pp. 104–5.

18. Phyllis Lee Levin, *Edith and Woodrow: The Wilson White House* (New York: Scribner's, 2001), p. 484.

Chapter 28. The Bloviating Warren G. Harding

1. Samuel Hopkins Adams, *Incredible Era: The Life and Times of Warren Gamaliel Harding* (Boston: Houghton Mifflin, 1939), p. 387.

2. Lillian Rogers Park, *My Thirty Years Backstairs at the White House* (New York: Fleet Publishing Corporation, 1961), p. 163; Ona Griffin Jeffries, *In and Out of the White House* (New York: W. Funk, 1960), p. 312; Francis Russell, *The Shadow of Blooming Grove: Warren G. Harding and His Times* (New York: McGraw-Hill, 1968), p. 437.

3. Russell, *Shadow of Blooming Grove,* p. 438; Patrick Mahony, *Barbed Wit and Malicious Humor* (Washington, D.C.: Institute for the Study of Man, 1956, 1983), p. 146.

4. Jeffries, *In and Out of the White House,* pp. 314–15.

5. Alice Roosevelt Longworth, *Crowded Hours* (New York: Scribner's, 1933), p. 324.

6. William Allen White, *The Autobiography of William Allen White* (New York: Macmillan, 1946), p. 619; Adams, *Incredible Era,* p. 217.

7. George Sullivan, *Presidents at Play* (New York: Walker & Co., 1995),

p. 49; Don Van Natta, Jr., *First Off the Tee: Presidential Hackers, Duffers and Cheaters from Taft to Bush* (New York: Public Affairs, 2003), pp. 217, 262.

8. Shepherd Campbell and Peter Landau, *Presidential Lies: The Illustrated History of White House Golf* (New York: Macmillan, 1996), pp. 55, 57; Van Natta, *First Off the Tee*, p. 262; Russell, *Shadow of Blooming Grove*, p. 445; Sullivan, *Presidents at Play*, p. 50.

9. Adams, *Incredible Era*, p. 80; Elise K. Kirk, *Music at the White House* (Urbana: University of Illinois Press, 1986), pp. 200, 205, 206; Doron K. Antrim, "Our Musical Presidents," *Etude*, May 1940, p. 337; Mel Peacock, "Music in the White House," *Etude*, January 1954, p. 54.

10. Carl Sferrazza Anthony, *Florence Harding: The First Lady, the Jazz Age, and the Death of America's Most Scandalous President* (New York: William Morrow, 1998), pp. 59, 89; Russell, *Shadow of Blooming Grove*, p. 230; Eric F. Goldman, "A Sort of Rehabilitation of Warren G. Harding," *New York Times Magazine*, March 26, 1972, p. 82.

11. Robert E. Gilbert, *The Mortal Presidency* (New York: Fordham University Press, 1998), p. 12.

12. Ibid.

Chapter 29. The Laconic Calvin Coolidge

1. John Hiram McKee, *Coolidge Wit and Wisdom* (New York: Frederick A. Stokes Company, 1933), p. 66; William Allen White, *A Puritan in Babylon: The Story of Calvin Coolidge* (New York: Macmillan, 1938), p. 35; Don Van Natta, Jr., *First Off the Tee: Presidential Hackers, Duffers and Cheaters from Taft to Bush* (New York: Public Affairs, 2003), p. 159.

2. Robert Gilbert, *The Mortal Presidency* (New York: Fordham University Press, 1998), p. 40; Robert Sobel, *Coolidge: An American Enigma* (Washington, D.C.: Regnery, 1998), p. 5.

3. Nathan Miller, *Star-Spangled Men: America's Ten Worst Presidents* (New York: Scribner, 1998), p. 89; Ona Griffin Jeffries, *In and Out of the White House* (New York: W. Funk, 1960), p. 318; Irwin Hood Hoover, *Forty-Two Years in the White House* (Boston: Houghton Mifflin, 1934), p. 125.

4. "The Bright Side of Calvinism: Those Coolidge Stories," in Paul F. Boller, Jr., *Memoirs of an Obscure Professor and Other Essays* (Fort Worth, Tx.: Texas Christian University Press, 1992), p. 114.

5. Van Natta, *First Off the Tee*, pp. 158, 159–60.

6. Ibid., p. 154; Shepherd Campbell and Peter Landau, *Presidential Lies: The Illustrated History of White House Golf* (New York: Macmillan, 1996), p. 74; Holly Miller, "Flex Time," *Saturday Evening Post*, July–August 1997, p. 96; Frank Cormier, *Presidents Are People Too* (Washington, D.C.: Public Affairs, 1996), p. 119.

7. Edmund W. Starling, *Starling of the White House* (Chicago: People's Book Club, 1946), p. 267; John Durant, *The Sports of Our Presidents* (New York: Hastings House, 1964), pp. 93, 95.

8. Hoover, *Forty-Two Years,* p. 131; Lindop and Jares, *White House Sportsmen,* p. 73; George Sullivan, *Presidents at Play* (New York: Walker & Co., 1995), p. 89.

9. Edmund Lindop and Joseph Jares, *White House Sportsmen* (Boston: Houghton Mifflin, 1995), p. 27; Mrs. Calvin Coolidge, "How I Spent My Days at the White House," Coolidge, "The Real Calvin Coolidge," *Good Housekeeping* (February 1935), p. 185.

10. Lindop and Jares, *White House Sportsmen,* pp. 150–51; Jeffries, *In and Out of the White House,* p. 324; Hoover, *Forty-Two Years,* p. 154.

11. Edward C. Lathem, *Meet Calvin Coolidge* (Brattleboro, Vt.: Stephen Green Press, 1960), p. 85; *The Autobiography of John Hays Hammond,* 2 vols. (New York: Farrar and Rinehart, 1935), vol. 2, p. 694.

12. Miller, *Star-Spangled Men,* p. 91; Doron K. Antrim, "Our Musical Presidents," *Etude,* May 1940, p. 349.

13. White, *Puritan in Babylon,* p. 440.

14. Ibid., p. 439; Ishbel Ross, *Grace Coolidge and Her Era* (New York: Dodd, Mead, 1962), p. 281; Claude M. Fuess, *Calvin Coolidge: The Man from Vermont* (Boston: Little, Brown, 1940), pp. 461–62.

Chapter 30. The Diligent Herbert Hoover

1. Theodore Joslin, *Hoover Off the Record* (Garden City, N.Y.: Doubleday, Doran, 1934), pp. 77, 194; Irwin Hood Hoover, *Hoover, Forty-Two Years in the White House* (Boston: Houghton Mifflin, 1934), p. 211.

2. Lillian Rogers Park, *My Thirty Years Backstairs at the White House* (New York: Fleet Publishing Corporation, 1961), p. 221; Elise K. Kirk, *Music at the White House* (Urbana: University of Illinois Press, 1986), p. 205.

3. Joslin, *Hoover Off the Record,* pp. 219–20, 230–31.

4. Herbert Hoover, *The Memoirs of Herbert Hoover: Years of Adventure, 1874–1920* (New York: Macmillan, 1951), pp. 13–14; Edmund Lindop and Joseph Jares, *White House Sportsmen* (Boston: Houghton Mifflin, 1964), pp. 70–71, 75.

5. Herbert Hoover, "An Interlude—Fishing," *The Memoirs of Herbert Hoover: The Cabinet and the Presidency, 1920–1933* (New York: Macmillan, 1952), p. 158; Bill Mares, *Fishing with the Presidents* (Mechanicsburg, PA: Stackpole Books, 1999), p. 198.

6. Hoover, "An Interlude—Fishing," *Memoirs, 1920–1933,* p. 158; George Sullivan, *Presidents at Play* (New York: Walker & Co., 1995), p. 87.

7. Will Irwin and Ken Herman, "Bush Is Known for His Commitment to Fitness," *Fort Worth Star-Telegram,* August 14, 2005, p. 5A.

8. Joslin, *Hoover Off the Record,* p. 56.

9. Ona Griffin Jeffries, *In and Out of the White House* (New York: W. Funk, 1960), p. 331; Martin L. Fausold, *The Presidency of Herbert Hoover* (Lawrence: The University Press of Kansas, 1985), p. 85.

10. Jeffries, *In and Out of the White House,* p. 334.

11. Hoover, *Memoirs, 1874–1920,* pp. 117–19; George N. Nash, *The Life of Herbert Hoover, the Engineer, 1874–1914* (New York: W. W. Norton, 1983), p. 499.

12. Joslin, *Hoover Off the Record,* p. 16.

13. Herbert Hoover, *Fishing for Fun—And to Wash Your Soul* (New York: Random House, 1963), pp. 18, 25.

14. Ibid., pp. 80–81.

Chapter 31. The Resourceful Franklin D. Roosevelt

1. Lillian Rogers Park, *My Thirty Years Backstairs at the White House* (New York: Fleet Publishing Corporation, 1961), p. 266.

2. Grace Tully, *F.D.R., My Boss* (New York: Scribner's, 1949), p. 2; John Gunther, *Roosevelt in Retrospect: A Profile in History* (New York: Harper, 1950), pp. 87–88.

3. Noel Busch, *What Manner of Man?* (New York: Harper, 1944), p. 151; Robert Jackson, *That Man: An Insider's Portrait of Franklin D. Roosevelt* (New York: Oxford University Press, 2003), pp. 7, 89, 13; Park, *My Thirty Years Backstairs,* pp. 265–66.

4. Tully, *F.D.R.,* pp. 8–9.

5. Arthur Bestor *et al., Three Presidents and Their Books* (Urbana: University of Illinois Press, 1955), pp. 96, 98, 104; Tully, *F.D.R.,* p. 11.

6. *Three Presidents,* pp. 96–97, 100–101; Edward Rothstein, "F.D.R. and the Stuff of His War," *New York Times,* February 3, 2006, p. B66.

7. Robert Cross, *Sailor in the White House: The Seafaring Life of FDR* (Annapolis, Md.: Naval Institute Press, 2003), pp. 29, 37; Gunther, *Roosevelt in Retrospect,* pp. 89–91.

8. Edmund Lindop and Joseph Jares, *White House Sportsmen* (Boston: Houghton Mifflin, 1964), p. 148.

9. Ibid., pp. 147–48; Gunther, *Roosevelt in Retrospect,* p. 91.

10. *Three Presidents,* p. 94.

11. Alexander Robbins, "When Presidents Cast a Line," *USA Today,* April 22, 1999, p. 10C.

12. Harold Ickes, *The Secret Diaries of Harold L. Ickes,* vol. 1 (New York: Simon & Schuster, 1953), pp. 449–50.

13. George Sullivan, *Presidents at Play* (New York: Walker & Co., 1995), p. 66.

14. Lindop and Jares, *White House Sportsmen,* p. 138; Frances Perkins, *The Roosevelt I Knew* (New York: Viking, 1946), p. 36.

15. Cross, *Sailor in the White House,* p. 67; Jackson, *That Man,* pp. 151–52.

16. Frank Cormier, *Presidents Are People Too* (Washington, D.C.: Public Affairs, 1966), p. 88; Park, *My Thirty Years Backstairs,* p. 267; Tully, *F.D.R.,* pp. 318–20.

17. James Roosevelt, *My Parents* (Chicago: Playboy Press, 1976), pp.

209–210; Samuel I. Rosenman, *Working with Roosevelt* (New York: Harper, 1952), p. 321.

18. Jackson, *That Man,* p. 13; Busch, *What Manner of Man?,* pp. 5–6.

19. Gunther, *Roosevelt in Retrospect,* pp. 94–95; Busch, *What Manner of Man?,* pp. 23–24; *Mother and Daughter: The Letters of Eleanor and Anna Roosevelt,* ed. Bernard Asbell (Geoghegan, N.Y.: Coward, McCann & Co., 1982), pp. 176–77.

20. Robert Hopkins, "How Would You Like to Be Attached to the Red Army?" *American Heritage,* July 2005, p. 34.

Chapter 32. The Plain-Speaking Harry S. Truman

1. Alfred Steinberg, *The Man from Missouri* (New York: G. P. Putnam's Sons, 1962), p. 231; Alan Schroeder, *Celebrity-in-Chief* (Boulder, Colo.: Westview, 2004), p. 80; Alonzo L. Hamby, *Man of the People: A Life of Harry Truman* (New York: Oxford University Press, 1995), pp. 286–87.

2. Elise K. Kirk, *Music at the White House* (Urbana: University of Illinois Press, 1986), p. 255; Steinberg, *Man from Missouri,* p. 26; Hamby, *Man of the People,* p. 15.

3. Ona Griffin Jeffries, *In and Out of the White House* (New York: W. Funk, 1960), p. 280.

4. Steinberg, *Man from Missouri,* p. 100.

5. Kirk, *Music at White House,* pp. 259–60.

6. Stuart Isacoff, "Eugene List: Presidents, Monsters, and Movie Stars," *Keyboard Classics,* July/August 1981, pp. 2–3.

7. Monte M. Poen, *Strictly Personal and Confidential: The Letters Truman Never Mailed* (Boston: Little, Brown & Co., 1992), p. 139; Margaret Truman, *Harry S. Truman* (New York: William Morrow, 1973), p. 52.

8. Merle Miller, *Plain Speaking: An Oral Biography of Harry S. Truman* (New York: G. P. Putnam's Sons, 1973), pp. 146–47; Margaret Truman, *Harry S. Truman,* p. 444.

9. Poen, *Strictly Personal and Confidential,* p. 139; Margaret Truman, *Harry S. Truman,* p. 52.

10. Hamby, *Man of the People,* p. 15; Steinberg, *Man from Missouri,* pp. 232–33; Bill Mares, *Fishing with the Presidents* (Mechanicsburg, Pa.: Stackpole Books, 1999), p. 44.

11. Frank McNaughton and Walter Hehmeyer, *This Man Truman* (New York: McGraw-Hill, 1945, 1948), p. 242; Ralph E. Weber, ed., *Talking with Harry: Candid Conversations with President Harry S. Truman* (Wilmington, Del.: Scholarly Resources Book, 2001), pp. 117–18.

12. Holly Miller, "Flex Time," *Saturday Evening Post,* July/August 1997, p. 76; George Sullivan, *Presidents at Play* (New York: Walker, 1995), pp. 13–15; Shepherd Campbell and Peter Landau, *Presidential Lies: The Illustrated History of White House Golf* (New York: Macmillan, 1996), pp. 238–39.

13. Sullivan, *Presidents at Play,* p. 24; Hamby, *Man of the People,* p. 473; Ken Hechler, *Working with Truman: A Personal Memoir of the White House Years* (New York: G. P. Putnam's Sons, 1982), pp. 22–23.

14. Hamby, *Man of the People,* p. 473.

15. Ibid., pp. 468, 484; J. B. West, *Upstairs at the White House* (New York: Coward, McCann, Geoghegan, 1973), p. 75; Margaret Truman, *Souvenir— Margaret Truman's Own Story* (New York: McGraw-Hill, 1956), p. 118.

16. Lillian Rogers Park, *My Thirty Years Backstairs at the White House* (New York: Fleet Publishing Corporation, 1961), p. 282; Steinberg, *Man from Missouri,* pp. 394–95; Hamby, *Man of the People,* p. 477.

17. Homer F. Cunningham, *The Presidents' Last Years* (Jefferson, N.C.: McFarland, 1989), p. 255; Kirk, *Music in the White House,* pp. 265–66.

18. Miller, *Plain Speaking,* p. 359.

19. Bernard Berenson, *Sunset and Twilight: From the Diaries of 1947–1958* (New York: Harcourt, Brace and World, 1963), vol. 1, p. 436.

Chapter 33. The Golf-Playing Dwight D. Eisenhower

1. Robert E. Gilbert, *The Mortal Presidency* (New York: Fordham University Press, 1992), p. 133.

2. Fred I. Greenstein, *The Hidden-Hand Presidency: Eisenhower as Leader* (New York: Basic Books, 1982), p. 45; Gilbert, *Mortal Presidency,* p. 132; John Eisenhower, ed., *Dwight D. Eisenhower, Letters to Mamie* (New York: Doubleday, 1978), p. 95.

3. Dwight D. Eisenhower, *At Ease: Stories I Tell My Friends* (Garden City, N.Y.: Doubleday, 1967), p. 7; Peter Lyon, *Eisenhower: Portrait of the Hero* (Boston: Little, Brown, 1974), p. 44; Edmund Lindop and Joseph Jares, *White House Sportsmen* (Boston: Houghton Mifflin, 1964), p. 17; Carl M. Cannon, "The Oval Office and the Diamond," *Atlantic Monthly,* May 2001, p. 33.

4. George Sullivan, *Presidents at Play* (New York: Walker 1995), p. 127.

5. William Mead and Paul Dickson, *Baseball: The President's Game* (Washington: Farragut Publishing Co., 1997), p. 93.

6. Ron Hutcheson, "Angle of Fore," *Fort Worth Star-Telegram,* June 11, 1997, p. 17.

7. Lindop and Jares, *White House Sportsmen,* p. 98; Sullivan, *Presidents at Play,* pp. 45–46; Don Van Natta, Jr., *First Off the Tee: Presidential Hackers, Duffers and Cheaters from Taft to Bush* (New York: Public Affairs, 2003), p. 65.

8. Shepherd Campbell and Peter Landau, *Presidential Lies: The Illustrated History of White House Golf* (New York: Macmillan, 1996), p. 106; Sullivan, *Presidents at Play,* p. 42; Lindop and Jares, *White House Sportsmen,* p. 94.

9. Campbell and Landau, *Presidential Lies,* p. 101.

10. Ibid.; Lindop and Jares, *White House Sportsmen,* p. 97.

11. Van Natta, *First Off the Tee,* p. 57.

12. Lindop and Jares, *White House Sportsmen,* p. 80.

13. Sullivan, *Presidents at Play*, p. 79.

14. Bill Mares, *Fishing with the Presidents* (Mechanicsburg, Pa.: Stackpole Books, 1999), p. 159; Alfred M. Lansing, "Ike's Fishing Secrets," *Collier's*, April 4, 1955, p. 33.

15. Merle Miller, *Ike the Soldier: As They Knew Him* (New York: G. P. Putnam's Sons, 1987), p. 25; Robert J. Donovan, *Eisenhower: The Inside Story* (New York: Harper, 1951), p. 204; Greenstein, *Hidden-Hand Presidency*, p. 26.

16. Donovan, *Eisenhower*, p. 196; Eisenhower, *At Ease*, p. 90.

17. Eisenhower, *At Ease*, pp. 340–41; Donovan, *Eisenhower*, pp. 204–205.

18. Eisenhower, *At Ease*, p. 341; Donovan, *Eisenhower*, p. 205.

19. Eisenhower, *At Ease*, p. 341.

20. J. Hoberman, "It's Always in 'High Noon' at the White House," *New York Times*, April 25, 2004, p. 11; Alan Schroeder, *Celebrity-in-Chief* (Boulder, Colo.: Westview, 2004), p. 185; J. B. West, *Upstairs at the White House* (New York: Coward, McCann & Geoghegan, 1973), p. 161.

21. Christine Sadler, *Children in the White House* (New York: Putnam, 1967), p. 292; Lillian Rogers Park, *My Thirty Years Backstairs at the White House* (New York: Fleet Publishing Corporation, 1961), pp. 338–39.

22. Eisenhower, *At Ease*, pp. 40, 42, 85–187.

23. Ibid., p. 43; Donovan, *Eisenhower*, pp. 207–208.

Chapter 34. The Dashing Young John F. Kennedy

1. William Mead and Paul Dickson, *Baseball: The Presidents' Game* (New York: Farragut Publishers, 1997), p. 118.

2. Ibid.; John Durant, *The Sports of Our Presidents* (New York: Hastings House, 1964), p. 124.

3. George Sullivan, *Presidents at Play* (New York: Walker & Co., 1995), p. 16; Pierre Salinger, *With Kennedy* (Garden City, N.Y.: Doubleday, 1966), pp. 239–47; Durant, *Sports of Our Presidents*, pp. 119, 129.

4. Thomas C. Reeves, *A Question of Character: A Life of John F. Kennedy* (New York: Harcourt, Brace, 1959, 1960), pp. 129–30.

5. Theodore C. Sorensen, *Kennedy* (New York: Macmillan, 1965), p. 42; Reeves, *Question of Character*, p. 39.

6. Sorensen, *Kennedy*, p. 41; Reeves, *Question of Character*, pp. 123–24.

7. Sorensen, *Kennedy*, p. 367; Jim Bishop, *A Day in the Life of President Kennedy* (New York: Bantam Books, 1964), p. 129; Lindop and Jares, *White House Sportsmen* (Boston: Houghton Mifflin, 1964), p. 137.

8. Sullivan, *Presidents at Play*, p. 41; Lindop and Jares, *White House Sportsmen*, p. 99; Shepherd Campbell and Peter Landau, *Presidential Lies: The Illustrated History of White House Golf* (New York: Macmillan, 1996), p. 119; Don Van Natta, Jr., *First Off the Tee: Presidential Hackers, Duffers, and Cheaters from Taft to Bush* (New York: Public Affairs, 2003), p. 44.

9. Sorensen, *Kennedy*, p. 378; Van Natta, *First Off the Tee*, pp. 15, 41–42; Campbell and Landau, *Presidential Lies*, p. 120.

10. Van Natta, *Presidential Lies*, p. 53.

11. Rose Fitzgerald Kennedy, *Times to Remember* (Garden City, N.Y.: Doubleday, 1974), p. 111; Sorensen, *Kennedy*, p. 23; John Hallman, *The Kennedy Obsession: The American Myth of JFK* (New York: Columbia University Press, 1997), p. 12; Seymour Hersh, *The Dark Side of Camelot* (Boston: Little, Brown, 1997), p. 25.

12. Pierre Salinger, *With Kennedy* (Garden City, N.Y.: Doubleday, 1966), p. 117.

13. Hallman, *Kennedy Obsession*, pp. 61–63; Irv Letofsky, "All the Presidents' Movies," *New York Times*, April 13, 1997, p. 29; Hugh Sidey, *John F. Kennedy: President* (New York: Atheneum, 1963), p. 64.

14. Alan Schroeder, *Celebrity-in-Chief* (Boulder, Colo.: Westview, 2004), p. 177; Sorensen, *Kennedy*, pp. 386–87; Reeves, *Question of Character*, pp. 315, 316; Arthur Schlesinger, Jr., *A Thousand Days: John F. Kennedy in the White House* (Boston: Houghton Mifflin, 1965), pp. 731, 738.

15. Reeves, *Question of Character*, pp. 316, 318; "Happy Birthday," *Time*, June 1, 1962, p. 13; Michael O'Brien, *John Kennedy: A Biography* (New York: St. Martin's Press, 2005), pp. 697–98; Richard D. Mahoney, *Sons and Brothers: The Days of Jack and Bobby Kennedy* (New York: Aracade Publishing, 1989), pp. 161–62.

16. William A. Degregario, *The Complete Book of U.S. Presidents* (New York: Wing Books, 1993), p. 545.

Chapter 35. The Frenetic Lyndon B. Johnson

1. Joseph A. Califano, Jr., *The Triumph and Tragedy of Lyndon Johnson* (New York: Simon & Schuster, 1991), p. 28.

2. Ibid., p. 29; Jim Bishop, *A Day in the Life of President Johnson* (New York: Random House, 1967), pp. 41–42.

3. Don Van Natta, Jr., *First Off the Tee: Presidential Hackers, Duffers and Cheaters from Taft to Bush* (New York: Public Affairs, 2003), p. 257; George Reedy, *Lyndon B. Johnson: A Memoir* (New York and Kansas City: Andrews and McMeel Co., 1982), p. 72.

4. Shepherd Campbell and Peter Landau, *Presidential Lies: The Illustrated History of White House Golf* (New York: Macmillan, 1996), p. 144; Jack Valenti, *A Very Human President* (New York: W. W. Norton, 1975), pp. 174–75.

5. Reedy, *Lyndon B. Johnson*, pp. 71–72.

6. Melissa Morison, "Between the Covers," *Dallas Morning News*, June 20, 1993, p. 3E; Liz Carpenter, *Ruffles and Flourishes* (Garden City, N.Y.: Doubleday, 1970), p. 209.

7. Ron Hutcheson, "Gang of Fore," *Fort Worth Star-Telegram*, June 11, 1997, p. 17; Van Natta, *First Off the Tee*, pp. 250, 253, 254; Campbell and Landau, *Presidential Lies*, p. 139.

8. Van Natta, *First Off the Tee*, pp. 258, 288.

9. "Mr. President, You're Fun," *Time*, April 10, 1964, p. 23A.

10. Califano, *Triumph and Tragedy*, pp. 20, 21.

11. Ibid., p. 22.

12. Ibid., p. 23; John L. Bullion, *In the Boat with LBJ* (Plano, Tex.: Republic of Texas Press, 2001), pp. 297–300.

13. Califano, *Triumph and Tragedy*, p. 24.

14. Elise K. Kirk, *Music at the White House* (Urbana: University of Illinois Press, 1986), p. 305; William A. DeGregario, *The Complete Book of U.S. Presidents* (New York: Wings Book, 1993), p. 574.

15. Kirk, *Music in the White House*, p. 305; Irving Bernstein, *Guns or Butter: The Presidency of Lyndon Johnson* (New York: Oxford University Press, 1996), p. 457.

Chapter 36. The Sports-Loving Richard M. Nixon

1. Richard Nixon, *In the Arena: A Memory of Victory, Defeat, and Renewal* (New York: Simon & Schuster, 1990), p. 104; Don Van Natta, Jr., *First Off the Tee: Presidential Hackers, Duffers and Cheaters from Taft to Bush* (New York: Public Affairs, 2003), p. 230.

2. Nixon, *In the Arena*, pp. 163–64; Shepherd Campbell and Peter Landau, *Presidential Lies: The Illustrated History of White House Golf* (New York: Macmillan, 1996), p. 154.

3. Van Natta, *First Off the Tee*, pp. 229–30; Campbell and Landau, *Presidential Lies*, p. 154.

4. Van Natta, *First Off the Tee*, pp. 231, 240; Campbell and Landau, *Presidential Lies*, pp. 151, 155.

5. Van Natta, *First Off the Tee*, pp. 231, 232, 240; William Safire, "A Columnist's Farewell," *New York Times*, January 24, 2005, p. 21A.

6. Van Natta, *First Off the Tee*, pp. 230, 233–34.

7. Ibid., pp. 236–37; Campbell and Landau, *Presidential Lies*, pp. 152, 159.

8. Nixon, *In the Arena*, p. 28; William Safire, *Before the Fall: An Inside View of the Pre-Watergate White House* (Garden City, N.Y.: Doubleday, 1975), p. 112.

9. Stephen E. Ambrose, *Nixon: The Education of a Politician* (New York: Simon & Schuster, 1987), p. 456; William Mead and Paul Dickson, *Baseball: The President's Game* (New York: Farragut Publishers, 1997), pp. 138, 139, 202, 210.

10. Ibid., pp. 134, 202; Ambrose, *Nixon*, p. 457.

11. H. R. Haldeman, *The Haldeman Diaries: Inside the Nixon White House* (New York: G. P. Putnam's Sons, 1994), p. 138; Kenneth O'Reilly, *Nixon's Piano: Presidents and Racial Policies from Washington to Clinton* (New York: Free Press, 1995), p. 7.

12. Richard Nixon, *The Memoirs of Richard Nixon* (New York: Grosset & Dunlap, 1978), p. 9.

13. Irv Letofsky, "All the Presidents' Movies," *New York Times*, April 13, 1997, p. H29; Mark Feeney, *Nixon at the Movies* (Chicago: University of Chicago Press, 2004), p. 279.

14. Feeney, *Nixon at Movies*, pp. 232, 279, 281, 294; Safire, *Before the Fall*, p. 621.

15. Nixon, *In the Arena*, p. 152.

16. Nixon, *Memoirs*, p. 15; Nixon, *In the Arena*, p. 156.

17. Monica Crowley, *Nixon in Winter* (New York: Random House, 1998), pp. 340–42, 349.

18. Nixon, *In the Arena*, p. 155.

19. Crowley, *Nixon in Winter*, p. 8.

20. Crowley, ibid., pp. 340, 351–52.

21. Nixon, *In the Arena*, pp. 163–65.

Chapter 37. The Agile Gerald R. Ford

1. James Cannon, *Time and Chance: Gerald Ford's Appointment with History* (New York: HarperCollins, 1994), p. 11.

2. Ibid., pp. 15, 21.

3. Yanek Mieczkowski, *Gerald Ford and the Challenge of the 1970s* (Lexington: University Press of Kentucky, 2005), p. 49.

4. James A. Henretta, David Broder, and Lynn Dumenil, *America's History* (Boston: St. Martin's, 2000), vol. 2, p. 1000.

5. Gerald R. Ford, *A Time to Heal: The Autobiography of Gerald R. Ford* (New York: Harper and Row, 1979), p. 289.

6. Ibid.; Mieczkowski, *Gerald Ford*, p. 49.

7. Ron Nessen, *It Sure Looks Different from the Inside* (Chicago: Playboy Books, 1978), pp. 163, 167; Mieczkowski, *Gerald Ford*, pp. 49, 51.

8. Nessen, *Looks Different from the Inside*, pp. 16, 169; Mark J. Rozell, *The Press and the Ford Presidency* (Ann Arbor: University of Michigan Press, 1992), p. 195.

9. Nessen, *Looks Different from the Inside*, p. 173; Don Van Natta, Jr., *First Off the Tee: Presidential Hackers, Duffers and Cheaters from Taft to Bush* (New York: Public Affairs, 2003), p. 97.

10. "At Play in the 'Dallas Alps,'" *Time*, January 6, 1975, pp. 46, 48.

11. "Puttin' with the President," *American Way*, October 15, 2000, p. 95; Van Natta, *First Off the Tee*, p. 81; Shepherd Campbell and Peter Landau, *Presidential Lies: The Illustrated History of White House Golf* (New York: Macmillan, 1996), p. 177.

12. Campbell and Landau, *White House Golf*, pp. 177–78, 184; Van Natta, *First Off the Tee*, p. 94.

13. Van Natta, *First Off the Tee*, p. 92.

Chapter 38. The Nature-Loving Jimmy Carter

1. Jimmy Carter, *An Outdoor Journal, Adventures and Reflections* (New York: Bantam Books, 1988), pp. 5, 6.

2. Ibid., pp. 35, 70.

3. Bill Mares, *Fishing with the Presidents* (Mechanicsburg, Pa.: Stackpole Books, 1999), p. 203; Howell Raines, "In Fly Fishing, Carter's Record Can't Be Assailed," *New York Times*, May 4, 1991, p. 28.

4. Mares, *Fishing with the Presidents*, p. 84.

5. Carter, *Outdoor Journal*, pp. 123–24.

6. Ibid., pp. 14, 91.

7. Ibid., pp. 127, 194, 262.

8. "I've Got to Keep Trying," *Time*, October 1, 1979, pp. 22–23; George Sullivan, *Presidents at Play* (New York: Walker, 1995), pp. 9–13; "One Race He Dropped Out Of," *Newsweek*, September 24, 1979, p. 33.

9. Betty Glad, *Jimmy Carter: In Search of the Great White House* (New York: W. W. Norton, 1980), p. 350; Elise K. Kirk, *Music at the White House* (Urbana: University of Illinois Press, 1986), p. 344.

10. Kirk, *Music at the White House*, p. 337.

11. Barbara Gamarekian, "All the President's Popcorn," *New York Times*, May 23, 1985, p. B12; Irv Letovsky, "All the Presidents' Movies," *New York Times*, April 13, 1997, p. 28.

12. Peter G. Bourne, *Jimmy Carter: A Comprehensive Biography from Plains to Postpresidency* (New York: Scribner, 1997), p. 41.

13. Glad, *Jimmy Carter*, pp. 483, 485–86.

14. Michael T. Kaufman, "Jimmy C., It Turns Out, Is a Poet Too," *New York Times*, January 18, 1995, p. B1.

15. Bourne, *Jimmy Carter*, pp. 479–80.

16. Stanley Cloud, "Hail to the Ex-Chief," *Time*, September 11, 1989, p. 60.

17. Hendrik Hertzberg, "Mr. E. President," *New Republic*, June 5, 1989, p. 4; "In Defense of the Carter Post-Presidency," *Washington Post National Weekly Edition*, January 2–8, 1995, p. 29; "One Very Busy Ex-President," *Time*, October 3, 1994, p. 36.

Chapter 39. The Movie-Struck Ronald Reagan

1. William Mead and Paul Dickson, *Baseball: The Presidents' Game* (New York: Farragut Publishers, 1997), p. 170; Michael Deaver, *A Different Drummer: My Thirty Years with Ronald Reagan* (New York: Harper Collins, 2001), p. 183.

2. Deaver, *Different Drummer*, p. 183.

3. Mead and Dickson, *Baseball*, pp. 167, 168.

4. Ibid., pp. 168–69; *Reagan: A Life in Letters,* ed. Kiron K. Skinner, Annelise Anderson, and Martin Anderson (New York: Free Press, 2003), p. 14.

5. Ronald Reagan, *An American Life* (New York: Simon & Schuster, 1990), pp. 89, 95, 116; Garry Wills, *Reagan's America: Innocents at Home* (Garden City, N.Y.: Doubleday, 1987), pp. 206–210; Carl M. Cannon, "The Oval Office and the Diamond," *Atlantic Monthly*, May 2001, p. 33.

6. Dinesh D'Souza, *Ronald Reagan* (New York: Free Press, 1997), p. 204.

7. Lou Cannon, *President Reagan: The Role of a Lifetime* (New York: Public Affairs, 1991, 2000), pp. 37–38.

8. Ibid., pp. 40–41, 43, 251.

9. Ibid., pp. 21–22; Wills, *Reagan's America*, pp. 196–97, 199–200.

10. William F. Buckley, "A Farewell to the Reagans," *Dallas Morning News*, January 19, 1989, p. 25A; Jerry Griswold, "I'm a Sucker for Hero Worship," *New York Times Book Review;* Edmund Morris, *Dutch: A Memoir of Ronald Reagan* (New York: Random House, 1999), pp. 40–42.

11. D'Souza, *Ronald Reagan*, pp. 75, 202; Donald F. Regan, *For the Record* (New York: Harcourt, Brace Jovanovich, 1988), p. 275.

12. Skinner, ed., *Reagan: A Life in Letters*, pp. 283–84.

13. Steven V. Roberts, "Reagan and the Russians: The Joke's on Them," *New York Times*, August 21, 1987, pp. A1, A6.

14. Ibid.

15. Reagan, *An American Life*, pp. 249–50; D'Souza, *Reagan*, p. 204; Robert E. Gilbert, *The Mortal Presidency* (New York: HarperCollins, 1992), p. 195.

16. Shepherd Campbell and Peter Landau, *Presidential Lies: The Illustrated History of White House Golf* (New York: Macmillan, 1996), pp. 187, 191, 192.

17. George Sullivan, *Presidents at Play* (New York: Walker, 1995), pp. 60, 91–92; Paul F. Boller, Jr., and Ronald L. Davis, *Hollywood Anecdotes* (New York: William Morrow, 1987), p. 358.

18. Sullivan, *Presidents at Play*, p. 91.

19. Cannon, *President Reagan*, p. 466; "So, Move Over, Jane Fonda," *Time*, December 12, 1983, p. 27; "Home, Home on the Range," *Newsweek*, August 24, 1981, p. 16.

20. Skinner, ed., *Reagan: A Life in Letters*, pp. 75, 89, 90, 814.

21. D'Souza, *Ronald Reagan*, p. 200; Cannon, *President Reagan*, pp. 32, 33.

22. Anthony Lane, "The Method President," *New Yorker*, October 18, 2004, p. 192; Robert Brustein, "Theater," *New Republic*, February 2, 1987, p. 27; David Thompson, *The New Biographical Dictionary of Film* (New York: Alfred A. Knopf, 2002), p. 716.

23. Cannon, *President Reagan*, p. 28; D'Souza, *Ronald Reagan*, p. 51.

Chapter 40. The Fast-Paced George H. W. Bush

1. Garry Wills, "The Ultimate Loyalist," *Time*, August 22, 1980, p. 24; Herbert S. Parmet, *George Bush: The Life of a Lone Star Yankee* (New York: Scribner, 1997), pp. 36, 66; George Plimpton, "A Sportsman Born and Bred," *Sports Illustrated*, January 2, 1989, p. 144.

2. Shepherd Campbell and Peter Landau, *Presidential Lies: The Illustrated History of White House Golf* (New York: Macmillan, 1996), p. 201; Maureen Dowd, "It's a Rare Sport That Bush Doesn't Like," *New York Times*, January 2, 1989, pp. 1, 11; Parmet, *Bush*, p. 36.

3. Plimpton, "A Sportsman," pp. 146, 160; George Sullivan, *Presidents at Play* (New York: Walker, 1995), p. 22.

4. Campbell and Landau, *Presidential Lies*, p. 201; Plimpton, "A Sportsman," p. 149.

5. Barbara Bush, *Reflections: Life After the White House* (New York: Scribner, 2003), p. 255.

6. Campbell and Landau, *Presidential Lies*, pp. 199, 200–201; Sullivan, *Presidents at Play*, p. 38; Don Van Natta, Jr., *First Off the Tee: Presidential Hackers, Duffers and Cheaters from Taft to Bush* (New York: Public Affairs, 2003), p. 288.

7. "Puttin' with the Pros," *American Way*, October 15, 2000, p. 91; Campbell and Landau, *Presidential Lies*, pp. 5, 200, 204, 208.

8. Michael Wines, "President Has Intestinal Flu," *New York Times*, January 9, 1992, pp. A1, A8; Bill Powell, "A Case of Political Flu," *Newsweek*, January 20, 1992, p. 30; Ann Devoy, "America's First Image of a Stricken President Bush," *Washington Post*, January 9, 1992, p. A1; Robert Gilbert, *The Mortal Presidency* (New York: Fordham University Press, 1998), pp. xiv–xv; Campbell and Landau, *Presidential Lies*, p. 201.

9. Gilbert, *Mortal Presidency*, p. xv; Pamela Kilian, *Barbara Bush: Matriarch of a Dynasty* (New York: St. Martin's Press, 2002), p. 193; Barbara Bush, *Barbara Bush: A Memoir* (New York: Scribner's, 1994), p. 449.

10. Gilbert, *Mortal Presidency*, p. xvi.

11. Dowd, "It's a Rare Sport," January 2, 1989, p. 1; Howell Raines, "Fishing with Presidents," *New York Times Magazine*, September 5, 1993, p. 28.

12. Bill Mares, *Fishing with the Presidents* (Mechanicsburg, Pa.: Stackpole Books, 1999), pp. 87–88; Sullivan, *Presidents at Play*, p. 55.

13. Plimpton, "A Sportsman," p. 158.

14. William Mead and Paul Dickson, *Baseball: The Presidents' Game* (New York: Farragut Publishers, 1997), p. 178; Sullivan, *Presidents at Play*, pp. 137, 139.

15. Mead and Dickson, *Baseball*, p. 171; Sullivan, *Presidents at Play*, p. 137.

16. Barbara Bush, *Reflections*, pp. 264–65; "Bush Pans Cliburn Piano Performance," *Fort Worth Star-Telegram*, February 28, 1992, p. 3A.

17. Plimpton, "A Sportsman," p. 158; John R. Greene, *The Presidency of George Bush* (Lawrence: University Press of Kansas, 2000), p. 141; Wills, "The Ultimate Loyalist," p. 24.

18. Drummond Ayres, Jr., "Bush Leaps into Open Sky, Again," *New York Times*, March 26, 1997, p. A10.

19. "Cue Parachutes for Bush 41," *Time*, April 12, 2004, p. 21; Barbara Bush, *Reflections*, pp. 284–86.

Chapter 41. The Unflappable Bill Clinton

1. Bill Clinton, *My Life* (New York: Alfred A. Knopf, 2004), p. 56.

2. Ibid., pp. 29, 40, 55.

3. Ibid., p. 36.

4. Ibid., p. 570; Hillary Rodham Clinton, *Living History* (New York: Simon & Schuster, 2003), p. 358; David Maraniss, *First in His Class: A Biography of Bill Clinton* (New York: Simon & Schuster, 1995), p. 45.

5. Nigel Hamilton, *Bill Clinton: An American Journey* (New York: Random House, 2003), p. 419.

6. Anthony Lane, "Politicians and Their Books," *New Yorker*, October 16–23, 2000, p. 175; Harold Evans, "White House Club," *New York Times Book Review*, January 14, 2001, p. 31.

7. Clinton, *My Life*, pp. 30, 522; Maraniss, *First in His Class*, pp. 66, 234.

8. Clinton, *My Life*, pp. 186, 614–15.

9. Maraniss, *First in His Class*, pp. 93, 101.

10. Clinton, *My Life*, p. 143; Maraniss, *First in His Class*, pp. 140–41.

11. Shepherd Campbell and Peter Landau, *Presidential Lies: The Illustrated History of White House Golf* (New York: Macmillan, 1996), p. 227; George Sullivan, *Presidents at Play* (New York: Walker & Co., 1995), p. 4.

12. Sullivan, *Presidents at Play*, p. 34; Campbell and Landau, *Presidential Lies*, pp. 218, 219, 224–25; Don Van Natta, Jr., *First Off the Tee: Presidential Hackers, Duffers and Cheaters from Taft to Bush* (New York: Public Affairs, 2003), p. 183.

13. Campbell and Landau, *Presidential Lies*, pp. 218, 226, 229; Van Natta, *First Off the Tee*, p. 192.

14. Van Natta, *First Off the Tee*, pp. 106–197; "Transition," *Newsweek*, June 24, 1996, p. 78.

15. Don Van Natta, "Taking Second Chances for Clinton's Course," *New York Times*, August 29, 1999, Sect. 4, pp. 1, 4; Campbell and Landau, *Presidential Lies*, p. 222; Frank Ahrens, "Our Nation's Fore! Fathers," *Washington Post*, June 4, 1997, p. D6; Van Natta, *First Off the Tee*, p. 223.

16. Todd S. Purdum, "Caution: Presidents at Play—Three of Them," *New York Times*, February 16, 1995, p. 1, D21; "Puttin' with the Prez," *American Way*, October 15, 2000, p. 95; Van Natta, *First Off the Tee*, pp. 1–5, 18–23.

17. Clinton, *My Life*, pp. 30, 36–37.

18. Irv Letovsky, "All the Presidents' Movies," *New York Times*, April 13, 1997, p. 28; Clinton, *My Life*, pp. 20–21.

19. Clinton, *My Life*, p. 21; *USA Today*, November 21, 2005, p. 6A.

Chapter 42. The Physically Fit George W. Bush

1. Bruce McCall, "Yo, Sparky, Yeah, You Know Who You Are," *New York Times*, February 18, 2001, p. 2.

2. Headlines about President Bush's fitness: *New York Times*, April 1, 2002 (p. A17) and July 31, 2005 (p. 4A), and *Fort Worth Star-Telegram*, July 31, 2005 (p. 4A) and August 14, 2005 (p. 5A).

3. *The White House Workout* (New York: Healthy Living Books, 2003); Ken Herman, "Bush Is Known for His Commitment to Fitness," *Fort Worth Star-Telegram*, August 14, 2005, p. 5A; "Laugh Lines," July 31–August 6, *New York Times*, The Week, August 7, 2005, p. 2.

4. "Running Man," *U.S. News & World Report*, March 14, 2005, p. 8.

5. Mike Allen, "President Touts Benefits of Running," *Fort Worth Star-Telegram* August 23, 2002, p. 4A; Elisabeth Bumiller, "A President Leaves No Doubt," *New York Times*, April 1, 2002, p. A17; Lawrence J. Knutson, "Bush Races To Set Fitness Example for Americans," *Fort Worth Star-Telegram*, June 23, 2002, p. 7A.

6. "Ride 'Em, Cowboy!" *Newsweek*, August 15, 2005, p. 6; Nedra Pickler, "Armstrong, Bush Ride Today," *Fort Worth Star-Telegram*, August 20, 2005, p. 4A; "Bush Prefers Pedal Power," *U.S. News and World Report*, April 18, 2005, p. 8; "From Tour de France to Tour de Crawford," *New York Times*, August 21, 2005, p. 15.

7. Elisabeth Bumiller, "Bush Makes Quick Work of Relaxing," *New York Times*, August 5, 2002, p. A10; Mike Allen, "Bush Tees Off with Mideast Discussion," *Fort Worth Star-Telegram*, August 5, 2002, p. 10A.

8. Jay Root, "Bass Haul: Feisty Fish Keep President Bush Reeling at his Crawford Ranch," *Fort Worth Star-Telegram*, November 23, 2001, p. 5B; ibid., May 8, 2006, p. 5A; David E. Sangler, "Bush Ventures Off Ranch to Court Steelworkers," *New York Times*, August 27, 2001, p. A13.

9. Scott Lindlaw, "Back at the Ranch," *Fort Worth Star-Telegram*, August 11, 2002, p. 25A; Maureen Dowd, "It's Not Personal, Jack. It's Strictly Business," *New York Times*, January 4, 2006, p. A21.

10. Eugenia Peretz, "High Noon in Crawford," *Vanity Fair*, November 2005, pp. 230–33; *Fort Worth Star-Telegram,* August 11, 2002, p. 25A.

11. Don Van Natta, Jr., "The Sporting Life at the White House," *New York Times*, September 9, 2001, p. 3.

12. Elisabeth Bumiller, "Measuring the Bush Family History and the President's Career in Innings," *New York Times*, April 18, 2005, p. A11; Van Natta, "Sporting Life," p. 3; "That's My Bush League," *Time*, May 14, 2001, p. 16; "A Real Man," *Fort Worth Star-Telegram*, November 6, 2001, p. 11B.

13. Katherine Q. Seelye, "Bush's Loss on Links Can't Dampen His Day," *New York Times*, August 8, 2001, p. A13; Scott Lindlaw, "Back at the Ranch," *Fort Worth Star-Telegram,* August 11, 2002, p. 25A.

14. Elisabeth Bumiller, "Bush and the Protesters: Tale of Two Summer Camps," *New York Times*, August 22, 2005, p. A9.

15. Maureen Dowd, *New York Times*, August 10, 2005, p. A21, and August 24, 2005, p. A21; "Punchlines," *Time*, August 29, 2005, p. 18; "Verbatim," *Time*, May 3, 2004, p. 17.

Index

Conner, Gen. Fox, 261
Coolidge, Calvin: at Amherst, 212,
218; and baseball, 217; and
books and reading, 218–19;
entertains, 217–18; and
exercise, 214–15, 217; and
fishing, 215–16, 224; formal
style of, 217; on golf, 212; and
hunting, 216; inactivity of,
212–13, 214; lack of hobbies,
215; and liquor, 218; as
multilingual, 218–19; and
music, 218–19; penuriousness,
212–14; political philosophy of,
213; as professional politician,
212; sense of humor, 214; and
smoking, 218; taciturnity,
212, 217, 225; targeted by
cartoonists, 215; and theater,
218–19; as unathletic, 212, 215,
284; as Vice President, 209;
and writing, 219
Coolidge, Grace, 217
Coolidge, John, 217
Costas, Bob, 354
cowboy: Theodore Roosevelt as,
175–76
Crédit Mobilier scandal, 141
Crook, William H: as presidential
bodyguard, 124, 131, 136, 152,
168, 186
crossword puzzles: Clinton and,
345
Crowley, Monica, 290, 291
Culbertson, Ely, 257
Cunningham, John S.: on Tyler,
76–77
Custis, Nelly, 8; on Washington, 2
Custis, Washington Parke, 9–10
Cutts, Mary, 40
Cutts, Richard, 40
Czechoslovakia: Clinton in, 338
Czolgosz, Leon, 172

Dana, Charles A., 122
dancing: Benjamin Harrison and,
161, 164; Jackson and, 59; John
Adams and, 15; Lyndon B.
Johnson and, 276–77, 278;
Taft and, 189; Tyler and, 76;
Washington and, 3–5
Daniels, Josephus: as secretary of
the navy, 233
David, Lord Cecil: *Melbourne,* 269
Davidson College: Wilson at, 196
Day the Earth Stood Still, The, 316
Deaver, Michael, 322; on Reagan,
313
Dempsey, Rick, 312–13
Depew, Chauncey, 191; on Arthur,
145
detective novels: Franklin D.
Roosevelt reads, 231; Truman
reads, 244
Dickinson College: Buchanan at,
101–2
Doctor Zhivago, 289
Donelson, Andrew Jackson, 58
Donelson, Emily: as Jackson's
White House hostess, 60
Dora Dean (Holmes), 141
Dostoevsky, Fyodor, 289–90, 340
Douglas, Stephen A.: debates
Lincoln, 109
Dowd, Maureen, 327; on George
W. Bush, 355
Drury, Allen: Reagan and, 318–19

Eaton, John: on Jackson, 56
Ed Sullivan Show, 337
education: Hayes on, 138
education, limitations in: Andrew
Johnson and, 123, 125;
Fillmore and, 91–92; Jackson
and, 61; Lincoln and, 115
Eisenhower, Dwight D.: and Army-
Navy football game, 251–52; as

history: Eisenhower loves, 261;
Nixon on, 289; Truman's
knowledge of, 243–44, 261
History of Britain (Schama), 339
History of the American People, A
(Wilson), 200, 202
Hobart, Garret: as Vice President,
167, 171
hobbies: Coolidge's lack of, 215;
Franklin D. Roosevelt's, 229;
Hoover's lack of, 215; John
Adams on, 13–14; Nixon's lack
of, 285
Hogan, Ben: on Eisenhower, 254
Holland: John Adams in, 13
Holmes, Mary Jane: *Dora Dean,*
141
Holmes, Oliver Wendell, Jr.: on
Jefferson, 24
Holmes, Oliver Wendell, Sr.: "The
Last Leaf," 117
Homage to Catalonia (Orwell), 340
Hone, Philip: on W. H. Harrison,
71–72
Honey Fitz [presidential yacht],
271, 275
Hoover, Herbert, 219; at Camp
Raridan, 222, 223; as
compulsive worker, 221–22;
denounces New Deal, 227;
early life, 222–23; entertains,
225–26; and exercise, 224–25;
and fishing, 222–24, 225, 226,
255–56; on fishing, 227–28;
*Fishing for Fun—And to
Wash Your Soul,* 227–28;
good health, 225; and Great
Depression, 221–22, 225–26;
gregariousness, 225–26; hates
wasting time, 226; hosts White
House conferences, 225–26;
Joslin on, 224–25, 227; lack
of hobbies, 222; plays with
medicine ball, 224–25; as

secretary of commerce, 223;
and smoking, 227; as social
conservative, 227; and theater,
226–27; and writing, 227
Hoover, Irwin, 200–1, 219, 221
Hoover, Lou, 225
Hoover Institution (Stanford), 227
Hope, Bob, 254, 300
Hopkins, Harry, 237
Hopkins, Mark, 143–44
Hopkinson, Francis, 8, 30
Horne, Charles Francis: *Great Men
and Famous Women,* 243–44
Hornet's Nest, The (Carter), 309–10
horse racing: Jackson and, 55,
57–59; John Quincy Adams
and, 50
horsemanship: Arthur and, 147;
Grant and, 127–31, 181;
Jefferson and, 25–26;
McKinley and, 166; Polk and,
84; Reagan and, 321–22, 323;
Theodore Roosevelt and,
181–82; W. H. Harrison and,
70; Washington and, 2, 4, 127
horseshoes: George H. W. Bush
pitches, 327–28; Truman
pitches, 246
Howells, William Dean: on
Garfield, 140; on Hayes, 134,
136
Huckabee, Mike: and George W.
Bush, 350
human nature: Theodore Roosevelt
on, 179–80
humor: Coolidge's sense of, 214;
Franklin D. Roosevelt's sense
of, 236–38; Lincoln's use
of, 106–8, 113; Lyndon B.
Johnson's sense of, 279–80;
Reagan's sense of, 319–20;
therapeutic value of, 108–9,
113; Wilson and, 199–200,
201–2, 203

Torre, Joe, 354
travel: Benjamin Harrison and, 164;
 McKinley and, 169, 171; Taft
 and, 192–93
Tristan and Isolde (Wagner), 307
Truman, Ben: and Andrew
 Johnson, 122
Truman, Bess, 240, 241, 247–48;
 and fishing, 245
Truman, Harry S.: Acheson on,
 247; and art, 249; and books
 and reading, 243–44; and
 cocktail hour, 247; Elsey on,
 243–44; good health, 246,
 248; informal style, 247–48;
 knowledge of history, 243–44,
 261; loses his temper, 248; and
 music, 240–43, 248–49, 307;
 and Paderewski, 241; Park on,
 247–48; pitches horseshoes,
 246; plays cards, 246–47; plays
 piano, 240–41, 287; reads
 detective novels, 244; and
 sports, 244–45; studies Latin,
 243–44; as Vice President,
 245; and walking, 245–46;
 work habits, 247; and World
 War I, 245
Truman, Margaret, 241–42, 248
Trumbull, John, 8, 30
Tulley, Grace: on Franklin D.
 Roosevelt, 229–30, 239
Turgenev, Ivan, 340
Twain, Mark, 119, 318; on Arthur,
 150–51; *The Gilded Age,*
 141–42
Tyler, John: and animals, 77–78;
 Cunningham on, 76–77; and
 dancing, 76; entertains, 76–77,
 79–80; and Jefferson, 75; and
 music, 78–79; political failure,
 79–80; puritanical personality,
 76; taste in books and reading,
 79; as Vice President, 73; at

William and Mary, 79; work
 habits, 77
Tyler, Julia, 77, 80; and music, 78;
 "regal" style of, 76; Thomas
 on, 76
Tyler, Letitia, 75–76
"Type A" personality: Lyndon B.
 Johnson as, 275

University of Michigan: Ford at,
 293–94, 295
University of Virginia, 40; Jefferson
 and, 29
U.S. House of Representatives:
 Garfield in, 139–41, 143;
 Hayes in, 136; John Q. Adams
 in, 52, 53–54; Kennedy in, 267;
 McKinley in, 168–69; Pierce
 in, 97
U.S. Marine Band, 79, 94, 111, 149,
 168, 205–6, 209
U.S. Military Academy:
 Eisenhower at, 251–52; Grant
 at, 128–29, 131
U.S. Senate: Kennedy in, 267; Van
 Buren in, 63
U.S. Supreme Court: Taft as Chief
 Justice of, 194

Valenti, Jack, 277
Van Buren, Hannah, 66
Van Buren, Martin: Alexander
 on, 65–66; and the "cheese
 excitement," 62; early life,
 63–64; in England, 65; in
 Europe, 68; formal style of,
 66–69, 73; Marryat on, 66; as
 professional politician, 64;
 Randolph on, 64; in Senate, 63;
 and sports, 64; and theater, 64,
 68; as Vice President, 59, 64;
 on W. H. Harrison, 70; and
 wine, 64
vaudeville: Wilson and, 203